Collaborative Projects

Studies in Critical Social Sciences Book Series

Haymarket Books is proud to be working with Brill Academic Publisher (www.brill.nl) to republish the *Studies in Critical Social Sciences* book series in pa perback editions. This peer-reviewed book series offers insights into our curren reality by exploring the content and consequences of power relationships unde capitalism, and by considering the spaces of opposition and resistance to thes changes that have been defining our new age. Our full catalog of *SCSS* volume can be viewed at www.haymarketbooks.org/category/scss-series.

Collaborative Projects

An Interdisciplinary Study

Edited by

Andy Blunden

Haymarket Books
Chicago, IL

First published in 2014 by Brill Academic Publishers, The Netherlands.

Published in paperback in 2015 by
Haymarket Books
P.O. Box 180165
Chicago, IL 60618
773-583-7884
www.haymarketbooks.org

ISBN: 978-1-60846-490-6

Trade distribution:
In the U.S. through Consortium Book Sales, www.cbsd.com
In the UK, Turnaround Publisher Services, www.turnaround-uk.com
In all other countries by Publishers Group Worldwide, www.pgw.com

Cover design by Ragina Johnson.

This book was published with the generous support of Lannan Foundation and the Wallace Action Fund.

Printed in Canada by union labor.

10 9 8 7 6 5 4 3 2 1

Library of Congress Cataloging-in-Publication Data is available.

Contents

List of Contributors

Igor Arievitch

is Professor at the Department of Education, the College of Staten Island, City University of New York. His research focuses on the role of teaching and learning in cognitive development. Dr. Arievitch has published on psychological regulation, internalization, cognitive tools, developmental teaching, and educational technology and has taught and researched at the universities of Moscow, Leiden and Bern before coming to New York.

Michael Arnold

is an academic in the Historical and Philosophical Studies Department at the University of Melbourne. He teaches Cybersociety and Science in Context and has published on a variety of subjects relating to digital technologies in the social context.

Lynn Beaton

has been an activist and commentator for over thirty years, participating in and writing on the anti-Vietnam War movement, the women's movement, trade union campaigns, the British Miner's Strike. She has published on issues associated with women and work, temporary employment and the history of worker organization and published three books. Her most recent work was a history of an asbestos cement plant in Tasmania, Australia.

William Blanton

is Emeritus Distinguished Professor of Teaching and Learning at the University of Miami. He is a continuing member of the original Fifth Dimension Project and conducts research on literacy and the application of telecommunications and digital tools in learning to teach.

Andy Blunden

is a writer and managing editor of the international journal *Mind, Culture, and Activity*. Andy is also Secretary of the Marxists Internet Archive and ran a Hegel Summer School in Melbourne 1998–2010. His book *An Interdisciplinary Theory of Activity*, was published by Brill in 2010 and *Concepts. A Critical Approach*, in 2012.

Michael Cole

was Professor of Communication and Psychology at the University of California, San Diego, and Director of the Laboratory of Comparative Human

Cognition (LCHC) until June 2013. His recent research within the 5th Dimension afterschool project, linking universities and local communities has been devoted to a longitudinal study of individual and organizational change, the dynamics of appropriation and the use of new technologies.

Brecht De Smet
has a PhD in Political Science, on contemporary Egypt from Ghent University, Belgium. He is currently a researcher in the Middle East and North Africa Research Group, doing extensive fieldwork in Egypt 2008–2011. His book on the Egyptian workers' movement and the 25 January Revolution will be published by Brill in 2014.

Natalia Gajdamaschko
was trained in Moscow and is a Senior Lecturer at the Faculty of Education of Simon Fraser University, Canada, where she has created and sponsors one of the first 2-year Masters Programs in North America based on Vygotsky and CHAT theories.

Virginia Gordon
worked as a community health activist, parent organizer and biomedical engineer before joining the Laboratory of Comparative Human Cognition. Her research interests include: the sustainability of educational innovation, busing and school integration, and international development and technology transfer. For 15 years she managed an in-school and afterschool 5th Dimension program.

Manfred Holodynski
is Professor at the Institute of Psychology for Teaching and Education at the Westphalian Wilhelms-University Münster, noted for his research on the cultural formation of the emotions.

Naja Berg Hougaard
is a PhD candidate in Psychology at the CUNY Graduate Center and teaches Human Development at Hunter College. Naja has a BA in Psychology from the University of Copenhagen and was a visiting scholar at LCHC. Naja's current work focuses on the emancipatory potential of critical-theoretical teaching in public higher education settings.

Vera John-Steiner
is Regents' Professor Emerita of Language, Literacy, and Sociocultural Studies and Linguistics at the University of New Mexico. She has published in psycholinguistics, cultural historical theory, creativity, collaboration and

bilingualism. Vera co-edited Vygotsky's *Mind in Society*, and her *Creative Collaboration* documents the impact of working partnerships in the human sciences. She has lectured in Latin America, Europe, and the United States.

Elena Kravtsova

is Director of Vygotsky Institute of Psychology, Head of the Projective Psychology Department, one of the authors of the "Golden Key" educational program for children of different psychological ages. Her research into the periodization of psychic and personal development, the zone of proximal development, and the developmental educational environment continue the research tradition of cultural-historical Psychology.

Gennadiy Kravtsov

is Head of the Psychology of Personality Department at the Russian State University of the Humanities. Gennadiy is a specialist in the methodology of cultural-historical psychology and regularly participates in international conferences and symposiums. He is an organizer of the Vygotsky Institute of Psychology and head of the research group that developed educational programs for children of pre-school, primary school and teen ages.

Ron Lubensky

earned his PhD in the School of Humanities and Communication Arts at the University of Western Sydney. His thesis *Citizens Make Sense in Deliberative Activity*, based on observation and analysis of an Australian Citizens' Parliament, explores public deliberation from the perspective of Activity Theory. Ron was Assistant Editor of the *Journal of Public Deliberation*. He lives in Melbourne, Australia.

Morten Nissen

teaches community psychology in Copenhagen, Denmark, and Fredrikstad, Norway. He investigates participation, subjectivity, "wild" social work, and addiction, with a focus on theories, standards, and practices. He edits *Outlines – Critical Practice Studies*, and heads the research center SUBSTANce-Subjects and standards. His book, *The Subjectivity Of Participation Articulating Social Work Practice with Youth in Copenhagen*, was published by Palgrave Macmillan in 2012.

Jennifer Power

is a research fellow at La Trobe University. She has published widely in the areas of sexual and reproductive health and HIV/AIDS, lesbian and gay issues and family studies. Jennifer's book on the community responses to HIV/AIDS in Australia is available through ANU E-press.

Mike Rifino, *Keiko Matsuura* and *Francisco Medina* are Psychology students at Hunter College.

Anna Stetsenko
is a Professor at the Graduate Center, CUNY, with appointments in PhD Programs in Human Development and in Urban Education. She came to CUNY after working at leading Universities and research centers in Russia, Switzerland, and Germany. Her research is situated at the intersection of human development, social theory and education including topics of subjectivity, collective agency, and personhood viewed through the lens of social change and activism.

Greg Thompson
is a Visiting Assistant Professor in the Department of Anthropology at Brigham Young University and was formerly a post-doctoral researcher at LCHC.

Chiel van der Veen
is a lecturer and PhD candidate at VU University Amsterdam, Department of Research and Theory in Education. His research focuses on oral communicative competence in young school children.

Eduardo Vianna
is an Associate Professor at LaGuardia Community College in New York. His research focuses on connecting teaching/learning and development to promote social justice and development among underprivileged groups. He has published on the developmental impact of teaching/learning and its central role in identity development, institutional transformation, and social change.

Lynne Wolbert
is a PhD student at the VU University Amsterdam, Department of Research and Theory in Education. The central aim of her research project is to investigate education for human flourishing.

Helena Worthen
is Professor Emerita of Labor and Employment Relations, School of Labor and Employment Relations, University of Illinois and teaches at the National Labor College in Silver Spring, Maryland. Originally a novelist, then a teacher of writing in colleges in San Francisco, she was active in the California Federation of Teachers and the National Writers Union and published widely in learning theory and employment.

Introduction: 'Collaborative Project' as a Concept for Interdisciplinary Human Science Research

Andy Blunden

The human sciences are fragmented into myriad disciplines, but a veritable *chasm* separates those disciplines which study the individual person and their actions from those disciplines which study human beings en masse: economics, history, political science and so on. The lack of a concept which meets the needs of science on both sides of this chasm mirrors the condition of modern life: individuals dominated by great processes of societal life in which they play no part. Could Activity Theory with 'project' as a *unit* of activity, provide a way to overcome this gap by using a shared conceptual language across both domains?

There are already many writers who address themselves to collaborative projects as part of their research, and among these, some who share a commitment to Activity Theory or the Cultural-Historical Psychology which underpins Activity Theory. However, these writers do not constitute a coherent current of thinking, as each writer does not take the concept of 'project' as central to their own project. Nonetheless, this literature provides a beginning for interdisciplinary research in the human sciences which can reach across the chasm between the sciences of the individual and the sciences of society.

The adjective 'collaborative' is meant to distinguish 'project' as a social formation in contradistinction to an individualistic conception of projects, but projects are *always* collaborative, and collaboration is *always* for a project.

In what follows I will outline the origins of 'project' as a unit for the human sciences and its value as an interdisciplinary concept, and then briefly review the foundation of the concept in different domains of theory, and conclude with a concise definition of the concept of 'collaborative project'.

Origins of the Idea of Project as a Unit of Activity

Very broadly, 'project' has arisen from currents of social philosophy whose origins lie in Hegel or Marx, rather than Kant or Frege, but the concept of 'project' as a unit of analysis for an interdisciplinary Activity Theory has its origins in the work of Vygotsky and his followers in the Soviet Union. It is this latter line of development which is the proximate origin of the approaches considered here.

Soviet psychologist Lev Vygotsky (1896–1934) approached the cultural formation of the psyche by means of a study of the collaborative use of artifacts which originate in a wider culture, in some social situation, also the product of the wider culture. He observed that a 'concept arises and is formed in a complex operation that is directed toward the resolution of some task', (LSVCW v. 1, p. 124) 'tasks that are posed for the maturing adolescent by the social environment – tasks that are associated with his entry into the cultural, professional, and social life of the adult world' (ibid., p. 132). But he did not investigate the processes of formation of the social environment itself. His units of analysis were the artifact-mediated action (such as word-meaning) and *perezhivanie* (a lived-experience), and he did not pursue the relation between these personal actions and experiences and the formation of the 'tasks…associated with…the social life of the adult world'. These were issues that were taken up by his younger associate A.N. Leontiev.

A.N. Leontiev (1904–1979) identified the concept of 'an activity' as follows:

> Thus, the principal 'unit' of a vital process is an organism's activity; the different activities that realize its diverse vital relations with the surrounding reality are essentially determined by their object; we shall therefore differentiate between separate types of activity according to the difference in their objects.
>
> 2009, p. 29

And an activity is 'a non-additive unit of the corporeal, material life of the material subject. In the narrower sense, i.e., on the psychological plane, it is a unit of life' (2009, p. 397). According to Leontiev, an activity was specified by the object to which all the actions composing it were directed, and in the light of which these actions can be made sense of. The problems arising from the future-oriented character of his definition, undoubtedly necessary for any study of the human mind, he resolved by means of a distinction between the *societal* motives/needs of the community as a whole and the personal sense of an object which motivates a person's actions. The harmonization of societal motives and personal meanings was a problem to be resolved by the formation of a mode of production, distribution and exchange which ensures that individuals are motivated to act in such a way that societal needs are met. But how can we make sense of 'societal motives' and 'societal needs'? There is no Central Committee authorized to determine the needs of the whole country – but nonetheless, individuals' actions are directed by their conception of the collaborative pursuit of more remote, societally developed ends, but these ends are realized only in the unfolding of the project itself. The object is not external to the activity, but is immanent within it.

In Russia in 1984, Fyodor Vasilyuk published a seminal book on psychotherapy: 'The Psychology of Experiencing' (1988) – 'the first important contribution to the field of psychodynamic theory made by a Soviet author in the last 50 years' (Kozulin, 1991). The key concept of the work is переживание (*perezhivanie*), translated somewhat inadequately as 'experiencing' or 'a lived experience', and understood by Vasilyuk as an active process of 'working over', or overcoming a crisis which has arisen in what he calls a 'отношение', translated as 'life relation', but which could also be translated as 'attitude to (something)' or 'life orientation'. I find it difficult to interpret Vasilyuk's отношение as anything other than commitment to a life-project (c.f. Stetsenko, 2003, 2012; Stetsenko & Arievitch, 2004a, 2004b; Vianna & Stetsenko, 2011).

Crisis situations arise in a person's life from failures of or blockages to life-projects, or conflicts between them. He says:

> During the period of acute pain [such as following the death of a loved one, or failure to win a desired career move] *perezhivanie* becomes the person's leading activity. We will remind you that psychology calls that activity leading which occupies a dominating position in the life of a person and through which his personal development is carried out.
>
> VASILYUK, 1988, p. 231

In his 1991 review of Vasilyuk's book, Alex Kozulin interpreted this as follows:

> The individual must bring about the unity of the self, and not only as an internal conscious project, but as an actual existence in a difficult world. The prototype of experiencing in this life-world is a creative experience of an author. Because the work of art is simultaneously present and not yet present at the moment of its conception by the author, the unity of the self first appears as life-intent or life-project. This intent as related to the system of values is felt by a person as a 'calling', and in its relation to the spatio-temporal actuality of existence it becomes 'life work'.
>
> p. 17

Vasilyuk constructed a four part typology of such crises in terms of an *internal* life-world which is either simple or complex, and an *external* life-world which is either easy or difficult. A *simple* inner world means that the crisis arises from the pursuit of just one activity without implication for any other project to which the person is committed. A *complex* inner world means that the subject is motivated by multiple projects which may be conflicting, or interdependent, and resolving a crisis becomes complex in that sense. An *easy* outer world means that the crisis arises from inner causes, not existential threats to the project or blockages having their origin independently of the subject. A *difficult* outer world means that a project to which the subject is committed faces a blockage or disaster. Vasilyuk's use of *perezhivanie* as a concept of an active, lived experience, thus rests on the conception of commitments to projects which are simultaneously features of their subjective life *and* objective, material projects in the external world.

The four types of crisis are (simple-easy) *stress*, (simple-difficult) *frustration*, (complex-easy) *conflict* and (complex-difficult) *crisis*. He says that *stress* is a 'hedonistic' or 'infantile' crisis – the subject is concerned only with the here and now and acquiring more; *frustration* is a 'realistic' crisis – the subject has to accept the unattainability of the object and determine what it is they *really* need, not just the specific thing which has the meaning for them of their real object; *conflict* is a 'crisis of values' – the subject is obliged to revisit the bases for their past actions and question their values which have led them into a tragic situation; *crisis* as such is a creative crisis, which forces the subject to transform the meaning of the absent object so as to make the psychologically impossible situation possible, so that the life-crisis resolved by creating a new life-world, a new self.

Resolution of the crisis in psychotherapy entails the patient engaging in an inner dialogue with themselves through which the object of the critical project(s) is reinterpreted in a more satisfactory way. His sketch of the stages through which psychotherapy passes resembles those outlined by Elisabeth Kübler-Ross (1969).

The concepts of 'an object-oriented activity' and 'a leading activity' are central to psychotherapy in Soviet psychology, whether or not it is called an 'activity', a 'project' or a 'life relation'.

In the 1950s and '60s in the Soviet Union, psychologists focusing on the problem of engineering design developed the concept of 'psychological projection'. In the concept of project arising from this work, the project is not simply the fulfillment of an original design, but rather the project develops in response to experience and realizes a process of collective intellectual development. Here arose the concept of the object as *immanent* to the project rather than being given to it externally. In the 1980s, the Moscow Methodological Circle further developed these ideas and broadened the scope and scale of the problems tackled. 'Projective psychology' also took root in educational psychology with the work of Elena Kravtsova and Gena Kravtsov (see Kravtsov

& Kravtsova, 2010). The projective method, as they see it, is the experimental-genetic method of instruction which aims to model developmental processes which are replicated in real life, and has been applied in their 'Golden Key' schools since 1992.

In the early 2000s, Anna Stetsenko utilized the concept of collaborative project, founded in Vygotskian Activity Theory, firstly in a review of a biography of A.R. Luria (2003), and later (2004) in an analysis of the Vygotsky's heritage. In these articles, Stetsenko used the concept of collaborative project both as 'the *leading activity* that organized and underpinned both [an individual's] life and...work', and as a broad social endeavor such as the Russian revolution, at the macro level, as well as particular collaborative activities at the meso-level. Here for the first time the concept of *project* spanned micro-, meso- and macro-levels of the human sciences.

While this Soviet current is the proximate source of the idea of 'project' as a unit for the concept of 'collaborative project' developed here, 'project' also has deep and broad roots in Western social science, most explicitly in the field of education.

The 'project method' of education originated in the education of architects in 17th century Italy, spread throughout Europe across a range of professions, and arrived in the U.S. in 1865 where it was adopted by the Massachusetts Institute of Technology (Knoll, 2012). Up till the 1930s, it was widely used in US elementary schools, where a project was described as 'a unit of educative work in which the most prominent feature was some form of positive and concrete achievement' (OED). The project method continues to be a favored approach in remedial education, and in science and technical education. John Dewey (1897/1981) pioneered an approach of this kind in his Laboratory School where all learning took place within projects closely connected to the tasks of everyday life. Paolo Freire (1921–1997) also used a project approach to learning, in the form of 'problem-posing education' in which the 'concrete, present situation [is posed] to the people as a problem which challenges them', (Freire, 1970/2011, p. 95) building knowledge through a collaborative enquiry into the real-life situation confronting them.

The Soviet educators went further in designing projects and lessons which 'modeled' child development, optimizing psychological conditions for a child's development, instead of the usual curriculum segregated by age and subject. Here the concept of a project as a societal product is merged with the concept of a project as a psychological projection in the formation of a personality.

But different concepts of project have been proposed independently elsewhere as part of a foundation for psychology and social theory in currents springing from Husserl's Phenomenology.

Alfred Schutz (1899–1959) was a European emigré at the New School in New York who aimed to extend Husserl's concepts for use in social theory.

> Conduct which is devised in advance, that is, which is based upon a preconceived project, shall be called *action*, regardless of whether it is an overt or covert conduct. As to the latter it has to be distinguished whether or not there supervenes on the *project* an intention to realize it – to carry it through, to bring about the projected state of affairs. Such an intention transforms the mere forethought into an aim and the project into a purpose.
>
> 1945/1970, p. 125

But despite Schutz's efforts to build a *social* theory, a project for him remained a product of the individual mind, directing a person's actions towards some imagined state of affairs, whereas for Activity Theory, the project is a societal process which usually already exists when it provides motivation for a specific person. Nevertheless, he had the key insight that in order to make sense of a person's actions, those actions have to be seen as arising from a subjective commitment to some project, from which a person draws their motivation.

Martin Heidegger (1889–1976) also began from Husserl's phenomenology, but put the artifacts which people produce and use in the course of their activity at center stage. According to Heidegger, we 'project' our concepts on to objects, although there is always something there, and we have a pre-intellectual or practical knowledge of how to use a tool, for example, and what it is for, prior to our projection. Heidegger developed his Existentialist concept of the project in 'Being and Time' (1927). Although Heidegger introduced the concept of 'project' into phenomenology, the artifacts which mediate our actions play the predominant role, rather than the activities which constitute the object, as a concept for Activity Theorists.

In his Existentialist phase, Jean-Paul Sartre (1905–1980) saw the self in terms of an individual having a 'fundamental project' which gives meaning to a person's life and what they do:

> For we mean to say that man primarily exists – that man is, before all else, something which propels itself towards a future and is aware that it is doing so. Man is, indeed, a project which possesses a subjective life, instead of being a kind of moss, or a fungus or a cauliflower. Before that projection of the self nothing exists.
>
> 1946/1989

Each of the projects in which an individual participates is a *part* of the subject's 'fundamental project'. For Sartre, the notion of identity formation was tied up with the discovery of a symbol of the person's being and the desire to realize that symbol which is their 'fundamental project', a quintessentially inner process. This phase of Sartre's work contributed to the development of Existential Therapy, which deals with conflicts arising in these inner projects. With the writing of his *Critique of Dialectical Reason* (1960), however, Sartre appropriated aspects of Marxism, and developed the categories of phenomenology as *social* formations. A 'project' he defined as a chosen way of being, expressed in *praxis*; groups were formed by a pledge or commitment individuals make binding them to a common goal, thus fusing their will to that of the group. A fused group passes through a phase of 'white heat' in which it is able to transform the world, after which it becomes a 'practico-inert' – a 'human object' or institution, no longer a living organism or project. Such practico-inerts form the world which we inhabit, the residue of fused groups of the past.

What distinguishes Activity Theory from Phenomenology and Existentialism is that for Activity Theory, the project has its origin and existence in the societal world in which the person finds themself; for Phenomenology and Existentialism the psyche projects itself on to the world. For Activity Theory, commitment to a project and formulation of actions towards it, are mediated by the psyche, but a project is found and realized as something existing in the world, be that an entire civilization, a single personality, or anything in between. (See MacIntyre, 1981, p. 146)

In the appropriation of Vygotsky's and Leontiev's ideas in Europe and the Nordic countries, the concept of 'activity system' was developed as a further elaboration of 'an activity' as it is understood in Leontiev's system. An 'activity system' is a system of actions directed towards some object, with its own norms, tools and division of labor. The concept is essentially the same as that of 'project' but is usually understood as some kind of functional institution, which develops as a result of contradictions within its structure.

A rebellion against objectivism in social theory also manifested itself in the emergence of Marxist humanism, originally with the Frankfurt School in the 1920s and particularly in Eastern Europe in the 1960s. In opposition to both Stalinized Marxism and Western sociology, these writers sought to restore a place for the active subject in social theory. Notable in this connection is Ernst Bloch. His major work, 'The Principle of Hope' (1938–1959/1986) traces a path which:

> leads via the little waking dreams to the strong ones, via the wavering dreams that can be abused to the rigorous ones, via the shifting castles in the air to the One Thing that is outstanding and needful.
>
> 1986, p. 11

Bloch rejects the hostility to 'utopianism' which the Marxist tradition counterposed to 'scientific socialism', pointing out that 'everybody lives in the future, because they strive'. More than any Marxist before him, Bloch understood that this striving for an imagined future is the motor of human history and must be placed at the center of science. It is this same humanist perspective which motivates the studies included here.

Writers have come to the notion of 'project' as an important concept in their work by various paths, from reflections on Cultural-Historical Activity Theory, social work, psychotherapy, Marxism or the study of social movements. But 'project' is also a concept which has become more and more prominent in the language of everyday life, whether talking about science and the arts, hobbies, political life or personal biographies. The combination of the philosophical sediment that the concept has acquired in the history of the human sciences, with the connotations that the word has accrued from everyday usage makes the concept of 'project' a powerful tool for interdisciplinary science. This is the idea I proposed in my book *An Interdisciplinary Theory of Activity* (Blunden, 2010).

Project as an Interdisciplinary Concept

Taking a cue from Hegel, projects can be seen as passing through four stages in their development. (1) Firstly there will be some group of people who by virtue of their social position are subject to some taken-for-granted or impending problem or constraint on their freedom. These are the conditions for a project to exist, but the project has not yet come into being. (2) On becoming aware of the problem there will be a series of failed projects arising from misconceptions of the situation, until, at a certain point: (3) An adequate concept of the situation is formulated and named and a social movement is launched to change social practices so as to resolve the problem or injustice. As the project unfolds and interacts with the social environment, its object becomes clearer and more concrete. (4) Eventually, the new form of practice becomes 'mainstreamed' as part of the social practices of the wider community. That is, it is institutionalized and its concept enters into the language and culture of the community. These stages are to be seen as ideal-typical, not proscriptive.

Hegel (1807; 1816) outlined this process in detail in his conception of a 'formation of consciousness', which Marx interpreted as a 'social formation'. Vygotsky and subsequent Activity Theorists used this same conception of concepts as both units of consciousness and the units of a social formation, and in their understanding of the genesis of projects. Here 'concept' does not reference a mental object (as it does for much contemporary psychology) but rather a system of actions which are united by their orientation to a common purpose. *Actions are both subjective and objective.* A concept is the ideal or normative form of that aggregate of actions which is implicit in the immediately given actions and interactions manifested in relation to some situation. Actions have the same relation to the project of which they are part as word meanings have to a concept. A concept, like a project, is a *larger* (molar) unit, which is implicit in each meaningful action, disclosing its motivation. The project inheres in the artifact-mediated actions, norms, rules and symbols flowing from the project's self-concept and underlying the actions which constitute the project. In my *Concepts, A Critical Approach* (Blunden, 2012) I examined these relations in some detail, but what is important here is how projects manifest themselves as *social movements* (in the broadest sense), before becoming, fully or partly, *institutionalized* as part of a social formation which is itself nothing but the product of many such social movements in the past.

In the course of their development projects objectify themselves, and there are three aspects to this objectification: *symbolic, instrumental* and *practical.* Firstly, the moment someone first communicates the concept of the project it is given a name or symbolically represented in some other way, after which the word or symbol functions as a focus for actions. The word eventually enters the language and acquires nuances and meaning through the development of the project and its interaction with other projects and institutions. Secondly, the project may be objectified by the invention and production of some new instrument or by the construction of material artifacts which facilitate or constrain actions in line with the project and facilitate its integration into the life of a community. The word in which the project is symbolically objectified may then be taken as referencing this artifact, reifying the concept as if it were an independently existing object, rather than an ideal functioning as the focus of a new form of social practice which constitutes it. Finally, and most important is practical objectification: once the project achieves relatively permanent changes in the social practices of a community, the project transforms from a social movement into customary and routinized practices – an institution. In this instance, the word may be taken as referencing the form of practice in which the project has been given practical objectification and normalized.

The projects I have in mind here might be a social movement, such as the women's health movement, or a campaign against asbestos production, or it might be a capitalist firm promoting a new product under its own brand name, or a fashion or youth trend, a government program, or a branch of science. But in every case, it is an evolving and expanding social practice which arises as a protest against and remedy for some problem. A project begins with a break from the former practices of the community. In particular, projects generally arise within some definite form of practice or institution which is sensitive and resistant to contradiction, so that overcoming a problem necessitates a self-conscious break, which is nonetheless eventually incorporated into the normal life of a community.

A project goes through a series of transformations. First is the immanent development of its conception of its object. Although launched with a certain conception of the nature of the relevant problem or opportunity, as the project unfolds and interacts with other movements and institutions in the community at large, it experiences the effects of its own activity, and its conception of its object changes. That is why I say that the object of a project is *immanent within the project itself.* The object is not some objective need existing independently of the project, which determines the project from outside. It might even be quite illusory. But it emerges from the activity of the project itself, as its immanent goal and self-concept.

In the process of flowing through a community, projects *sediment* symbols, material artifacts and institutions, which remain as testaments to their activity. Such sediments may be a *technological* inheritance which will benefit subsequent generations, *institutions* – such as the legal system, universities, and scientific institutions, nation-states, firms, and so on, or words and symbols embedded in our *language* and symbolic culture. The legacy might also be climate change, polluted rivers, linguistic abominations, an obesity epidemic or some other 'social problem'. But, whatever form they take and whatever their legacy may be, projects are what makes and constitutes the world we live in.

It should be noted that like a branch of science, a project has its own norms: theoretical norms, semantic norms and practical norms. Such norms not only ensure that actions carried out within the project are meaningful for participants but also insulate participants from countervailing norms of the wider community. Soldiers mobilized for war while recklessly risking their own lives; asbestos workers expose themselves and others to the lethal fiber sharing the belief that the material is harmless; priests may feel free to abuse children in their charge, who in turn submit to the abuse – it is likely that in any project which sanctions hierarchy, abuse will flourish to the extent that the internal life of the project is insulated from public discourse. Participants in a project may evolve a unique jargon incomprehensible to outsiders, while, especially if they are successful, introducing new words to the lingua franca. These norms are not just a means of creating internal bonds and distinction from outsiders (though they may be this as well): they instantiate the self-concept of the project and give meaning to all the individual actions which constitute the project as a whole. The norms may even apparently supplant the object itself, which exists only as an abstraction from the norms.

Ethics

One of the great strengths of Activity Theory with 'collaborative project' as the unit of analysis is that collaboration is not only an observable phenomenon which can be a means of scientific description and explanation, but it is also an *ethic*, and one with powerful normative force in contemporary, secular society. Having a concept which is both a unit of analysis for science and a secular ethical norm gives it a special place in social science and its practical application, particularly in sciences such as economics, jurisprudence and sociology whose subject matter is ethical life.

For example, economic science assumes that economic agents will act 'rationally' within the bounds of the information available to them at the time. But the definition of 'rational' assumed by economic science is contrary to the ethics of large sections of social life. When governments make policies and laws based on a conception of what is ethical, then such laws function so as to *propagate* the ethic which is built into the science. This process, which has gone on since governments began to take policy advice from economists in the 18th century, has had deleterious effects on human welfare.

In 1981, Alasdair MacIntyre published *After Virtue*, which, despite the fact that MacIntyre had converted to Catholicism in 1980, became a reference point for secular ethics. MacIntyre situates ethical norms in 'practices' which he understands much as I understand 'projects': 'Every activity, every enquiry, every practice aims at some good' (1981, p. 139). MacIntyre distinguished between 'internal goods' 'realized in the course of trying to achieve those standards of excellence which are appropriate to, and partially definitive of, that form of activity' (1981, p. 175) and 'external goods' such as prizes, monetary rewards and wages which are used to sustain the practice, and are associated with the transformation of the form of practice into an institution. In this connection, MacIntyre refers to the 'corrupting power of institutions' (1981, p. 181). For MacIntyre also, the concept of 'project' extends from organizations such as a school or hospital to entire political communities, 'concerned with the whole of life, not with this or that good, but with man's good as such' (1981, p. 146). The virtue ethics which MacIntyre builds on this conception of social life is precisely consistent with the 'project' approach to Activity Theory.

One qualification to MacIntyre's ethical project which is important to the task at hand is Agnes Heller's (1987) contrast between the sense of equality which prevails within the 'dense ethos' uniting participants in a project, and the 'loose ethos' which characterizes the marketplace of public intercourse. Heller observes that the obligation to treat others as equals is not universal. While we are obliged to treat equals equally, within the practices of an institution 'equals should be treated equally and unequals unequally' – the boss gets paid more, managers give orders to subordinates, parents bear the burdens of care for their children, etc. Utopian dreams notwithstanding, there is no real project within which equality is truly the norm. Consequently, Heller points out that the ongoing displacement of the formerly dense ethos of institutional life by the loose ethos of modernity which underlies MacIntyre's concerns is *not* a regressive development. However, the critical problem of developing a universal ethos which can sustain a genuinely human life still lies before us. Since human freedom can only be attained through mediated self-determination, i.e., participation in projects, the ethics of *relations between projects* must be central to our concerns.

Finally, I will briefly touch on discourse ethics (Habermas, 2001) which requires that 'all those affected' be counted as participants in a discourse. This requirement is not only vague and abstract, but untenable. Who decides who is affected, and how exactly does an individual remote from the discourse participate? But more significantly, what are the discussants *doing together* which gives a purpose to the discourse? Seyla Benhabib (1992) reminds us that 'discourse ethics...is not to be construed primarily as a *hypothetical* thought process, carried out singly by the moral agent...but rather as an *actual* dialogue situation'. Moral maxims based on the hypothetical interests of a generalized other are meaningless. To be meaningful at all such an ethics presupposes state or supra-state institutions, as representatives of the generalized other, to mediate social action, which is an unwarranted restriction on the moral standpoint. Rather, the real relations between any two individuals is given by the projects in which they collaborate, whether that 'collaboration' entails cooperation or conflict over the object. Collaboration is a strong ethical norm, but encompasses a complex variety of nuances according to the mode of collaboration. The complex ethics entailed in consultation, attribution, privacy, sharing, ownership, division of labor, negotiation of norms, consistency, and so on, provide a real basis for the construction of an ethics for the modern, secular world.

One of the corollaries of Benhabib's (2002) approach is that the concept of nation-state has to be disentangled into the several distinct projects which are conflated in the notion which has pertained since the Treaty of Westphalia. This is a task which can only be resolved by a social theory which takes projects and not abstract general categories as its basic units.

Methodological Individualism and Dichotomies in the Social Sciences

Every science has for its foundation one concept, either a 'unit of analysis' which characterizes the smallest entity which constitutes a whole in the theory, or a 'system concept' of a multitude of such units, a 'molar unit', constituting its conception of a *Gestalt*.

The unit of analysis for many human sciences, especially those in the analytical tradition, is the individual person. And for the most reductive strands of psychology and medicine generally the individual is also the *Gestalt*. The raising of a person by this or that family, into this or that historical epoch, speaking this or that language, are taken to be external, contingent processes, like the pressing of wax into a mold. Alongside the concept of the individual is a system concept of the 'social group', the unit for the social sciences, generally conceived of as an aggregate of individuals sharing some attribute in common, be that ethnicity, place of residence, gender, age, occupation, income or whatever. But for a growing body of human science, this analytical approach is unsatisfactory.

Accordingly, twentieth century researchers introduced a range of system concepts for social interaction: discourse, activity, genre, language game, frame, tradition, figured world, activity system, idioculture, social formation, network, ideology, ideological apparatus, field, habitus and so on. All such conceptions provide insights into the formation of the human mind, but rarely extend to considering the collectives represented in the relevant 'system concepts' as themselves *units*, subject to transformations and interaction with *others*.

Likewise researchers with a broader resolution took nation, state, market, community, economy, culture, people, social class and so on as objects of study. As Sylvia Scribner observed:

> Psychologists, for example, tend to conceive of the individual as a dynamic system while assuming in their research designs that history on the societal level is static; anthropologists often make the reverse assumption.
>
> 1985, p. 140

'Methodological collectivism', which takes such suprahuman entities as its units must take for granted the nature of individuals acting out the behavior of the collective, which in turn can only be the subject of abstract empirical description. Either a logical circle in which the individual – a parody of a real human being – behaves as required to reproduce the macrophenomena, or a logical circle in which *descriptions* of the collective are elevated to the status of laws *governing* the collective.

The 'rational economic agent' of economic science, for example, cannot withstand criticism from the standpoint of psychological science. The results are even more desultory when this parody of the human being is extended for example to social movement theory. This is the case with most American social movement theorists who try to understand the actions of individuals in relation to social movements in terms of individuals pursuing individual goals and performing a cost-benefit analysis as they do so (Jamison & Eyerman, 1991, p. 24ff). Such approaches treat human beings as automatons, and lack any defensible ethical insight into what motivates human life. Outside the boundaries of his or her own discipline, the scientist most often resorts to folk conceptions of the smaller or larger unit of analysis, as the case may be – a simple boundary condition beyond the horizon of critique. A concept is needed which is concerned equally with how a person's mind is shaped by their social situation and cultural context, *and* how social formations and cultural constellations are shaped by the actions of individuals. The same concept must facilitate scientific investigation at *all* levels of aggregation.

Such a concept must meet certain requirements. It must be able to represent a self-sufficient *Gestalt* of social life at the individual level, the meso-level with which 'project' is normally associated in common parlance, *and* the cultural-historical level. It must embody movement and change, not some functional or structural conception of 'dynamic equilibrium'. And it must capture both how the individual human psyche is determined by a person's social situation *and* how individual persons participate in real social change. Finally, it must express both a viable ethical conception of modern life *and* a unit of scientific analysis for the formation of modern life and its conduct.

Such a concept is the collaborative project.

'Project' may be understood just as it is understood in books on 'project management' written for engineers and producers in the arts and sciences.

It also encompasses 'life projects' which form the core of a person's identity, and projects in the sense of historical projects such as nation-building, the Enlightenment, Science and so on.

Such a conception must give maximum scope for the co-formation of individual persons and the forms of life to be lived by those persons. By taking 'project' as a unit of analysis a number of other notorious dichotomies become manageable. For example, if we replace the conception of 'social structure' with that of the world as a fabric woven from interacting projects, and at the same time, understand that a project is the only possible manifestation of the human will as a collective will, then the agency/structure dichotomy can be resolved. If we understand that the object of a project is immanent within the development of the project itself, the real unfolding of which is equally a learning process, then there is no dichotomy between development and immanence. There is no quandary between determinism and contingency, because in commitment to projects the individual's life is itself a determining factor. Because projects both create and instantiate concepts, and are therefore, like actions, are both subjective and objective, this ancient dichotomy is no longer problematic.

The study of collaborative projects is open to any method of analysis, be it discourse analysis, behaviorism, rational choice theory or whatever. The are no axioms for projects; the insights from any of the approaches to understanding social action can contribute to the study of projects. In this way, the wall between the various analytical approaches can be broken down, by shedding light on the nature of a formation of human action which in turn can function as a unit at the micro-, meso- and macro-levels of the human sciences.

'Project' as a unit of Activity and as a starting point for Activity Theory is an interdisciplinary concept for the following reason. A project is the focus for an individual's motivation, the indispensable vehicle for the exercise of their will and thus the key determinant of their psychology *and* the process which produces and reproduces the social fabric. Projects therefore give direct expression to the identity of the sciences of the mind and the social sciences. Projects belong to both; a project is a concept of both psychology *and* sociology. Social and political theory resting on the concept of 'project' is humanist because it gives realistic expression to the agency of individuals in societal affairs and concrete content to social relations.

The Project Conception of the Person

Cultural-Historical Psychology and Activity Theory (CHAT) is a rich and living tradition of research and education across a wide range of psychological disciplines: psychology, psychotherapy, vocational training, counseling, education, child development as well as meso-level disciplines such as town planning, community development, work organization, etc. Everything that has been established within this scientific tradition stands with the adoption of 'project' as the unit of activity. To a great extent, the present exercise is the *extension* and *strengthening* of Activity Theory in those disciplines which deal with human beings en masse. But nonetheless, 'project' as a unit of activity contributes new insights to our conception of the individual person and the psyche and enriches the work already done by CHAT researchers.

The unit of a social group is an individual, but the unit of a project is an *action*, just as the unit of an activity is an action. A project is constituted by the actions of different people at different times, whilst individuals participate in different projects. 'Project' is not another name for a 'group'. A project is an aggregate of actions, a unit of social life.

It is a common criticism of psychology that emotion and reason are treated as two distinct processes, independent of one another, and many theorists have considered how to 'connect' reason and emotion. But if we begin from actions, actions whose meaning and value are manifest in the project of which they are a part, then before cognition or emotion can be abstracted, we have something which is neither emotion nor cognition but which underlies both. It is only by means of reflection that the affective and cognitive aspects of an action can be abstracted from one another. But the project is the source both of motivation for action and conception of a means by which the end may be attained. Participation in collaborative projects therefore provides for the unity of cognition and emotion and their subsequent differentiation.

There are many theories of identity and some CHAT researchers locate the source of identity in the projects a person is committed to and in the roles a person takes in pursuance of those projects. This leads us to a humanist conception of identity, which is in contrast to structuralist theories of identity based on difference and likeness. A person's identity is that central, concrete project (or narrative) which is realized and concretized through a person's life, subsuming the diversity of projects to which a person commits themselves over their lifetime: furtherance of their family, a profession, national or community goals, and so on. So a person's identity is not just formed *by* collaborative projects, it *is* a collaborative project. Projects create selves at the same time as they create social bonds.

A central and defining aspect of the personality is the will. Growth from infancy to adult citizenship entails the development of self-mastery and a will moderated by consciousness of one's social position. Exercise of the will is in principle possible only through collaborative projects – the person as a sovereign subject comes into being only thanks to communicative self-determination achieved in the realization of shared goals in collaboration with others. The study of projects provides insights into the formation of will. As human beings are formed as sovereign subjects, so also are the social bonds which will sustain them formed. Mental problems, if not resulting from injury or disease, can generally be traced to the frustration or failure of projects or the person's collaboration in them, or in conflicts between projects themselves or a person's commitments to projects, or exploitation of a person's commitment to a project in the 'thick ethos' prevailing within a project. Understanding personal crises therefore leads directly to a consideration of the projects to which they are committed and their position within those projects.

Even the conception of knowledge is radicalized by the project approach. Knowledge as it is usually offered in schools nowadays is a fragmented mosaic of disconnected material, grouped in subject areas, reflecting the fragmented character of modern capitalist society. In the project approach, knowledge is seen as practical, taking the form of problem/solutions at this or that point in the realization of projects to which a person may be committed. Knowledge in this conception expresses a person's interest and capacity to change the world. This different conception of the mind reflects a different conception of social life.

The Project Conception of Social Life

Generally speaking, for the dominant currents of social theory, the unit of a social formation is taken to be a *social group*, and the unit of the social group an individual. Fear, antipathy or indifference to outsiders may be explained in terms of 'difference' – people of one social group distrust or fear others speaking a different language, looking different, adopting different norms of dress, etc. This approach (which has a sound enough basis in both casual observation and social theory) leads to a picture of the political community as a kind of mosaic of distinct groups, cemented into fixed positions, held together if at all, by residual shared attributes, or at best by mutual interest and exchange. There exist any number of theories, some of them very powerful, which explain how such social groups cohere and reproduce themselves over generations. Some theories, such as that of Bourdieu (1979), see social groups as actively constructed by their members, rather than as abstract general categories, but even in such cases the individuals remain trapped in a social structure whose dynamics lie beyond their horizon of action. But Activity Theory sees a social group as but the *product* of a project, as the *appearance* of a project at one stage in its development. The representation of social formations in terms of social groups (however defined) is abstract and static. Social structure and especially social *change* can only be grasped by means of the concept of 'project'. Equally, social structures can only be properly understood through the process of their formation and change. A coherent community is an integral fabric, woven together by projects: not a quilt of multi-colored patches, but a rich and moving tapestry of diverse intertwining threads. The personality and identity of every individual is formed through the multiplicity of projects to which they are committed and through which they have fashioned collaborative relations with others.

In political life, the social form in which world-transforming projects can manifest themselves is historically circumscribed. In my essay 'Forms of Radical Subjectivity' (Blunden, 2003), I traced the particular forms of collaborative self-consciousness through which projects have formed themselves since the advent of modernity. 'Radical subjects' are those projects which have identified themselves as Other to the dominant social subject and set out to overthrow existing social conditions. These forms have been, in succession: the spontaneous uprising, the secret society, the class-based movement, the mutual aid association, the (Paris) Commune, the mass political party, the workers state, the popular or united front, the national liberation front, new social movements (such as the Civil Rights and Women's Movements), the more ephemeral protest movements, identity politics and, more recently, alliance politics. Each successive form sublates and subsumes those forms which have preceded it: the front presupposes the party, the alliance more often than not is made up of 'affinity groups', a.k.a., secret societies, etc.. Each form, as it is overtaken by later forms, continues to exist within and beside the new forms of subjectivity. In each case the mode of collaboration is adapted to the social and political landscape of the time. Conditions of civility, freedom from repression, social cohesion, the available means of communication as well as the resources and existing forms of activity among the radicalized social layers all determine that projects for radical change will adopt different forms of 'cognitive praxis' (Jamison & Eyerman, 1991) in different historical circumstances.

Writing in the 1920s and '30s, at a time when the tactics and strategy of the workers' movement in Europe was facing a crisis, Antonio Gramsci (1937/1971) addressed himself to the problem of the formation of a *collective will*. In particular, he saw the need for workers to form themselves into a project with a consciousness that would transcend their own 'corporatism' (i.e. fraternity to their immediate peers) and establish relations of solidarity and collaboration with other workers and other sections of the community, notably the peasants in the South of Italy and intellectual fellow travelers. Gramsci's approach to social problems, like the project approach advocated here, does not take social interests and social consciousness as given, but rather as processes to be developed in *praxis* (i.e. critical activity). Gramsci took as his inspiration Machiavelli's *The Prince*. According to Gramsci, in the modern age of mass politics, the Prince is not any concrete or even ideal individual, but rather a utopian image which can only be instantiated by a 'party' – in the broadest sense of an organized faction of society – or more precisely, a 'project'. The Prince is the realization of a collective will, which Machiavelli had personified in the image of the ideal political leader. The modern Prince entails the immanent formation of a 'philosophy of praxis': a coherent world view that emerges from the mutual interpenetration of everyday class practices and philosophical critique. In order to consolidate the working class social movement, Gramsci recognized the need for internal differentiation of directive, cultural, and technical functions within the class project. However, he also emphasized that if the Prince is to be an emancipatory power, 'dialectical pedagogy' – i.e. a reciprocal and democratic relation between the educators and the educated – is required.

A central problem for activism and political struggle today is the modalities by which distinct projects (social movements or institutions) may lend aid with one another or enter into alliance to gain some specific objective. Collaboration is the birthplace of creativity (John-Steiner 2000), and new developments of all kinds very often arise through the penetration of one project by another or the formation of a collaborative alliance between projects. There are three basic ways in which one project may lend assistance to another project.

Colonization: In this scenario, a subject rescues another subject by subsuming their activity into their own project. The aim may be exploitative, but may also be philanthropic. As a result the colonized subject no longer controls its own destiny and to one degree or another must abandon its self-consciousness, ideals and norms, in return for survival.

External Reward (*or Exchange*): In this scenario, the labor of another subject is incorporated into the subject's own project by offering external rewards (see MacIntyre, 1981, p. 181), such as wages, prestige, trade or reciprocal support in their own project. Cooperation for mutual benefit is encompassed by this mode. This leaves the other subject free to pursue their own object, and may even gain resources for that purpose while providing resources for the 'host' project. But this is an arm's length relationship which leaves the independence of both subjects intact and does not generate a relationship of genuine collaboration or reciprocal critique.

Solidarity: In this scenario, another subject is assisted by voluntarily lending one's own labor to the support of the other's project according to the other's direction. Solidarity is the opposite of philanthropic colonization, because in assisting an other, the other remains the owner of the project and is thereby assisted in achieving self-determination. The project lending solidarity sacrifices part of its autonomy for the benefit of the struggling project and creates the basis for trust and mutual understanding, thereby opening the way for a creative alliance based on collaboration.

Given that social movements (and projects generally) set out to change social practices, social movements must transform institutions. This may entail abolishing or overthrowing an institution, but almost always the aimed-for transformation is achieved by forming an alliance with at least a section of the institution and ultimately the institution itself, facilitating the institution's self-transformation. In the project approach, an institution is a project: *a social movement which has become mainstreamed.* In this view an institution is not simply a practico-inert (Sartre 1960), but an arena within which an institution has the potential to re-discover its concept and reform itself. Scientists do not become scientists and work long hours in the laboratory just to get good pay, travel opportunities and prestige, even if on a day-to-day basis, as individuals, they are motivated by these goals. According to Activity Theory participants in an activity have an understanding of the motive of the activity, even if it figures only mediately in setting their day-to-day goals. Jamison's (1991) otherwise excellent approach to social movements falls down where he sees the objectification of a social movement in institutions as simply the 'break-up' of a social movement as part of its decline and fall. But as former social movements, institutions are always open to a 'paradigm shift' to use Kuhn's (1962) very apt expression. Because different projects have different norms of action, belief and meaning, any kind of alliance generates friction and often misunderstanding, the norms of an institution or social movement flow from its self-concept and have meaning which transcends immediate misunderstandings.

Yrjö Engeström (2001) has theorized the process of mutual transformation of 'systems of activity' (i.e., projects) through the idea of a 'shared object'. In Engeström's approach the shared object facilitates the collaboration of two distinct systems of activity.

The Project Conception of Economic Life

With the emergence of the modern era, bourgeois (civil) society rose up in the gap which opened up between family and state. It has given us a domain in which the ethic of exchange is dominant, rather than collaboration and command. Economics may give us scientific knowledge of economic activity by taking as its unit of analysis the exchange of commodities. This is all very well, but critics have pointed out that exchange of commodities fails to take account of 'externalities', in particular the natural and social pre-conditions for economic life. But even *within* its own domain, economics covers only a fraction of the activity through which people's needs are met by social labor.

The project approach takes the *company* as the unit of analysis of capital, and it takes the company to be a project. That is, a unit of capital is a social relation, specifically a project whose object is the expansion of capital by putting commodities into circulation and withdrawing money at a profit. The measure of capital – the 'molar' unit of value – is the proportion of the total social labor which is commanded by the company. In general, a company is constituted as a project through instrumental, symbolic and practical objectification so as to command labor from which profit can be accrued and accumulated.

But companies (or more broadly, 'corporations', including statutory and not-for-profit enterprises which are active within the economy) are far from being the only projects active in economic life. Further, companies have an internal life of their own which is not based on the ethic of exchange.

There are three basic modes of collaboration which constitute labor activity as projects.

Command: this is the dominant relationship existing within companies (or not-for-profit projects), constituting the line management. The stream of command begins with a Board of Directors or CEO (legally, the 'directing mind' of the company) and flows along with funds down the tree to the 'coal face' employees. Command is a strong archetypal mode of project collaboration which has characterized projects from nation-states to families down the centuries. It is a limiting case of collaboration: a *non-collaborative mode of collaboration*.

Exchange: this is the dominant relationship in the marketplace, but is increasingly found within commercial projects via the use of one-line budgeting, out-sourcing, franchising and so on. This is the other limiting, *non-collaborative mode of collaboration* in which each party retains its independence and formal equality by regulating the relationship through payment or exchange. The flow of command is accompanied by the flow of money, but the parties retain their freedom to refuse, and thereby their mutual independence.

Collaboration: this is the relationship which is normative among the productive employees of a company as well as within the 'directing mind' of a company. In both cases, 'working together', consultation, mutual critique, sharing work and attribution are the norms. Profit-making companies rely on the collaborative labor not only of their employees during working hours, but of the working class communities who collaboratively produce the labor power made available for exploitation.

In the market, command and collaboration are subsumed under exchange, while within companies, collaboration and exchange are subsumed under command, and in the voluntary sector, normally exchange and command are subsumed under collaboration. A complete picture of economic activity is possible only by recognizing the mutual subsumption of these three modes of collaboration, including both normative collaboration and 'non-collaborative' modes of collaboration, which are normative within hierarchical organizations.

For all its faults, 'social capital' research (Coleman 1990; Putnam 2000) has demonstrated that modes of collaboration other than exchange are amenable to quantification, and confirms that projects other than companies need to be considered to get a full picture of economic life and its preconditions. A project-based approach has the potential to introduce some clarity into 'social capital' research which currently lacks a rigorous foundation. The same holds for corporate law and the legal theory surrounding corporate action generally. As MacIntyre pointed out: 'Every moral philosophy has some particular sociology as its counterpart' (1981, p. 209), and the same is true of Law.

This conception of the three paradigmatic modes of interaction between projects also encompasses A.N. Leontiev's conception of the 'merely understood' and 'really effective' motives in psychology. For example, if a child is *commanded* to do their reading, seeking to commit the child to this project which is important for their development, the child resists, and does not embrace the motive of completing the reading. Then the child may be offered in *exchange* for doing their reading that they can go and play with their friends. This creates an 'external' commitment to the reading project. But a genuine *collaboration* between teacher and child in which the child is motivated to read, does not arise from rewards, even rewards closely connected to the task. The child has to discover the task's value in relation to existing 'really effective' motives. Collaboration is possible only when the effective and merely understood motives coincide.

Summary

'Project' may function as a unit of analysis for activity in a range of disciplines from psychotherapy to political science and historiography, because *one and the same concept* may be used in each discipline. 'Project' is not just a metaphor or a polysemous word, whose meaning is different in different contexts, but a genuinely interdisciplinary concept. 'Project' functions explicitly to theorize *the connection between human actions and the societal context* in which individual actions are meaningful. Since no social phenomena are possible other than through the actions of individuals, and no meaningful individual action is possible other than in and through the larger cultural and historical context of action – the concept of 'project' is applicable in all the human sciences. The concept of 'a project' is a further development of the concept of 'an activity' developed by A.N. Leontiev, or 'system of activity' developed by Yrjö Engeström and others based on cultural-historical research in psychology by many thousands of researchers, and facilitates bringing the entire tradition of Activity Theory to bear on a wide range of subject matter beyond the normal disciplinary bounds of psychology.

The Concept of Project

A 'project' is *an activity*, that is, a *unit* of activity, and as such is the basic concept of Activity Theory. To say 'collaborative project' is simply to emphasize that 'project', as the basic relation which brings people together, indicates not a common attribute, but a shared commitment.

Activity Theory has its roots in Classical German philosophy especially that of Hegel, in particular as appropriated by Marx (1845), as set out in *Theses on Feuerbach*. The proximate source of Activity Theory is the Cultural Psychology of Lev Vygotsky. On these foundations, A.N. Leontiev first set out a framework for Activity Theory, elaborated, for example, in *The Development of Mind* (2009) and *Activity, Consciousness and Personality* (1978). These foundations were further developed by a number of Soviet writers, by Yrjö Engeström with his *Learning by Expanding* (1987) followed by numerous journal articles and book chapters, and separately by a number of researchers in Europe.

An activity or project is an aggregate of actions, so the conception of a project rests on the conception of an *action*. In Activity Theory actions are both subjective and objective – behavior is not abstracted from consciousness. Consequently, an aggregate of actions is also equally objective and subjective. Implicit in the concept of 'action' is that actions are artifact-mediated; that is, all actions are effected by means of tools or symbols meaningful within the project and usually within the wider culture. Consequently, activities are also inclusive of the material conditions they both create and presuppose.

Activity Theory with 'project' as the concept of 'an activity' is continuous with all the research conducted in this scientific tradition and incorporates its insights. Briefly, the concept of an activity which was first formulated by A.N. Leontiev, can be defined as follows:

> Activity is a molar, not an additive unit of the life of the physical, material subject. In a narrower sense, that is, at the psychological level, it is a unit of life, mediated by psychic reflection, the real function of which is that it orients the subject in the objective world.
>
> LEONTIEV, 1978

'Molar' means a large mass of material of some quality, in contrast to 'molecular' which means the smallest unit of material of some quality. The concept of a molar unit in psychology originated in German Romanticism and is implied in almost every action of a human being which is not directed towards its immediate object but to some relatively distant motive. Nonetheless, 'molar unit' is a concept with which modern social science has a great deal of trouble. In Activity Theory there is nothing in an activity other than human actions, and this is a thesis with which contemporary interactionist theories would be in agreement, eschewing recourse to biological determinism, religious or structural fatalism or any other force outside of human action as determinants of human life. But because there is nothing other than human actions to be found in an activity this does not mean that an activity is simply the additive sum of actions. In fact, the activity is generally a *precondition* for any of the component actions which instantiate it: when we act we do not generally *create* an activity, we *join* it. So Activity Theory recognizes that there are aggregates of actions which have a unity of their own for which, as the saying goes, the whole is greater than the sum of the parts. The question then is *what is it that gives an activity its unity*?

An activity is defined by a universal, societal concept of its object, instantiated in its principal symbols and name. Individual participants may be aware of the motive of the activity in which they are participating, but the sense they have of it, and their motive for participation in the activity, is individual. The harmonization of the contradiction between societal and individual needs is resolved by the development of a social division of labor and a societal system for the circulation and distribution of the products of labor. Each individual action is motivated by a goal which may not be the same as the motive of the activity which it realizes. An individual action which serves an individual's goal, such as 'Go to point A', realizes the motive of the activity of a large number of individuals thanks to a social division of labor and a socially produced means of the supervision of labor.

The above outline has a number of problems chief among which is that the context from which it originated was a 'planned economy' such as was known to the Soviet writers, and it does not extend well to life in the capitalist world, or for that matter, to any really existing 'planned economy'.

Yrjö Engeström freed Activity Theory from some of the shortcomings of this first model, introducing his 'expanding model' of activity. Here the elements mediating subject and object are introduced at the 'ground floor', so to speak, of analyzing an activity. The subject and its object are mediated by instruments and the community. In turn the relation between the subject and the community is mediated by norms and rules, and the relation between the community and the object of the activity is mediated by a division of labor. Engeström thus introduced into the concept of an activity, explicit consideration of the culturally produced artifacts used in the activity, the community engaged in the activity, and the norms and division of labor. Engeström describes this model as 'expanding' because each mediation arises in response to contradictions and an iterative process of new mediations and new problems bring about an expansion of the activity system and changes in the object.

What the notion of Project is intended to do is to bring the concept of an activity back to a simple concept which can also mobilize everyday meanings, and at the same time give greater emphasis to the dynamic nature of activities and a vision of the social fabric in which the unlimited agency of individual human beings is manifest. To this end two important concepts of Hegel have been brought to bear, namely the concept of immanence and Hegel's mediation of the molar/molecular relation in a logical concept.

How is the relation between a project and its object to be understood? If we take the object to have an independent, objective existence, then we are left with a number of problems. Is the object to be determined by the Central Committee or does it suffice to say simply that it arises from human activity in the past? An aim or 'human need' cannot be added to an activity otherwise lacking in motive, and nor can an activity added to a pre-existing need. The object of a project is *immanent within the project itself.* The project arises in response to some contradiction or problem within a social situation. However, the object cannot simply be conceived of as 'to solve problem X'. The problem stimulates efforts to find a solution but it is not in itself sufficient to form a concept (Vygotsky, 1934/1987, p. 126). Quite different, even mutually hostile projects may be directed at one and the same situation and solve one and the same problem. The formation of a project with a concept of the problem is an original and creative social act. From that time forward the project, with its object, continues to develop according to its own logic, so to speak. Where a project may 'end up' cannot be determined in advance. The plot unfolds according to its own dynamic and through interaction with the wider community. This is what is meant by immanence.

How can we understand the relation between the motivation of individual actions on one hand, and on the other hand, the immanent objective of the project which forms the unifying principle of the project uniting all the disparate individual actions into a single activity? Hegel resolved this problem in his solution to the problem of the subsumption of any number of individual actions under a concept, but there is no criteria other than the concept itself determining this subsumption. The relation between an action and the project which gives to the action its rational meaning is the same as the relation between any individual discursive act and the concept which it instantiates, and the same as the relation between any individual thing and the category under which the thing is subsumed. The relation between the individual and the universal is mediated by the particular, that is by praxis, and is not to be conflated with the subjective-objective relation which is a quite distinct relation. The universal has no separate existence, but exists only in and through its particularization by individuals.

It is the failure to grasp this conception which has meant that interactionist discourses fail to see the forest in their fascination with the trees. Attempts to replace the individual/universal relation with the categorization of individuals according to contingent attributes leads away from Activity Theory and projects to the theorization of society in terms of social groups made up of like individuals – a truly postmodern, fragmented view of the world. Activity Theory with Project as a unit of activity can, on the contrary, grasp the real participation of the individual in the universal and the universal in the individual. But *any* research, not just Activity Theory, which sheds light on the dynamics of collaborative projects will contribute to the understanding of social cohesion and social change, and facilitate interdisciplinary research.

References

Benhabib, S. (1992). *Situating the Self. Gender, Community and Postmodernism in Contemporary Ethics*. New York, NY: Routledge.

Benhabib, S. (2002). *The Claims of Culture. Equality and Diversity in the Global Era*. Princeton, NJ: Princeton University Press.

Bloch, E. (1938–1959/1986). *The Principle of Hope. Volume One*. trans. N. Plaice, S. Plaice and P. Knight., Cambridge, MA: The MIT Press.

Blunden, A. (2003). *Forms of radical subjectivity*, http://www.academia.edu/1968764/in *For Ethical Politics*, Melbourne, Australia: Heidelberg Press.

Blunden, A. (2010). *An Interdisciplinary Theory of Activity*, Leiden Netherlands: Brill.

Blunden, A. (2012). *Concepts. A Critical Approach*, Leiden Netherlands: Brill.

Bourdieu, P. (1979/1984). *Distinctions. A Social Critique of the Judgment of Taste.* translated by Richard Nice, Cambridge MA: Harvard University Press.

Coleman, J.S. (1990). *Foundations of Social Theory*, Cambridge MA: Harvard University Press.

Dewey, J. (1897/1981). "My pedagogic creed," pp. 442–454, *The Philosophy of John Dewey*, ed. J.J. McDermott, Chicago IL: University of Chicago Press.

Engeström, Y. (1987). *Learning by Expanding*, http://lchc.ucsd.edu/mca/Paper/Engestrom/expanding/toc.htm.

Engeström, Y. (2001). Expansive learning at work: toward an activity theoretical reconceptualization, *Journal of Education and Work, 14*(2).

Freire, P., (1970/2011). *Pedagogy of the Oppressed*, trans. Ramos, M.B., London UK: Continuum

Gramsci, A., (1937/1971). *Selections from the Prison Notebooks*. Trans. Hoare, Q. & and Nowell Smith, G., New York, NY: International Publishers.

Habermas, J., (2001). *The Inclusion of the Other. Studies in Political Theory*, Cambridge MA: M.I.T. Press.

Hegel, G.W.F. (1807/1910). *The Phenomenology of Mind*. Trans, with an Intro & notes J.B. Baillie, London UK: George Allen & Unwin Ltd..

Hegel, G.W.F. (1816/1969). *The Science of Logic*, trans. A.V. Miller, London UK: George Allen & Unwin.

Heidegger, M. (1927/1962). *Being and Time*, translated by Macquarie, J. & Robinson, New York: Harper and Row.

Heller, A. (1987). *Beyond Justice*, UK: Basil Blackwell Ltd.

Jamison, A. & Eyerman, R. (1991). *Social Movements. A Cognitive Approach*. University Park, PA: Pennsylvania State University Press.

John-Steiner, V (2000). *Creative Collaboration*. New York: Oxford University Press.

Knoll, M. (2012). "I had made a mistake": William H. Kilpatrick and the project method, *Teachers College Record*, 114(2), p. 1–45. http://www.tcrecord.org ID Number: 16242, Date Accessed: 10/4/2013.

Kozulin, A. (1991). The psychology of experiencing: A Russian view, *Journal of Humanistic Psychology 31*(3) 1991, 14–19.

Kravtsov, G. & Kravtsova, E. (2010). *Department of Projective Psychology webpage* http://psychology.rsuh.ru/kf_proekt.html

Kropotkin, P. (1902). *Mutual Aid: A Factor in Evolution*. http://www.marxists.org/reference/archive/kropotkin-peter/1902/mutual-aid/index.htm

Kübler-Ross, E. (1969). *On Death and Dying*, New York: Macmillan.

Kuhn, T. (1962/1996). *The Structure of Scientific Revolutions*. Chicago, IL: University of Chicago Press.

Leontiev, A.N. (1978). *Activity, Consciousness, and Personality*, Prentice-Hall.

Leontiev, A.N. (2009). *The Development of Mind*, Pacifica, CA: Marxists Internet Archive Press.

MacIntyre, A. (1981). *After Virtue*, Notre Dame, IN: University of Notre Dame Press.

Marx, K., (1845/1975). 'Theses on Feuerbach', *MECW* 5, London, UK: Lawrence & Wishart, 3–5.

Putnam, R.D. (2000). *Bowling Alone: Collapse and Revival of American Community*, New York, NY: Simon & Schuster.

Sartre, J.-P. (1946/1989). "Existentialism is a humanism," in *Existentialism from Dostoyevsky to Sartre*, ed. W. Kaufman, NY: Meridian Publishing Company.

Sartre, J.-P. (1960/2004). *Critique of Dialectical Reason, Volume 1, Theory of practical ensembles*, trans. A. Sheridan-Smith, with a foreword by F. Jameson, London, UK: Verso.

Schutz, A. (1945/1970). *On Phenomenology and Social Relations, Selected Writings*, edited and with an introduction by H.R. Wagner, University of Chicago Press, excerpt reprinted from "On Multiple Realities," in *Philosophy and Phenomenological Research*: 1945.

Scribner, S. (1985). 'Vygotsky's uses of history', *Culture Communication and Cognition. Vygotskian Perspectives*, ed. Wertsch, J., pp. 119–145, New York: Cambridge University Press.

Stetsenko, A. (2003). Alexander Luria and the cultural-historical activity theory: Pieces for the history of an outstanding collaborative project in psychology, *Mind, Culture and Activity 10*(1), 93–97. New York, NY: Routledge.

Stetsenko, A. (2012). Personhood: An activist project of historical Becoming through collaborative pursuits of social transformation (invited paper for the Special Issue on Personhood, edited by Jack Martin and John Bickhart), *New Ideas in Psychology* 30, 144–153.

Stetsenko, A. & Arievitch, I. (2004a). Vygotskian collaborative project of social transformation. History, politics, and practice in knowledge production, *The International Journal of Critical Psychology 12*, 58–80. Basingstoke, UK: Palgrave Publishers Ltd.

Stetsenko, A., & Arievitch, I. (2004b). The self in cultural-historical activity theory: Reclaiming the unity of social and individual dimensions of human development. *Theory & Psychology 14*(4), 475–503.

Vasilyuk, F.E. (1984). *The Psychology of Experiencing. The Resolution of Life's Critical Situations*. Progress Publishers Moscow. English translation (1988), Hemel Hempstead, UK: Harvester-Wheatsheaf.

Vianna, E., & Stetsenko, A. (2011). Connecting learning and identity development through a transformative activist stance: Application in adolescent development in a child welfare program. *Human Development 54*, 313–338.

Vygotsky, L.S. (1934/1987). "Thinking and speech," *Collected Works*, Volume 1, New York: Plenum Press, p. 39–285.

Overview

Twelve writers were invited to contribute a chapter in their area of expertise to a book on the theme of collaborative projects as a concept for interdisciplinary human sciences. The areas of interest covered micro-, meso- and macro-levels of the human sciences. Authors were required to provide reports on research which had both empirical data and analysis. The editor then wrote the introduction, which was developed in response to several rounds of critique by the participants. After the research reports had been written, they were circulated to all the authors and several others who were then invited to submit short reflections on either individual chapters, or the concept as a whole. In the concluding remarks the editor then reflected on the reflections.

Research Projects

The first three chapters describe initiatives in which children and young people are engaged in projects as the centerpiece of a developmental approach to pre-school and primary education, college education and social work respectively.

Elena Kravtsova and *Gena Kravtsov* outline the *projective method* for a continuous education system as it is applied in the Golden Key Schools in Russia. The projective method is the experimental-genetic method of instruction which aims to model the developmental processes which are replicated in real life. This method concerns the potential of each child within the developmental process, and works for the highest potential of each student. True to Vygotsky's conception of 'height psychology', the projective method represents a concrete approach to determining the highest level of personality development, and uses 'projection' models to help children imagine goals/solutions to various tasks, with the guidance of adults.

In the Golden Key Schools, lessons are not divided along subject lines; the semantic core of the lesson is the *plot*, very often located within a special play situation, where the children become totally involved, and acquire real skills in the course of acting out tasks arising from the central plot. The traditional division of lessons by subject in primary school education puts the cart before the horse; children obtain fragmented knowledge that has no meaning or personal sense. Through participation in the projective method, children acquire contextualized knowledge in a form which has the potential to develop into conceptual knowledge at a later stage in their development. This potential results from the conception of human life as a project.

In 'The Dialectics of Collective and Individual Transformation', *Eduardo Vianna, Naja Hougaard* and *Anna Stetsenko* describe a collaborative project centered on developing a Peer-Supported Activist Learning Community in an urban community college. Fashioned on Activity Theory expanded through a Transformative Activist Stance, this project implemented critical-theoretical teaching-learning (bridging Freirean and Vygotskian pedagogies) focused on closing the gaps between students' learning goals and their overall life pursuits by using knowledge as a mediating tool for students' evolving activist agendas and agency. Cultural mediation includes theoretical conceptual tools to (a) critically examine and interrogate the historical social practices leading to inequality, racism, sexism and other forms of discrimination, (b) facilitate students to take a stance on these issues while (c) developing activist agendas of contributing to practices that could bring about social transformation, averting injustices while drawing on the knowledge traditions and experiences of students as members of marginalized groups. In addition to a participatory action methodology of teaching-learning, the study draws on interviews, group discussions and ethnographic observations. With its focus on learning identities emerging within collaborative activist pursuits, this study illustrates the role of collaborative projects in human development and learning.

Morten Nissen discusses a video produced and displayed on the internet by a Copenhagen facility for young drug users. This analysis is part of a collaboration with the counselors that articulates 'user-driven standards of social work'. In the context of this book however, it is first of all a prototype of the theoretical approach to collaborative projects that the author has developed. In the first step, the video production is explored as not only a vaguely circumscribed practice, but as a singular collective. This requires facing issues of power. Next, it is described how the collective is framed in powerful discourse. It is, however, argued that the fashionable totalizing and anonymous view of power must be developed through the concept of recognition, and that this facilitates a fuller realization of the complicity of research in the constitution of collectives and their participants. Finally, the anticipatory nature of this collaborative project is discussed in connection with the concept of hope, stressing the kind of 'blues hope' that goes beyond common sense.

Moving from the domain of projects designed by professionals in which to engage young people to promote their personal development, into the adult world as such, the next chapter is devoted to a study of collaborative projects in the arts and sciences.

Vera John-Steiner notes that within the last decade, large scale collaborative projects have grown in number and importance. For instance, biomedical research nowadays relies on the close collaboration of clinicians and laboratory scientists in examining the sources of various illnesses. These trends are manifestations of the deeper reality of human innovative projects, which are rooted in our socially interdependent existence. This realization has been challenged by advocates of individual contributions and introversion, and the debate about 'groupthink' vs. solitude has entered conversation in the mass and social media. The controversy between individual activity and social interdependence may reflect the current virulent political divisions between proponents of personal success and communal responsibility.

In this chapter, John-Steiner challenges this argument by providing a fuller picture of long-term, carefully nurtured collaborative projects. The three aspects of collaboration focused on are the rhythms and cycles of collaboration, the notions of complementarity, and mutual appropriation. Interview data from the partnership of a chemist and physicist whose joint work has gained international renown will illustrate the complex dynamics of periods of collaborative productivity interspersed by individual elaboration. Mutual appropriation is how collaborators learn to expand their own methods of working with different concepts and research tools in engagement with their partners.

From this point on, the focus shifts from Psychology to projects as the producers of the social fabric itself. The next chapter began as a project to develop practices to combat educational inequality, but came up against problems which transcended the scope of educational and psychological theory. Instead the problems of resistance to social change came to the fore.

In their chapter on the 5th Dimension, *Michael Cole*, *Virginia Gordon* and *Bill Blanton* examine the development of a line of research referred to as the 5th Dimension Project. The 5th Dimension is traced from its origins as an element in an educational experiment three decades ago to its widespread implementation in diverse universities and community settings in the United States and abroad at present. Special emphasis is placed on the relatively long time span of the project which, it is argued, provides insights into a variety of issues of concern to students of learning and development. In particular, viewing the 5th Dimension on the scale of a multi-decade project allows for longitudinal as well as cross-sectional analysis across implementations revealing new information about why seemingly successful innovations fail to survive and the multiple factors entailed in the long-term sustainability of educational change.

The next two chapters continue the focus on what might be called 'finite projects', that is to say, projects involving a finite number of people over a finite time-span, but having the objective of introducing some specific change in social practice.

Andy Blunden and *Michael Arnold* tell of a project launched in 1999 by staff at the University of Melbourne which introduced a the concept of a new type of centrally allocated teaching space – the Collaborative Learning Space, and changed the University's policies for the maintenance and construction of shared teaching spaces. The concept of Collaborative Learning Space has spread across Australia and internationally and is now institutionalized in the practice of building university teaching spaces. The authors review the various forms of objectification which are necessary to institutionalize a new concept within the life of a community.

All such finite projects which aim to change social practices, insofar as they succeed, become part of long-term, historical projects which are themselves a part of the social fabric. An example of such a project is given by *Helena Worthen*.

In her study of how workers defend their working conditions in the US, Helena Worthen offers the example of a healthcare institution in deep Central Illinois. Like 94% of the workplaces in the US, this one is non-union. The culture of the region is politically conservative and profoundly anti-union. Following the sudden announcement of a change for the worse in their working conditions, these workers attempt to organize. They are motivated by a sense that a longstanding non-adversarial relationship between workers and employer has been betrayed. Unlike workplaces where workers have experience in the practice of representation and neighboring examples of how to develop their project and what to expect, workers here have to invent their participation structure from scratch, learning as they go along. The leadership of two workers, one whose brother is a union electrician and one who previously worked at a unionized factory, is critical. So is the support of a national union, which becomes involved later on. Her narrative about how these workers got organised in the teeth of the worst kind of repression, and finally got their contract, which regularized and stabilized their relationship with their employer, is based on interviews and participation in the struggle.

Ron Lubensky has been extending the interdisciplinary vision of collaborative projects to the practice, advocacy and study of public deliberation. For decades, political theorists have trumpeted the benefits of public participation in political decision making as a treatment for the inadequacies of representative government and the democratic deficit that results from arbitrary executive power. A cottage industry of public participation practitioners is active in many countries, especially at the local government level, to design and facilitate processes that bring the full diversity of public values and lived experience into the policy generation process. However, for all the academic fanfare, the deliberative enterprise is stalled, with few examples of concrete political influence. Recent empirical work has attempted to prove the benefits of public deliberation to legitimize its application, but Lubensky claims that public acceptance of the deliberative enterprise will rise on normative rather than epistemic claims alone. This chapter presents public deliberation as archetypal *collaborative projects*, providing insight into the barriers to its mainstream adoption, and opening pathways for more compelling narratives and improvement of the enterprise.

According to Lubensky, the project approach reveals that deliberative theorists and practitioners must make their object of activity the social movement that brings public deliberation into the mainstream.

This brings us to the consideration of those projects which transcend the life span and activity of a finite number of individuals, beginning with Vygotsky's collaborative project of social transformation in the early Soviet Union, a project to which many of the authors of this book remain committed.

Anna Stetsenko and *Igor Arievitch* discuss how the history of Vygotsky's work has been mostly portrayed from the standpoint of outdated – cognitivist and individualist – views on science and history, including in the 'Great Man' version that focuses on sole giants purportedly creating knowledge in ivory towers of purely academic pursuits of little political and practical relevance. The chapter presents an alternative approach to Vygotsky's legacy that is compatible with the very spirit of his theory which evolved as a collaborative project unique for its practical, political, and civic engagement and ideological commitment to ideals of social justice, equality, and social change.

Moreover, this project went beyond the narrow confines of psychology in its traditional guise of an ivory-tower enterprise separate from sociocultural transformative practices and instead resulted from, participated in, and contributed to the giant social experiment that was taking place in Russia. Remarkably, Vygotsky's approach embodies, in its real life history, the very theoretical principles central to it, such as the inseparability of knowledge and action, theory and practice, and the collaborative nature of knowledge. Analysis reveals the proximity of the Vygotskian project to newly evolving perspectives on science as cultural practice. It also draws attention to knowledge being an outcome and vehicle of ultimately practical, inevitably ideological, and collaborative engagements with the world that comes out of, participates in, and contributes to specific collaborative projects.

The final three reports concern projects played out on the global social and political arena involving masses of people. Here projects are essentially engaged in conflict with the dominant projects in a society and collaborative relations with other projects. As demonstrated, the social changes achieved are not just legal or institutional changes, but changes in the consciousness of masses of people.

Jennifer Power shows how the AIDS Movement changed people's minds in Australia, where affected communities, notably the gay community, established the first 'safe-sex' campaigns, created large volunteer-based care and support networks for people living with HIV/AIDS, and established a presence at the forefront of public health-policy making regarding HIV/AIDS.

AIDS activists successfully convinced the Federal Government to provide funds to enable them to take a lead in HIV-prevention and permanently enshrine the concept of community participation within the Australian public health system, including a measure of expert status equal to that of medical professionals in scientific and clinical decision making regarding HIV/AIDS.

Much of the social and political history of HIV/AIDS in Australia can be understood in terms of the relationship between three projects: community-based AIDS activists, the Federal Government and the medical profession. These projects were by no means neatly distinct: there were many individuals who sat in more than one camp – doctors who were also activists, activists who were also bureaucrats, but there was also mistrust and often competing agendas. However, the collaborative project that developed between these three projects was an important feature of the AIDS response, and built important strategic bonds and a sense of trust between the disparate groups involved.

Lynn Beaton and *Andy Blunden* examine how asbestos, once regarded as a 'miracle fiber' was exposed as a lethal carcinogen and banned in Australia.

As early as 1935, prominent asbestos user, James Hardie, reorganized their company structure to protect against compensation claims from asbestos disease sufferers, and yet it wasn't until 2003 that asbestos was banned. For 70 years, people handling asbestos products remained ignorant of the dangers, while medical scientists, governments, public regulators, trade unions, and the media, to a greater or lesser degree aware of the dangers, were rendered impotent by a concerted campaign by the Industry.

How did leaders of the asbestos industry live with the knowledge that they were bringing death and misery to hundreds of thousands of people? How were those responsible for public health and medical science made complicit? How could people daily engulfed in asbestos dust ignore public information warning of the danger to their own life? But more importantly, how was the more adequate concept of asbestos as a deadly airborne poison finally brought to public consciousness and objectified in law? The deadly effects of asbestos only came to be widely known because of the collaboration of two projects, drawn from the union movement and medical science, which was able to recruit individuals from the media, victims, lawyers involved in litigation and the wider community, to construct the Anti-Asbestos Movement as a collaborative project.

Finally, *Brecht De Smet* examines the emergence of the Egyptian revolution from the collaborative project in Tahrir Square, to defy expectations, bring down the Mubarak regime and open a way to democracy. De Smet investigates the complex relations between different projects and importantly shows how a project's concept of itself develops immanently from its activity.

The developmental logic of a multifaceted process of demonstrations, occupations, strikes, sit-ins, and street fights in various cities, neighborhoods, workplaces and rural villages is analyzed through the unit of 'Tahrir'. Midan Tahrir was not only a physical space where the first demonstrations on 25 January 2011 started, it also constituted an emancipatory, *collaborative project* which absorbed, unified, and developed the fragmented projects of protest that existed since the beginning of the 2000s. The original object of the 25 January movement, a protest against police violence, was quickly overshadowed by a much more radical demand which emerged from the revolutionary activity itself: 'the people want the end of the regime'. The project of Tahrir was a projection of a new type of society, the cell-form of the revolution.

De Smet shows the limits and constraints of project Tahrir. Rather than transforming the whole Egyptian social formation into the 'Republic of Tahrir', both the social space and spirit of the Square have been disassembled by the 'transition' government. The soft coup of the army that deposed Mubarak and the subsequent passive revolution of the election process constitute predicaments for the further development of the popular Subject. In order to overcome these obstacles the revolutionary neo-formations which emerged in Tahrir Square have to be collectively matured and shared – if not, the Egyptian social formation may again develop a strong authoritarian pathology.

Reflections

The first two reflections look at how the relationship between social projects and the broader community changes over time, whilst each changes the other. *Brecht De Smet* criticizes the conception of 'prefiguration' embraced by anarchists in the contemporary Alterglobalization Movement. In this conception, the desired form of society is immediately implemented on a small scale, with the hope that it may be imitated and quantitatively expanded. De Smet shows that this 'flat' conception of development fails to see that both the project itself and the concept it has of its end point are transfigured over time in the process of interaction with other projects.

In her reflection on the history of the Feminist Movement, *Lynn Beaton* looks at how the project of women's emancipation has changed the world and itself has changed in response to changing times. Beaton sees that the struggle of women in recent decades is wrongly discounted due to a misperception about the 'second wave' feminist movement and its relation to the broader community. 'Second wave' feminism was a creature of its times, but while times have changed, feminists have never stopped struggling. The present is always a work in progress.

The next two reflections respond to the Peer-Supported Activist Learning Community (PALC) described by Vianna et al. Firstly, a group students participating in the Community describe their own transformation, and then Ron Lubensky reflects on how the space for such activist learning has been restricted since his own days as a student.

Mike Rifino, Keiko Matsuura and *Francisco Medina* tell how they came to participate in what became an activist learning community at Hunter College, New York. They relate how their view of themselves, their college and the world around them was transformed. The conception of the tasks they faced at the start of this project – centered on their own inadequacy and/or the insuperable barriers erected against them – were gradually transformed, at first through interactions within the group but later through active and effective efforts to change conditions in the college and surrounds, in the process transforming themselves into self-assured advocates for social justice.

Ron Lubensky further explores the foundations of the TALC practice in the concept of collaborative projects and looks at the ethical dimensions of this project. Drawing the connection with his own project of deliberative democracy, Lubensky criticizes the norm of neutrality imposed on educators and facilitators of all kinds. He recognizes in TALC 'the same sort of reciprocity that facilitated deliberation relies upon for constructive progress'.

Natalia Gajdamaschko reflects on the benefits that the concept of 'project' brings to research on children's play. Play, like a project, is based on imagination, and in that sense 'thrown forward', exercising imagination to overcome the lack of the child's means to participate in adult life and laying the basis for the development of the higher psychological functions.

Chiel van der Veen and *Lynne Wolbert* continue the focus on developmental education, this time in Dutch pre-school and primary education, engaging with the concept of collaborative project at two levels. Developmental education has been built up in the Netherlands thanks to a collaborative project launched in response to the one-sided focus on transmission of knowledge in mainstream early education. The approach of these educators is reminiscent of the 'projective method' practised in the 'Golden Key' schools described in the first chapter. Van der Veen and Wolbert use the Aristotlean notion of *eudemonia* (human flourishing) to theorize the aims of developmental education, towards a good life for pupil, teacher and the community as a whole. This adds a new ethical dimension to the notion of 'collaborative project'.

The next three reflections engage with the affective, cognitive and practical aspects of the internal dynamics of projects. *Vera John-Steiner* explores a number of themes across various chapters, in particular pointing to the importance of mutual appropriation and complementarity within collaborative projects. These relations draw on individual differences in life-experience to promote successful projects as well as the transformative development of the participants themselves.

Greg Thompson explores past challenges to the individual/social dichotomy through Rousseau, Hegel, Marx and Durkheim. Drawing parallels between Vygotsky and Durkheim in terms of symbolic mediation, Thompson opens up the prospect of appropriating Durkheim's ideas about the emotional power of symbols and rituals to investigate the 'spiritedness' of collaboration and the spirited nature of ideas themselves.

After outlining the range of issues implicated in project sustainability (also dealt with in Cole's chapters), *Manfred Holodynski* turns to the motivational and emotional aspects of commitment to and participation in collaborative projects. Holodynski utilizes A.N. Leontiev's ideas on the difference between personal sense and an individual's motivation, on one hand, and the project's objectives on the other. He offers important pointers to the analysis of actions within a project and the impact of breakthroughs, stumbling blocks, recruitment and transgressions which projects encounter.

The next two reflections enter deeply into the implications for research of the concept of 'collaborative project', and return us to the theme of time and activity. *Helena Worthen* makes the point that the distinctive feature of all the reports in this book is that they are almost all narratives. Worthen sees this use of narrative in social science as a welcome move which introduces the element of time which is absent in much social science nowadays. However, she questions exactly how the concept of 'collaborative project' may be put to use in social scientific activities. Moreover, she questions the loss of concepts such as norms, division of labor, contradiction, etc., utilized in Engeström's Activity Theory, and goes on to suggest further directions for research in Activity Theory with 'project' as the unit of analysis.

Michael Cole reflects on his own research with the 5thD afterschool program and sketches what he calls a mesogenetic methodology. Furthering the tenet of

Cultural-Historical Activity Theory, that phenomena can only be understood in their development, including both growth and decline, Cole looks on the activity setting created by 5thD as an 'idioculture'. Research over 30 years has allowed Cole and his co-workers to reconstruct the narrative of the rise and fall of implementations of this learning environment. This provides invaluable insights into the cultural formation of mind which are otherwise inaccessible because of the long time-scale over which cultural change unfolds.

In his concluding remarks *Andy Blunden* also reflects on the narrative character of the research reports and claims that 'project' has introduced a new dimension of time into Activity Theory. He claims that further research is needed on both the internal dynamics of and interactions between projects. Finally, he emphasizes that taking 'project' as a unit of analysis obliges Activity Theory to develop a new conception of the object of activity and its relation to the other elements such as norms.

PART ONE

Research Projects

CHAPTER 1

The Projective Method as the Basis of Continuous Education

G.G. Kravtsov and E.E. Kravtsova

The projective method is a calling card of both L.S. Vygotsky's cultural-historical theory and his "non-classical" psychology. On one hand, this method was rarely used by Vygotsky's students and disciples with the exception of D.B. Elkonin and V.V. Davydov (Davydov, 2000; Elkonin & Davydov, 1966), who used this methodology to create a system of continuous education for primary school.

On the other hand, recently, a lot of terms and concepts which used the word "projective" have appeared – project, projective psychology, forming method, etc. This situation obliges us, once again, to return to the psychological content of the conception of "projective method."

In Vygotsky's theory the projective method was initially called the experimental-genetic method. It opposed itself to the cross-sectional method and allowed, in Vygotsky's words, the modeling of the processes of development in experimental conditions.

It does not, even slightly, coincide with the understanding of the projective method as the complex of projective tests used in the studies of personality.

Also, the described approach to the projective method is not related to the various usages of "project" in modern life, which do not consider the changes in psychic and personal development of individual.

In Russian (Soviet) psychology, the projective method became, mainly, the synonym of the method of formation, introduced by P. Ja. Galperin. According to Galperin (1998), on one hand, the establishment and development of mental actions and concepts takes place in and through formation and, on the other hand, the formation itself reflects real processes of person's development.

The analysis of the concept of projective method and other concepts close to it, allows us to mark out the common characteristics and specific features of Vygotsky's experimental-genetic method.

It seems that the concepts of "projective method" and "projective test" have one thing in common. Both of them are *methods of research*. The projective method and projective tests, in first place, study personal features. However, the projective tests reveal already formed, shaped features, while the main task of the projective method is to look into the dynamic of individual features or characteristics. In other words, projective tests study features in stasis, while the projective method does it in motion.

There are two principal differences between the projective method and the widely used method of projects. The method of projects is aimed at the final result of project's implementation, while the projective method is aimed at the mechanisms and conditions of origination of the various qualities of the psyche and the personality. Besides, the basis and content of most projects are not related to the processes of one's psychic development or to psychic development in general.

There are also qualitative differences between the projective method and the method of formation. Firstly, the result of the method of formation concerns a particular quality or feature. For example, this method allows one to form mental actions, concepts, qualities, like the ability to type a text on a computer or a typewriter. The projective method, by contrast, allows research and study, and not just the achievement of some, even important and necessary, result. Secondly, formation helps the child acquire the results, which *should be*, according to researcher's "plot," while projecting allows us to understand who the person *can be* according to the laws of psychic development. Thirdly and finally, the method of formation always has an experimenter, who, on one hand, determines which features and qualities need to be formed and, on the other hand, creates conditions for their formation. In the projective method, the one who carries out the experiment and the one whose psychic processes are being modeled are in the same box, at least in relation to the results of education and development. Thus, if those who organize a project's implementation are not developing themselves, then this method will not model the developmental processes of this project's other participants. Besides, it is one of the substantial characteristics of non-classical science's method that there is no strict differentiation between experimenter and subject.

The features of the experimental-genetic method and its differences from other methods do not mean that it should be used separately. The experimental -genetic method allows one to utilize all existing psychological methods and tests. At the same time, the projective method is not a set of finished tests and questionnaires, but the creation of conditions of a person's development, which can be modeled and corrected according to both general laws of development and individual developmental features of the particular person.

The experimental-genetic method manifests the scientific nature of psychology on a new level. Science, which deals with general patterns, assumes that different scientists who use one particular test will get the same results.

At the same time, it is well known that experimental data may vary greatly, depending on the particular experimenter and experimental conditions, depending on their personal features.

By its external characteristics, the experimental-genetic method looks like A.F. Lazursky's (1918) natural experiment. But the natural experiment allows one only to manifest revealed features and qualities of a person, while the projective method makes it possible to actively create them in the process of research. And during this process, all participants – researchers and subjects – are developing.

The projective method helps to solve the problem of correlation between the theoretical and the practical in research. So, in the first stage of using the projective method the theoretical model of development needs to be constructed. This model is based on the analysis and study of the existing psychological data, including theoretical and practical research, which allows us to understand the features of the studied subject, specific to its development – age features of the particular activity's formation, etc. This model is of a theoretical nature and assumes deep *theoretical* analysis. The implementation of the model in practice is the second stage of the projective method. It is critical, once again, to draw attention to the research nature of this method. It is not mandatory, even contraindicated to try to fully implement in practice the theoretical model created. The model is being checked, specified, corrected and even radically changed in the process of experimental tests and implementation. For example, in the "Golden Key" educational program, developed by authors, primary-school age children don't study in a common school by the traditional educational program, but, instead, they master school knowledge during a specially organized life in a large "public family" – a complex of kindergarten and primary school. But during the implementation of this program we have faced many unexpected problems and questions which were not foreseen by our theoretical model. Thus, we have had to pay special attention to the forms of initiation of former preschool children who have graduated to inclusion in school life and school education.

The cardinal difference between the projective method and all others is that the developing work is aimed not at the individual child or group of children but at the whole environment and all spheres of children's and adults' life. We came to the conclusion that full-fledged development of preschool and primary-school age children is hardly possible if restricted to education only. In other words, even if we should create and try to implement an innovative educational program, for example, the developing mathematics program for primary-school students, their development wouldn't change a bit, even if they were to use the corresponding terminology and master the general ways of solving the particular tasks. In this connection, we can remember the deplorable conclusion of H.M. Teplenkaya (1968), who showed that all attempts to replicate Piaget's phenomena and the development of conceptual thinking of senior preschool age children contributed nothing to the development of their thinking and general psychic and personal development.

This conclusion relates to both the theoretical model and the manner of its implementation. This feature of the experimental-genetic method provides its interdisciplinary nature. Thus, researchers who use the projective method and create educational or remedial programs, always stray beyond the limits of a particular a psychological area and, involuntarily, become pedagogues, psychotherapists, doctors, even, in some sense, "parents" for the children they work with, because of considering children's interests in the research. Use of the projective method assumes that a psychologist may and should be able to understand a doctor or a pedagogue, who often takes part in the experiment – either as an organizer or as a direct participant. More than that, a psychologist should be able to take on, of course with particular limitations, the roles, attitudes and relevant knowledge of these other professions.

So, if we consider the experimental-genetic method as a way of modeling psychic processes in experimental conditions, we can say that the projective method – its continuation and development in modern psychology – acts as the theoretical-methodological base of the system of continuous education.

The Golden Key Schools

In this paper we'd like to describe one particular program of continuous education. It concerns preschool-age children, school children and students who study psychology.

There are two types of institution working in the "Golden Key program." One part of them are private and financed mainly by the parents of the children who study there. The other part are state institutions and they are financed from the regional budget.

The first "Golden Key" kindergarten was opened in Moscow in 1992. At the present moment there are around 25 institutions working by this program. But due to the implementation of new state standards of preschool education this year, the program has become very popular. Besides this, various parts and themes of the program (for example play, communication, organization of education in primary school etc.) are used by kindergartens and primary schools, which are based on different educational principles.

The main goal of this program is to help children to reveal their individuality, to realize their ZPD (zone of proximal development). The most important moment for us is to work with their ZPD making it broader (and ultimately to change their ZPD depending on its dimension). We consider these three ideas as one goal since the development of a personality realizes the individuality to which instruction is directed. The realizing of their ZPD means that education leads development whilst changing the ZPD makes the education spontaneous. It means that the adult's program is transformed into the child's program.

This program is based on the cultural-historical conception of Vygotsky. As this theory concerns practically all the aspects of psychological development we want to stress its three main ideas which we tried to realize in all periods of the child's development.

We think Vygotsky's (1998) idea about communication as a main source of psychological development in ontogenesis is very important. It means that all child education must be presented as different forms of communication in two systems: between only children and between adults and children. At the same time the realizing of this idea of Vygotsky's makes education developmental. Vygotsky wrote that we can see the ZPD when a child can't do something by himself but can do it with adults helping (when the adult organizes a special communication with him). When an adult can help a child in this way, in the near future the child becomes able to do it by themself. When we put the communication in the center of the educational system we help the pupils to both study different subject contents and become subjects of communication. Please note, when we say "subject of communication" we mean that child is able not only to take part in communication but manage this process according to their own goals.

The second idea of the cultural-historical conception which is realized in our program is the unity of affect and intellect. Vygotsky (Vygotsky, 1993; Kravtsov, 1995) thought that education becomes personal when it develops affect and intellect at the same time. It means that the content of education has to be very emotional for children, has to be connected with their interests and needs and must not have an alien character.

The third idea of Vygotsky's (1935) which is embodied in our program concerns two different forms of education – spontaneous, when a child studies in accordance with his own individual program, and reactive, when a child studies in accordance with the adult's program. In the first type of situation the child himself wants to study, he has his own goals for learning – this is spontaneous education. In the other situation, the child doesn't have such a goals but the adult does – that is reactive education. Spontaneous education is more efficient and is less tiring for the children. On the other hand, spontaneous education cannot be used for the building of an instructional program because it does not include any special organization or management from the adult side. It turns out that reactive education must be transformed in a special way into a spontaneous program and only then we can use the advantages of both kinds of education.

The essential condition for creating the continuous education program is that from one side the principles of the program construction must be common for every period of psychological development. But from other side these principles must be realized in different ways according to the specifics of each psychological age. For example, the thesis that communication is the center of education in preschool childhood is realized by the organizing of mixed-age groups. In this way we can organize different conditions where each child can be in different roles: in one position he is above somebody and he teaches somebody, in the other position he is under, and he is taught by somebody. In the third way he has an opportunity to do something on equal footing even with an adult and sometimes he does something and studies something by himself in an independent position. As Vygotsky thought, the basis of all these positions is the position "grand-grand-we" (*Ur-Wir*), when a child acts in concert with his partner as a collective subject.

In early school-age this thesis is realized in another way. Now children of equal age are divided into structured groups and each get a different role position. Now they can use their role in communication according to the actions which a child realizes. At the same time the child begins to use in real life the knowledge which he has received at school: he teaches a poem with his younger friend or together with his classmate, calculates how much petrol a car needs for getting to a certain place, and so on.

In teenage communication, the educational process realizes itself in the third aspect: children begin to study work communication, where they may hitherto have had no role or their role appeared only in connection with their point of view. Such roles are the center of different discussions. These discussions finish when some real result is achieved. So if in preschool childhood children have some conditional result, in early school ages we can see a transition from a conditional result to a real one, but they can use their real result only in special activity, for example, in games. In their teenage, children have real results too, but their real result helps them to realize either their own opinions or the results of common discussion in real life.

In the eldest school classes (15–17) work communication between teenagers becomes a form of their communication and at the same time the content of their communication becomes connected with interpersonal relations and other persistent philosophical and moral problems. The main result of such discussions becomes ideals and values. Children begin to sense the world around them and to change this sense in different ways. At the same time they study consciously imitating or studying different subjects.

When we teach student-psychologists, communication remains the center of education early on, but now students study to take roles in communication volitionally, to analyze it in different kinds of activity and use it for purposeful development or correction.

Vygotsky's statement of the unity of affect and intellect in preschool childhood is realized as a unity between family and public education. In this way we have an assimilation of both: a family-as-a-kindergarten and a becoming-kindergarten-like local public family. For example, children live in mixed-age groups as in an extended public family, their life in this family has the same outward appearance as in real life and their real parents take part in their life in the kindergarten. It gives the children an opportunity to feel themselves comfortable and to go from kindergarten to family and back without psychological problems. Besides, life in the kindergarten is constructed in different events. These events have a very emotional character and preparation for these events is the real subject content of preschool education. For example, in the public family a new toy appears. This toy is a brown bear, which suddenly goes to the North Pole to find its mother. The children decide to return this bear to the kindergarten. And in order to do it they study where the North Pole is on the map, how to find it with a compass, who lives over there, what the weather over there like is, how they can get there and so on. Besides in the kindergarten this preparation also takes place in their real family. So we can have the unity between the child's emotions (children want to return the bear very much) and intellect, when children study knowledge as such.

In primary school the unity between affect and intellect is realized in another way. So far as early school-aged children do not have such emotional relations with a family as preschool ones and while for the most part of their school life a child dreams of becoming a teacher, the adults organize some specific conditions where a child can teach others in reality. Besides that, children from primary school get the opportunity (and this becomes a real emotional component) to realize their knowledge in different activities. For example when a child has studied to read and to count we ask him to read for everybody some letters from a magician or to write a poster about a performance or to take money enough for buying ice-cream for all his friends.

In teenagers the principle of unity between affect and intellect is realized in working in some special workshops where a child together with other children and an adult can make some chairs or sew some dresses or make something else useful and to realize it in their real life. The main idea of this is for the child to study how to do it and how to use his knowledge in his or her real work – for example they may measure the size of a chair or they can find the place where the buttons should be. In this way it turns out that the child's knowledge and his learning activity can be used as material or a tool to achieve a real goal.

The students of the eldest classes have the emotional component of their education in the opportunity for analysis and reflection. We think that this age is the most sensitive for studying practical psychology, which everybody needs independently of their future profession.

The unity between affect and intellect for student-psychologists presupposes including them in real practical psychological work from the very beginning. We can do it with the help of projective psychology. When students study this psychology they can create the program of development or correction for various real children, to begin their psychological diagnoses, to construct a developmental environment for them. Students do this real psychological work with the professional supervision of a psychologist.

Vygotsky's idea about spontaneous and reactive education in preschool childhood means that till the end of this period the child needs only spontaneous education. In other words, till the crisis of seven years it is impossible to use the reactive form of education for children. In this context, preschool children can study only in the spontaneous way.

But spontaneous education has many limitations. If each child has only his own program we can't teach them together. So, adults must transform reactive education into spontaneous education. If we take from our previous example the bear traveling to the North Pole, we can say that first of all adults have done some special work with the children and the bear and the result of this work was that the children start to wish to know everything about the North Pole, and they begin to wish to go to there and to save the bear. In this way the adult's reactive program of teaching children some ideas about the North Pole and climate changes into the spontaneous program of the child.

In early school childhood, on one hand, we have the same mechanism but on the other hand, through their interest in the bear, the real result appears. Gradually the result is to discover how long the trip to the North Pole takes or whether it takes more time to get the North Pole or to Africa becomes more interesting for children than to bring the bear back.

Through the crisis that occurs in a child's development normally between the ages of 6 and 7, a child's communication becomes volitional and context-sensitive. This facilitates the child's transition from spontaneous education to, at first, spontaneous-reactive and then, to completely reactive education.

If children have had the seven years crisis it is easy to introduce some situations connected with reactive education (Kravtsova, 1991).

For example, in the situation to do with traveling to the North Pole, schoolchildren have decided to do a surprise for the pre-school children: they want to show the younger children the Northern Lights. So, they find out everything about the Northern Lights and study so as to imitate it in reactive form. As children grow up, adults can use reactive education more and more. However, reactive education must not supplant spontaneous education because even adults have a more effective result in spontaneous education than in reactive education. The main role in transforming reactive education into spontaneous education belongs to teaching dramatic play and games.

On the one hand, in early school childhood play activity has a good level of development. But on the other hand, new games appear in this period. Most of these games have some practical results: to get something, to find somebody, to get a definite number of points and so on.

That's why there is a competitive motive in these games, and the child tries to do his best to win in them and if he wants to win, he must acquaint him- or herself with the rules and techniques of this activity. In one situation the activity may be to throw a ball into a basket. In another situation the activity may be writing or the counting of something. In a third situation the activity concerns the translation of a text. So, we can regard a game as a possibility for transforming reactive education into spontaneous education. It is very important for young schoolchildren to realize their knowledge and skills in practice. If a pre-school-age child has written some text he or she becomes very proud of it and will forget about the instruction which is in this text. The early school child writes or reads in such situations only to do something or to win something.

Teenagers have a well developed form of reactive education. However, in this period spontaneous education is very important again. According to our program for middle school the main form of the teenager's education is in workshops. During the lessons in workshops teenagers make something with their hands and during the usual lessons they can discuss some problems or rote knowledge and skills got from the workshop. Besides at usual lessons, they receive new information which they must check and realize in the workshop. For example, during the usual natural science lesson the teenager gets new material about the dependence of living creatures on their environment and they test this information in the "young naturalists' workshop": they discuss with each other how the bird breathes and the place where it lives, how the fish breathes and why it can't breathe on the land. At the same time in the "young naturalists' workshop," children construct different planets with inhabitants and during school lessons they discuss the differences between conditions on their planets and between the manners of different planets' inhabitants and their breathing. In this way they start to understand very difficult notions: climate, geographic areas, poles and so on. According to the correlation between lesson and workshop adults use different forms of education. If a teenager gets knowledge from practical work, he studies in a spontaneous form, but this spontaneous education was transformed from reactive education. When a teenager gets new information from books or from teacher's stories, from adults explanations, he studies in reactive form.

When we teach pupils in the eldest classes, we use both spontaneous and reactive education. At the same time, reactive education is transformed into organized spontaneous education in the same way as earlier. We use different kinds of discussion as a form of organized spontaneous education. Another way spontaneous education is used in creating different kinds of education where students must teach younger students to analyze their own behavior and activity. Otherwise organized forms of spontaneous education allow students to reproduce the context of different situations. In other words, students become able to perceive some concrete situations to imagine what has been earlier with every participant of situation, to recreate participants' biography and so on.

When we educate student-psychologists we create some special forms of organized spontaneous education – personal programs. First of all it is "experimental psychological theater." In this form of study students may acquire fundamental knowledge of psychological science by playing and modeling different situations. From the very beginning in "experimental psychological theater," fundamental knowledge is a tool for solving different psychological programs but not "knowledge only for the sake of knowledge." The main result of such teaching is that a student can *appropriate* this knowledge, and that knowledge is more secure and can be used in psychological professional activity more easily.

The Program of Continuous Education

The program of continuous education consists of three independent programs. The first of them is called the "Golden Key." The name of this program, which we have taken from a famous children's tale, gives us the opportunity to define its specific features. First of all, according to this program preschool and primary-school children spend the greatest part of their time in folk tales and dramatic play. Secondly, adults who work in this program have the ability to find the key for every child's heart. And last, thirdly, by the end of the program every child has acquired his own golden key from and to whole world.

The main feature of this program is that it consists of events that are constructed with a definite logic. For example, the kindergarten group is completely renewed every 4 years and during this time, children take part in events, related to space (1st year), time (2nd year), object world (3rd year) and finally, reflection on events they have experienced. These may be events related to the child's personal life, which have priority, or events that are planned by an adult.

There is also the logic of event-planning in regard to the children's psychological age, events related to the children's common life and, also, events which introduce a child to the culture of the wider world. These events allow the organizing of a rich, shared life for both adults and children, and this life gives us the opportunity to include in it the children's family.

This fact is very important for us because it is a real chance to teach not only children but their parents too. It is a real way of creating a developmental social space. In mixed-age groups pre-school children and students of primary school live together; in particular, such a type of group includes children from three to ten years old. Note that pre-school children study only by means of events, but the young school-children beside that, go to a school which is situated in the same building. So in the morning young school children come to their group family and then go to study and after then return to the group family again.

The main specific feature of the education of young school children in our program is that they study both at school and in groups. But at the beginning of education at school, children appropriate new *forms* of leading activity – learning activity. And in groups, children appropriate new subject *contents* which are necessary for them. In the appropriation of learning activity children begin to use it for new subject contents. This helps us on the one hand to promote the unity of affect and intellect and on the other hand lets us transform reactive education into spontaneous education.

The second program is for the children from 11 to 15 years and is called the "Master" (as in "master craftsman") program. This name is not unintentional. First of all, it symbolizes that at this age children study mainly at lessons that are organized as a workshop. In workshops there is a *real* activity, some real tasks and an adult who is master craftsman and who can do this activity and solve these tasks at a very high level. In the workshop, this master craftsman and the children are always busy preparing some real product. The main aim of this program is concerned with children acquiring the mechanism of scientific thinking.

The third program is constructed for children who are from 15 to 17 years of age. It is called "Discovery." The specific feature of this age period is discovering. The teenager becomes aware both of the surrounding world, people and himself in this world. We have noted that the usual modern school does not give teenagers the possibility for this realization. Students often don't know how to construct their future life. Sometimes students change their professional domain after several years of studying at high school. Others decide to work after school in order to discover their own area of interest, but we see quite often that with time they still fail to understand themselves better, moreover they lose hobbies and interests that they had before, without acquiring new ones.

We consider that we can say this because the main aim of the usual schools is to give knowledge to children but not require them to study how to use this knowledge, and so do not prepare children for their future life. So we have constructed our own program on opposite principles. When we were describing the general principles of our programs we said that this period is very sensitive for real life practical psychology. The students must not know that they are studying psychology. The teacher gives the students some special tasks and problems and they must solve them by psychological means. This means that they must take into account the psychological specifics of the situation, the participants and many other aspects of the problems and tasks.

Certainly, the "Discovery" program has large subject contents but these subject contents are not the program's aim, they are the program's *tool*. If a student acquires both psychological goals and the subject tools for these aims he or she becomes able to manage his or her own personal development.

Studying Psychology

Besides these three programs we have a new program for the student-psychologists. The content of this program is connected with the new structure of Institute where the students are studying. This is the Vygotsky Institute of Psychology at the Russian State University for the Humanities. There are departments that have responsibility for teaching and pedagogy. In other words, it is connected with the contents and methods of studying. At the same time we try to have different subjects in every department. This makes it possible to negotiate the same psychological concepts from different sides.

For example, in the department of personality psychology we offer courses that belong to different domains of psychology (for example, pedagogical psychology, art psychology, development psychology, clinical psychology and so on), that have personality as a subject.

We have divided all psychology subjects into three groups according to both cultural-historical theory and the content of psychological and personality development. In connection with it we have departments of common regularities of development – a department of personality psychology and a department of social and pedagogical psychology. A third one has courses where conditions for common and individual development are researched.

Besides these departments there are special workshops in our Institute where students can study different forms of practical work. We have a workshop for the psychology of art, where students study experimental psychological theater, communication by literature, etc. Another workshop works with diagnostics and correction. In the beginning in this workshop the student can observe a professional psychologist work with the help of Gesell's mirror. Then they begin to help the psychologist: to play with a child, to talk with an adult, to fill protocols and so on. Ultimately, they can do consultation work by themselves, but only under the supervision of our professor-psychologist.

Finally, the third workshop is called "Projective Psychology." It is connected with the experimental-genetic method of Vygotsky where one can make models of processes of psychological development. Examples of this method are the programs I have just described.

The third branch of education of psychologists is connected with scientific research work. This work takes part in special laboratories that are divided according to classic knowledge about psychological life. It includes the laboratory of cognitive processes, the laboratory of emotional processes and the laboratory of the psychology of the will.

All participants in the educational process of the Institute (students and professors) at the same time take part in different aspects of Institute's structure (at departments, at workshops and at laboratories). We consider that this way helps us to prepare the specialist in psychology who doesn't separate theoretical fundamental knowledge and practical psychological work from each other and understands their unity. We consider that this way helps our graduates work successfully in various areas of modern psychology.

Problems of Psychology

Use of the projective method in the creation and practical implementation of this model of continuous education has allowed us to get particular practical results which help to solve a number of problems. Thus, firstly, this system of continuous education solves the problem of succession between different levels of education and, at the same time, the problem of children's psychological readiness for each new stage of development and education. Secondly, the implementation of the program leads to the promotion of children's health.

It turned out that children who attended kindergartens and schools working by our program, fall ill significantly less often than their peers from traditional educational institutions. Thirdly, working by our program leads to the development of both children and adults – teachers and parents, which, according to Vygotsky's (1998) thinking, is the necessary condition for full psychic and personal development.

Besides practical results, the use of the projective method also helped us to acquire data, which allows us to interpret many problems, formulated by Vygotsky, in a different way, specifically one of the central problems of his theory – the concept of Zone of Proximal Development.

In traditional psychology, as a rule, we build an education program with orientation towards the following words of Vygotsky: what a child does today with an adult's help, tomorrow he can do himself. We understand this as whatever is the content of the zone of proximal development today, tomorrow must become the content of actual development. In this context education which is oriented towards the ZPD is a really a process of transformation of the ZPD into actual development. We do not want to sow doubt in the importance of this transformation, but nevertheless, it should be noted that this kind of education is directly connected with a child's ability to study, not with his development. There are scientists who believe that each person differs from others in this ability. One child is very smart, quick-witted, while others can realize this process only very slowly. But it is interesting and important to note that even when we get similar results – that is, if students can fulfill tasks given to them equally well by themselves, tasks with which they couldn't cope with before – they will continue to be different in their levels and peculiarities of their learning ability. In other words, this kind of education does not have any developmental effect. It only helps to transform the potential that students have into real abilities.

Those researchers who work on such a paradigm do not pay attention to the problem: what is the main thing? – ability to do something on your own taken as a mechanism of getting a new level of development, or a new level of development as a mechanism for person's ability to do something on their own. In classical psychology we won't find the solution to this problem and cannot answer the question why different people have different levels of ZPD or how we can change this level. I think this is the main reason for which many scientists think that the ZPD is more a metaphorical than scientific term. Analysis of the concept of ZPD along with the data acquired in the process of implementing the projective method, has allowed us to form a new understanding of this conception.

According to Vygotsky (1935), the content of the ZPD is what a child has but still cannot use by himself. That's why he needs adults' help. The adult, or those who play this role, help the child only to use the content that he already has. On the contrary, if a child does not have abilities, skills, knowledge, information, nobody can help him to use them in his own activity.

We believe that the term "ZPD" from the very beginning supposed there is another kind of development, not only the proximal kind. We can call it the zone of potential development, or the zone of further development. This space of development differs qualitatively from the ZPD. Its content still excludes some definite features, characteristics and skills that with the help from outside can be used to fulfill tasks. However, it nevertheless includes the sources of these, the conditions under which these skills, features and characteristics can appear.

So, the sources of the ZPD are in the zone of potential (or further) development; this kind of zone is responsible for some of the psychological grounds of the ZPD. But the fact that these sources are available, and that there is some psychological readiness does not mean that something constructive will appear, and the process of mature growth (созревания) of psychological processes and functions will begin.

The process of transformation of the zone of potential development into the zone of proximal development is directly connected with the general logic and mechanisms of cultural-historical development in non-classical psychology.

One of the main ideas of the cultural-historical approach concerns the mechanisms of transformation of natural psychological functions into the higher ones (Vygotsky, 1997). Those tools that a person acquires in the process of education are directed towards his or her own self. In other words, in the context of the cultural-historical approach, the changes that take place inside of a person are much more important than the skill, knowledge or information that he acquires during his education. A person can learn to solve very difficult tasks and problems but it does not mean that they will bring this to change in their development. On the contrary, no matter that a person cannot fulfill tasks and solve problems which he or she couldn't before so long as he develops psychologically. According to this idea, the contents of the term "the zone of potential development" and the term "potential development" and the ZPD can be presented as the characteristic of a personality and development of individuality. At the same time, the zone of potential development is not connected with the development of a definite person. It's just the soil, and what kind of fruit will grow on it depends on the personal characteristics of a definite person. For instance, a preschooler has imagination as the basis for a play. But he can realize it, his imagination can be developed into a play, and thus become the ground for further psychological and personality development, or it can become the reason for fears or even autism. For instance, two five-year-old girls with equal levels of imagination are drawing pictures. They've painted very angry men. One of them draws a magician who will help make this angry person kinder. The other girl stops drawing and goes under the table and says: "I won't draw any more!" – she is afraid of this angry man. Such understanding of the zone of potential development and the ZPD, as well as the relations between them, means that transformation of the zone of potential development into the zone of proximal development means that the content of the mechanism, skill, etc. produces the personality characteristic of a person. So developmental education and the cultural-historical approach appear to be directed towards the potential development.

There's no need to prove that the ZPD has definite borders. Its lowest border is connected with the actual development (ZAD) of a person. Its highest border divides the ZPD and the zone of potential development. This kind of understanding allows us to tell that developmental education and its results widen the borders of the ZPD. First of all, the borders are widened by the change in interrelation between the zone of potential development and the ZPD. Of course, and this is the second factor – in developmental education we have changes in interconnection between the ZPD and the ZAD. But we think that people with a small ZPD have problems with their ability to study.

Vygotsky didn't write anything about what kind of help must be rendered to a child to help him to cope with a task on his own. But if we orient towards the main role of communication in psychological and personality development in the cultural-historical approach, we will see that this help may have different directions. One of them is to help a person to use his subject content for task-solving. The other one is to help a person to get help from outside. Parents, psychologists and educators know as a fact that many children and adults have problems with taking help from outside. When the other adult appears and begins his activity near him, he can do it easier. So, we have two kinds of help. One is called a subject help. It is directed towards helping a person to use a subject knowledge, skills or abilities, etc. to solve definite problems and fulfill tasks. The other kind of help is of a communicative character. It helps a person to take help from outside when needed.

So, if we have a person who cannot take help from outside to solve problems or fulfill tasks, we conclude: this content is outside of his ZPD. But when we have the second kind of help, sometimes a person has an ability to take help from outside. So, we can come to the conclusion that now this content is inside of the ZPD. In this way, we have the process of the development of the ZPD itself. Results that were acquired with the help of the projective method leads to the conclusion that the developmental education means such a type of education that develops the ZPD.

Unlike modern, "classical" psychology, the structure of which is like its natural science twin, which considers a person from the viewpoint of what he must be, non-classical psychology and first of all cultural-historical approach research those characteristics that show what a person can be. This difference has a very deep psychological sense.

We cannot construct any developmental, educational or correctional system without understanding the laws of psychological and personality development. Also, we cannot understand problems of a person, construct conditions that he needs for his or her development, build a space for his life and activity without understanding the laws of personality and psychological development. But when we try to understand a person while being oriented only towards laws of psychological and personality development, to create conditions to develop his weak and strong aspects of his development and construct the education aimed at his acquisition of the characteristics they must obtain and being oriented only at statistical data, then we omit the main problem of psychology – the problem of personality.

The projective method gives an opportunity to give a new sense of the content of non-classical psychology. Non-classical psychology, as Elkonin (1998) wrote, transformed psychology from a science which fixes real characteristics of the object under research to a science that allowed us to create some subject of development, to project life in such a direction which it should be in accordance with the laws of psychological development. It begins from the old psychology which didn't know the problem of personality and transformed it to projective psychology which allowed us to construct conditions for personality development.

References

Davydov, V.V. (2000). *Types of Generalization in Education: Logical Psychological Problems of School Students' Construction*, Moscow: Russian Pedagogical Society.

Elkonin, D.B. (1998). Epilogue. In Vygotsky, L.S. *Collected Works, Volume 5*, pp. 297–317, New York: Plenum Press.

Elkonin, D.B. & Davydov, V.V. (1966). Eds. *Age Abilities of Knowledge Mastering* (*Primary School*), Moscow: Prosveschenie Publications.

Galperin, P. Ja. (1998). *Psychology as the Objective Science*, Voronezh: Institute of Practical Psychology Publications.

Kravtsov, G.G. (1995). *Psychological Problems of Primary School Education*, Krasnoyarsk.

Kravtsova, E.E.(1991). *Psychological Problems of Children's Readiness for School Education*. Moscow. Pedagogika.

Lazursky, A.F. (1918). *Natural Experiment and its School Application*, Petrograd: K. L. Rikker Publications.

Teplenkaya, H.M. (1968). "To the problem of concept formation of preschool age children," *Dependence of Education on the Type of Object-oriented Activity: Collection of Articles*, ed. P. Ja. Galperin, N.F. Talyzina, Moscow: Moscow State University Publications, pp. 124–152.

Vygotsky, L.S. (1935). *Mental Development of Children in the Process of Education*, Moscow: Uchpegiz.

Vygotsky, L.S. (1993). "The problem of mental retardation," *Collected Works, Volume 2*, pp. 220–240, New York: Plenum Press.

Vygotsky, L.S. (1997). "The history of the development of the higher mental functions," *Collected Works, Volume 4*, pp. 1–259, New York: Plenum Press.

Vygotsky, L.S. (1998). "The problem of age," *Collected Works, Volume 5*, pp. 187–207, New York: Plenum Press.

CHAPTER 2

The Dialectics of Collective and Individual Transformation: Transformative Activist Research in a Collaborative Learning Community Project

Eduardo Vianna, Naja Hougaard and Anna Stetsenko

Introduction

In this chapter we describe the implementation of a transformative activist research project designed and carried out in collaboration with students in a community college in the New York City metropolitan area. The inspiration for this project was the critical need to expand current educational approaches for community college students, many of whom struggle in college. Guided by ideals of democracy and social justice, our aim was to move beyond instrumentalist conceptions of higher education that seek to only prepare students to fit in with existing social structures by meeting the expected demands of the job market. Inspired by cultural-historical activity theory (CHAT, see Leontiev, 1978; Vygotsky, e.g., 1997, 1998a, 1998b) expanded by the transformative activist stance (TAS, Stetsenko, e.g., 2008), we collaboratively implemented a project in which both students and faculty/researchers endeavored to move beyond the goals of adapting to the world to instead develop activist projects of social transformation in college and beyond. The specific goal was to work in solidarity in striving to break away from a narrow, commodified educational agenda focused on utilitarian learning outcomes geared toward future employability. Our method was based on co-constructing with students, based on critical-theoretical pedagogy (Vianna & Stetsenko, 2011), a collaborative space and tools for activist learning and development to expand active engagement in transforming alienating and oppressive educational practices in the college and in their community practices. Thus, this project consisted in bringing together students and researchers to collaboratively investigate and promote the development of their transformative activist stance, through the tools of learning, by expanding the contribution of each participant to a widening range of community practices, sociocultural practices and discourses. In other words, we invited our participants to engage in the collective project of developing a genuine learning community committed to dialectically changing institutional practices by changing and empowering themselves as activists who understand and commit to their indispensable role as agents of social change. The implementation of this project illustrates the core notion of TAS about the dynamics of individual and collective layers in collaborative projects as ontologically co-extensive, mutually co-evolving, bi-directionally related, and synergetically defining and sustaining each other. As we discuss below, this project integrates some elements of, but also radically transcends constructivist-inspired educational models that are fast becoming the hallmark of institutional reform in postsecondary education.

By describing the co-evolution of this project at the intersection of mutually embedded transformations in multilayered practices and the emerging activist agendas of the participants, our aim is to shed light on the dynamics of individual and collective levels of "collectividual" (as defined in the next sections) transformations within such collaborative projects. Thus, we describe how the emergence of activist agendas of the participants, though instantiated at the level of individual agency, was supported by, and at the same time itself supported, changes at the level of collective dynamics as part and parcel of an emerging collaborative activist project understood as a unity of individual and collective layers. In other words, as unique individual contributions to the collaborative project, the growth and expansion of individual agency was both called for and realized as the expansion of the collaborative project and vice versa – the collaborative project was both called for and realized as the expansion of individual agency embedded within the project development. It is the development of this indissoluble synergy and mutual constitution of individual and collective learning and agency that we aim to capture in this chapter.

In order to provide a contextualized account of the developmental dynamics of this collaborative project, we will first situate it in the context of competing educational agendas that have shaped the organizational structure and practices of community colleges. We will also briefly discuss how the liberal education reform movement currently underway in American postsecondary education has impacted higher education agendas, which has led many colleges to revise their mission and organizational structure (AAC&U, 2002). Because our project was situated in a community college whose leadership fully embraced the liberal project of educational reform, we will briefly describe how this movement has drawn on constructivist principles to address gaps and contradictions in higher education institutions that arguably create barriers for student learning and development. This brief overview will highlight the unique positioning of our project vis-à-vis this constructivist reform as it dialectically, both embodied and contributed to this reform agenda while radically reconstructing it, based on a transformative activist stance. We will focus on the distinctive dialectics of learning and development in our project wherein these processes are shown at once to be instigated by and result from participants' activist contributions to creating their educational and other community practices. We then describe the implementation of our collaborative project as an emerging (i.e., growing and shifting in the process of implementation) collective endeavor that was launched with the goal of addressing institutional gaps at the intersection of a broad range of sociocultural practices as instantiated in the structures and practices of the community college. Our project addressed how these gaps were manifest and instantiated in each participant's positionings and stances toward their community practices, including toward learning and college activities, toward their future, and toward social and community practices more broadly. In addressing these gaps, the goal was not only to document them but also to implement activities through which participants and the overall project could transcend the limitations associated with these gaps. Then we present examples to demonstrate how participants' evolving and growing engagement with and contributions to the collaborative project led to shifts in their own positionings and stances at various levels (i.e., in their learning goals and broader life agendas) and how these changes, in turn, spurred changes in the collaborative project itself. In sum, the emphasis is on reciprocal and synergistic, collectividual dynamics encompassing participants' activist contributions to the collaborative project (at varying levels) and the growth of this project itself. One of the levels at which this dynamics became salient is the participants' expanding activist stance as the grounding on which learning and development became integrated.

Theoretical Grounding of the Project

Transformative activist stance (see Stetsenko, 2008, 2010a, b, 2012, 2013a, b, in press; and for its applications, see Vianna & Stetsenko, 2011; Vianna & Stetsenko, in press) has been developed in an extension of Vygotsky's project (e.g., 1997, 1998a, b) interpreted through a political-ideological, rather than value-neutral, lens. This interpretation highlights this project's exemplary close ties with the egalitarian practices of social transformation premised on a commitment to ideals of social justice and equality. Given the historical and sociopolitical circumstances of how this theory emerged and developed, and how it became assimilated in Western approaches, its revolutionary meaning and implications (both theoretically and methodologically) still await full explication.

TAS has been specifically developed as a perspective that opens up ways to understand human development that integrates notions of social change and activism into the most basic assumptions of how human beings come to be, to act and to know the world.

In a continuation of a programmatic transformation, endeavored by Vygotsky, of the foundational premises on which traditional theories of human development are built, and towards developing a fully dialectical approach predicated on the notions of social change and activism in place of adaptation, TAS takes collaborative transformative practice aimed at changing the world as a constitutive core grounding for all forms of human being, knowing and doing. In accordance with the broadly interpreted Marxist and Vygotskian positions, but at the same time in expansion of those (due to re-fashioning them to more centrally focus on synergies of individual and collective subjectivity and agency), the central premise is that people come to know themselves and their world and ultimately come to be human *in and through* (not in addition to) the processes of collaboratively transforming their world in view of their goals and purposes. In similarity with other practice-based perspectives, this approach views human development as embedded in sociocultural practices and contingent on them, including their power dynamics, ideologies and discourses. Furthermore, expanding on these perspectives, and also explicitly integrating Bakhtin's approach (in its focus on *postuplenie*, see Stetsenko, 2007), TAS posits *transformative historical and ideological Becoming through activist contributions* to historically unfolding collaborative social practices (and their instantiations in specific projects) as a radically new *ontology and epistemology* that unites being, knowing and doing as aspects of one unified process of human development. This ontology and epistemology views processes through which humans change their world as primary and foundational in the sense that all other phenomena of human life are seen as grounded in these transformative collaborative practices, growing from them, constituting their dimensions, serving their goals, and never completely breaking away from these practices. Furthermore, because this approach affirms that all human activities (including processes of knowing and doing) represent instantiations of contributions to collaborative *transformative* practice, the vision for the future and commitment to bringing this vision to life are posited as central and inherent, rather than additional or supplemental, dimensions of human development, therefore revealing this process as being profoundly infused with ideology, ethics and values.

In capturing dimensions of ethics, responsibility, commitment, and directionality central to human social practices, TAS highlights the need for an activist stance vis-à-vis the world, embodied in goals and commitments to social transformation, as the key constituent of human development. On this premise, activist positioning and taking a stand can be conceptualized as an ineluctable dimension and a primary condition for development, already present at the level of "elementary" processes such as perception – whereby even 'simple' acts of seeing are determined by one's goals and orientations to change – all the way to higher forms of subjectivity and intersubjectivity. The argument is that it is the realization of this activist stance through answerable deeds – itself made possible only within ongoing collaborative projects and as defined through them – that forms the path to personhood and knowledge.

From a transformative activist stance, persons are agents not only for whom "things matter" but *who themselves matter* in history, culture, and society and, moreover, who come into being as unique individuals exactly through their own activism, that is, through and to the extent that they take a stand on matters of social significance and find ways to make a difference in these processes by contributing to them.

The transformative ontology of social practice – augmented by the notion of individual contributions to this practice as its carriers and embodiments – can be seen as superseding the very distinction between collective and individual levels or dimensions of social practices. What is offered instead is one unitary realm or process in need of new terms to convey the dialectical amalgamation of the social and the individual – "*the collectividual practice.*" This term suggests that individuals always act together in pursuit of their common goals, being inescapably bound by communal bonds and resources, yet each individual acts from a unique socio-historical position (standpoint) and with a unique commitment (endpoint), though always coordinated and aligned with the social projects/practices to which this commitment contributes. That is, the TAS reinstates the centrality of personal agency, commitment, and responsibility *on a new foundation* of a communal view about human development as a collective and collaborative socio-historical project.

Therefore, our TAS-based research project was a catalyst of a bi-directional and synergistic, simultaneous transformation that was social *and* personal at once, with both forms serving as facets of *one and the same process* of changing community practice *and* its participants. Not only do individuals change in the course of collaborative projects, they do so while and through instigating important changes in their community practices. That is, based on the dialectics highlighted by TAS, social change and individual development appear as directly connected to social practices and their specific collaborative projects; yet self-change, conceived non-individualistically, is not eschewed either. Understood not as an individual "psychological" endeavor, personal transformation instead is carried out as part and parcel of collaborative practice. This perspective therefore affords ways to reconcile emphasis on personal and collaborative dimensions of collaborative projects at the intersection of individual and collective agency, thus overcoming the outdated dichotomies of agency versus structure and of sociality versus individuality.

Situating the Peer-Supported Activist Learning Community (PALC): Gaps and Contradictions in US Community Colleges

Established in the beginning of the previous century in response to a demand for a more skilled labor force, community colleges now comprise the largest single sector of American postsecondary education, enrolling more than 40 percent of all undergraduates (Schulman, 2000; NCES 2006–184, 2006; Phillippe & Sullivan, 2005). These two-year colleges typically maintain open admissions policies that provide access to postsecondary education regardless of high school preparation and performance (Griffin & Hurtado, 2011). As Solorzano, Villalpando, & Oseguera (2005) point out, community colleges attract students who are unable to enroll directly into four-year colleges because they have not met admissions requirements. According to them, "[t]his is often because of poor college preparatory counseling and the cumulative effects of having been tracked into non-college-preparatory curricula in elementary, middle, and high school" (p. 281). Moreover, as community colleges are less expensive than four-year colleges, they seem to offer working-class students the opportunity to pay low tuition while working. Consequently, community colleges enroll predominantly low-income students, who constitute the most diverse students in terms of age, race and ethnicity, ability, and career aspirations.

Throughout their history community colleges have been fraught with three primary competing agendas, namely, to provide vocational educational, to confer terminal Associate of Arts or Science degrees, and facilitate transfer to four-year colleges (Solorzano et al., 2005). Such competing goals also reflect the broader political divergence of educational agendas that have shaped how colleges and universities define the purpose of higher education. Regarding their function to facilitate transfer to four-year colleges, community colleges offer students opportunities to complete the general education requirements of many baccalaureate-granting institutions. On the other hand, as higher education scholars have noted, "[m]any two-year institutions perceive themselves as being in service to local community learning needs – duplicating missed opportunities at previous levels of education as well as introducing new subject matter that is practically and oriented or technical in nature" (Griffin & Hurtado, 2011, p. 28). Recently, the Obama administration weighed in on this debate by initiating a highly funded program entitled *Skills for America's future* that encourages community colleges to engage in more private business partnerships, suggesting that the private sector should be more involved in the curriculum development in the community colleges based on the assumption that community college students are their future work force (US Chamber of Commerce Foundation, 2013). Critics contend that these types of private-public partnerships often funnel students into low-skilled, low-paid jobs and thus not allowing them to achieve higher education (Beach, 2011). Importantly, this type of initiative raises concerns that the focus of educational practices will fall on narrow skills, which is at odds with the liberal education project's response to the demands of the twenty-first century – demands for more college-educated workers and more engaged and informed citizens (AAC&U, 2002).

Despite the growing national attention they have recently received, community colleges across the United States continue to struggle with disappointing graduation rates. Traditionally, community college students have faced significant barriers to success, from need of remedial classes to financial and housing problems. Not surprisingly, many fail to complete their studies, which is reflected in stubbornly poor retention rates. According to a large study, while 70% of the incoming community college students express an intention to transfer to a four-year college in order to pursue a bachelor's degree, only 15–25% actually end up transferring within a 4-year period (NCES, 2001–197). Moreover, a recent study found that 45% of community colleges students had left the institution without a credential after 3 years (NCES, 2009–152). This confirms a trend of continuously high dropout rates of which minority and first-generation college students make up a disproportionate level (Seidman, 2007).

In order to negotiate their conflicting agendas, meet the multifaceted needs of their students, and respond to pressures to increase the effectiveness of retention efforts, community colleges offer a wide array of academic support programs and student services, from tutoring and peer support programs, to academic advisement and counseling. However, such services are usually provided in a poorly coordinated manner due to the colleges' divided organizational structure, disciplinary priorities, and competing missions to educate students effectively (Whitt, 2011). In the next section we briefly review recent trends in higher education research that have attempted to bridge gaps in institutional practices with a range of instructional and organizational innovations. A key theme this work has underscored is how fragmentation of programs and services negatively impacts student success (King & Baxter Magolda, 2011; Kuh, Kinzie, Schuh & Whitt, 2005; Pascarella & Terenzini, 2005). This review allows us to both draw parallels with and highlight main differences between our TAS-based research project and recently emerging approaches rooted in the constructivist tradition.

The Shifting Landscape of American Higher Education Practices

A broad reform movement is currently underway in response to sweeping social changes impacting postsecondary education in the United States. Driven by economic and political interests, there is mounting pressure on higher education institutions to increase access, accountability, equity, and excellence. These pressures have intensified as American colleges and universities have been challenged by a dramatic diversification of the student population, diminishing funds and financial support for college students, and the increasing uncertainty of the job market (Keeling, 2004; Thelin & Gasman, 2011). On the one hand, a conservative agenda of accountability, underpinned by the neoliberal ideology championed by business leaders and politicians, has exacerbated the vocational-academic divide by casting doubt on the employability value of a broad, liberal education and seeking to steer a large segment of the student college population into technical degrees that train students for the entry-level job market. On the other hand, the liberal education project[1] has responded to these challenges by launching a reform movement that has sought to expand and redefine learning in broader terms. Its chief concern is to disavow such narrow views of learning as tailored to specific skills whose success is measured with standardized tests to, instead, expand the core values of liberal education. Considered to have always been America's "signature educational tradition," liberal education aims at "expanding horizons, building understanding of the wider world, honing analytical and communication skills, and fostering responsibilities beyond self" (AAC&U, 2007). As the rationale for the liberal agenda is to prepare students for an increasingly global economy and society, the goals of college education have been recast in terms of higher order competencies deemed as indispensable requisites for the 21st century, such as integrative learning, intercultural knowledge and global citizenship. For instance, the Carnegie Foundation, a major funder of higher education research, recently published a statement on integrative learning that

1 Liberal education project is used here to refer to a broad coalition of higher education researchers, scholars and policy makers affiliated with institutions aimed at promoting liberal education in postsecondary institutions. Liberal education is usually defined as "a philosophy of education that empowers individuals with broad knowledge and transferable skills, and a strong sense of value, ethics, and civic engagement" (AAC&U).

defines "[d]eveloping students' capacities for integrative learning is central to personal success, social responsibility and civic engagement in today's global society. Students face a rapidly-changing and ever-more-interconnected world, in which integrative learning becomes not just a benefit but a necessity." Interestingly, liberal educators in higher education have argued, based on research with employers, that understanding of global issues is a highly valuable skill in today's job market (AAC&U, 2013).

The emphasis on active engagement and integration has dovetailed with the notion of transformative education based on bridging learning and identity development. Proposed as a self-authorship process, learning is viewed as becoming meaningful when it starts with students' own knowledge and engages them in reflecting on their discourses or frames of reference, a central dimension of students' identities (Baxter Magolda, 1999; Kegan, 1994). In this sense, learning must be "included in a much larger context that requires consideration of what students know, who they are, what their values and behavior patterns are, and how they see themselves contributing to and participating in the world in which they live" (Keeling, 2004, p. 9). To this effect, student-centered, holistic education is posited as the remedy to transform utilitarian learning outcomes, which, according to this view, is responsible for the failures of higher education as it reifies education as a commodity. Focused on the "whole student," this approach calls for developing wide-ranging and cross-disciplinary knowledge, higher-level skills, an active sense of personal and social responsibility, and a demonstrated ability to apply knowledge to complex local and global problems (AAC&U, 2007). Moreover, the collaborative and social nature of learning has gained wide recognition, casting further doubt over the traditional view of learning as an individual, primarily cognitive, activity.

Spearheaded by influential scholars and professional organizations, the liberal agenda in higher education has led to an impressive and growing body of research on constructivist-inspired innovative educational agendas that are fast becoming the hallmark of institutional reform in postsecondary education. Inspired by the metaphors of engagement and integration, constructivist researchers in higher education have decried the narrowly cognitive focus of learning and the conspicuously fragmented organization of higher education institutions (Bass, 2012; Keeling, 2004; Kuh, 2008, 2010). This body of work has yielded research evidence that the greatest impact of colleges and universities "appears to stem from students' *total* level of campus engagement, particularly when academic, interpersonal, and extracurricular involvements are mutually reinforcing and relevant to a particular educational outcome" (Pascarella & Terenzini, 2005, p. 646; emphasis in the original). This constructivist-inspired reform movement has led to a plethora of instructional innovations in postsecondary education. Among these, the

American Association of Colleges and Universities has recently identified a set of so-called high impact practices, which has been demonstrated to be most effective in promoting robust learning outcomes (AAC&U, 2008). Those practices include first-year seminars and experiences, learning communities, collaborative assignments, writing-intensive courses, undergraduate research, community-based learning, internships and capstone courses and projects. As most high impact practices are not part of the formal curriculum but rather constitute co-curriculum activities, this body of research has furthered policy calls to transform and reconfigure the organization of higher education institutions. As Bass (2012) has noted, the currently underway expansion and reconceptualization of learning has clashed with the time-honored structures of higher education, as colleges and universities have been funded and organized with the formal curriculum as the center of learning.

Couched in terms of constructivist principles, into which sociocultural tenets have been incorporated, these high-impact practices clearly embody many progressive notions such as active, collaborative, experiential, inquiry-based, transformative learning. As such, our project shared many features of high-impact practices, such as bringing groups of students together with faculty and community-based learning that engages students with ongoing efforts to analyze and solve relevant problems in their communities (Kuh, 2008). However, while we concur with the need to expand the prevailing technical-utilitarian and primarily cognitive view of learning, our collaborative transformative project sought to go significantly beyond liberal approaches. Specifically, instead of merely adding the notions of transformation and contribution to an essentially constructivist agenda, our TAS-based project was inspired by a radically different understanding of transformation and contribution based on a dialectical approach to learning and development as grounded in activist pursuits of social transformation. This is a significant departure from constructivist approaches in higher education, which moreover lack a solid basis on which to link learning and development. As one leading researcher contends, despite the established association between a plethora of educational practices and self-transformation, "the mechanisms of development that reflect progress toward this transformation are not precisely understood" (King & Baxter Magolda, 2011).

A Collaborative Project in the Community College: Developing the Peer-Supported Activist Learning Community (PALC)

We turn now to how the two first authors implemented as lead researchers a collaborative project in the community college in New York City where the first author teaches.[2] The student population of this college, like most others community colleges in the US, consists mainly of low-income first generation students who face myriad challenges (Engle & Tinto, 2008). In this particular college, 81% of students report household income less than $25,000 and over 50% of students are foreign born with over one hundred native languages spoken in this population. Given students' social-economic status, immediate concerns related to emerging out of poverty, financial stability and upward mobility powerfully shape, and in many instances dominate, institutional discourses and practices, fostering pragmatic learning goals among students and instrumental notions of student success among many faculty and staff. However, such a narrowly instrumental orientation to learning, with its emphasis on narrow skills and technical training, clashes with the competing liberal-constructivist educational agenda, which emphasizes longer term, broader goals such as life-long learning and transfer to four-year institutions based on developing higher-order competencies such as integrative learning, civic engagement, and so on. Based on his direct experience with students and fellow faculty and administrators as a psychology professor, the first author witnessed first-hand how many students, caught in the midst of such competing agendas, vacillate between these two opposite positions and struggle to take a coherent stance toward learning, especially those uncertain about their career and overall future aspirations. Not surprisingly, many experience a high degree of alienation and oppression in their college education, which often seems to them either too broad or too narrow and, consequently, at odds with their respective instrumental or liberal life agendas.[3]

As soon as they began meeting with participating students, the researchers directly witnessed, as the literature on higher education has amply documented, conspicuous gaps between academic learning, especially in general education courses that focus on broad learning objectives, and students' personal lives and professional aspirations. These gaps and contradictions, in addition to institutional discourses about students as deficit learners, seemed to be implicated in problematic patterns regarding how students positioned themselves towards (1) *academic learning* as either marginally relevant to their

2 While the third author did not directly carry out the data collection and related research procedures, she contributed as a consultant from the inception of this project, from developing its rationale to methodological and analytical suggestions and recommendations.

3 While a smaller group of students who take an activist and even radical stance toward their community practices and society in general tend to identify with some faculty and staff engaged in activist endeavors, they too experience a high degree of disconnect in many classes and from the majority of other students.

personal lives or as an instrument to conform to the status quo and adapt to existing social structures, towards (2) *their peers*; characterized by a sense of individualism and a lack of solidarity in spite of shared struggles, towards (3) *the faculty*; leading to antagonistic or barely connected relationships, and also (4) toward college life and activities from which most felt disconnected and avoided participating in.

In response to students' anxiety regarding the disconnect between their current educational activities and future aspirations, we sought to address gaps and contradictions in their positionings and inconsistent agendas through a collaborative project, akin in some ways to a participatory action research project,[4] that would foster synergistic links between learning and identity via the development of activist agendas. Organized around weekly meetings, our project initially consisted of bringing students together with the researchers to critically reflect on their college experiences in light of their learning goals and future aspirations. The recruitment of participants began with students who had taken a course with the first author. Some were invited to join the project because they seemed to be working below their potential, whereas others had approached the first author seeking career advisement or personal guidance. We started with a group of 6–7 students but soon the participants began to invite their peers. In a matter of weeks the group grew to more than ten students. As we already mentioned, we found an array of positionings among our initial participants, ranging from passivity to rebelliousness, though virtually all participants shared a general sense of disconnect, uncertainty and contradictions in regards to their courses and overall college experience. In terms of their future goals, they were either confused or unsure about this or could not meet the demands of their majors and projected careers. Moreover, they experienced a constrained sense of agency in their courses, characterized by lack of engagement and feelings of resignation, usually accompanied by resentment toward their instructors, which had roots in their experiences in middle and high school. In sum, we found a common pattern among participants of experiencing a high degree of disconnection and feelings of alienation in institutional activities that extended to their peer relations and personal lives.

Though students were critical of their courses and other institutional practices, and viewed society as egregiously unjust, they tended to approach their problems as their own personal issues, which they thought required individual

---

4 For a comparative analysis between our model of transformative activist research and participatory action research see Vianna & Stetsenko in press.

remedy, not collective action. Though some frequently shared their issues with a few peers, our participants typically did not even attempt to establish collective ways of tackling their problems. Accordingly, they sought the collaborative project, primarily, as an opportunity to develop personal skills and knowledge in order to be able to deal with the tough reality of their lives and education. In other words, virtually all students took an adaptive stance to institutional and community practices. As their discourses revealed, they related to social structures, including the college, as practically immutable. This seemed to reinforce their instrumental view of learning, which in turn led them to see any effort of investing in college activities beyond their courses, such as nurturing peer relationships, as futile at best. Even though many were struggling to complete their coursework as scheduled, they would frequently repeat that they wanted to get out of the community college as quickly as possible. Such statements indicated their commitment to a pragmatic view according to which "things are the way they are" (i.e., institutional practices) and there is not much anyone can do about it. Therefore one must not get distracted trying to resist or change the status quo but, instead, focus on one's own narrow goals and complete the coursework. Not surprisingly, realizing this individualist stance was a struggle for the participants. Thus, the appeal of our project, which many perceived as an opportunity for receiving personal guidance or counseling. This was also evident in that some participants would volunteer personal advice to others on hearing their struggles with instructors, administrative offices, and even personal matters.

Our project was grounded in Stetsenko's transformative ontology (as an expansion of Vygotsky's legacy), which posits that people develop and learn by *contributing to ongoing continuous transformations* of community practices. Thus, our research was based on the notion that processes of learning and identity, as activist pursuits of seeking to transform community practices, necessarily entail the development of and commitment to future-oriented agendas or "endpoints" (Stetsenko, 2012, 2013a, b and in press; Vianna & Stetsenko, in press). In contrast to much research that avoids directly addressing the value-laden nature of research, our project was firmly grounded in the notion that collaborative transformation is always purposeful, intentional and as such shaped by political and value-laden projects. In this sense, the collaborative project as established in PALC was about *projecting* to allow students to engage in the process of "throwing forth" (cf. etymology of the noun "project") into the future.

Inspired by Vygotsky's claim that learning leads development, and the TAS notion that people develop and learn by forming activist stands and finding ways to matter in their community practices, we conceived of this collaborative project as the pathway to expand students' agency by acquiring the tools of taking a stand on and making a contribution to ongoing community practices. Insofar as human development and learning are understood (per TAS) to be inextricably tied to activist contributions to changing and moving beyond existing practices (based in knowing about those practices), we aimed at reclaiming learning as an indispensable facet of overall human development in its unity of being, doing and knowing. To this effect, we invited students to join as co-investigators in an innovative educational collaborative project, to be created with and for them, wherein they could investigate and develop ways to become activist learners through learning about and contributing to their community practices. Specifically, our goal was to turn learning into a meaningful quest for personal and social transformation by developing (through active reconstruction) tools for activist positionings, or stands, which afford contributions to transformations of ongoing community practices.

The specific paths to this goal included developing the tools for activist learning about, critiquing, and discussing ways to transform existing community practices including their courses and activities in the college while connecting those to other social practices and their histories. Our collaborative project consisted of an original co-curricular program comprising a voluntary peer-based learning community, which we, in collaboration with the students, came to name the peer activist learning community (PALC). Building on previous work that applied TAS to research with and for underprivileged youth (Vianna, 2009; Vianna & Stetsenko, 2011; Vianna & Stetsenko, in press), our method was based on critical-theoretical pedagogy, which merges Freirean (Freire, 1970) tenets with Vygotsky's inspired approaches, in particular Galperinian systemic-theoretical instruction (Galperin, 1985; for overview, see Arievitch & Stetsenko, 2000). Thus, we focused on co-constructing with students tools for activist learning and development to expand each other's active engagement in transforming alienating and oppressive educational practices in the college and in their community practices. Thus, PALC focused on closing the gaps between students' learning goals and their overall life pursuits by using knowledge as a mediating tool for students' evolving activist agendas and agency. Specifically, we sought to engage students in (a) critically examining social practices and discourses (e.g. educational practices – starting with critically examining the immediate relationships and practices of the students in the context of the community college) leading to inequality, poverty, racism, sexism, and other forms of discrimination; including their own knowledge and assumptions; in order to (b) facilitate students' positioning (taking a stance) on these issues, including toward learning; and (c) develop activist agendas of contributing to social practices that could bring about social transformation.

Connecting Individual Action with Sociocultural Practices through Critical-Theoretical Learning

By having students share their individual struggles we expected that we could begin developing a communal sense of solidarity, insofar as that would facilitate their realization of the collective nature of their individual plights. Thus, we shared with students our early finding of how disconnected they were, which generated the theme of alienation as a topic of learning. One student had encountered Marx's concept of alienation in his sociology class, so we suggested reading about that in Fromm's *Marx's concept of Man*. We coupled that with the concept of purpose in life, to which another student had been introduced in his psychology course. Another student, an English major and a fan of Charles Bukowski and beatnik poetry, suggested poems and films wherein nihilism featured as a key theme. Learned together, these concepts provided the students with tools to critically examine some of their discourses and how they position themselves toward learning and other sociocultural practices. Hence, they began to develop a growing awareness of themselves as social, cultural, and historical agents who contribute to social practices. One student in particular experienced a strong epiphany as he connected those concepts to his job situation as a cashier in a retail store. Whereas he had previously taken his negative feelings toward his job, including a generalized lack of enthusiasm associated with fears of not having better options for future employment, as a personal foible, now he saw himself as positioned by powerful social forces as merely "another cog in the machine," as he put it. Though the empowering effect of such consciousness raising ("conscientização" in Freire's terms, see Freire, 1970) is hard to overestimate, many students were still not convinced that committing to build collective agency was worth their individual efforts. In fact, some openly expressed skepticism that anything beyond self-preservation and personal gains could ever bear fruits.

Despite these reservations, the weekly discussions mediated by critical-theoretical concepts opened up the participants to reflect on their stance toward their community practices as co-constitutive of those very practices. To this end, we added to our discussions a focus on the concepts of agency and contribution. While acknowledging students' experiences of discrimination or oppression, either in the college or in society at large, as part of broad structural patterns of oppressions, we simultaneously introduced the notion of agency as a way to underscore their individual participation in and contribution to reproducing or changing the very conditions they felt oppressed by. This notion became especially concrete for them with regards to their stance toward their courses, including their relationship with instructors and peers and vis-à-vis their families' expectations. One of the most touching moments in this process happened when the first author asked Chris,[5] who became one of PALC's most committed members, what kind of contribution he would like to make to social practices, to which the student answered: "I never thought of myself as capable of making a contribution to anything." This amounted to nothing less than a profound epiphany for this student who had been diagnosed while in middle school as having ADHD. Through group discussions, Chris began to realize how he used to view his mental abilities as his own individual and permanent deficits, including his shyness, which he viewed as a fixed trait, and his struggle with writing effective academic texts. Thus, Chris came to regard his "experiential knowledge" not only as his appropriation of an ideologically charged discourse within his community practices but also as a misleading individualist conception about his mental abilities whose generalized influence in his identity impeded the growth of his agency. As we describe below, Chris's transformation mediated by collaborative critical-theoretical learning, had a great impact in the collective dynamics of the group as it served as a case study through which many layers of educational practice were collaboratively analyzed via critical theories of education and human development. Thus, rather than being limited to one case of personal transformation, as important as that was, Chris's transformation was not only communally celebrated and a cause of collective pride, but it became embodied in narrative form as a symbolic (cultural) tool to both introduce incoming members to critical analysis of educational practices and models and to disseminate PALC's mission and accomplishments.

Gradually, a common sense emerged among participants that their individualist stance, mediated by reductionist and individualist conceptions of mind and identity, was not only integrally connected with institutional and other community practices, but that it was in fact through such a stance that the very practices that alienated and oppressed them were reproduced. Thus, we reached a paradoxical moment when the participants realized the *collective impact of their individualist stance*. With that, they also began to realize that even by passively accepting the status quo they were contributing to perpetuating it.

One important achievement of the project during this initial phase (in the first semester) was that learning concepts and theories in the social sciences became increasingly meaningful to participants as they began to apply them to understand their own circumstances. Based on these dialectical notions of

5 All names used in this chapter are pseudonyms.

agency and contribution, we invited students to position themselves as co-authors of their educational and other community practices through our project, based in the college, in which together with the researchers they could *collaboratively* investigate and expand their contribution to a widening range of community practices.

With the emphasis on the centrality of the notion of individual contribution to social practice in human development, as articulated in Stetsenko's work on the transformative activist stance, a shared activity emerged in PALC that consisted of discussing each participant's positioning toward a range of community practices in light of developing an activist agenda to transform those practices. Typically, each participant would bring up an immediate concern with a practice or relationship, such as a particularly problematic course, their struggles reconciling work and studies, or difficulties with family members. Under the guidance of the researchers, the group empathetically (i.e., non-judgmentally) embraced each member's personal concerns while challenging them to position themselves as agents who make a difference, even if only on a small scale, in their community practices and relationships. On the one hand, the group accepted each participant's feelings (whether it was anger, frustration, resignation, etc.), helping them to relieve the emotional burden and build solidarity around their common experiences with oppressive conditions and relationships. On the other hand, no matter how constrained participants viewed their participation in their educational and other community practices, the group encouraged and even challenged them to consider the ways in which they actively contributed to those practices – and sometimes emotionally charged discussions ensued. In this context, not only resistance but also, paradoxically, passivity were taken as expressions of participants' agentic stance and, hence, amenable to at least some degree of change and as a launching pad for transformation. The upshot was that the group's shared activity, instantiated by each member's personal commitment to building the group's collective practice, served as a platform for each participant to develop new personal goals and agendas to realize their changing activist stances. Central to these discussions was that each participant's stance, seemingly exclusively personal and solely individual concerns, including the researchers', were addressed as situated within and emblematic of larger societal patterns, structures and processes and open to be challenged.

This phase of the project, centered on critical-theoretical learning, was the starting point from which an array of bi-directional developments ensued, which increasingly merged students' developing agendas and stances with the collaborative goals of PALC, thus giving rise to a truly collectividual project. While the researchers initiated the project with the aim of developing a critical learning site committed to an explicit agenda of social justice through implementing a critical-theoretical curriculum, the project gradually changed as students began actively participating in and contributing to the weekly meetings. As participants' trust and solidarity within the group grew, they began to feel supported and empowered, though often still feeling vulnerable and anxious, to try out more activist and agentic forms of participation in and contribution to their community practices. One common pattern in the group was to encourage and instigate students who were shy and lacked the confidence to actively contribute to classroom discussions in their courses to take advantage of PALC to start doing so. Although some members took many weeks (in one case even a couple of months) to feel comfortable to speak up in group sessions and take an active role in PALC, those who maintained their participation long enough (at least a couple of months) eventually became active contributors to the group. Thus, each group member actively contributed to collective decisions regarding the curriculum and to carrying out the diverse activities of the group. This was facilitated by the practice of collectively establishing the agenda of weekly meetings, including tasks and assignments (e.g., writing for the group's blog, assigning readings, doing group presentations). At this level, the group's agenda began to merge with each participant's agenda, which was now based on activist contributions to their community practices. Thus, whether it was about making suggestions to improve their courses or to change gender dynamics in their families, the participants began to take an increasingly transformative activist stance toward a widening range of social practices. This included a growing commitment not only to strengthen PALC but also to find ways for PALC to contribute to college activities and practices.

Throughout this process some participants underwent a dramatic shift in their learning identities clearly manifest in an increasingly agentic and activist positioning in their learning and courses. In one striking case a struggling, timid student changed his participation in his courses during one semester so thoroughly that his performance and grades increased to the point of causing great surprise among PALC members. At first, this student was reluctant, given his remaining shyness and aversion to being at the center of attention, to serve as a role model for PALC. However, under the collective encouragement of the whole group, the student accepted the invitation of the faculty mentor to give a presentation with the first author at the college's psychology club. This presentation caught the attention of a member of the college's center for teaching and learning and a brown bag presentation followed, which was attended by the dean of academic affairs as well as many departmental chairs and other faculty and students, including PALC members. The remarkable success of these presentations for the college community served as a powerful incentive for participants to realize the potential of their work to contribute to institutional practices. As a result, not only was a new way to recruit students to join PALC established, but also participants began making connections with faculty and programs in the college as well as with other student organizations. Drawing on their own transformation, PALC members created a collective support system for them to find their unique voices in an expanding range of educational practices.

By providing students with a collaborative space and community resources for critical-theoretical learning, including for voicing their individual struggles, the PALC project served as a site for participants to formulate individual agendas (endpoints, visions, projects) while also merging them with the collective goals and endpoints in the project by sharing these during PALC meetings. Thus, we sought to explicitly position students as active and indeed activist agents of learning and of wider community practices and critical inquirers, rather than merely "undergoers" of the very struggles they were facing. As such, students were encouraged, once they began formulating issues such as discrimination, to pursue these as topics of social critique, reflection, and analytical investigation, thereby making it possible for them to develop their personal projects while at the same time contributing, through this very work, to the larger project of PALC. Through this model of activist research we encouraged all students to pursue their personally most pressing issues while, through presentations and discussions in the group, always seeking to place their individual experiences and questions within a larger societal context as well as within the social justice agenda of PALC. Increasingly, students' emerging activist agendas began to hinge on transforming their educational practices and stances, which called for them to join their individual efforts with PALC's collective agenda of activist transformation of educational and related community and social practices.

Inspired by critical theories of human development and learning, including TAS and related Vygotskian perspectives and critical pedagogy, PALC discussions focused a great deal on critiquing educational practices, past and present, whose myriad pitfalls participants knew all too well from having suffered their negative impact first hand. Throughout the process of reflecting on educational practices, the researchers shared their perspectives, experiences, and stances on the limits of transmission models of learning. These discussions entailed reimagining new possibilities for educational practices, which in turn called forth participants to take an activist position toward learning and other college activities. As participants shared and documented their individual experiences, a common pattern began to emerge where they could see the connection between their educational experiences and stances, existing educational models, and broad social practices.

Students as Emerging Activist Scholars and Agents of Change

As participants continued to expand their understanding of the complex, historical links between educational and other social practices in connection with their emerging activist agendas and stances, they began to seek ways to collectively contribute to changing those practices. Their concerns and efforts centered on challenging and seeking alternatives to the transmission model of education, which became all the more evident to them in many of their courses, and its corollary view of knowledge as acquisition of information and skills. Despite participants' increasingly agentic and activist positioning in their courses, including taking much more initiative to build relationships with instructors and form alliances with those who were more progressive, they simultaneously began to see the constraints of the classroom as a site for transformative education. This growing realization, mediated by learning critical theories of education, led them to not only seek alternative practices and sites, as an expansion of PALC, where critical-theoretical teaching-learning could be realized, but also to consider the need for broader changes in the educational system and in society as a whole. Thus, the participants began articulating a desire to engage in and develop collective forms of activist contributions to college and other interrelated community practices. At this point, PALC had become a collective site for activist identity development, especially for those more committed to it. As a consequence, the more their communally shared personal sense of belonging to this activist project grew, the more they sought ways to intensify and broaden their social contributions, via PALC's collective initiatives, by seeking to give voice to their emerging activist stances and to channel them into practical changes. One way this materialized was through presentations such as the ones described above, which later expanded to other venues, such as in seminars and conferences at the social science department, in college-wide, and later in professional academic conferences.

Moreover, progress toward more cohesive collectividual dynamics was facilitated by addressing an important contradiction in our relationship with participants. Specifically, we decided to confront head on and pose as a collective goal the need to resolve the persisting gap between the authors as the researchers and the participants as the researched. One important way in which this happened was through discussing and learning about research models in order to define PALC's research methodology and establish it as a legitimate research site. This was initially instigated by Hikari, a Japanese student who joined PALC after having taken a class with the first author, and entered the project with an interest in epistemology and a deep skepticism of research committed to non-positivist paradigms. Troubled by what she perceived as PALC's glaring violation of objectivity, Hikari began vocally questioning the validity of PALC as a research project. In order to address the questions she posed, the researchers suggested that she explore feminist epistemology and participatory action research. As the highly committed student she had always been, Hikari soon began devoting herself to learning about non-positivist models of science. As soon as she learned the basic critique of neutral, dispassionate models of scientific endeavors, Hikari turned into an ardent proponent of non-positivist research committed to social justice and social transformation. As Hikari became particularly disgusted with what she now saw as the thinly disguised and highly ideological character of mainstream psychological research, she began inviting her peers to join her in a project to critique and expand the curriculum of psychological courses and to find ways to reach out to other students. Since directly engaging their instructors in such critical discussions was often difficult, Hikari and other participants became interested in establishing a student conference for psychology students.

The establishment of the psychology conference, an inaugural event in the college (now in its third year), was crucial to strengthening the collective ties among participants culminating in a collective identity representing the lengthy transformation of their stances from recipients to critical producers of knowledge. Since each member had already developed her or his topics of interest and relied on PALC to learn about them, we spent a full semester helping participants to turn their topics into research and/or research proposals, many of which they worked on collaboratively. Thus, students worked on developing symposia, roundtable, and paper presentations. Moreover, they coordinated their efforts with the psychology club into a complex web of activities from preparing the call for proposals and the conference poster to recruiting students through classroom visits as well as faculty and staff to serve as discussants and moderators. In the following semester, some of these presentations were published in the first psychology student journal, published by the psychology club and inspired by this first psychology conference. In the wake of the success of this conference and journal publication, PALC and psychology club members began planning a college-wide social science conference, which took place the following semester. The implementation of the social science conference was emblematic of the expansive changes that PALC underwent as students contributed to and pushed the agenda of the learning community. The nature of how PALC developed was always spurred by finding solutions to the contradictions that the project inevitably faced, as formulated first by the researchers, and later by the larger learning community. In seeking to engage these contradictions, the project's goals and activities continuously changed and expanded from first being primarily discussion-based to later critical engagement with academic literature, discussing and presenting it in the group and finally writing papers reflecting their own views presented at collective forums.

Expanding PALC through Activist Participation in Social Movements

One example of how students' individual as well as collective and collaborative contributions expanded over time is how PALC members became involved in social movements, and how this involvement fed back into and expansively propelled the project itself. This involvement occurred first in a struggle against tuition hikes and later in the Occupy Wall Street protest movement that was sweeping the United States from its beginning on September 17, 2011. As a part of our non-neutral critical-theoretical curriculum committed to an agenda of social justice we had been exploring the financial crisis in various ways (e.g. through watching a documentary called "Plunder," reading a text by David Harvey on neoliberalism etc.) in order to create a larger context in which to place our discussions of students' immediate experiences in the college. During discussions about the financial crisis in the spring of 2011, we were addressing the concept of austerity measures and ways in which the financial crisis was manifesting in our everyday lives, such as through public transit hikes. When the university announced that it would be implementing an array of tuition increases, the second author and a number of the students decided to show up for a university board meeting as part of a growing movement amongst faculty and students against the tuition hikes. Antonio, a Puerto Rican student who became involved in both the struggle against tuition hikes as well as in the Occupy Wall Street movement, was a student who despite doing well academically, was struggling to connect with other students and expressed feeling disconnected with his family and his overall community. Initially upon entering PALC, he was very shy and avoided participating in group discussions to the point of making the whole group uncomfortable with his self-effacing positioning. Gradually, Antonio began to express his issues, such as his resentment towards Puerto Ricans and how he understood his own academic success as a unique and individual achievement, which made him feel disconnected from his community. Through discussions during the weekly PALC meetings and through the introduction of academic readings on issues of race, Antonio began to develop an agenda of exploring critical race perspectives and soon made presentations on both Puerto Rico and critical race perspectives in PALC. During his own personal transformation of committing to a critical race perspective and through becoming increasingly knowledgeable on the topic, Antonio brought a critical race discourse to the meetings and as such brought other PALC members into his own personal pursuit on the topic. Through this process, Antonio not only became a leader and a teacher within PALC, but ultimately contributed to developing the collective endpoint of PALC to now include a shared commitment to becoming increasingly aware of and taking a stance on racial justice issues. When the opportunity to enter the Occupy Wall Street movement arose, Antonio was particularly interested in how racial dynamics were played out in the Occupy structures and immersed himself in a fraction of the movement that sought to tackle questions of exactly this nature. Like Antonio, also Hikari, the PALC member who propelled the inquiry on the epistemological validity of PALC, became part of the struggle first within the college and later in OWS. The personal endpoints of both Antonio and Hikari, while quite different, were similar in their overall critique of the status quo and as such their different stances allowed them both to participate and become engaged in movements engaged in envisioning new futures. During their participation in PALC, Antonio and Hikari, by taking their individual, personal inquiries as starting points for their development, both actively contributed to the changing goals and activities of PALC as their own personal leading activities expanded and changed. The PALC project fostered students' developing individual endpoints while at the same time and exactly through this process contributing to the changing endpoints and activities of PALC. Central here is that the critical-theoretical learning catalyzed students' stands, which led to their changing views and activities, including participation in movements for social justice, which then again called for more learning. As Antonio became involved in the struggle against austerity measures in the college, he became curious about how political decisions in the college were made and, encouraged by PALC, he pursued it as a topic of inquiry. He presented his findings during a PALC meeting, including a critique of both the political process by which board members are chosen as well as a questioning of the racial and gender make-up of the board. Important to mention here is that throughout the process of students' transformative development, growing out of their changing activities from conference presentations to participating in social movements, the role of the researchers shifted and changed accordingly. As students pursued their own topics of analytical investigation and became more knowledgeable on specific topics, the power dynamics in PALC between members and the two authors shifted. Thus, as students increasingly developed their personal endpoints and contributed to the agenda of PALC, they transformed not only their position within the project but also the collective power configuration of PALC. This entailed transforming the positions of the researchers into learners alongside other PALC members. Even though such transformation does not negate the power dynamics within the collective project, insofar as power differential between student and teacher identities were never completely transcended, this does reveal how gaining knowledge compels authoring agendas.

Conclusions

In this chapter we have laid out the rationale for a TAS-based model of research that asserts the impossibility of neutral, disinvested research and posits the need for researchers to not only be clear on their commitments (political, ethical, and ideological) but also to engage in spurring social transformation in community practices as being at the crux of research aimed at social justice and social transformation in support of this goal. With the description of a transformative activist, collaborative research project, based on mediation by critical-theoretical teaching-learning, we made the case for how the students' changes in their positions and learning identities were initially spurred by their participation in the project and how, then, these very changes helped to further propel and strengthen the project in its mission, its goals and its outreach. Critical for the TAS-based research is that the researchers' initial commitments and endpoints of seeking to transform the educational setting in which they positioned themselves as agents of change first set the ground for the changing endpoints and activities of the collaborative project, which ensued as the project grew and expanded. This was made possible because the initial endpoints of contributing to the transformation of learning practices in the community college were neither statically nor dogmatically formulated but instead, were intentionally left open for collaborative transformation to which students contributed in significant ways.

Our aim was to demonstrate the importance of spiral, bi-directional dynamics of individual and social levels in this collaborative project, what Stetsenko (2010a; 2013a,b) has termed the collectividual dynamics. At the core of this approach, which tackles head on the traditional and arbitrarily dichotomous split between the individual and the collective, is that people develop and become human *in and through* collectively acting on the world and *contributing to collaborative projects of their communities*, as captured by the "collectividual" dynamics. Engendering a collaborative project aimed at social justice thus necessarily entails allowing personal, historical paths to come together in a collaborative effort. The implementation of the PALC and its ensuing transformation, once initiated, served as a strong illustration of how TAS-predicated research in the context of a community college facilitated the collectividual dynamics. Specifically, we showed how students' individual as well as collective and collaborative contributions expanded over time as they increasingly mastered the critical-theoretical knowledge and developed their stance first *within PALC,* as contributors to the critical-theoretical curriculum within the group. Later on, through developing their individual, personal projects of inquiry and identity and their life agendas, the merging of participants' activist stances with PALC's collective activist stance began to manifest *in the broader context of the community college* and its structures. This dynamic was exemplified as students began to change their stance from passive recipients of education to activist scholars who can and do make a difference in their own community and learning including by finding their own voice such as through presenting their diverse, yet connected and collaboratively developed "endpoints" at the social science conference (e.g. through interrogating objectivity, deficit models of learning, and critical race perspectives to mention a few). Finally, PALC's contribution expanded and changed *in and through larger societal projects and contexts* (e.g., Occupy Wall Street, Board of Trustees meetings) as its members participated in and contributed to larger social movements aimed at a social transformation, outside of the initial collaborative project. The ways in which PALC expanded as members became engaged in both the struggle against tuition hikes and later the Occupy Wall Street movement, bring forth the complex paths in which projects aimed at social change necessarily need to stay open to connecting with and being transformed by other projects while at the same time transforming these projects too. In this case participants' expansive engagements with political projects outside of the core, initial project (such as participation in and contribution to OWS) fueled the research project's initial commitment to challenging and transforming educational practices and ultimately brought a new perspective connected to the need for larger societal change, not unconnected to the struggle in the college, yet beyond its bounds. While the emergence of such a movement that students ultimately participated in could not have been predicted, PALC always sought to connect and place the immediate critique of the college within a larger context that allowed this project to connect with other social transformative projects with similar goals of social justice like that of the OWS movement. The open-ended nature of the PALC project, while being fiercely committed to an agenda of social justice, allowed exactly for this unforeseen expansion that took place as students entered the OWS movement. To this end, the critical-theoretical learning played a central role. By drawing on critical-theoretical knowledge, students developed tools to systematically connect their diverse everyday experiences with current events and to link those with larger societal patterns and their unfolding histories and conflicts. Thus, our project created a space in which tools needed for engaging in activist pursuits aimed at not only transforming practices within the context of the community college but beyond, could be explored, created and agentively appropriated. Critical to this joint collaborative project between researchers and participants and its iterative cycles of change and expansive growth, was the expertise students contributed, with this expertise stemming especially from their membership in marginalized groups and their associated first-hand experiences of social struggles and conflicts. This provided invaluable insights and propelled the project as it interrogated community practices, including power dynamics within and beyond the research site. Developing the collective endpoints for social change was accomplished through critically interrogating strengths and contradictions of positions taken by all parties involved, of both students and researchers, in the continuous expansive and collaborative dynamics of the PALC project.

We believe that the new model of educational practice implemented in our project offers a viable and more thoroughly democratic alternative to prevailing instrumentalist conceptions of higher education. Inspired by the transformative activist stance, our project centered on providing students with an open-ended learning community where mediation by critical theories served as tools for students to develop activist pursuits of social transformation in college and beyond. In this sense, our approach simultaneously embodies and expands the goals of integrated learning, which seeks to prepare students to be informed citizens who understand their role in and act responsibly in a globalized world. To this effect, our project explicitly and critically addressed the limitations inherent in the liberal educational agendas that ultimately seek to adapt students to the status quo. Thus, instead of preparing students to fit in with existing social structures, we invited our participants to engage in the collective task of developing "*collectividual practice*" committed to dialectically changing institutional and related community practices. This in turn called for them to change and empower themselves as activists who understand and commit to their indispensable role as agents of social change. Thus, the model of educational practice proposed here, based on working in solidarity with disadvantaged students, goes beyond the liberal educational agenda in that it directly attempts to break away from a narrow, commodified educational agenda focused on utilitarian learning outcomes. Instead, our model is predicated on a more equitable and democratic agenda grounded in a dialectical theoretical approach to learning and development that focuses on how *individuals not only change in the course of collaborative projects, but do so while and through instigating important changes in their community practices*. In sum, following TAS, our project directly addressed how individuals always act from a unique socio-historical position (standpoint) and with a unique commitment (endpoint), though always coordinated and aligned with the social projects/practices to which this commitment contributes.

To conclude, central to this collaborative project, and to the underlying TAS approach, is the premise that social change is possible and that students and researchers, through committing to activist projects of social transformation and working to implement their agendas, can and do make a difference in their own development and learning *and* in the larger social processes and community practices (with these being bi-directional, recursive, and synergistic processes). Our hope is that the work in the PALC project, with its lessons regarding the role of activist stance in promoting expansive growth at both individual and collective layers within collaborative projects, will inform other activist scholars in our shared pursuit of the new political imagination and social transformation aimed at social justice.

References

Arievitch, I.M., & Stetsenko, A. (2000). The quality of cultural tools and cognitive development: Gal'perin's perspective and its implications. *Human Development, 43*, 69–92.

Association of American Colleges and Universities – AAC&U (2002). *Greater Expectations: A New Vision for Learning as a Nation Goes to College. National Panel Report.* Washington, D.C.: AAC&U. Retrieved September 3, 2013, from http://greaterexpectations.org.

Association of American Colleges and Universities – AAC&U (2007). *College Learning for the New Global Century. National Report.* Washington, D.C.: AAC&U.

Association of American Colleges and Universities – AAC&U (2008). *Liberal Education and Global Citizenship: The Arts of Democracy.* Retrieved September 3, 2013, from http://www.aacu.org/globalcitizenship/index.cfm.

Association of American Colleges and Universities – AAC&U (2013). *It Takes More Than a Major: Employer Priorities for College Learning and Student Success.* Retrieved September 3, 2013, http://www.aacu.org/leap/public_opinion_research.cfm.

Bass, R. (2012) Disrupting Ourselves: The problem of learning in higher education. *Educause Review 47*(2), 23–33. Retrieved September 3, 2013, from http://www

.educause.edu/ero/article/disrupting-ourselves-problem-learning-higher-education.

Baxter Magolda, M.B. (1999). Constructing adult identities. *Journal of College Student Development 40*(6), 629–644.

Beach, J.M. (2011). *Gateway to Opportunity: A History of the Community College in the United States*, Sterling, VA: Stylus Publishing.

Engle, J. & Tinto, V. (2008). *Moving Beyond Access: College Success for Low-Income, First-Generation Students*. Washington, D.C.: Pell Institute for the Study of Opportunity in Higher Education

Freire, P. (1970/1993). *Pedagogy of the Oppressed*. New York, NY: Continuum.

Galperin, P. (1985). *Metody obuchenija i umstvennoe razvitie rebenka* [Methods of Instruction and Mental Development of the Child]. Moscow: Izdatelstvo MGU.

Griffin, K.A. & Hurtado, S. (2011). Institutional variety in American higher education. In J.H. Schuh, S.R. Jones, S.R. Harper & Associates (Eds.), *Student Services: A Handbook for the Profession*. San Francisco: Jossey-Bass.

Keeling, R. (Ed.). (2004). *Learning Reconsidered: A Campus-Wide Focus on the Student Experience*. Washington, DC: American College Personnel Association and National Association of School Personnel Administrators.

Kegan, R. (1994). *In Over Our Heads: The Mental Demands of Ordinary Life*. Cambridge, MA: Harvard University Press.

King, P.M. & Baxter Magolda M.B. (2011). Student learning. In: P.M. King, M.B. Baxter Magolda, J.H. Schuh, S.R. Jones & S.R. Harper, (eds.) *Student Services: A Handbook for the Profession*, 207–225, San Francisco, CA: Jossey-Bass.

Kuh, G. (2008). *High Impact Educational Practices: What They Are, Who Has Access to Them, and Why They Matter*. Washington, D.C.: AAC&U, 2008.

Kuh, G. (2010). High-impact Practices: Retrospective and prospective. In J.E. Brownell & L.E. Swaner, *Five High Impact Practices: Research on Learning Outcomes, Completion, and Quality*. Washington, D.C.: AAC&U, 2010.

Kuh, G., Kinzie, J., Schuh, J., & Whitt, E.J. (2005). *Student Success in College: Creating Conditions That Matter*. San Francisco: Jossey-Bass.

Leontiev. A.N. (1978). *Activity, Consciousness and Personality*. Englewood Cliffs, NJ: Prentice Hall.

National Center for Education Statistics (2001). *Community College Transfer Rates to 4-year Institutions Using Alternative Definitions of Transfer*. (NCES 2001–197). Washington, DC: E.M. Bradburn; D.G. Hurst & S. Peng. Retrieved from http://nces.ed.gov/pubsearch/pubsinfo.asp?pubid=2001197.

National Center of Education Statistics (2006). *Profile of Undergraduates in U.S. Postsecondary Education Institutions*, 2003–04: With a Special Analysis of Community College Students (NCES 2006–184). Washington, DC: Horn, L., Nevill, S. & Griffith, J. Retrieved from http://files.eric.ed.gov/fulltext/ED491908.pdf.

National Center for Education Statistics (2009). *On Track to Complete? A Taxonomy of Beginning Community College Students and their Outcomes 3 Years After Enrolling: 2003–04 through 2006.* (NCES 2009–152). Washington, DC: Horn, L. & Weko, T. Retrieved from http://nces.ed.gov/pubs2009/2009152.pdf.

Pascarella, E.T. & Terenzini, P.T. (2005). *How College Affects Students,* San Francisco, CA: Jossey-Bass.

Phillippe, K., and Sullivan, L.G. (2005). *National Profile of Community Colleges: Trends & Statistics.* Washington, D.C.: American Association of Community Colleges.

Seidman, A. (2007). *Minority Student Retention: The Best of The Journal Of College Student Retention: Research, Theory and Practice.* New York, NY: Baywood Publishing Company.

Schulman, L. (2000). *The Carnegie Classification of Institutions of Higher Education.* Retrieved August 31, 2013 from http://classifications.carnegiefoundation.org/downloads/2000_edition_data_printable.pdf.

Solorzano, D.G., Villalpando, O. & Oseguera, L. (2005). Educational inequities and Latina/o undergraduate students in the United States: A critical race analysis of their educational progress. *Journal of Hispanic Higher Education, 4* (3), 272–294.

Stetsenko, A. (2007). Being-through-doing: Bakhtin and Vygotsky in dialogue. *Cultural Studies of Science Education, 2,* 25–37.

Stetsenko, A. (2008). From relational ontology to transformative activist stance: Expanding Vygotsky's (CHAT) project. *Cultural Studies of Science Education, 3,* 465–485.

Stetsenko, A. (2010a). Standing on the shoulders of giants: A balancing act of dialectically theorizing conceptual understanding on the grounds of Vygotsky's project. In W.-M. Roth (Ed.), *Re/structuring Science Education: ReUniting Psychological and Sociological Perspectives* (pp. 53–72). New York, NY: Springer.

Stetsenko, A. (2010b). Teaching-learning and development as activist projects of historical becoming: Expanding Vygotsky's approach to pedagogy. *Pedagogies: An International Journal, 5,* 6–16.

Stetsenko, A. (2012). Personhood: An activist project of historical becoming through collaborative pursuits of social transformation. *New Ideas in Psychology, 30,* 144–153.

Stetsenko, A. (2013a). Theorizing personhood for the world in transition and change: Reflections from a transformative activist stance. In J. Martin & M.H. Bickhard (Eds.), *The Psychology of Personhood* (pp. 181–202). Cambridge, UK: Cambridge University Press.

Stetsenko, A. (2013b). The challenge of individuality in cultural-historical activity Theory: "Collectividual" dialectics from a transformative activist Stance. *Outlines – Critical Practice Studies,* Summer. Special Issue on "Transformative social practice and socio-critical Knowledge" (ed. by I. Langemeyer & S. Schmachtel).

Stetsenko, A. (in press). Transformative activist stance for education: Moving beyond adaptation to the status quo through critical activist scholarship. In T. Corcoran (Ed.), *Psychology in Education: Critical Theory-Practice.* Rotterdam: Sense Publishers.

Thelin, J.R. & Gasman, M.R. (2011). Historical overview of American higher education. In Schuh, J.H., Jones, S.R., Harper, S.H., & Associates. (Eds.). *Student Services: A Handbook for the Profession (5th ed.).* San Francisco, CA: Jossey-Bass.

US Chamber of Commerce Foundation (2013). *Skills for America's Future.* Retrieved August 31, 2013, from http://education.uschamber.com/initiative/plan-develop-skills-americas-future.

Vianna, E. (2009). *Collaborative Transformations in Foster Care: Teaching-learning as a Developmental Tool in a Residential Program.* Saarbrücken: VDM Verlag Dr. Müller.

Vianna, E., & Stetsenko, A. (2011). Connecting learning and identity development through a transformative activist stance: Application in adolescent development in a child welfare program. *Human Development, 54*, 313–338.

Vianna, E., & Stetsenko, A. (in press). Research with a transformative activist agenda: Creating the future through education for social change. In J. Vadeboncoeur (Ed.), *National Society for the Study of Education.*

Vygotsky, L.S. (1997). The history of the development of higher mental functions. In R.W. Rieber (Ed.), *The Collected Works of L. S. Vygotsky. Vol. 4* (pp. 1–278). New York: Plenum Press.

Vygotsky, L.S. (1998a). Pedology of the adolescent. In R.W. Rieber (Ed.), *The Collected Works of L. S. Vygotsky. Vol. 5. Child Psychology* (pp. 1–184). New York: Plenum Press.

Vygotsky, L.S. (1998b). The problem of age (M. Hall, Trans., original work written 1933–1934). In R.W. Rieber (Ed.), *The collected works of L. S. Vygotsky. Vol. 5. Child Psychology* (pp. 187–205). New York: Plenum Press.

Whitt, E.J. (2011). Academic and student affairs partnerships. In J.H. Schuh, S.R. Jones, S.R. Harper & Associates (Eds.), *Student Services: A Handbook for the Profession.* San Francisco: Jossey-Bass.

CHAPTER 3

Could Life Be... Producing Subjectivity in Participation

Morten Nissen

The Video *Could Life Be*...as Prototype

In May 2013, a video was posted on the website of the Copenhagen facility for young drug users, *U-turn*, under the heading 'Narratives by Youths'.[1] It is titled 'Could life be ...'. If we click on it, we first read a sort of poem:

I grew up in chaos and confusion
Stuck in a destructive relationship
On a travel I met a young Turkish man – with bleached hair.
He sang for me on the beach, under the stars
Old Turkish folk songs
About moving on[2]

Then we witness a young woman – the motion pauses as her name *Berrin* appears in print – walking towards, climbing, and finally jumping from, a diving tower in an indoor swimming-pool, all the while singing in Turkish, accompanied on the saz by a Turkish-looking man sitting on the pool edge in swim shorts.Danish subtitles appear as she sings:

I'm on a long narrow road
I walk all day, I walk all night
I don't know what state I'm in
I walk all day, I walk all night

Berrin does not look like a professional singer or model, and the room is visibly ordinary. Yet the overall impression strikes one as aesthetic: beautiful images with interesting cuts and camera angles, including a vertical shot from the

1 By October 2013, the URL was http://www.uturn.dk/fortael_unge_kunnelivet.html, but at the time you read this, the homepage may have been rearranged, so that the video may be found somewhere else on U-turn's or Copenhagen City's website, or may be gone.

2 All Danish text is translated into English by MN.

bottom of the pool through the shiny surface to the artfully patterned ceiling, suddenly broken by Berrin's plunge.

At the website, we can read that the script was written by a 'Youth from the evening group', and that Lotte Svendsen, a famous Danish film director, participated, along with Kristian Kofod, psychologist at the facility, whom we can also see in a set snapshot, holding a camera on the diving tower, facing Berrin.

What's the point? In a recent article in *STOF*, the Danish journal for drug treatment professionals, Kofod and one of his colleagues explain:

> When the young people, through creative work, make new narratives, this leads to reflection and experiments with acting differently. ... Many of the young people we meet carry identity documents from schools, welfare offices or clinics. ... These documents tell strong stories about failed persons and negative identity, when they are based on deficits or psychological symptoms. ... But many of the young people we meet also bring along a wish to make creative narratives through creative activity. ... By working from these interests we try to help the kids create identity narratives that match their preferred self-image. This way, we try to give them a stronger position from which to act on their use of drugs and the relations that this use is part of.
>
> NIELSEN & KOFOD, 2013, pp. 33–34

This video, and the reasons for making and showing it, is one of the things we currently (2013) analyze as instances of 'User-Driven Standards in Social Work' as part of our research on 'SUBSTANce – Subjects and Standards'.[3] At a time when drug counseling is increasingly standardized – not least, through representing clients by using validated standard tests such as the 'Addiction Severity Index'/the 'Euro-AdAd' (Carpelan & Hermodsson, 2004) or the 'Outcome Rating Scale' (Miller et al., 2003) – aesthetic objects of this kind, and the practices of producing and using them, are visibly unorthodox as images of drug treatment and its clients. They seem to be completely idiographic and subjective. And where are the drugs? Yet they do suggest standards of some weight for social work with young drug users: Even though it goes against the dominant trends, the Ministry of Social Affairs have declared the 'U-turn' approach a *model* to be implemented in other Danish towns, and we are following and analyzing this process in collaboration with the social workers. Among other things, we have noticed that the video may well be unorthodox and 'idiosyncratic', but it is also not only state-sanctioned but reproduced on

3 See http://substance.ku.dk.

numerous computer screens and presented in a journal read by hundreds of drug counselors.

The concept of 'standard' speaks to the current waves of standardization, and to the 'science and technology studies' (STS) that investigate that process (cf. e.g. Bowker & Star, 1999; Busch, 2011). But it also has a deeper tradition in philosophies and social theories of practice and language (Jensen, 1987; Thorgaard, 2010; Wartofsky, 1979; Ilyenkov, 1977), including the Vygotskian. As such, a standard is a form of practice, perhaps immanent to a singular practice, and perhaps objectified as a model (or prototypical) artifact taken to regulate that practice, and potentially other practices.

Uffe Juul Jensen (1987) writes, under the heading 'The ideal as a prototype governing a practice' – using the example of a car:

> The ideal is that particular car which, produced by the manufacturers, serves the function of a prototype for the production of cars in the particular practice, with a range of uses in mind….
> a prototype (or a copy of a prototype) also serves an essential function in the learning process; it can be regarded as an embodiment of the standard procedures of the practice. … The ideal is public, using prototypes as a realization of standard procedures for doing certain things, and it is collective, that is shared by members of a particular practice.
>
> pp. 92–93

Thus, in our example, 'members of that particular practice' of U-turn-style drug counseling can regard the video as a 'shared' prototype, a realization of its standard procedures, and use it to learn and 'govern' their practice. In the Vygotskian tradition, we might come to think of Leontiev's example with the child for whom the spoon, as an objectified meaning, is a not just an immediate instrument, but prototypical of the cultural standards for eating that the child is learning (Leontiev, 1981).

Jensen studies health care practices. On his account, one kind of clinical practice that is currently struggling for recognition in health care is what he calls the 'situation-oriented' practice. This is the practice of helping individual persons cope with particular life-situations. That practice may include identifying and treating diseases, as defined in diagnostic manuals and guidelines, but it is different in its overall scope and orientation. Here, the main point is in fact to go from 'file selves' to 'real selves' and 'let the individual person become his or her own standard' (1987, p. 158).

The U-turn model represents a similar movement in social work, from the stigmatizing disease-oriented 'file selves' toward the 'user-driven standards' of 'identity narratives that match (the) preferred self-image' of girls like Berrin. What they do at U-turn is (among other things, such as conducting parent groups, supervising professionals in other institutions, and providing secondary school teaching and physical training) arrange various activities where such preferred narratives are cultivated. Making the video is a way of helping Berrin by engaging her as participant in creating a prototype that not only embodies standards of a 'situation-oriented' social work, but also Berrin's personal standards.

This description of the practices at U-turn is one of many instances of the U-turn *as model*. It resonates in many ways with that given on the U-turn website, and even, to some extent, with the one rendered on the Ministry homepage. But, as we shall unfold throughout this chapter, such articulations are far from innocent, since they are the artifacts that objectify the U-turn as the 'U-turn model'. So, dear reader, if you are impatient for a simple, concrete description of the youth social work at U-turn, I shall have to disappoint you: There isn't such a thing.

Moving On: Collectivity, Power, Recognition, and Hope

Whenever I watch that video, I am moved almost to tears. In the introduction you just read, I have tried to reproduce this movement, for a readership of more or less critical, more or less Vygotskian social theorists. The tricks I used were to set a scene in which 'we' – the readership-as-audience – identify with the 'good guys' who help a disadvantaged young person in dire need, while struggling against the anonymous machine-like forces that generate an oppressive common sense; and to imply that our common project, in our local research collaboration, *and* in this book, is to theorize the exceptional and beautiful scenery of human practice that those good guys are able to uphold, and in which Berrin can develop and flourish as participant.

I did this because it is a true story that displays an important prototypical practice and useful analytical concepts, and because I still think there is good reason to be moved. But I also did it because, if we really want to theorize what goes on, in ways that help those social workers, and ultimately girls like Berrin, we must develop our approach. While being moved is crucial, moving on is no less so.

So, like Berrin's old Turkish folk song, this is about moving on – not quite knowing the state we're in, perhaps, but with the hope of strengthening our position by reflecting on the stories we tell of ourselves.

We could move in many directions, of course, but, given the line of theoretical work I have taken part in developing,[4] *and* given the kinds of issues that face people who work to create 'User-Driven Standards of Social Work', my suggestion – and my plan for this chapter – is to go on to raise questions of *collectivity*, *power*, *recognition* and *hope*.

In brief:

(1) *Collectivity*: The kinds of 'we' that are summoned and aligned – such as 'U-turn' and its 'evening group', the community of Danish drug counselors who identify with the 'U-turn model', and the society of researchers who theorize their practice – each and all of those collectives are both vital and precarious. Even if we do approach them as 'particular practices', simply designating them as such is to obscure or sanctify the ways they emerge and exist as *singulars* – as not just kinds, but things of which there exists only one exemplar in the world.[5] We must keep asking also how any given collective is constituted and recurrently reconstituted.

(2) *Power*: We may spontaneously think of these collectives of 'good guys' in terms that push aside power as only relevant outside them, or at their borders. But in fact, the outside is deep inside, and the border is at the core. What we are dealing with are practices, collectives and identities that are formed and framed through being objectified with 'discursive' artifacts that mediate inter-subjective relations including selfhoods.

(3) *Recognition*: Although we can arrive at some understanding of the 'power of doing good' by thus stepping out of our spontaneous standpoint of solidarity, it also leads to a reductive approach to collectivity and power, and to another way of avoiding a reflection on the impact of what we do. The full concept of power goes beyond the idea of framing or discursive ordering and addresses processes of recognition of singular collectives and participants, and this, in turn, requires that we, as writers and readers of social theory, admit to being involved.

(4) *Hope*: The narrative question 'Could life be…' is not only key to personal identity. Collectives, too, are *collaborative projects*, defined by hopes such as that of 'user-driven standards'. All too often, such hopes are reduced to rational plans, within the parameters of the given state of affairs, or, often

---

4 This work is presented at length in Nissen (2012a).

5 Although this may appear to be a tricky logical category, it is one we use every day: Things like Turkey and Berrin are singulars, unlike, for instance, Turks, clients or artists, which are particulars (See Harré, 1998). In general, I use Hegel's logical categories Einzelnes, Besonderes, and Allgemeines translated as Singular, Particular, and Universal.

in a counter-move, denied in favor of a purely negative vision of process. Yet that choice is barren if nothing can be created beyond schedules and disturbances. Instead, just like Berrin and her helpers, we must cultivate our hopes.

The Collective

Let us begin with the collective, in two steps: First, sketching an interpretation of the video as a particular collective practice, and second, asking how that collective is constituted as singular unit.

The video is contemporary in its strong focus on the person, expressed, among other things, by its many close-up shots of Berrin's face. The same focus seems to characterize the drug counselors' methodology of identity narratives. In fact, it seems more obvious to call this kind of practice 'person-oriented'. Clearly, this is all about Berrin, and all for Berrin's sake.

Yet, it is more than that. If this were the whole story, why would a famous film director help make it beautiful? And why would it be posted on the internet?

If we ask the counselors, they are experimenting with 'aesthetic documentation':

> When the youth is engaged in working on the 'product' or the 'document', the problem is bracketed. ... Just as narrative therapy investigates preferred identity narratives, making them stronger, richer, and more elaborate, we try with aesthetic documentation to strengthen the narrative. But here it is through the creation of *the product*, which sustains or *freezes* meaning. ... If the document is given an artful form, many seem to be more keen to expose it than if it were a letter, which is typically more private. Thus, the document helps the youth bring her story to others, and to hear their response to the story.
>
> NIELSEN & KOFOD, 2013, pp. 36–37

The bracketing of the problem – addiction – is achieved by working on a product. The set shots on the website hint at the simple fact that creating a beautiful video is hard and complicated work. There are many things to learn: How long should the silent initial frame be? How do you hold a camera at the bottom of a pool? How do I sing in clear tone without strain or pretense? Etc.

If Berrin were to describe her problems, her hopes, and her cultural tradition in a group therapy session, that, too, would be a kind of skilled production. But we wouldn't notice because we would take it so much for granted. Or perhaps we *would* notice, if it turned out – as it sometimes happens at

U-turn – that Berrin is *not* skilled in this kind of verbal self-presentation; and soon, we could add an intellectual dysfunction to her long list of diagnoses….

Here, the production process is amplified, and the product itself is emphasized, by valuing an aspect that appears to lack any therapeutic rationale: its aesthetic properties. In this production, Kofod's and Nielsen's amateur skills in photography and music are expanded by Lotte Svendsen's know-how as film director. Berrin's drug problem is bracketed as she learns by participating in a practice, the procedures and objects of which embody the standards, not of counseling or even drug abstinence, but of cinema.

The sense Berrin makes of herself is mediated and cultivated by cinematic – not therapeutic – standards. This is meaningful. In Leontiev's terms (borrowed through Vygotsky and Paulhan from Gottlob Frege), sense is developed into meaning. The meaning of a work of cinematic art is complex and open to multiple reinterpretations, but it is also, as the counselors note, 'frozen', stabilized and generalized across situations and communities.

As an aesthetic product, the video connects the production team, through the internet, with mixed audiences of Berrin's peers, family, social workers, management, researchers etc. These connections are multiple, but not endless; they still guide the process, just as a view to traffic would guide the manufacture of a car. Importantly, the artfulness of the product is something to be proud of, for Berrin as for all members of the team. For those audiences, and together with the rest of the team, Berrin is showing off, displaying herself not only as main protagonist, but also as writer, actress and co-producer of a work of art.

Thus far, we have reconstructed the video production as a kind of collective practice. We remarked how one kind of practice – aesthetic documentation – is substituted for another kind, which would be more typical in drug treatment institutions – counseling or therapy.

The 'kind' or 'form' of practice, or in other words, its standards, can be grasped in four dimensions: agents, object-focus, ends and means. Who, what, what for, how? Since these are dimensions of intentional practice and are always defined in relation to each other, they can be said to make up the *intentional structure* of a collective (Nissen, 2012a, ch. 5). When we opened the U-turn website, we expected to learn about therapists using counseling techniques to cure addictions in young people. Instead, we enjoyed a music video over a Turkish poem, made by a film crew with camera and saz.

In both cases, one could argue, the object-focus is a person, and the same person would also participate as agent. But the differences are great between the person as the site of a disease or as the protagonist of a poetic cross-cultural journey – and between that person as client-user or as actress-singer-scriptwriter. These differences are not only between categories that describe the person. They are first of all differences between the practices in which those categories make sense, and the person's ways of participating in them. The client category is part of a clinical practice in which Berrin, safely within a confidential therapeutic space, learns to deal with herself in terms of her drug problem; her trajectory points toward leaving the practice behind and keeping the experience mostly to herself. In the film production, Berrin learns by peripheral participation in a *community of practice* defined by aesthetic standards; though she is not likely to become a professional, aesthetic practices are everywhere and she will probably go on to boast the video to her friends and family.

The difference between the closed circuits and self-reference of the treatment institution, and the open communities of aesthetics is important if we take a broad, contextual view of the life and development of a girl like Berrin. Still, we would not be quite fair if we claimed that it is only the clinical practice that is circumscribed as a unit, or that only the aesthetic practice opens to the world. The institution only closes on itself as it simultaneously connects to the clinical world of professions, sciences, and also users, relatives, and even the soaring lay culture of addictions. And conversely, the existence of a singular unit has been presupposed all through our account of the aesthetic practice, or designated with everyday terms such as 'the production team', or indeed, we have used – along with the counselors – the given terms for the institutional entities such as 'U-turn' and its 'evening group'.

I also borrowed the term 'community of practice' (COP) from the situated learning tradition (e.g. Lave & Wenger, 1991; Wenger, 1998). This was deliberate: As a theoretical concept, the COP is meant to open just the sort of questions we have been addressing in this section ... except the very last. The COP is not supposed to be identified in singular instances. When, in 2008, Jean Lave reflected on the fate of the concept, she explicitly refused to accept that a COP is 'a thing to look for'; instead, it was only 'a way of looking'; and that way of looking would always see a 'complex practice' never existing but always 'under construction' (Lave, 2008, pp. 290–291).

This is a strange situation. Precisely when we focus on participation, learning and identity, the question of the unit of practice, the collective, appears obvious. And of course, for the counselors at U-turn, the establishment of a video production team with proper relations of 'old-timers' with 'newcomers' was no small feat at all. In fact, while a drug treatment institution is a fairly standard unit, it takes some skill and effort to form and uphold an aesthetic production team that is at the same time part of a drug treatment institution.

So why would Jean Lave shy away from that question?

In the first instance, we might think it had to do with the basic contradiction between the finite, situated nature of any singular collective, and the universality and transcendence of human practice as such.[6] What 'we' do, and who 'we' are, always make sense in *this situation*; it is situated, and this is basically how we engage, participate and learn. Yet as we saw, that sense depends on it being continuously developed into meaning that goes beyond the situation, and on conversions the other way, of such objectified meaning into local sense. Is Lave, perhaps, eager to avoid the trap of severing the local from the global?

She is indeed. But at a closer look, we can see that this contradiction is easily overcome/superseded in the concepts of exchange and cross-contextuality. People and things simply move between situations. For this, the question of unit need only be answered by its most unspecific qualities: the here and the now. This approach to practice is unfolded by Ole Dreier (2008), who has worked closely with Jean Lave. To him, an 'action context' is circumscribed in time and place, just as a subject is always coextensive with a human body. This way, he turns away from structural abstractions, toward what he calls the concrete.

Of course, as testified by a respectable phenomenological tradition that stretches back to Schütz, Husserl and Heidegger, these are indeed fundamental qualities of being in the world, and they will not quite yield to even the most radical cyber-globalization. Still, this – as it were: 'physiocratic' – way of understanding the singularity of collectives is unsatisfactory. The time when collectives were always locally delimited, and those limits were directly given physically, has long since passed, if ever there was such a time. Even Heidegger had to learn that Germany was not guaranteed by its blood and its soil. Time and place are always part of the story, but they do not in and of themselves explain how human practice is sliced up, between people and between times and places. Perhaps Jean Lave's retreat to a nominalist epistemology (the CoP is only 'a way of looking', etc.) is because she realized that this move to the hyper-concrete is really a hyper-abstraction from the real life of abstractions.

But there is something more going on to justify it. Like the social phenomenology he draws on (though often unacknowledged), Dreier highlights spatio-temporality as a reaction to the obvious alternative, which is structuralist. Just as Garfinkel reacted to the Parsonian functionalism of his day (Heritage, 1984), so, Lave and Dreier sought alternatives to structural-functionalist versions of

6 In the dialectical tradition, 'human practice as such' is often termed Praxis (Bernstein, 1971). The problem of unit only arises because it *contradicts* Praxis. Without Praxis, units would be simply given as accidental things – groups, aggregates of individuals – as in most mainstream social psychology.

Marxist social theory, not least those that had become part of the cultural-historical tradition to which they both contributed. A structuralist approach to social units would simply derive them from the standard intentional structure, as given in a functional division of labor. From Leontiev to Engeström, Hedegaard and many others, the unit of an activity would be defined by its 'object' or 'object-motive' (Engeström, 1987; Hedegaard, 2011; Leontiev, 1978). The collective in question is circumscribed as either a therapy group with the object of cure, or a film crew with the object of a music video.

The structure of practice, which Ilyenkov (1977) called the 'objective form of subjective activity' is thus declared *identical* with that subjective activity itself. The conversion of meaning into sense is no longer problematic. This has the great advantage that we can know directly about subjectivity, including the motives of participants – unless, of course, those motives are deviant...

Or, to put it in less ironic and more direct terms, it tends to substitute normativity for understanding.[7] And this precisely becomes problematic when we approach unorthodox units such as U-turn's 'evening group/production team', and unusual kids like Berrin. Especially when both are struggling with powerful and problematic ways of being defined.

So the phenomenological reaction is understandable. At least, in a situated approach we can allow for multiple and contradictory standards to coexist, and we can sympathize with those who struggle with them. The only trouble is, we have to look the other way when units are constituted.

This impasse can be regarded as a utopian way of dealing with the issue of *power*, in two opposite versions.[8] Either we pretend that defining a collective unit by its structure is innocent, or we pretend that there is an innocent collective unit, always-already given, beneath those structures – when in fact, the constitution of a collective, a 'we', is a crucial exercise of power, and in fact the attribution of intentional structure is a key aspect of that constitution.

And because it is, we, as researchers, are participants in this process. This most likely explains the utopian preference for innocence. Not that the researchers stand back from engagement in worldly affairs, but more that a

---

7 See also, to this critique, Nissen (2011).

8 See also, to this, Nissen (2013). I should add, however, that in both traditions, this set of problems has been discussed intensely and various strategies have been developed to handle it. To some extent, my critique is unfair toward later works of Engeström (2008) and Lave (2011). I claim, however, that if it rests on popular, skewed readings of their earlier work, those widespread misreadings are not accidental, and have not quite been remedied by their later work in these respects.

deep and understandable solidarity with practitioners makes it hard to identify with power.

Power

The second part of my analysis of the video will focus on discourse and power, on the framing of collectives and subjectification of their participants. If, in the first part, the ethos was one of a utopian identification with practitioners, this second part will start with a cynical break with that solidarity, in a perverse, Foucauldian or Goffmanian identification with power – which I will then criticize.

Inspired, first, by Erving Goffman (1986, 1986a), we can note that participants *frame* their interaction, that is, they take the attribution of structure to regulate it, to constitute its singular instance, and from that, they learn who they are. This is of course the point in the counselors' counter-framing of what goes on in the U-turn evening group: Berrin is identified, and takes part in identifying herself, not as client but as participant of a video production team, carrying a rich Turkish culture.

But with Goffman, things soon get a little more complicated. The story of Berrin, the film crew apprentice, reminded me of a paradox that we came across two decades ago in a similar research collaboration with social workers who took their inspiration from Goffman, but who were never quite sure that they managed to achieve a counter-framing (cf. Nissen, 1997; 2012a: ch. 5). What if they didn't? Did they in fact perform what we came to call the 'paradox of the horny hooker'? It goes like this: In prostitution, the main premise for both participants is that the prostitute's sexual desire is irrelevant. Yet precisely for that reason, she puts up a show of sexual arousal. The pretense does not fool anyone, but it keys and makes possible the exchange. So, in order to do A, we must pretend Not-A. Could it be the case that social work sometimes needs to be framed as 'not social work' in order to be realized?

It could indeed, if we learn from Foucauldian studies of social work (Dean, 1999; Philp, 1979; see also Nissen, 2012a, ch. 3). Characteristic of social work is just the kind of utopian humanism that moved us in the first section above.

In the first instance, we should not underestimate the power of the disciplinary apparatus of which the U-turn is part, no matter how progressive its professionals want it to be. When they, as we saw, refer to '…identity documents from schools, welfare offices or clinics (that) tell strong stories about failed persons and negative identity, …based on deficits or psychological symptoms' – those documents tell strong stories because their meaning is fixed, frozen and stabilized, not just in material artifacts, but also in the constellations of power that they mediate. For instance, the diagnosis of some students' failure is a necessary structural aspect of the way the institution of the school is built, and the way this is part of class structure, labor market organization etc. in present Western societies (Varenne & McDermott, 1998). Similarly, the individualized diagnosis of addiction as a minority trait, rather than as a problematic aspect of late modern life, congeals strong social interests in institutional habits and material conditions that are not easily transformed (Alexander, 2008; Schüll, 2012).

Secondly, these power structures do not only work at political levels or as the strategies of oligarchic individuals bestowed with a uniform capacity we call power. Rather, they are discourses that people generally adopt to order how they deal with people – that is, with other people or even with themselves.[9] Subjectification ensues when people take up the agent-positions they provide, including the reflexivity highlighted by Goffman: When I am objectified – e.g. as client – then I relate to myself as such, and display that I do, within those therapeutic relationships.

But, on top of this, those discourses work to subjectify because they are at the same time *humanistic*. This is where it really gets nasty. In modern times, we do not kill criminals or cut off their hands; instead, we install the disciplinary structures of the prison because we want to empower the poor criminals by teaching them how to behave, so they can unfold their human potentials (Foucault, 1997). And all the grotesque humiliations of psychiatry were always meant to help the madmen finally assume responsibility for themselves as human beings (Foucault, 1967). And then, when perhaps we have realized that schools, prisons and asylums do not quite emancipate all their inmates – since labels such as dyslexia, deviance and madness prove to be stronger than their hosts – social work is invented to invoke the true, *holistic* human subject. This is done by drawing on discourses such as Vygotskian or Critical Psychology, where the subject is at her most universal, free of any specific qualities, since she is regarded as the subject of *social* problems. It is precisely by setting itself off as critical, as different from the apparatus of power – and by thus reforming and expanding that apparatus – that social work is constituted (Philp, 1979).

If we take another look at the video, we might note the strange juxtaposition of *laminations*, or layers of reference (Goffman, 1986, ch. 3). The beauty of the images and the song is set within the website of a treatment facility, and the poem at the start reminds us that, if 'life could be…', then it is probably not quite there yet, for the Berrin who 'grew up in chaos and confusion' and has

---

9 This, for Foucault, is ethics. In *The History of Sexuality* (Foucault, 1985), he suggests a set of analytical concepts to study ethics, or 'technologies of the self', that are almost identical with what I call intentional structure above.

been 'stuck in a destructive relationship'. What we enjoy is not the beauty of the film as such, or of Berrin as such, but of a *movement* away from the 'strong stories about failed persons and negative identity'.

Further, the three dots in the title nicely convey the fact that, what precisely life could be, is extremely open, or even arbitrary. As Berrin sings about moving on, not knowing the state she's in, the cinematic symbolism of her open face, looking out into nowhere, is as obvious as that of her plunge into the unknown.

In other words, the video is prototypical, not of treatment, nor of filming, but of a collective defined in terms of a critical social work humanism. As we have established in many user interviews at U-turn and similar places, being an 'alternative' facility, struggling for recognition of itself and its users, has a very strong kind of appeal. This is also how it works to invite us, readers and viewers, into communities, not just of practice, but of social problems and social movements to address them.

If we follow the Foucauldian approach further along this track, we do not imagine that we escape from power. Rather, what we encounter is a form of governance and mentality – in short: governmentality – that is now rivaling discipline for socio-cultural importance: pastoral power. The counselors Nielsen and Kofod are like priests who engage Berrin in a transcendent community, free of the constraints and passions of worldly institutions, but with obligations and resources to become the author of her own life. They have not just taken Berrin's motivation as premise (as in a disciplinary practice), but worked to elicit and enhance it. They have exercised the 'powers of freedom' by carefully staging a process where Berrin is 'inventing herself' (Rose, 1996, 1999). And although she is now recognized in a new way as a human being, absolutely free to define what life could be, it is understood that this life will be adapted to society's demands, not because of a force wielded against her, but because of her own responsible self-care. 'User-driven standards', perhaps, but it would be naïve to regard those as values simply grown authentically somewhere within Berrin and now free to unfold as they please.

Now we begin to sense how the Foucauldian approach, beyond a certain point, is barren. We have broken our solidarity with the counselors and revealed that, when they imagine themselves to be breaking new ground and setting new (user-driven) standards, all they do is perform the prevailing, pastoral form of power. But, they might ask us back, does that mean they should rather stigmatize and discipline Berrin, or just leave her alone with her drugs? If they did, we would have no other Foucauldian answer than to say no, no, by all means, please go ahead and do whatever best suits the powers that be, only now with the stoic awareness that this is, indeed, what you are doing. Foucault's famous injunction to 'refuse what we are' was never meant as a practical advice – only an ironic stance.

Precisely that kind of cynical pragmatics is currently rising to dominance as ruling ideology. And, just like the functionalism that fed into the disciplinary apparatuses of the twentieth century, part of how it rules is by overlooking struggles and contradictions. Even though all the key writers in the Foucauldian tradition claim to cherish fractures and multiplicity, the upshot is invariably the cynical reduction of any struggle, any progressive movement, to expressions of humanism viewed as a smoother and more economical power structure.

Some post-structuralists attempt to counteract this impending return to structuralism by highlighting the interactionist problematic of how agents deal with discourse by framing, positioning, etc. (e.g. Davies & Harré, 1990). No doubt, much can be learnt from taking up the interactionist legacy, just as I have done with Goffman. But in theoretical terms, the problem of structural homogenization is not solved by invoking the infinite vicissitudes of situations. We still have nothing to work with apart from the given and well-known structures and discourses. And since, at this point, we are no longer lured by the phenomenological dream of the here-and-now beneath or beyond structure, we are immediately sent back to discursive ordering, in an infinite regress: What frames the framing? In which discourse is the subject who manages discourse subjectified? Who are we who define ourselves the way we do? Etc.

Of course, that perpetual evasion can be attractive. Currently, much post-structuralism seems to be stuck in a futile exercise of inventing ever new terms that are meant to defend subjectivity by being purely negative, by not yet having been colonized in positive determinations imbued with power (heterogeneity, heterotopia, multiplicity, lines of flight, affectivity etc. etc.). It is as if a utopian flame is still seen to flicker in all that which we have not yet determined, except as indeterminate. Yet, as it fails to provide any substantial hope of change, it feeds a dystopian powerlessness: Even if the light gets in through the crack in everything, as post-structuralists are fond of quoting Leonard Cohen saying, we are still prisoners of precisely 'everything', in a world thus totalized.

Thus it turns out that cynicism, no less than innocence, is a way of evading ourselves – that is, of not addressing how the standpoints that we assume as researchers form part of the struggles we are witnessing.

Recognition

Let us pick up the argument from before it went astray with the totalizing hypothesis of governmentality. We identified a collective struggling for recognition.

In this section, I suggest we grant it recognition, as far as it is in our power to do so.

The video does not simply provide an example of contemporary 'pastoral', neo-liberal counseling. Certainly, a range of approaches do exist that aim to develop clients' motivation for self-care in drug counseling, by focusing on solutions rather than problems, and by emphasizing the client's autonomy while at the same time assuming social adaptation as common sense – e.g. 'solutions-focused therapy' (de Shazer, 1991) or 'motivational interviewing' (Miller & Rollnick, 1991).[10] These are in fact part of the professional background at U-turn.

But that background also includes approaches that are explicitly framed as critical, and which problematize the institution of counseling itself. One such approach is 'narrative practice' (White, 2007), which is developed with inspiration from, among others, Foucault, Derrida, Bruner, and Vygotsky. In this tradition, diagnostic discourse is not only treated as potentially counterproductive in a therapeutic sense, but also as something which can itself be part of a social problem. Thus, White writes of addiction:

> In that contemporary culture is a culture of consumption, and in that there is an ever increasing range of substances available to us, it should not be so surprising that addiction and/or the excessive consumption of these substances is so prevalent, and that this is destroying the lives of so many persons, traumatising their families, and wreaking havoc in our communities. In view of the burgeoning nature of this situation, I believe that it is unrealistic to expect that individual therapeutic responses will ever be able to respond adequately. The need for organised community responses is urgent.
>
> WHITE, 1997, p. 5

Could the video be regarded as prototypical of a collective struggling for recognition as an organized community response to a general social problem?

We noted at the outset that the video became data in our research because the state has proclaimed U-turn's approach a model for Danish work with young drug users. But also that it is, nevertheless, unorthodox. Most of what is thus sanctioned is standardized, individualized and evidence-based drug counseling. If we zoom out to contemplate the recent changes in public

10 Certainly, if we were to study instances of counseling that could be described with these names, we would also have to slow down analysis and recognize much that would go or point beyond this ideological form; but that is not a matter for this chapter.

management in Denmark and similar countries, this is no surprise. 'New Public Management' (NPM) is the neo-liberal attempt to reorganize state activities in the forms of market and civil society, and, apart from outsourcing activities to private enterprise, and the 'pastoral' appeal to the self-responsibility of citizens as users and self-helpers, a very important kind of NPM governance is through standardization (Busch, 2011; Du Gay, 2000).

The point in standardization is to govern by descriptions of what works best, as judged by available effect studies. As simple as it sounds, that tends to veil political issues about what is the problem, for whom, in which situations, etc. In other words, each time a standard is defined, a particular intentional structure is taken for granted and the question of its relevance is excluded from awareness, in the interest of pragmatic simplicity.

In the field of drugs and addictions, like in many other fields, this means that the social problem that Michael White identified above is transformed into a problem with and for individuals, and aggregates or populations of individuals. That is, it is indeed possible, in terms of NPM, to address social problems as such, as long as they are viewed statistically. It is thus likely that the more liberal 'harm reduction' approach to drugs will prevail in many countries such as Denmark, because it is more effective measured by effects on populations of diagnosed addicts – and so, methadone clinics, street nursing, syringe programs, heroin trials etc. will thrive, although even the harm reducing effects of some such interventions are paradoxically curbed by their having to meet the gold standard of evidence from randomized controlled clinical trials (Houborg, 2012).

But a 'social problem' in the sense exemplified by Michael White, and as reconstructed in Mark Philp's (1979) genealogy of social work, is more than that. This becomes evident if we do not limit our focus to that circumscribed by a given diagnosis, within the standard of drug treatment. As soaring numbers of addicts are diagnosed or define themselves as such, it is increasingly debated whether that is the best way to conceive of the phenomenon. This resembles closely the development which is emerging in child psychiatry as another drug problem – only from the opposite side, as it were – as the deluge of drugs is that prescribed by doctors, often the same drugs that some of these children will later buy in the streets (Keane, 2008).

The 'organized community response' has got to go beyond the narrow standard of drug treatment to address these broader questions. And this requirement is not only felt at the community level. When the clients are young people whose lives have not long been defined by their specific deviance, professionals are often encouraged to zoom out to what Jensen would call a situation-oriented view and practice. Youths like Berrin, users of U-turn, typically have a broad range of problems in their life. They also have a range of abilities, resources and dreams to build on. But it takes more than a standard counseling situation to address those problems and to elicit those resources. The knee-jerk reflex idea of staging a 'talk about your problems and your targets' just does not work with Berrin and her likes at U-turn. And, in each case, the social workers anyway work with networks of professionals, peers, and relatives. So they are almost pushed by the nature of their work to experiment beyond 'what works' in terms of the narrow standard, with practices such as 'aesthetic documentation'.[11]

But they have to struggle to do it. While counseling methods such as 'solution-focused therapy' and 'motivational interviewing' fit smoothly into NPM, 'aesthetic documentation' is far too wild and fluffy to be standardized and evidence-based. Even if Berrin and her peers in the 'evening group', along with Kofod, Svendsen and their colleagues, had a crucial learning experience, this does not necessarily translate to evidence of efficiency as a drug treatment method. For that translation to occur, we would be faced with questions like these: How many addicts have an interest in Turkish folk songs? What would it cost to hire famous film directors in every Danish counseling facility? Etc. Such questions are absurd; but we only notice that absurdity because we venture far enough beyond the standard for them to be exoticized.

The collective formed around the practice of creating the video was *unique*. It formed itself, and it was formed through its relations to others, as an alternative kind of practice. They knew quite well, as a collective and as participants, that they were doing something different from what normally happens at treatment facilities like U-turn. That is, the collective did not emerge innocently, beneath formal structures, only in my analysis to be attributed with an alternative quality. And it also did not simply perform a fashionable governmentality. Instead, it was constituted in a struggle for recognition, as a unique part of a singular state agency that organized a new kind of community response to a social problem. By performing and embodying such a response, like many other agencies in the history of social work, U-turn forms part of a precariously democratic, expanding welfare state – not a mechanism in a uniform apparatus of power.

This way of regarding the collective finally provides a way of approaching the question of unit that we could not address if we ignored power, nor if

---

11 I have unfolded this point more in Nissen, 2012, where I also take up the concept of 'life' in different articulations. This could be another way of discussing the meaning of "Could Life Be…": The 'life' that is recognized here is well beyond that which emerges in harm reduction policies.

we totalized it. Collectives are forged as singulars in relations of recognition. To understand this, I have taken up the 'dialectics of recognition' that was first sketched in Hegel's Phenomenology (Hegel, 1977; Nissen, 2012, 2012a, ch. 7).[12]

The concept of recognition is not simply cognition – the identification of a person or a collective as contingently autonomous, self-reflective participant – but includes social consequences: power. This power is mediated by structural attributions – recognitions are always recognitions *as* – but they are never *only* that, since they are always singular and, we might say, situation-oriented, and they always co-constitute collectives to which both parties belong. The full concept of power is a dialectics that continuously unfolds between the singular, the particular, and the universal. Meaning is converted to a sense that is common – to the recognized and the recognizing – only then to be reconverted in the production of new meaning that challenges and overcomes this common sense, in a process of ongoing ethical universalization. As we put together references from music videos and addiction counseling to make (common) sense of the video, we are invited to treat Berrin – along with Kofod, Svendsen, and U-turn – in a new way that critiques the elitism of cinema and the stigma of treatment.

This gives us a way to reinterpret the Foucauldian concept of subjectification (and the Althusserian 'interpellation'). It was indeed naïve to conceive of 'user-driven standards' in absolute liberal terms, but it was unhelpful to just flip the coin and mock them as subjection to a given discursive structure. Rather, participation implies relations of recognition between collective and participant, 'Us' and 'Me'. Like in Hegel's allegory, this must go through opposite logical moments: First, a superficial, mutual recognition; then, the submission of the participant to the collective; and finally, the transformation of both participant and collective through the practical realization of this participation that also substantiates the recognition.

Berrin's plunge is symbolic of her surrender to the logic and the ethics of 'aesthetic documentation'. If she is to take part in this, she must submit to the standards of this practice, and indeed, to 'this practice' as a singular collective. But 'this practice' is precisely *emergent*. Although Berrin probably learned some very old tricks of the trade of video production, her participation was

12 Although there is no space here to unfold it properly, I should mention that this requires a reading of Hegel's concept of recognition that does not reduce it to Kantian formalism, nor set off a zone of purely psychological dynamics, but which regards it as constitutive of an ethics in a wide sense (as in Højrup, 2003; Musaeus, 2006; Taylor, 1995; Williams, 1997).

crucial to the advent of the novelty we are discussing here: The collective practice of 'Could Life Be...'.

Conversely, our discussion of it also has implications. Although the collective was already self-consciously struggling for recognition as alternative before I came along (at least, as author of this text), articulations in research like this are part of this recognition, too. Especially at a time when 'scientific knowledge' and 'evidence' are otherwise increasingly taken, as relevant to practices like that of U-turn, to mean models that purify instrumental cause-effect-relations, that is, abstract standards. If this text and the likes of it are recognized as 'scientific knowledge', then the U-turn model can be said to be 'evidence-based', although in a way that expands that concept considerably.

Just so: *If*. Now we can see how this works the other way, too. If my texts are important to U-turn, U-turn's work is just as important in my struggles for recognition, not just of this particular theory, but, more generally, of social research in a dialectical, cultural-historical tradition.

Hope

In the final part of my argument, I will suggest that this reciprocal inter-subjectivity is best conceived in terms of hope. Not the kind of hope that is immediately reinscribed into the dominant discourse, nor the kind that only thrives in a sheltered dreamland of abstractly concrete being-in-the-world – but the kind that grows from the way real struggles for recognition make real subjectivities.

With the formula 'Could life be...', our video is all about hope. But which kind of hope?

As mentioned, to anyone acquainted with drug treatment, the video might appear to be just another instance of the emphasis on targets and solutions in contemporary counseling.

Of course, this emphasis can be done in different ways. 'Motivational Interviewing' and 'cognitive-behavioral therapy' provide ways to help clients set their targets rationally, directly in connection with their problems. Compared to such rationalism, our video appears more to the dreamy, romantic side, and the drug problem is not really present at all.

So perhaps a better way to articulate it could be solution-focused therapy, which is famous for the 'miracle question': 'Suppose you woke up one morning and your problem, by some miracle, was gone. How would you notice?' The idea is that the 'language game' of solutions is different from, and does not depend on, that of problems. One of its key writers, Steve de Shazer, nicely deconstructs dynamic and structural approaches to therapy and their focus on understanding the problem that the client presents as signs of some structural defect (in the psyche or in the family system) (de Shazer, 1991). But, characteristically, what he substitutes for this is a pragmatics of communication that, in the end, rests on common sense:

> Clients are seeking practical results when they come to therapy; they are pragmatists. They are 'in pain', and they want to get rid of the ~~problem~~, plain and simple.
>
> IBID., p. 110

De Shazer writes 'problem' in strikethrough to signify the intention of deconstructing it. But it still figures as an anchor to the 'plain and simple' hopes that define therapy. The common sense in terms of which counselors and clients meet and recognize each other, in this field, is standard drug treatment that positions them as provider and user of a service. Consistent with NPM, this resembles a commercial 'service relation', even though it is state-financed and imbued in many ways with state power, including the power to define deviance (cf. to this, Goffman, 1961, p. 321 ff.). The hope of cure, in and of itself, is negatively defined: It is the absence of addiction. If it works better to focus on positive targets, then *anything* the client wants will do. So, you like to picture yourself singing a Turkish folk song and jumping from a diving tower? No problem...as long as it works.

The video could in fact be articulated that way. But where would that lead? That is not so hard to predict. If cost-efficient treatment is guiding us, there are much cheaper ways to achieve a formulation of the clients' targets that 'works'. We wouldn't actually need the director and the rest of the 'aesthetic documentation' practice. Except, perhaps, if we think of it all simply as a way of 'branding' and 'marketing' U-turn. This would make sense if they wanted to attract clients from richer municipalities, or those whose parents could pay the bills. In other words, the sense this would make would match the current drift of welfare states like Denmark toward the class-divided health and social care known from many other rich countries, such as the USA.

Instead, through this text, I have articulated the video in terms of a quite different kind of hope. This is the kind of hope that drives an aesthetic practice were dreams are precisely no longer just 'anything', but carefully cultivated as meaningful, in the framework of a collective that struggles for recognition of a new level of responsibility for the real social problems of communities and persons, far beyond the common sense of efficient addiction treatment.

Along with Cheryl Mattingly (2010), I suggest that the most important kinds of hope should be understood on the background of its dialectical counterpart, despair. These are the kinds that go beyond common sense. Since they imagine a more profound change than that which fits into the given state of affairs, their shadow of despair is never quite out if sight. Mattingly takes up the term '*blues hope*' from Cornel West to portray a genre of narrative among poor, African-American users of health care, in which hope figures as

> ...a journey that requires not merely a transformation of the body but the transformation of a person's, a family's, or even a community's whole life.
>
> IBID., p. 73

Imagine a community where the most disadvantaged, immigrant girls were allowed to work with famous film directors to cultivate their dreams into beautiful works of art! The true beauty of the video lies in the blues it sings, even with a Turkish folk song: The shadow of despair is felt all along. We can easily sense the precarious nature of Berrin's dream because we feel it ourselves, as the radical utopia of this kind of aesthetic documentation being the practices of a municipal drug treatment facility.

Yet, the utopia of the video is at the same time concrete, in Ernst Bloch's terms (Bloch 1995). It points to a radical transformation, but it is also a continuation of a lived narrative, a historical tendency that has a *real possibility* of materializing. The video is actually there on the website, and the story it tells of 'aesthetic documentation' as a kind of social work is a true story of 'user-driven standards' that are not arbitrary and free in an absolute liberal sense, but a carefully cultivated prototype that intervenes in the development of drug treatment practices in Denmark.

The abstract utopia of various arbitrary miracles may be very efficient in pragmatic terms, as the long history of religion testifies, but their pragmatic efficiency is as conservative as their images are kept separated from worldly life and practice. Although the Foucauldians, as we saw, do have a point when they regard social work as continuous with that history, they are mistaken if they do not recognize social work also as part of real social transformations. This is one of Bloch's main reasons for reconstructing a long cultural history of utopia in his *Principle of Hope*. Abstract utopia cannot be simply replaced by factuality, since we are always nurturing hope, not least, various kinds of blues hope that we have to balance between despair and abstraction. Instead, they must be cultivated, rearticulated as part of real history.

As mentioned, the U-turn model – as exemplified here by the video production – is not only an answer to real needs that are felt in practice for going beyond a narrow conception of addiction counseling, but also state-sanctioned, as unorthodox as it is. It does not represent the dominant standard – the evidence-based counseling methods that fit into NPM – but it does provide a model of some significance, which is why I have articulated it here.

The story of Danish public services is not only a story of NPM, but also that of a welfare state attempting to respond to social problems, and continuously and precariously emerging in such attempts. As any state practice, it is contradictory. Different state *projects* clash, coexist, and are continuously rearticulated. Each singular agency is torn by such contradictions, and as such always emergent. This is part of why the collectives they form are responsive in their recognition of participants. Berrin plunges into a submission to the aesthetic documentation of U-turn, but in the same movement, she takes part in forming it.

Identities are formed in anticipation. Not just the identities of persons, but also of collectives. The understanding of collectives as *collaborative projects* implies not only that social units are first of all units of practice, but also that they are forged in struggles for recognition to which cultivations and articulations of hope are crucial.

And this is the point in writing and reading a book like this: We take part in articulating hopes of the kind that build on real tendencies yet suggest radical transformations.

References

Alexander, B.K. (2008). *The Globalisation of Addiction. A Study in the Poverty of the Spirit.* New York: Oxford University Press.

Bernstein, R.J. (1971). *Praxis and Action. Contemporary Philosophies of Human Activity.* Philadelphia, PA: Universty of Pennsylvania Press.

Bloch, E. (1995). *The Principle of Hope.* Cambridge, Mass, USA: MIT Press.

Bowker, G. & Star, S.L. (1999). *Sorting Things Out. Classification and its Consequences.* Cambridge, Mass./London: MIT Press.

Busch, L. (2011). *Standards – Recipes for Reality.* Cambridge, Mass: MIT Press.

Carpelan, K.S. & Hermodsson, A. (2004). *ADAD och utvecklingen av ett dokumentationssystem för ungdomar.* [ADAD and the development of a documentation system for adolescents]. *Nordisk Sosialt Arbeid,* 24, 110–123.

Davies, B. & Harré, R. (1990). Positioning: The discoursive production of selves. *Journal for the Theory of Social Behaviour,* 20, 43–64.

de Shazer, S. (1991). *Putting Difference to Work.* New York: W.W. Norton & Co.

Dean, M. (1999). *Governmentality. Power and Rule in Modern Society.* London: Sage.

Dreier, O. (2008). *Psychotherapy in Everyday Life.* Cambridge, Mass, New York: Cambridge University Press.

Du Gay, P. (2000). In *Praise of Bureaucracy*. London: Sage.

Engeström, Y. (1987). *Learning by Expanding. An Activity-Theoretical Approach to Developmental Research*. Helsinki: Jyväskylä.

Engeström, Y. (ed.) (2008). *From Teams to Knots: Activity-Theoretical Studies of Collaboration and Learning at Work*. Cambridge, Mass.: Cambridge University Press.

Foucault, M. (1967). *Madness and Civilization. A History of Insanity in the Age of* Reason. London: Routledge.

Foucault, M. (1985). *The History of Sexuality II*. New York: Vintage Books.

Foucault, M. (1997). *Discipline and Punish. The Birth of the Prison*. New York: Vintage Books.

Goffman, E. (1961). *Asylums. Essays on the Social Situation of Mental Patients and Other Inmates*. London: Penguin Press.

Goffman, E. (1986). *Frame Analysis. An Essay on the Organization of Experience*. Boston: North Eastern University Press.

Goffman, E. (1986a). *Stigma. Notes on the Management of Spoiled Identity*. New York: Touchstone.

Harré, R. (1998). *The Singular Self*. London: Sage.

Hedegaard, M. (2011). The dynamic aspects in children's learning and development. In M. Hedegaard, A. Edwards, & M. Fleer (Eds.), *Motives in Children's Development. Cultural-Historical Approaches* (pp. 9–27). Cambridge, MA: Cambridge University Press.

Hegel, G.W.F. (1977). *Phenomenology of Spirit*. Oxford: Clarendon.

Heritage, J. (1984). *Garfinkel and Ethnomethodology*. Cambridge: Polity Press.

Højrup, T. (2003). *State, Culture and Life-Modes. The Foundations of Life-Mode Analysis*. Aldershot, UK: Ashgate.

Houborg, E. (2012). The political pharmacology of methadone and heroin in Danish drug policy. *Contemporary Drug Problems*, 39, 192.

Ilyenkov, E.V. (1977). *Dialectical Logic. Essays on its History and Theory*. Moscow: Progress Publishers.

Jensen, U.J. (1987). *Practice and Progress: A Theory for the Modern Health Care System*. Oxford: Blackwell.

Keane, H. (2008). Pleasure and discipline in the uses of Ritalin. *International Journal of Drug Policy*, 19, 409.

Lave, J. (2008). Epilogue: Situated learning and changing practice. In A. Amin & J. Roberts (Eds.), *Community, Economic Creativity, and Organization* (pp. 283–296). Oxford: Oxford University Press.

Lave, J. (2011). *Apprenticeship in Critical Ethnographic Practice*. Chicago: University of Chicago Press.

Lave, J. & Wenger, E. (1991). *Situated Learning. Legitimate Peripheral Participation*. New York: Cambridge University Press.

Leontiev, A.N. (1978). *Activity, Consciousness, and Personality.* Englewood Cliffs: Prentice Hall.

Leontiev, A.N. (1981). *Problems of the Development of the Mind.* Moscow: Progress Publishers.

Mattingly, C. (2010). *The Paradox of Hope: Journeys Through a Clinical Borderland.* Berkeley/London: University of California Press.

Miller, S.D., Duncan, B.L., Brown, J., Sparks, J., & Claud, D.A. (2003). The outcome rating scale: A preliminary study of the reliability, validity, and feasibility of a brief visual analog measure. *Journal of Brief Therapy*, 2, 91–100.

Miller, W.R. & Rollnick, S. (1991). *Motivational Interviewing: Preparing People to Change Addictive Behavior.* New York: Guilford Press.

Musaeus, P. (2006). A sociocultural approach to recognition and learning. *Outlines – Critical Social Studies*, 8, 19–31.

Nielsen, S.K. & Kofod, K.H. (2013). *Æstetisk dokumentation af unges selv-fortællinger* [Aesthetic documentation of young people's narratives of self]. *STOF*, 33–37.

Nissen, M. (1997). *Conditions for User Influence in a Social Development Project. Nordiske Udkast*, 25, 45–64.

Nissen, M. (2011). Activity theory: Legacies, standpoints, and hopes: A discussion of Andy Blunden's An Interdisciplinary Theory of Activity. *Mind, Culture & Activity*, 18, 374–384.

Nissen, M. (2012). Recognizing life – A study in the atheist micro-bio-politics of drugs. *Subjectivity*, 6, 193–211.

Nissen, M. (2012a). *The Subjectivity of Participation. Articulating Social Work Practice with Youth in Copenhagen.* London: Palgrave MacMillan.

Nissen, M. (2013). Beyond innocence and cynicism: Concrete Utopia in social work with drug users. *Outlines – Critical Practice Studies.*, 15, 37–51.

Philp, M. (1979). Notes on the form of knowledge in social work. *The Sociological Review*, 27, 83–112.

Rose, N. (1996). *Inventing Our Selves. Psychology, Power, and Personhood.* Cambridge: Cambridge University Press.

Rose, N. (1999). *Powers of Freedom. Reframing Political Thought.* Cambridge: Cambridge University Press.

Schüll, N.D. (2012). *Addiction By Design. Machine Gambling in Las Vegas.* Princeton, NJ: Princeton University Press.

Taylor, C. (1995). The Politics of Recognition. In C. Taylor (Ed.), *Philosophical Arguments* (pp. 225ff). Cambridge, Mass.: Harvard University Press.

Thorgaard, K. (2010). *Evidence, Patient Perspective and Deliberative Clinical Decision-Making.* PhD, Aarhus University.

Varenne, H. & McDermott, R. (1998). *Successful Failure. The School America Builds.* Boulder, Colorado/Oxford: Westview Press.

Wartofsky, M.W. (1979). *Models. Representation and the Scientific Under*standing. Dordrecht/Boston/London: D. Reidel.

Wenger, E. (1998). *Communities of Practice – Learning, Meaning, and Identity*. Cambridge, Mass.: Cambridge University Press.

White, M. (1997). Challenging the Culture of Consumption. Rites of passage and communities of acknowledgement. In M. Raven (Ed.), *New Perspectives on Addiction*. Adelaide, Australia: Dulwich Centre.

White, M. (2007). *Maps of Narrative Practice*. New York: W.W. Norton.

Williams, R.R. (1997). *Hegel's Ethics of Recognition*. Berkeley/Los Angeles/London: University of California Press.

CHAPTER 4

Rhythms of Collaboration

Vera John-Steiner

In this book devoted to the notion of collaborative projects many different definitions are provided. In our previous work on collaboration we have suggested different intensities and dynamics for joint endeavors. A collaborative project where the participants' roles are shifting will be different from one in which there is a strong complementarity that characterizes collaborators' activities. In scientific projects with the need for a highly developed discipline-linked knowledge base we frequently find that a shared purpose is accompanied by complementary knowledge bases. The necessity for relying on more than one domain of expertise is widely recognized in today's science and provides one of the clearest examples of collaborative projects. Here, the interdependence of the participants is clearly articulated, and their working together ranges from informal discussions to general plans leading to clear division of labor and, in some cases, to the discovery of new facts, solutions, or laws.

A The Dynamics of Joint Endeavors

One example of a highly successful collaborative project consists of the joint work of the physicist Geoffrey West of the Santa Fe Institute and biologist James Brown from the University of New Mexico. In the course of an interview they reconstructed their early interests and the history of their continuing research. Their highly regarded work on biological scaling started in different contexts. Dr. West recalled, "I had given colloquia on scaling back in the '80s, but sometime in the '90s, my interest became more intense. I became intrigued with the problem of aging: Why it is that we die and what causes aging? Why do we live 100 years, and not a million years, or three months?"

In 1995, Jim Brown had just finished a book on micro-ecology. His graduate student, Brian Enquist, took the book with him while doing fieldwork in Costa Rica. After his return, Brian questioned his mentor about size-related variations in metabolic rates. The literature they examined revealed, both in plants and among animals, a 3/4 power scaling relationship. Brian was pushing for an explanation of this power ratio, which was somewhat counter-intuitive. (As the Santa Fe science writer Dennis Jarret put it: "You would think that a creature twice your size needs twice your energy, but that is not the case.") Brown and Enquist started to seek the underlying principle of quarter power scaling, but at one point it became clear that they needed help from a mathematical physicist. The collaboration with West was then brokered by a Santa Fe Institute intermediary.

Early in their meetings they just started talking about what each of them had been thinking, and as they both had an interest in scaling, their conversations were rewarding. They were able to go from what we have called distributed collaboration in our examination of patterns to that of complementarity (John-Steiner & Mahn, 1996). Their *cycles and rhythms* consisted of taking from the joint discussions emerging ideas that needed further reflection, frequently accomplished in different (sometimes solo) settings. But what is neglected in such a description is that the material that they were working with was based on their shared discussions. While the external cycle moves between physical proximity of the collaborators to separation, the internal dynamics are dialogic, where the physicist is mastering biological concepts and his partners are acquiring physical and mathematical approaches. These appropriations lead to new insights. There is, then, in the course of most collaborative projects, movement between social and individual poles, which are part of a sustained process and cannot be isolated from each other. This position is contrary to the frequent practice of dichotomizing solo and joint activities based on superficial criteria.

Another example of the smooth shift from solo to shared explorations of ideas is the collaboration between the brothers Dreyfus, the philosopher Hubert and the engineer Stuart. Their best-known work is the co-authored volume *Mind Over Machine* (1988). They were always close and provided each other emotional support and intellectual stimulation. While working on their book, they met in Hubert's office in the mornings using some notes that Stuart prepared while thinking about their common work at night. "Their ideas emerged during conversations. And while they preferred to talk in their offices with the tape recorder on, they found themselves engaged in talk during walks, while at airports, or whatever." Hubert described some of their interactions: "Sometimes we type. I start a sentence and he finishes it, and then he starts a sentence and I finish it."....Hubert further added that "the process was so dialogical that thinking and talking could not be differentiated" (John-Steiner, 2000, p. 29).

Both the Dreyfus brothers and West and Brown relied productively on their disciplinary differences. Their *complementarity* partly derived from their disciplinary cultures. "The culture of physics is to look for the generalities of the universals, sort of the cosmic view of things. Biology, by its very nature, has evolved, so far, to look at the detail, the diversity, the particular. And except for natural selection, there are no great laws. Many biologists think in very particular terms. The great thing about Jim is that he is a physicist at heart. I mean he really wants to think in generalities, wants to know the fundamental reason" (John-Steiner, 2008, interview). But there are differences between them as well. While West is very sophisticated in mathematics, Brown's background in this discipline is more limited. They also differed in their reliance upon information collected in the field (Brown and Enquist) and information collected from large existing databases (West).

At the start, their discipline-based approaches created the partnership. Brown's wide knowledge of biology and West's sophisticated knowledge of mathematics and physics were complementary. But it was their scientific and personal beliefs that were the "glue"—the colla that made their partnership so robust. (Colla is Latin for glue: interestingly, a word embedded in "collaboration.")

West, Brown, and Enquist started to meet at the Santa Fe Institute which provided them with office space and some financial help. Their process was dialogic; West recalled that the biologists Brown and Enquist asked some very basic, "marvelous" questions, and West responded by clearly presenting relevant mathematical ideas. But they had to be careful that they were, as Brown put it, "on the same page." As West recalled, "The nub of the whole thing was the dialogue: Jim asking the questions, then my having to get down to the basics of making these sophisticated mathematics into something that could be understood at a very elementary level. And that was very, very important" (John-Steiner, 2008, personal interview). Complementarity requires negotiation in language and sufficient information about the other's discipline to avoid false moves. They were working in a domain which is rich in descriptive literature which Enquist was constantly exploring. But while other researchers focused on detailed descriptions, these collaborators examined scaling phenomena from a systems perspective, synthesizing the necessary details into a holistic, adaptive, and integrated view. Their work was governed by their shared scientific style and values.

As they faced challenging problems they built on each other's expertise. They spoke of their sense of trust, a component basic to good collaborative relationships. The work was going well, and by 1996 they identified some of their crucial concepts, including the pervasive role of metabolic rates, the notions of area preserving and fractal branching. Some of these concepts were not new, but the integration of them in the theoretical and mathematical argument for 3/4 power scaling is their major, breathtaking achievement. As the collaborators were getting ready for their first joint publication, they were facing one troubling issue, that of mammalian circulatory systems which involve pulse transmission. They could have published the paper without examining this issue, but they did not. The resulting *Science* paper, which appeared in 1997, had made, in science writer's Jarrett's words, "a big splash in science worldwide."

When I asked Brown and West whether their collaboration encountered any difficulties, neither of them could think of any immediately. When I rephrased my question, West recalled that writing together was difficult at the beginning. He was surprised that his writing style was more complex, even "flowery" while Brown preferred a terse prose. As they published more together, including their co-edited book *Scaling in Biology*, their writing styles blended more completely.

This partnership illustrates a concept we have used extensively in our analyses in *Creative Collaboration*, that of *mutual appropriation*. This is a process of internalization, of making one's own some aspect of one's partner's knowledge and styles of work. Mutual appropriation is the result of sustained, intense engagement during which partners hear, struggle with, and reach for each other's thoughts, domain expertise, and objectives. Brown and West and their increasing number of collaborators continue to be committed to doing science together. As they search for first principles, they change each other as they change the scope of contemporary science.

Geoffrey West has brought the culture of physics and a particular way of mathematical reasoning to this partnership. His identity as a physicist and the respect of colleagues in his field matter to him. But, as he travels, he finds that he is more and more intrigued by what biologists have to say to him. He has become a profoundly interdisciplinary researcher. After completing the research with Brown, West initiated a new collaboration with Luis Bettencourt on urban organization and dynamics. The questions that drive their work bear a certain analogy to the scaling issues in biology. They envision cities analogically as large mammals where roads and boulevards are like the artery systems of an organism. In this project, like in the previous ones, the researchers' interest is in fundamental rules. They are concerned with the energy needed to sustain a metropolis and found that, similar to animals, when a city doubles in size it does not double its requirements for survival, but only needs 85% of the resources. It is interesting that one of the advantages of city living is that it offers a positive environment for social interaction and collaboration. Jane Jacobs, the urban activist and author of *The Death and Life of Great American Cities* (1961) describes the value of such urban areas: "they facilitate the free flow of information between city dwellers" (In Lehrer, 2010). Collaborative projects are not limited to city life, rural areas have long been known for mutual assistance among villagers and farmers, but cities provide a close proximity for the diversity of talents, interests, and institutional resources so essential to the demands of contemporary living.

B Collaboration is not Groupthink

The rapid tempo of contemporary life, its noise, aggressiveness, and incessant sociability is severely criticized by Susan Cain the author of *Quiet: The Power of Introverts in a World That Can't Stop Talking* (2012). Cain raises some interesting concerns about the desire for quiet and deep reflection that motivates her and many others. But her approach is one-sided and ignores the more basic interdependence of humans. In contrast, in *Creative Collaboration* (2000) I have argued for rhythms and cycles of joint and solitary periods of work which are embedded in the challenge of solving difficult problems in our society.

Cain, along with many others, reduces the notion of the social to the random collection of a number of individuals in the same environment engaged in casual and frequently superficial interactions. Viewed from a Vygotskian framework, the concept of the social is not restricted to people gathered in a small space and engaged in a face-to-face encounter. It refers to the fundamental connectivity of human life that makes survival possible. In a complex, technologically developed society some of this interdependence is not visible, but it requires but brief reflection to realize that no single individual can take care of all of his/her needs without others, whether these are for food, shelter, economic means, or, most basically, the physical reliance of the young on their elders.

The concept of collaboration put forth in *Creative Collaboration,* and one that I still advocate, is the voluntary joining of individuals with complementary knowledge, temperament, attention to detail, and shared vision. Such collaboration attracts people with different temperaments, some who discover their promising ideas through long periods of reflection to be shared with members of their thought communities. Others need the face-to-face stimulation of conversation, debate, working side by side in a laboratory, or the rich exchanges in an effective classroom. The concern with being silenced while living in a 24/7 chattering world is a legitimate one, as articulated by Cain. Solitude and sociability are both needed for human survival. But those of us who emphasize the social sources of development take a developmental perspective where humans individually and collectively build upon their joint intellectual, artistic, ethical, and practical legacies. The emphasis on complementarity is also linked to different modes of expression. Some people with a more extroverted temperamental makeup excel in teaching, projecting their thought and that of others in an alive, often dramatic, mode of communication. Others achieve similar objectives by writing, often a more solitary endeavor, where the audience is removed and its needs and interests are imagined by the writer. But in both cases, the social origins and functions of knowledge are shared among a multitude of recipients who actively adapt and transform what has been transmitted to them. These considerations are ignored by Cain who equates the social with "new groupthink" which she describes as "teamwork above all else. It insists that creativity and intellectual achievement come from a gregarious place" (2012, p. 75).

In American classrooms children are encouraged to be independent, self-assured, and competitive in order to function effectively in the marketplace. But recently, cooperative groups have also been introduced into classrooms, and, at times, this has been done in a mechanical way. Cain criticizes the highly verbal emphasis on teamwork which she says results in a neglect of originality or insight. Her argument is undermined by the many successful group projects, both verbal and visual, that enrich the traditional classroom where the teacher is the guiding influence behind all activity and the children's enjoyment and enthusiasm for shared activities is maximized (Connery & John-Steiner, 2013).

Cain gives voice to an old, standing dichotomy between individual and social which is so pervasive in our thinking. Rather than accepting the dichotomy, my way of suggesting a synthesis between these two modes is akin to Renaissance painters and their apprentices. When they were confronted with the task of finishing a very large painting, they relied on a division of labor: a special area was assigned by the leading painter to an apprentice for more intensive work. That individual's contribution became part of the larger painting. More generally, when we appropriate a new idea, experience, or tool from the socially constructed environment, we focus on and transform this novelty and connect it to the joint endeavor. The bracketing of a particular problem or challenge from the larger context allows for focused attention and elaboration. Once the bracketed part is completed, the individual contribution becomes social, as it is linked to the work of one's peers. By seeing the individual-social polarization as a process rather than the fixed locus of an activity we can deal more productively with this false dichotomy that haunts us so persistently.

The tension between the individual solitary thinker and a community of interdependent individuals is partly based on the Cartesian principle of "I think, therefore I am." Descartes' experience of temporary isolation has become the model for thought. Rather, thinking is the culmination of endless small and large interpersonal acts that makes it possible for reflection to begin. An interesting example of a shift in mathematics, a field usually described as solitary, was initiated in 2009 by Tim Gowers in what has become known as the *Polymath Collaboration.* Gowers presented a mathematical problem on his blog and invited anyone interested to contribute to its solution. After 40 people participated in this internet collaboration and three months had passed, the problem was solved. It was written up with the author identified as D.H.J. Polymath (Polymath, 2012). Part of the success of this interesting new practice was that Gowers presented some suggestions as to how the process should proceed. He argued for comments that were short and not too technical, easy to understand, at an early stage of formulation, followed by a trusting way of criticizing each other's ideas which should focus on incremental suggestions. He further urged that the participants keep the discussion focused: avoid sidetracks except if the participating community encourages such a direction. His last point was that the paper be submitted under a collective pseudonym with a link to the entire online discussion (Gowers, 2009).

Since this original project, there have been others that followed it, and there is growing interest in analyzing these online discussions to identify the kind of comments that accompany specific mathematical suggestions. These include examples, conjectures, proofs, strategies (including induction, generalization, and analogy), and some clarifications and purely social comments "which all help to create a friendly, collaborative, informal, and polite environment" (Martin & Pease, 2013, p. 11). The participants have acquired interactional strategies that make focusing on the intellectual challenge effective. Their efforts contradict Cain's view of collaborative activity as one that tends to accept simplified and sometimes false conclusions; rather it shows that carefully planned collaboration can vastly expand the resources of individuals and that it is an increasingly important organized form of problem solving and creative discovery.

But in the popular representations of creative individuals, the vividness of the experience of intense solitary thought overshadows the pervasive reality of human interdependence. The pencil or the computer with which we write, the chair in which we sit, the thoughts that nourish our own reflections are all products of joint labor. Vygotskian scholars struggle with their own experience of temporary isolation while recognizing, as Stetsenko and Arievitch (2004) point out:

> The social collaborative nature of human mind, the paramount role of social context and history in the production of psychological processes and outcomes such as knowledge, the embeddedness of knowledge in practical transformative engagements with the world, and the inextricable link between practical and theoretical, material and mental,

> political and intellectual, social and individual – all of these principles characterize both the real life history of [the] Vygotskian project and the very gist of a theory developed in it. In this sense, the congruence between Vygotskian project creation and the foundational principles developed in it provides a living proof of a direct connection between intellectual constructions and the practice, of which these constructions are a part.
>
> p. 60

Social scientists in the West have been raised in a culture that focuses on individual achievement. It is difficult to break out of such a value system. And while the social nature of our reality is increasingly recognized by contemporary thinkers, it is still a recognition that chafes against a lifelong focus on the self as the agent of knowledge construction, creative works, and human development. It may be this conflict that has resulted in implementations of teamwork that are superficial and are belittled by Cain as groupthink. She equates being alone as the definition of the non-social even while describing a violin practice in solitude (2012, p. 81). She overlooks that the young violinist is playing a composition by another person. When Cain speaks of books, she emphasizes the experience of quiet focus while ignoring that she's reading something written by somebody else. The act of reading is a social joining of the writer and the reader that then provides new possibilities of exploring deeply and thoughtfully what has been read and to transform the consequences. The power of collaboration lies in the combination of the life sustaining interdependence of humans with its flexible practice across many settings. These settings present a continuum from solo activities (where the collaborative partner is not present) to carefully organized long-term collaborative projects (in which two or more individuals join their vision and talents in a shared project). The range of this continuum contributes to the polarization of solo and social activities; it hides the multifaceted social nature of existence. Thus, the amount of time that people spend in private spaces or in face-to-face groups is not what determines the social nature of human activity, but it is the fact of profound interdependence between people which makes survival and creativity possible.

C Developmental Issues

The first of the three features of collaboration that are mentioned in this chapter is the rhythm between face-to-face activity and solo activity. This aspect of human collaboration, which is easy to identify in long-term scientific and artistic projects appears very early in children's lives. It is an interesting feature of language acquisition that children use gaze, gesture, context, as well as words they have acquired from their caregivers to make their own utterances which are then expanded and interpreted by their elders into longer and more comprehensible sentences (Zukow-Goldring, 2006). But children's practice of language is not limited to interactional settings. They also practice their words when alone trying to catch the intonation and the cluster of consonants of the language they heard from their parents and siblings. In *Narratives from the Crib* (2006), Katherine Nelson documented these pre-sleep monologues of children reliving their daily events, repeating conversations with their parents, and practicing difficult words. If one focused only on these tape-recorded segments of speech, one might say this is language produced in isolation, that it is not social. However, what the child is working on is the approximation of the input received in interactions with others and then improved by repeated effort in privacy. This, then, is another example of the rhythms and cycles of a co-constructed social process which is refined when the child is alone. Cain looks only at the immediate context (which sometimes is a solo one) in which an activity is taking place, not at its source and the effectiveness of its development.

Another feature of collaboration discussed above is complementarity, the way in which people with different skills, experience, and temperament add to each other's individual potential. In studying pre-school children's music-making abilities, Patricia St. John (2010) provided age-appropriate instruments for the participants to explore. The children were intrigued by the instruments' tonal qualities and tried various rhythms as they played with them. An unexpected finding of her longitudinal study was that the young musicians engaged in intense pretend play and that they imposed a "script" on their explorations. One of these scripts used the instruments for parade music and another was a creation of a story about soup-making. St. John writes, "Serving as a mediating artifact, the stir xylophone became the 'bowl'...Abby, seemingly otherwise occupied, could be heard making up a spontaneous song about the soup's contents while marching around the perimeter of the circle. She kept a steady beat with her feet as she marched and simultaneously improvised with Chinese bells" (2010, pp. 70–71). In such a script, one child becomes a chef, one a waiter, another a customer. By assuming different roles they complement each other and create a small drama. Complementarity is essential to collaboration. In many beginnings people bring their previous experience and skills to their joint endeavor. While at other times the participants change by learning from each other new methods, bodies of knowledge, and roles which contribute to a fully realized collaborative project and new constellations of complementarity emerge.

Closely related to complementarity is the concept of *mutual appropriation*: "a result of sustained engagement during which partners hear, struggle with, and reach for each other's thoughts and ideas…the stretching of human possibilities through the collaborative partners' shared experiences that sustains their endeavors" (John-Steiner, 2000, p. 199). Intergenerational collaboration is a good example of mutual appropriation. In the American Southwest, traditional relationships still exist in some Pueblo communities. In a study conducted a few decades ago, we found that observational learning was prevalent among Pueblo children who deeply respect and closely follow their elders' activities. During the hot summer months, cool water is a highly desirable gift from child to grandparent. In order to greet a hard-working grandfather after a long day in the fields, some children learn how to make cups in which to collect water to be placed in a cold corner in their adobe-walled homes. When asked why they were concerned about their elders' need for refreshment at the end of the day, the children answered, "In the winter he tells us stories and this is the way in which we can thank him" (John-Steiner & Osterreich, 1975). In addition, in order to make the cups that hold the water, the children can model the body of the vessel without much adult assistance. But once they try to make the handle, they need to appropriate their relatives' modeling of cup-making. Thus, they are provided with assistance from more mature members of their community. In return, their enthusiasm and eagerness is of help to their tired elders and is part of the intergenerational transmission of a mutually respectful way of living under challenging circumstances.

These are but three features of the many forms that interdependence and collaboration take. They need to be further examined and analyzed in different settings to counter the frequent distortions of collaboration into "teamwork." In the latter, the careful arrangement of the choice of partners and the richness of complementarity that they bring to the project are often ignored. Similarly, the need for adequate length of time for joint activity, which facilitates mutual appropriation, is seldom incorporated in arbitrarily assembled teams. And, most importantly, the neglect of differing styles, backgrounds, temperament, and rhythms of work make novel outcomes unlikely.

With the rapid increase in collaborative projects, the study of the aspects examined in this paper and additional ones becomes possible. As many of these collaborations, such as the Polymath Project, take place on the Internet, part of the process has become more visible. We can now look forward to greater precision in specifying which characteristics contribute to productive collaborative projects and by providing richer description, such as those included in this volume, highlight the complexity of the social in our representation of human generativity.

References

Cain, S. (2012). *Quiet: The power of introverts in a world that can't stop talking*. New York, NY: Crown Publishers.

Connery, C., & John-Steiner, V. (2013). The power of imagination: Constructing innovative classrooms through a cultural-historical approach to creative education. *Learning Landscapes, 6*(1), 129–154.

Dreyfus, H.L., & Dreyfus, S.E. (1988). *Mind over machine: The power of human intuition and expertise in the era of the computer*. New York, NY: Free Press.

Gowers, T. (2009). Gowers's Weblog. http://gowers.wordpress.com/2009/01/27/is-massively-collaborative-mathematics-possible/

John-Steiner, V. (2000). *Creative collaboration*. New York, NY: Oxford University Press.

John-Steiner, V. (2008). Personal interviews Geoffrey West and James Brown.

John-Steiner, V., & Mahn, H. (1996). Sociocultural approaches to learning and development: A Vygotskian framework. *Educational Psychologist, 31*(3/4), 191–206.

John-Steiner, V., & Osterreich, H. (1975, October). *Learning styles among Pueblo children*. NIE Research Grant, Final Report, University of New Mexico, Department of Educational Foundations.

Lehrer, J. (2010, December 17). A physicist solves the city. *New York Times Sunday Magazine*, p. MM46.

Martin, U., & Pease, A. (2013, May 4). Mathematical practice, crowdsourcing, and social machines. arXiv:1305.0900v1 [cs.SI]. To appear, Springer LNCS, *Proceedings on Intelligent Computer Mathematics*, CICM 2013, July 2013 Bath, UK.

Nelson, K. (2006). *Narratives from the crib*. Cambridge, MA: Harvard University Press.

St. John, P. (2010). Crossing scripts and swapping riffs: Preschoolers make musical meaning. In M.C. Connery, V.P. John-Steiner, and A. Marjanovic-Shane (Eds.), *Vygotsky and creativity: A cultural-historical approach to play, meaning making, and the arts* (pp. 63–82). New York, NY: Peter Lang Publishing.

Stetsenko, A., & Arievitch, I.M. (2004). Vygotskian collaborative project of social transformation: History, politics, and practice in knowledge construction. *International Journal of Critical Psychology 12*(4), 58–80.

Zukow-Goldring, P. (2006). Assisted imitation: Affordances, effectivities, and the mirror system in early language development. In M.A. Arbib (Ed.), *Action to language via the mirror neuron system* (pp. 469–500). Cambridge, UK: Cambridge University Press.

CHAPTER 5

Seeking to Combat Educational Inequality: The 5th Dimension

Michael Cole, Virginia Gordon and William Blanton

This chapter examines the development of a line of research we refer to as the 5th Dimension Project. We trace the 5th Dimension from its origins as an element in an educational experiment three decades ago to its widespread implementation in diverse universities and community settings in the United States and abroad at present. We place special emphasis on the relatively long time span of the project which, we argue, provides insights into a variety of issues of concern to students of learning and development. In particular, viewing the 5th Dimension on the scale of a multi-decade project allows for longitudinal as well as cross-sectional analysis across implementations revealing new information about why seemingly successful innovations fail to survive and the multiple factors entailed in the long-term sustainability of educational change.

The 5th Dimension – Origins

The project described here is a part of the program of the Laboratory for Comparative Human Cognition (LCHC). The overall mission of LCHC is to understand the role of culture in human development in order to understand more deeply the social sources of social inequality and methods of promoting social equity.[1] The 5th Dimension project grew out of a moment of crisis in the overall LCHC project of which it was a part (LCHC, 1982; Cole, 1996, chapter 10; Nicolopolou and Cole, 1993).

This moment occurred in the middle of an attempt to extend earlier LCHC research into a broad study of the behaviors that call forth the diagnosis of "learning disabled." Our preliminary research had indicated clearly that children diagnosed as learning disabled in school display no special difficulties and are not considered learning disabled in many other situations, where they appear to be effective learners, even circumstances that involve print. (Cole & Traupmann; 1981; Hood, McDermott & Cole, 1980).

1 For descriptions of the overall program of LCHC and its history, see http://lchc.ucsd.edu.

On the basis of this prior research we had obtained funding to trace the behaviors of a group of children enrolled in a special class for the "learning disabled" over a broad range of social environments. We sought not only to videotape class sessions, but to accompany the children into various other classes, the playground, their afterschool activities, their weekends – in short, to map out the social ecology of the children's encounters with print and other people.

This enterprise was brought to an abrupt halt when the teachers involved in the special classrooms, realizing that someone was videotaping them as they failed to teach the children despite their special circumstances, asked us politely to take our cameras elsewhere and stay away from their classrooms. We could sympathize with the teachers. By our own assessment the children in fact represented many potential psychological diagnoses and individualized teaching challenges, but they fit no single pattern and the challenge of teaching them to read in normal classroom settings within existing pedagogical norms seemed a daunting task to us.

What to do? Terminate the project as hopeless given the emerging resistance to us making the kinds of observations that our research methodology required? Or seek to address the challenge of creating an effective literacy environment for such a diverse group of children, whose one apparently common characteristic was that they were not learning to read, even when enrolled in school-based special classrooms?

Mindful that the salaries of our colleagues depended in no small measure on the way the problem was solved, it was decided to continue the project under an entirely new arrangement. Instead of observing others try to teach these children to read, we would undertake the task ourselves, but outside of the regime of formal schooling.

More or less on the spur of the moment, we agreed with the school personnel that we would institute an after-school program for 2nd–6th graders they found it too difficult to teach – the problem kids.[2] In a very short period of time, Peg Griffin, who had extensive background in the theory and practice of reading instruction, came up with four different, small group, reading activities, each of which allowed children to move around, talk to each other, and work together if they wished in trying to "win" the reading games that Ms. Griffin had organized. It was characteristic of all these activities that they involved at least one competent reader in addition to the "teacher." This role

2 At the time, local teachers' contracts required that they demonstrate progress for at least 80% of the children in their classrooms. Our request was that they provide us with the remaining 20%.

was played by undergraduates doing special research classes, graduate student assistants, and other researchers. Active meaning making through print was the common core of the different activities underlying, implemented in a manner to keep it interesting for the kids.

Still, reading is reading and the children have just spent the past 7 hours and many years failing to learn to read, in game-like situations or not. We needed to build more "fun" into the setting – it was afterschool and voluntary. In addition to building physical activities of various kinds into the activity (run around the track at breaks in the action), we also made wide use of computer games.

While the reading activities proved to be of enormous interest to us as researchers, the data were difficult to analyze and describe. We claimed (correctly) that we had found a way to create systems of reading that are both diagnostic and re-mediational at the same time. We thought this a potentially powerful tool that could be used on a broader scale, but it was not this potential that charmed those who read our work. It was the fact that a part of our program was carried out on computers – a new and controversial medium at the time.

Elsewhere the reader can follow the fate of the reading instruction program and its theoretical significance (Cole, 1996). Here, because it became the standard bearer around which a great deal of LCHC activity was organized, we focus on the 5th Dimension.

The Conception and Implementation of the 5th Dimension

The year was 1981 and microcomputers had only recently come on the market causing a stir about the effect on children's brains of playing Pacman. The popular imagination worried about whether this was a new addiction to replace television or a new medium with great potential for promoting the intellectual development of children. Focus on the potential of the new medium for creating interesting learning environments, when appropriately orchestrated, was the route that LCHC took, so including "edutainment" computer games fit well with efforts to help struggling kids to mastery literacy.

The computer activities we began with were certainly popular with many of the children. There were, however, two major shortcomings of the pattern of their interests from our point of view as developmentalists. Firstly, the interested children were almost entirely boys, reinforcing stereotypes about gender and technology that we explicitly wanted to counteract. Secondly, the children were mostly interested in playing shoot-em-up games with no discernible redeeming educational value. They eagerly brought such games to the afterschool program in their backpacks, anxious to play.

When we realized that we were simply re-inscribing gender norms and that access to the computers for game playing was threatening to disrupt the kind of balanced play/education environment we were seeking to design, the challenge became to harness the new medium to the task of promoting literacy, numeracy, and academic thinking more generally. The answer was the 5th Dimension.

The initial prototype of the 5th Dimension was created by Peg Griffin and Catherine, King over a long spring vacation. Extensive descriptions and video materials from the 5th Dimension are available free online, (http://www.uclinks.org, tclclearninglounge.org, lchc.ucsd.edu) so I will not spend a great deal of time describing the general initial idea here, but will focus on several theoretical commitments which were significant in the design of the project.[3]

The 5th Dimension was fashioned loosely on a "Dungeons and Dragons" metaphor, which was popular with children at the time we began this work and has continued to have a life of its own in cyberspace. A large space was arranged with computers scattered about, often near the walls, in such a way as to allow two or three people to use a single screen to work together. A physical maze was placed in a prominent position, with a few entrances and exits and many doorways between rooms.

Each room contained a card with the name of two activities on it, at least one of which was likely to be a computer game. The children would each have a physical avatar, a "cruddy creature" they could use until they demonstrated some proficiency in achieving a high level of performance in some minimal number of 5th Dimension-related tasks. There were many artifacts provided to encourage literacy and numeracy: a "task card" specified the performance necessary to move up levels within the 5th Dimension (including, of course, the game itself), a hints book contained tips for people who wanted to succeed quickly, tips that the children wrote to complete task cards.[4] A playful Wizard would sometimes appear on the rickety computer network we had set up to enable chat with the children, and to give an air of mystery to the 5th Dimension

3 The name, 5th Dimension, was chosen to promote the idea that the children had entered a new realm of experience (beyond dots, lines, space, and time) where play and learning were combined. A "pretend" wizard really corresponded with the children and provided interesting games.

4 When a game was too "school like" or too "arcade like" various artifacts were introduced into the activity that balanced the competing demands of school and arcade. If the game was too school-like, a task card used to guide playing of the game in the 5th D became more playful, and if the game seemed too mindlessly shoot-em-up, a task card could guide the players to trip over intellectual obstacles that induced them to engage in literacy, numeracy, and other forms of academic, intellectual activity.

itself. And so on. Lots of enticing tasks, lots of choice, undergraduate students present to help out when the going got tough or participants just hung around and chat while waiting for someone to finish using a game. An afterschool micro-world/club, with its own local cultural norms, favored practices, standout personalities was created. An enormous diversity of children contented to spend their time engaging with the program and each other several times a week participated.

We judged the 5th Dimension to be a marked improvement over the spontaneous choices of the children with respect both to the acquisition of academic skill and socioemotional predispositions to participate in activities where print mediated the interactions they were enjoying. Feedback from parents was quite positive. Initially suspicious, the teachers reported that several of our children showed improved performance in the classroom. And kids kept on coming, improving their ability to deal with a wide range of appropriately challenging academic tasks.

At this point, the 5th Dimension became an object of intense interest to us. Kids liked it, adults responsible for children outside of school seemed to like it, we liked it both as a way of studying new ways to engage children with intellectual matters and because of the enormous impact it appeared to have on the undergraduates who participated in the activities as an apprenticeship in research.

From a Prototype to a Project

For the next few years we sought continued government funding from the Bureau of the Educationally Handicapped (BEH) and the National Science Foundation (NSF). But the shift in methodology we had adopted – immersion in the specially designed activities as simultaneously a means of diagnosis and a medium for remediation of academic disabilities – was declared "cutting edge" but too "basic" for BEH while the fact that the procedures appeared to be clinical applications made the work ineligible at the NSF.

To our good fortune, we found support for our work from private sector foundations. One such organization was the Carnegie Foundation, which had supported earlier research at LCHC, and whose staff members took an interest in our efforts to design new modes of reading instruction incorporating computers and computer networks. They were also interested in our methodological approach that brought together scholars from several different social sciences to wrestle with understanding how it can be that normally developing children find learning to read, let alone acquiring a disposition to read, an insurmountable task. Carnegie also supported efforts to link this general question to the very specific issue of ethnic and social class inequalities in academic achievement which were at the heart of the LCHC research program. The support of the Spencer foundation, which was interested not only in issues of technological change and education, but our focus on out-of-school time as a resource for educational improvement was another essential in those earlier days.

Out of these resources, during the 1986–1987 academic year, the 5th Dimension Project under examination here was officially launched. In contrast with 1981–1982 when the 5th Dimension emerged from the collective imaginations of Peg Griffin, Catherine, King, and the band of colleagues and students with whom they worked, it now re-emerged as "the 5th Dimension Project," with all the essential features of its canonical forbearer but a new identity. It was now a "successful educational innovation," born as part of a project on understanding the phenomenon known as "learning disability" at a time when the public was fascinated by the potential and perils of computer games for children.

The 5th Dimension as a Tool of Research

We pursued several goals when we once again took up the 5th Dimension as an object of research in 1986. The American educational community was a-buzz with concerns that the U.S. was a "nation at risk" and educational researchers were spending a lot of time and effort trying to figure out how to get American children to spend "more time on task" (Denham & Lieberman, 1980; Frederick & Wahlberg, 1980). Despite professional and policy concerns, it was not clear how to get children to sit longer at their desks or to do more homework. Nor was the public sufficiently concerned to vote funds for a longer school day or a longer school year.

We knew from our research with the 5th Dimension as well as collateral research by other members of LCHC that there are a variety of ways to attract children and engage them in intellectually engaging, academically relevant activities after school (Anderson, Diaz & Moll, 1984; Levin, Riel, Rowe & Boruta, 1984). But we did not know what the essential dimensions of the variety of such activities were, either with respect to potential host community institutions, child populations, or ways of mediating the activity. Based upon our experience with the 5th Dimension, we thought it provided both a potentially effective attractor of children who could benefit from "more time on task" and at the same time allowed us to investigate any special qualities of instruction that might be provided by computer mediated activity.

Here is how we made our case in appealing for support.

> The basic strategy of this approach is to focus on contexts of instruction rather than psychological tasks as the basis for research and instructional intervention. It uses two basic methods for promoting development of contexts that support higher levels of academic learning.
>
> 1. Reorganization of activity within contexts.
> 2. Reorganization of the relations between contexts.
>
> A key to both forms of educational reorganization in the present world circumstances is the potential of new information technologies to solve some of the problems that have grown up as a byproduct of technological success e.g., massive underachievement in school. Our evidence shows that the communicative potential of new information technologies has been drastically underutilized in the rush to improve classroom practice. While not ignoring advances in software design, the special focus of a cultural context approach is on re-connecting existing institutions so that they work synergistically to create educational innovations within institutions.
>
> This orientation provides a concrete framework within which to reconfigure children's educational experience along lines proposed by Goodlad (1984) ("educative communities"), Cremins (1976) ("ecology of education") and others (e.g., Fantini, 1985). Within each institution that will be a part of the proposed experiment there will be a variety of educational activities, each of which affords different mixes of educational tasks and technology; comparisons made across institutional settings will help to specify the conditions needed to create maximally effective instruction in each. Our use of the communicative potential of new information technologies provides for coordination of resources along two crucial dimensions: horizontal integration is achieved by site-to-site connections; vertical integration is achieved by inclusion of small children, university students, and adults in a single interactive network. The data gathered from educational activities within contexts provide one essential stream of data for analysis of the processes characterizing the impact of new technologies in the teaching-learning process. Additional process data come from the flow of discourse between sites. The products are measured in terms of change in standardized test scores, teacher and parent evaluation, and increases in community support. The ultimate goals of this project are:

1. To research the power of a cultural context theory to engineer powerful reorganizations of educational activity within a variety of community and school contexts;
2. To investigate the power of communication between sites as a method of fomenting within-context change;
3. To create a new kind of educational activity system which can be taken up and maintained by the community with its own resources.

The last of these goals deserves special attention, because as we made progress on the first two (effective organization of activities for the children at a site, effective interaction among sites), the issue of sustainability mentioned third constantly challenged us, methodologically, theoretically, and practically, eventually becoming central to the project of the 5th Dimension.

The Value of Focusing on Sustainability

As recounted elsewhere, Cole's interest in the issue of sustainability as a goal of educational reform was piqued by earlier work in West Africa (Cole, 1996). During the interval when we were searching for funds to continue research on the 5th Dimension, our interest in sustainability was rekindled because LCHC had been commissioned to write a monograph for the National Research Council to identify barriers to the participation of women and minorities in technological fields of study. While immersed in gathering information for the report, an NRC staff member sent us a report prepared by the American Association for the Advancement of Science about successful technological education programs targeting women and minorities, the very topic we were supposed to be researching (AAAS, 1984). The report identified 16 characteristics of the successful programs, which, if implemented, indicated that: "if minorities and women are provided early, excellent and sustained instruction in these academic areas...then their achievement levels parallel those of white males" (p. iv).

The 16 "characteristics of the successful programs" were:

1. Strong academic component in mathematics, science, and communications, focused on enrichment rather than remediation.
2. Academic subjects taught by teachers who are highly competent in the subject matter and believe that students can learn the materials.
3. Heavy emphasis on the applications of science and mathematics and careers in these fields.

4. Integrative approach to teaching that incorporates all subject areas, hands-on opportunities, and computers.
5. Multiyear involvement with students.
6. Strong director; committed and stable staff who share program goals.
7. Stable long-term funding base with multiple funding sources.
8. Recruitment of participants from all relevant target populations.
9. University, industry, school, etc. cooperative program.
10. Opportunities for in-school and out-of-school learning experiences.
11. Parental involvement and development of base of community support.
12. Specific attention to removing educational inequalities related to gender and race.
13. Involvement of professionals and staff who look like the target population.
14. Development of peer support systems (involvement of a critical mass of any particular kind of student).
15. Evaluation, long-term follow-up, and careful data collection.
16. 'Mainstreaming' integration of program elements supportive of women and minorities into the institutional programs.

We could not help asking ourselves why our report was necessary given that the answers we were seeking were presumably known? Why were new programs, many of which lacked the essential characteristics identified in the AAAS report, being reinvented every year, including programs at our own universities? Why, in short, were proven, effective, programs not sustained?

The simple answer in both the American and Liberian cases (see Cole, 1996) seemed to be that the successful programs could not be integrated into the normal operation of educational institutions because they required extra effort in terms of creating the conditions that enabled a sufficient proportion of those 16 success markers to be present. Such "admirable experiments" were tolerated by the social institutions where they were developed only so long as they "paid their own way"; when outside funding dried up, they could not compete successfully for internal resource demands.

Taking this perspective as a starting point, here was a new challenge. If we could demonstrate the effectiveness of the 5th Dimension and have it win acceptance in a host institution, could we do so in a way that was sustainable "over the long haul"? As Cole later posed the question,

> Obviously all innovations don't go away. Some come and stay for a long time, such as the use of IQ-like tests as measures of academic achievement or Thorndikian drill and practice methods to teach basic academic skills. What are the factors involved in the process by which an innovation is taken up or rejected, even if it fulfills society's expectations of it?
> COLE, 1996, p. 288

A research plan was born. We would create several afterschool computer-mediated programs modeled on the original 5th Dimension in different institutions that hosted children during the afterschool hours. These activities would provide the highly desired "more time on academic tasks." We would run a practicum course in child development at UCSD as a source of "older siblings" to provide academically able and motivated personnel to enrich the afterschool settings and opportunities for creating zones of proximal development. We would trace each system over time to observe the processes of development that we were attempting to create. During this same period we would learn as much as we could about the history of the institutions we worked with, their current organization and practices. The "object" (5th Dimension) was studied in its "context" (its institutional center, the place of that center in its community, the place of that community in the larger, regional social order).

The goal of sustainability was specified as the continuation of community-university collaboration modeled on the 5th Dimension after the special research funds ran out. Note that we did not propose total University withdrawal from engagement. Rather, we specified a cost sharing plan in which both sides would continue involvement but the presumed costs of continuing would be greatly reduced for each partner because of the resources provided by the other and routinization of the partnership.

We planned for the project to last for four years. Year 1 would be devoted to goal formation – staff at each community institution, in collaboration with the project staff, would investigate a broad range of potential computer-mediated activities for children suitable to their site. Years 2 and 3 would be devoted to designing and running the system. Finding methods to improve and evaluate our activities would be uppermost during this period. Year 4 would be the "uptake year" during which each institution would seek to make adjustments needed to continue the project once the startup funding had been terminated. By analyzing the patterns of success and failure (assuming there was at least one success) we thought we would have something interesting to say about the conditions that enabled or doomed sustainability of the 5th Dimension as an inter-institutional educational innovation.

The Mixed Fate of the Initial Cohort of 5th Dimensions

During the initial, goal-formation year of the project, the staff held workshops periodically with various community organizations to decide on just what sort of collaborative program they would like for their institution. At the end of that year the research group conducted interviews with the directors of each institutions that showed a strong interest in collaboration: the School, the Childcare Center, the Library, and the BGClub.

Diagnostically, whatever goal formation had gone on during the workshops, little was in evidence at the time that the program opened. The School decided not to go ahead with their involvement because they feared for the safety of their computers; they offered to help the Childcare Center instead. The BGClub and Library personnel had enjoyed the 5th Dimension and thought their kids would like it too. The Library personnel expressed the hope that this could be done in a way to involve the children with library functions, and we agreed it was a good idea. Then the process of development and attrition began.

Childcare Center

The first 5th Dimension to expire was at the Childcare Center, where our activities continued only 2/3 of the 1987–1988 academic year. The demise of the Childcare Center's 5th Dimension was not the result of the failure of the activity to please the children or the staff. In fact, not long after starting the program we were asked to modify our procedures to expand the number of the kids who could get a chance to participate.

The stress point that led to the demise of the 5th Dimension at the Center was fear of child abuse combined with the relatively rapid turnover of undergraduates (UCSD classes run for only 10 weeks a quarter). As a result of publicity surrounding an alleged child abuse case in Los Angeles and a high level of concern about child abuse more generally, the agency that licensed the Childcare Center insisted that all adults working in a day care facility register their fingerprints with the Department of Justice and obtain a TB test. Money was not a problem but time was; the quarter was well under way by the time all the paperwork was completed, and the undergraduates could go to the site. As a consequence of these complexities, the Center's Director was grateful when we suggested, prior to the start of the third quarter, that we suspend the project.

The Library

The Library 5th Dimension was located in a back corner of the library. When it was not in session, the computers, the maze, and other paraphernalia were stored in an adjacent closet. Because it was located across a freeway from the elementary school, children who attended the Library 5th Dimension were generally dropped off and picked up by their parents and it took a few weeks for the new activity to catch on. By midway through the first quarter we had a steady complement of 6–7 children attending twice a week. In the second year, we accommodated increased demand by running two shifts of the 5th Dimension for an average of 8–9 children per session, four days a week.

The Library 5th Dimension was the most successful of our systems from the perspective of its impact on the children (see Nicolopolou & Cole, 1993). Students and children formed close personal bonds; interactions at this site were marked by the high level of task involvement that developed among the children and the undergraduates.

From early in the project we worked with the Library staff to build expertise in the running of the 5th Dimension and we helped them raise money locally to begin the process of providing hardware and software. We created special activities that required the children to acquire library skills and we met with the staff periodically to review progress in the program. The librarian was helpful in seeing that a phone line was placed near the 5th Dimension to facilitate communication with the Wizard.

At the end of the third year of the project we met with the staff at the Library to discuss the future. We could guarantee that students would keep coming (because I could teach the classes or arrange for someone else to), but we could not continue to provide a site coordinator and we could not be responsible for computer upkeep, purchases, etc. The local Friends of the Library agreed to pay for a site coordinator, but the Library staff decided that they did not want to continue the program. There were many reasons for this decision: the Library was short of space, the children sometimes got noisy, parents often failed to pick up the kids on time, there were administrative difficulties in handling the money needed to pay a site coordinator, they did not have time to train people to work with the children, etc. Each of these problems could have been solved, but the fact of the matter was that the librarians had come to the conclusion that the 5th Dimension did not fit closely enough with their main goals as librarians. And that was the end of the 5th Dimension in the Library.

The Boys and Girls Club

The 5th Dimension at the BGClub took place in a large room that well exceeded our initial, modest capacities to accommodate children. We slowly added to our 4–5 computers and undergraduates came in larger numbers, so our capacity to handle larger numbers of children increased. As soon as we had the person power, we kept the program open four days a week. Since the space was not being shared with other programs, we had the luxury of leaving things set up between sessions. We could also put the maze in a prominent place in the center of the room and put children's artwork and posters relevant to 5th Dimension activities on the walls.

The number of children who sought admission to the 5th Dimension fluctuated from a low of 4–5 to a high of 12–13. In accordance with the norm of the Club, children came and went as they pleased; some came only once a week while other were habitués, depending upon their life circumstances and interests. The rapid flow of children, both within and between days, made it difficult for children and undergraduates to get to know each other. In addition, the undergraduates and researchers found it difficult to keep track of which games children had completed at each level. As a consequence, the undergraduates had difficulty grasping the rules and conventions they and the children were supposed to follow. As a consequence, some children (and undergraduates) felt that the rules were coercive and external to them, so they either resisted or ignored them.

Researchers and undergraduates tried various strategies to simplify the operation of the 5th Dimension but our attempts were a total failure. Before long the children settled into playing whatever games suited their fancy at whatever level. Despite these difficulties, the children kept coming, the Club personnel were pleased, and the students continued to sign up for the class.

That summer we ran a special summertime 5th Dimension at the BGClub in which we returned to the original 5th Dimension structure, elaborating new artifacts to deal with the complexities of the BGClub setting (record-keeping devices, a carefully worked out organization of the games within the maze, improving task cards, for example). When the 5th Dimension re-emerged in its elaborated form, it proved a gratifyingly sturdy tool.

During the second year, ambitious undergraduates opened a new 5th Dimension in one of the neighboring BGClubs, and soon thereafter a third Club asked for and got a 5th Dimension. The Clubs gave the program an award and embraced it as an important new addition to their program. Most importantly, they provided the needed support for computers and telephone lines.

When we met with the directors of the Boys and Girls Club at the end of the third year they were committed to continue the program. They did not shy away from picking up responsibility for paying a site coordinator part time and they had already started to provide the needed support for computers and telephone lines. However, a recession caused cutbacks at all the clubs and at UCSD we cut back to the "main 5th Dimension" at the original Boys and Girls Club.

For the next two years, the 5th Dimension at the BGClub, "treaded water," so to speak. The practicum class continued to be taught at UCSD and we continued to send students to the 5th Dimension at the BGClub. We focused heavily on both keeping the activities developing in a healthy way and in documenting the changes we were (and were not) observing. We wrote articles about what we were seeing and sought financial support to continue our efforts.

The 5th Dimension Goes International

At this point, the "Project of the 5th Dimension" underwent a period of rapid growth when several factors came to together. The first was the widespread excitement, in society at large and the educational community in particular, about the potential educational benefit of personal computers. Within the academic community many colleagues, both in the US and abroad, sought us out to join with them in undertaking their own, similar projects. The second factor was Cole's own long-term interaction with Soviet/Russian psychology which included not only involvement in the publication of translations but academic diplomacy when he became responsible for Soviet-American academic exchanges in Psychology for a number of years in the 1970s and 1980s. The third was LCHC's adoption of the cultural-historical psychological view, greatly influenced by the Muscovite Vygotskians, mixed with American cultural anthropological and pragmatic social science both of which resonated strongly with the international community of educational researchers at the time.

The interest of the academic community manifested itself most clearly in invitations to engage in joint research projects with people living in Europe, Asia and Latin America. In each case, for varied reasons, some colleagues believed that the notion of building 5th Dimensions under different local constraints, and then comparing the difficulties that each group faced and the changes wrought would be instructive intellectually. And in the international circumstances of the time, everyone seemed to think that having youth discussing their different experiences was a good idea. They believed that the 5th Dimension had promise of providing opportunities not only to explore the power of computers for education, but the value of the 5th Dimension for studying both the organization of activities locally and (using the communicative potentials of the nascent internet) and globally. As a consequence, a variety of intra-national and bi-national collaborations began to take shape.

The 5th Dimension as a Tool of International Science Diplomacy[5]

By about 1985 it was clear that it was technically possible to patch together various pathways that mixed the store-and-forward e-mail systems based on university mainframes with private satellite facilities. It had also been demonstrated that such activities had valued educational consequences. Consequently, it seemed technically possible to conduct the same sort of work with Moscow that LCHC was conducting with people in other parts of the world based around some common activity, sometimes involving children, sometimes an entirely an adult-focused activity.

In March of 1985, David Hamburg, President of the Carnegie Corporation, went to Moscow to participate as a member of a bi-national Committee on International Security and Arms Control set up by the National Academy of Sciences in Washington and the Soviet Academy of Sciences. He was anxious to establish connections with the Soviet leadership in which scientists could promote "second track diplomacy."

The chairman of the Soviet counterpart committee was Evgenii Velikhov, President of the Academy of Sciences and science advisor to Mikhail Gorbachev. In a private conversation with Velikhov, Hamburg inquired about ways in which leaders in the US and USSR might take advantage of the new situation caused by the advent of Gorbachev to power to promote mutual understanding and cooperation. Velikhov identified the need of all advanced industrialized countries to deal with the accelerating scientific and technological changes which were then occurring as a common problem and specifically emphasized the need to introduce knowledge about computers into the schools as a topic of special concern. The two men agreed to pursue this theme by an exchange of relevant scholars and the Velham (Velikhov-Hamburg) Project was born.

As a follow up, Hamburg organized for a delegation representing Carnegie, including Fritz Mosher, who headed the relevant Carnegie Program and Cole, to travel to Moscow, meet with Velikhov, and formulate a concrete project. The transfer of computer technology to the USSR was a sensitive issue of national security, so it took some negotiation to come up with a workable, in-principle reciprocal project. The eventual solution was that a project would use the 5th Dimension (which, after all, purported to use Soviet ideas such as the "zone of proximal development") as a common object of research. The research in the USSR would be housed in the Institute of Psychology of the Academy of Sciences, and its participants would include leading developmental psychologists with whom Cole and his colleagues wanted to swap ideas about how to

5 For a fuller account of this project, see http://lchc.ucsd.edu/Histarch/velham.html.

make optimal use of the new mediational means represented by microcomputer and computer networks.

They minimized the problems of technology transfer by using computers that were "low tech" and by seeking to insure that their Soviet partners came up with most of their own equipment. The use of the still-nascent internet was much more problematic because of security concerns, but we prevailed in the end – the computer interactions, occurring in written form as they all had to at the time, involved easy surveillance to see that no national secrets were being given away as children corresponded with each other about how to survive in an ecology simulation game or write an algorithm to guide a jumping frog.

In the summer of 1987 the Soviet and American groups succeeded in moving to a "trial balloon" phase during a special summer camp conducted not far from Moscow during which we were able to institute a version of the 5th Dimension including the potential for the kids to interact via a store-and-forward messaging system. The child-to-child correspondence ranged from comparative strategies about how to win at a commonly experienced game, more personal exchanges involving various kinds of cultural display, including riddles, poems, and comparisons of favorite objects The adult discussions were also useful. Scholars on the two sides jointly discussed a wide range of topics including the strengths and weaknesses of various software the children were being exposed to, the best ways of organizing interactions between the children and particular games, and ways to take advantage of telecommunications to stimulate children's active engagement in learning and communicating.

From approximately the fall of 1988 to the beginning of the 1990–1991 academic year we conducted a wide range of studies in and around the 5th Dimension which complemented work we had already begun in the United States. We placed a high premium on being able to motivate child-to-child correspondence; the internet was still too primitive to allow transmission of video cheaply, so we complemented 5th Dimension engagement with various projects to engage the children's imaginations about each other's lives and common problems, such as the armed conflicts that broke out in both Estonia and Iraq. Overall, we learned a lot about how difficult it could prove to organize child-to-child correspondence outside of school-like settings, sometimes succeeding, sometimes failing. Having a reliable foreign partner also allowed us to separate problems in organizing collaborative activities across sites *within* a country and a shared language from complications arising from unshared language and time delays between opportunities for communication (American sites were specially organized in a Chicago housing project, a New York Community Center, a working class suburban New Orleans afterschool program, and a Southern California free school).

The Velham project advanced our research agenda in several ways. First, vis-à-vis our ability to do interesting design work, we were fortunate to create a unique international team that included a private American software company, Soviet computer scientists and developmentalist-educators. They re-designed a popular program for teaching children to create algorithms in a manner that mixed Soviet and American ideas on maximization of the program's potentials (Griffin, Belyaeva, Soldatova & the Velikhov-Hamburg Collective, 1993).

With respect to sustainability issues, the matter was more complicated. The existence of the 5th Dimension in Moscow was always something of an anomaly, kept together by the project directors on the two sides within the political agenda of the late Soviet era and in particular, Velikhov and Hamburg. The Velham project enabled us to engage others in pursuing our research goals and it certainly made our work visible, but at the same time it fell outside of the scope of our sustainability analysis because of its direct, politically entangled, origins.

Continued International Expansion of the 5th Dimension Project

All during the 1990s and continuing to the present day, institutions not only in the United States, but around the world, have created similar activities vastly increasing the range of sociocultural ecologies within which it has been implemented. For example, Berthel Sutter at the Blekinge School of Technology in southern Sweden was interested in using the UCLinks-5th Dimension model to prepare undergraduate students to be software designers. Another researcher from the Blekinge School of Technology, Monica Nilsson, started a 5th Dimension as a means of studying ways to transform and develop school structures and activities.

Projects inspired by the 5th Dimension model sprouted up in several locations in the Nordic countries, in Spain, Mexico and Brazil. Some focused on technological skills, some on literacy, some on play as a foundation for later education; some on preschoolers, some on high school youth. The range of home departments was equally as diverse.

Almost immediately the European projects formed networks of their own. For example, the Nordic Network was instrumental in securing grants for collaborative research and in developing two new networks of 5th Dimension sites – one a project supported by the European Union, the other a collaboration between the European sites and American sites. The increased demand for initiating collaborative projects in different parts of the world continued to build, and with it financial and collegial support for expansion of the project (Nilsson & Nocon, 2005).

Perhaps most important in terms of sustainability of the 5th Dimension, the Velham project provided ongoing support for new implementations of the 5th Dimension in an unusual mix of cultural/institutional settings *within the United States*. Issues of educational equity had not ceased to be a part of Carnegie's mission, so the involvement of poor people of color in genuine tele-mediated exchanges with Russian children was of paramount importance and proved to be one of the most powerful sources of educationally valuable inter-site interactions during the course of the project.

From the 5th Dimension to UCLinks

By 1991, our focus on the 5th Dimension in connection with the Velham project was diminishing. The momentous events in the USSR naturally shifted focus to the rapid dissemination of the internet within the former Soviet Republics as part of a process of state re-formation in which ethnic tensions and national disputes were playing out. Velham continued, but continuation of second track diplomacy as it had existed in the age of Perestroika lost its appeal. If the 5th Dimension was going to continue to develop, it had to do so on the basis of other funding sources.

By this time in our research, we had come to appreciate much more fully the complexities of sustaining, let alone scaling up an educational innovation such as the 5th Dimension, despite its many attractions. We had seen three of the four initial sites we began with disappear because, despite their acknowledged virtues and the money to conduct the program, the work of coordinating with the University schedule on top of the need to maintain the local organizations' core, institutionalized functions was simply too great. We had seen new 5th Dimensions come into being, heightening our sensitivity to the uniqueness of each 5th Dimension in its institutional and geopolitical setting. And we had the ongoing 5th Dimension at the original Boys and Girls Club to contend with (along with a new version of the activity especially designed for immigrant Latino children that began not far from the Boys and Girls Club (see Vasquez, 2003).

To our great good fortune, the funds to conduct a more expanded, more systematically diverse set of 5th Dimensions made its appearance in form of a grant from the Mellon Foundation, administered by the Russell Sage Foundation. Mellon funded an expanded exploration of the 5th Dimension as part of its larger set of program focused on the promotion of literacy. They wanted a more serious investigation of the potentials of the existing 5th Dimension research and educational design practices using computer-based activities to promote literacy on a large scale.

The Distributed Literacy Consortium

Funding for a new project entitled "Capitalizing on Diversity, a Proposal for the Distributed Literacy Consortium" began in 1991, just as support for 5th Dimension activities with the Russians was coming to an end. The basic idea was to create a team of researchers in different kinds of institutions of higher learning and different academic departments in order to begin to get a handle on the question of the kinds of ecologies that could provide sustained support to the 5th Dimension, assuming they were convinced of its utility.[6]

Participants were chosen (in addition to their willingness to participate!) to provide as a broad a sample of organizational relationships and target populations as possible. At the same time, of course, we would be adding to our samples of the conception, birth, and presumably death of a great many more 5th Dimensions than was true when we came out of the first round of implementations with only one of the original partners left standing.

Evaluation had been built into research on the 5th Dimension from the beginning, but it became a focal preoccupation of the Consortium. Evaluation was a tricky business. First, what do you use for control groups? What should one be testing for? How can one document processes of learning and development in a manner that addresses ongoing controversies about these processes with a lot of policy implications?

To take on these many tasks, in addition to the implementers of individual 5th Dimensions, the evaluation work was conducted by three "evaluation teams." A Language and Culture group focused particularly on sites that were located in neighborhoods with lots of English Language Learners, but also more generally on the development of idiocultures and idiolects of the different sites they studied. A Cognitive Evaluation team focused on creating useful measures of performance, experiments, and quasi-experiments, as conditions allowed. A Process team focused on documenting actual processes of teaching and learning as they occurred in those settings where we could meet the needed level of technical support.

---

6 The partners were: UCSD/LCHC (Cole & Vasquez), working with a Boys and Girls Club and a bilingual bicultural site called La Clase Mágica, both located in the same costal suburban community near UCSD, CSU San Marcos, (Pat Worden and Miriam Schustack) working with another local Boys and Girls club site in North County San Diego; Michigan State University (Margaret Gallego) working with a community site also called La Clase Mágica undertaking ethnographic study of the impact of their educational activity system on the children and their families; Appalachian State University in North Carolina (Bill Blanton); UC Santa Barbara (Richard Duran and Betsey Brenner); Whittier College (Don Bremme).

By design, the three teams interacted with each other and often gathered data from the same sites. But they collaborated in particular to be able to take advantage of the different affordances of the different kinds of sites. For example, in those sites in which activities were sufficiently structured and participation was regular enough to make pre- and post-testing meaningful, quantitative assessments were used. By contrast, in sites where the site idioculture reflected the "drop in" policies of the host organization so that children were constantly coming and going, the use of videotaped interactions of dyads and ethnographic analyses of fieldnotes was more appropriate.

Because the idea was to create dense enough interaction among the different implementers so that they could effectively help each other, the consortium constituted itself as what subsequently became referred to as "Co-laboratories." We instituted a norm of reporting weekly on an email listserv about the doings of the day, the problems encountered, the insights gained. We also created a staff position for a person whose major job was to promote discussion on the internet and chase after people too caught up in the local to find time for writing updates. Although not entirely effective, these measures produced a steady stream of participant accounts of their projects over time. The listserv was also used to cook up joint projects that might engage children across sites. In those earliest days of the internet, these simple organizational practices were still an anomaly.

The second major focus of the consortium was to identify the common characteristics of 5th Dimension sites. This topic was visited and re-visited repeatedly by the Consortium members. By the mid-1990s various formulations had converged on a minimal set of principles couched in the following terms:

- A 5th Dimension is a joint project between a university/college and a community institution. The university provides supervised undergraduates to the community institution as labor while the community institution provides necessary space, equipment, and supervision of the activities to provide the students with a valuable research experience.
- The activity is a mixture of "leading activities" (as proposed by cultural historical activity theorists) including affiliation, play, learning, and work as multiple sources of motivation for participation.
- Participant structures are designed to minimize power differentials between the participants, particularly the undergraduates and the children with whom they work.
- Heavy emphasis is placed upon the value of communication in a variety of media including computers, conversation, and writing in the service of meeting goals that are provided within the activity setting.

- Participation by children in the activity is voluntary. Children are free to leave at any time. Consequently, the games and other activities that participants engage in must adhere to goals that the children find interesting.

The Distributed Literacy Consortium 5th Dimensions often incorporated the artifacts of the initial LCHC prototype site: a maze for distributing tasks, cruddy creatures (avatars) that represented children's progress, task cards that balanced educational and entertainment productively, and a mythical/virtual entity various referred to as a "wizard," "maga," "volshebnik," or a mythical cat, depending upon the choices of local participants.

The Mellon-sponsored project lasted for 6 years, an unusually long period to be allowed to conduct social science research of this interdisciplinary, labor intensive form. During this period, a great many researchers put vast energy into developing new ways to use computers for educational purposes, and computer rooms of various quality sprouted up in youth clubs and after school programs in several locations. The 5th Dimension was one among many such projects being formulated around the world and a new level of technological innovation involving digital technologies had appeared in the public's imagined future. These changes coincided with political events in the State of California, that directly affected UCSD and even more directly, affected LCHC. The 5th Dimension was again re-purposed in the service of the larger LCHC project of which it was a part: it became a vehicle for a state-wide program to promote eligibility of under-represented youth to gain admission to the University of California.

The Birth of University-Community Links (UCLinks)

In the summer of 1995, the Regents of the University of California made a controversial change in statewide admissions policies. In a special resolution they declared that:

> Effective January 1, 1997, the University of California shall not use race, religion, sex, color, ethnicity, or national origin as criteria for admission to the University or to any program of study.

Although there were a variety of University programs that sought to encourage minority enrollment through informational outreach, and some local and regional research units devoted to study of barriers to educational achievement among ethnic minorities and the poor, this decision left the University with no plausible mechanism for addressing the obvious and continuing inequities in educational access that characterized California's educational system.

To those of us who had been a part of the Distributed Learning Consortium, the timing seemed right to offer the overall 5th Dimension model system as a pro-active measure for our colleagues in the UC who shared their desire to find new ways to bolster the skills associated with UC eligibility and competitiveness among California youth. The case seemed a strong one because it offered a publicly visible way of demonstrating faculty commitment to the three-fold mission in the charter of the University of California as a public institution: to combine research, teaching and community service.

The President of the University at the time was Richard Atkinson who had at one time served as Cole's advisor while he was obtaining his BA at UCLA, and with whom he had been in touch over the intervening years. Atkinson had just been promoted to the Presidency from his position as Chancellor at UCSD. He knew of the 5th Dimension program and its involvement of UCSD students and faculty in local under-represented communities. Confronted with the Regents' rejection of affirmative action, he needed to demonstrate that the University had a commitment to equity and diversity despite legal restrictions on how that commitment could be implemented.

Atkinson provided seed money to permit Cole and Olga Vasquez, a colleague at UCSD who had designed La Clase Mágica, the adaptation of the 5th Dimension model for Latino immigrant children near the Boys and Girls Club, and who was a central member of the Mellon phase of the project, to travel around the state to identify and recruit faculty who might be interested in a state-wide effort to implement the 5th Dimension as at least the start of a response to the Regents' new policies. Charles Underwood, an outreach specialist at the UC President's Office traveled with them to help formulate a workable plan. They found support for the idea not only among their colleagues from the Distributed Learning Consortium, but from scholars located in various departments on all nine campuses of the University.

Even as plans were being made to implement UCLinks programs across the UC system, the situation with respect to affirmative action programs became more acute. During the 1996 election, California voters amended the California Constitution through an initiative known as Proposition 209, or the "California Civil Rights Initiative." The proposition included the following crucial section:

> The State shall not discriminate against, or grant preferential treatment to, any individual or group on the basis of race, sex, color, ethnicity, or national origin in the operation of public employment, public education, or public contracting.

With implementation of new, less supportive, policies only months away, the newly formed "UC Links Project" was elaborated into a state-wide program to be initiated in the fall of 1996 on campuses where it did not already exist. Funding had once again appeared for the 5th Dimension Project, but now it was re-purposed to provide a means for the University to make a positive response to the removal of affirmative action as a remedy for the inequitable situation it found itself in. Money was allotted from the UC Office of the President which officially housed the project and the services of Charles Underwood, whose expertise as an anthropologist with extensive experience working in the area of university-community collaboration to promote K-12 academic preparation, UCLinks swung into operation.

The UC Links program exists to the present day. It grew from 14 sites in 1996–1997 to 30 sites in 2013. In the last 17 years, UC Links has engaged over 15,000 youth in diverse communities across the State of California as well as over 8,000 undergraduates from not only from UC campuses, but from a number of Links programs that sprouted up in the California State University and Community College systems. Although the amounts of money provided to support local implementations are modest (averaging about 25–35,000 dollars per campus over the years), they have been sufficient to allow a flowering of a broad variety of models of University-Community collaboration, some of which have remained close in spirit to the original programs begun in 1996, and some of which have branched out to take advantage of the many different ways in which UC faculty and students could engage youth from underrepresented communities in educationally enriching collaborative activities (see http://uclinks.org).

The Current Situation

The term, "current situation" in the age of Internet 2.0 is more or less guaranteed to be behind the times by the time these written words appear in a book. At the time of this writing (Summer, 2013) the 5th Dimension Project has encompassed over 100 sites in over 10 countries and is still generating new "offspring" in different parts of the United States and abroad even as some seemingly effective and long-standing sites cease to function. For projects associated with UCLinks, there continues to be a modest level of funding within the broad scope of the University of California's efforts to promote diversity at all levels of University life. Characteristic of both long enduring sites and the new initiatives that are emerging is a proliferating diversity of the particular activities that the children and youth engage in, incorporating the rapidly changing opportunities for use of the internet and mobile, social media tools and practices.

Reflections on the Project as Mode of Research

This essay appears in the context of a volume meant to draw attention to projects as useful units of analysis in developing the ideas of cultural historical activity theory. It seems only appropriate, then, that in these reflections we focus on the potentials and difficulties for both theory and practice in adopting this mode of research.

At the most general, theoretical, level, a major advantage of a project such as the 5th Dimension is that it makes available for analysis, and thereby evaluation, theoretical principles and speculations that could not be as effectively addressed by other modes of research. In our case, the theoretical approach we use has come to be called CHAT – the broad family of cultural, historical, activity-based, theories that have blossomed in recent decades, with intellectual roots that reach back into Russia, Western Europe, and Anglo-American traditions of scholarship (Rogoff, 2003; Sannino, Daniels, & Gutiérrez, 2009; Toulmin, 1978; Wertsch, 1985).

A central tenet of this approach, its "cultural-historicalness," comes from its basic assumption that human lives must be understood simultaneously on different time scales, including phylogeny, cultural history, the process of child development over years (ontogeny), and the moment by moment changes that occur in culturally mediated, human interaction (microgenesis). A second basic assumption is that one needs to study "behavior in its context" or in CHAT terms, "mediated action in activity." In the case of the 5th Dimension, additional "layers of context" means a given 5th Dimension in its institutional context, and the larger/longer term nature of that institution's sociohistorical circumstances. A long term project such as the 5th Dimension provides excellent opportunities to extend our knowledge with respect to both the temporal and synchronic organization of activity: Diversity in the temporal and synchronic organization of such environments is the norm, not the exception.

Taken individually, every implementation of an activity that took the 5th Dimension as its point of origin, has allowed its implementers to investigate basic processes of learning and development that are clearly relevant to traditional CHAT concerns: myriad forms of mediated interaction through computers to promote learning and development, the influence of organizing interactions between participants of different ages and levels of expertise, how to organize inter-site communications in activity-enhancing ways, methods for *in situ* analysis of learning, the dynamics of site/institutional setting interactions, and more. (Cole & The Distributed Literacy Consortium, 2006).

As useful as this research has proven to be, it certainly required a long-term project involving all sorts of complicated institutional arrangements and large numbers of participants. A good deal of useful information is to be had by implanting and running 5th Dimension-like activities for the conventional funding period of 2–3 years (although the start-up costs of creating such a "laboratory" might be considered prohibitive). However, one of the key research questions that motivated the 5th Dimension project was to how account for the processes by which such seemingly useful forms of activity – useful in producing more time on task and academically more successful children – loses its allure and sinks back into oblivion. *The ONLY manner in which to address this question is to follow the longer-term project route.* So it is this process that we concentrate on in reflecting on the lessons learned thus far by the 5th Dimension Project.

Re-Viewing Sustainability through the Lens of the 5th Dimension Project

Having described the development of the 5th Dimension project over a quarter century, it is now time to re-view the benefits of project-based research, particularly with respect to our understanding of the sustainability of "successful educational innovations." For the purposes of this essay, as we look back at the history of the 5th Dimension, we are going to assume that it was, in fact, and remains a successful educational innovation as conventionally measured. Those who wish to dig more deeply into the difficulties of quantifying causal variables and how they have been dealt with, see the summary in Cole & The Distributed Literacy Consortium (2006) and more recent evaluation data provided under the aegis of UClinks (at www.uclinks.org).

In choosing to focus on sustainability, we are mindful, following Vygotsky and the CHAT tradition, that concepts emerge and take the form they do in the course of people's everyday struggles to solve a problem that confronts them. In our case, the problem is how to sustain activities governed by a set of principles that constitute a theory of how to design development-enhancing environments for children and youth.

As we re-view the path of the 5th Dimension project, our concept of sustainability, given to us "in the beginning" by our academically-mediated experience can be seen as more or less the sort of definition that one finds as the primary definition of sustainability in the current Wikipedia entry: "the capacity to endure." In our case, it was not the endurance of an object, such as the Parthenon, that we were concerned with, but endurance of a system of activity and its core principles, that themselves were formulated as a set only after many years into its implementation.

We also had at least some vague notion of the Wikipedia definition, "to maintain or support." We thought we understood "the need to supply with sustenance: nourish." Here the habitual use of our physical ecology, and agriculture, as the source of understanding "sustainable" played (and continues to play) a strong role in our thinking. However, our knowledge was "only theoretical," it had still not encountered the living reality, which would markedly enrich our notions of sustainability as endurance (!).

If both a system of activity, a "Fifth Dimension," and its nourishing context are conjoined, "endurance" in all its senses is the result.

In short, to study sustainability, we need agreement on what is being sustained, what the system of supports is that feeds and supports it, and how that joint, institutional activity maintains that relationship over long periods of time. Simultaneously, when the activity disappears, we need to be present to observe how a working activity system is disassembled, re-purposed. As Vygotsky emphasized, development is seen both in the growth and decline phases of a human life span. And so it is at the cultural historical level of a project.

So, let the story begin, keeping in mind that the meanings of the core term of discussion undergo change in the course of the project itself.

Partnerships as the Unit of Analysis

Perhaps the biggest surprise looking back is how "Institutional-o-centric" our early view of the project was. Our documents read more or less as if the Fifth Dimension was an activity that occurred "out there" in the community. The University just "did it" there. This attitude is clearly evident in the grant proposal we wrote to the Spencer Foundation that ultimately made the project possible.

In the section of the proposal about our plans, should the sites be sustained (against our expectations), we imagined residual costs, but judged these irrelevant from the University's point of view:

> No additional, unfunded staff positions [on the university side] are required to run the sites (the fact that we need research staff money to create the system and conduct the basic research should not be equated with the maintenance costs if our basic strategy proves effective).

In an important sense, our fundamental understanding of the basic structure of the 5th Dimension as a University-Community collaborative joint activity began to develop because the Boys and Girls Club violated our expectations and continued to run their program. Only then were we faced with the implications of claiming that no special funds would be needed for the University to continue the course (and hence sustain the partnership). In particular, it meant that the University was committing itself to pay for a relatively small "laboratory" or "field experience" course all year long. That might not mean costs in money, but it meant reallocation of University resources, a process that is never certain. Theorizing the University's role in sustainability became a major concern.

The fact that it was the Boys and Girls Club that wanted to continue the program usefully provoked our thinking about the University as being a crucial part of the process of sustainability, no less than it had been a part of initiation.

There is some paradox in this outcome. Relatively speaking, we did not place a high value on the academic benefits associated with the Boys and Girls Club. Many children passed through, the surrounding environment was a free play room with its own norms of social life, and our carefully crafted pedagogical structure was constantly being shaken. At best, sustainability in this case meant enduring more hard work and research to improve an activity we found difficult to justify in terms of measurable developmental influence.

We were left to contemplate the finding that the library, our most successful 5th Dimension from a "learning outcomes" point of view was not sustained but a less successful one was. What is valued at one level of context is not attractive on another.

There was another puzzle we had not been able to explore in the fact that only one community organization continued the project with us. In our sustainability plan, we had also imagined that if three community organizations survived, they might be able to create a collaborative structure to deal with the relatively modest monetary costs of the program. But with only one such institution, no community group evolved. It would take another long round of research before we saw what impact such a community organization could have on sustainability.

Sustainability and Social Context

The period following this initial round of research, from the perspective of sustainability and long term projects, illustrates the way in which events at a world scale influence events at a quite local scale and seemingly tiny threads of connectivity can result in project sustainability. The convergence of interests around the Velham project could never have been foreseen or planned for. But because of the existing relations built around issues of culture, education and inequality, and the world's fascination with the educational potential of computers, the Fifth Dimension provided an extremely useful tool in the arena of international diplomacy, provided LCHC members contact with Russian and other European colleagues versed in cultural-historical theory, and, crucially, supported continued development of the Fifth Dimension in the United States. The addition of sites in New York, Chicago, and New Orleans allowed us to expand beyond the middle-class town in which the initial project began. Now ethnicity, social class (and in the case of the Russians, language) all came into play in ways we had not previously been able to observe.

Core Principles and Diversity in Implementation

The six years of support from the Mellon Foundation, supplemented by the Spencer foundation, were central to complicating our understanding of sustainability. It was at this time that a specified set of core principles emerged.

These years also allowed us to see more Fifth Dimensions disappear and we came to believe that the kind of institution of higher learning and the kind of community organization were not critical either to the creation or the sustainability of the Fifth Dimension. Rather, success of implementation appeared to depend critically on working out *mutual agreement* between the organizations on the shape of the locally constructed Fifth Dimension and the specific configuration of challenges it was able to overcome.

Also important to the expansion that occurred during these years was the felt need to create a networked organization of implementers and to adopt the Swedish notion that all such collaborations should have a role for a "spider" whose job it was to constantly traverse the network of relations and be certain that no threads were dropped. All useful in designing for sustainability of the kind of project into which the 5th Dimension had developed.

UClinks and the Current State of the Fifth Dimension

Throughout the project's history, the 5th Dimension, and the wide variety of UClinks systems that have sprung up around the world, has attracted new but compatible interests as socioeconomic and political conditions changed. With the end of Affirmative Action in California, 5th Dimension became part of a large multi-university system as a tool for increasing the enrollment of underrepresented youth.

Perhaps the most impressive lesson to emerge from these many years of experiences has been the amazing variety of ways in which new participants fashioned activities that went far beyond anything imaginable when the project began. The core principles acting as "cultural genes" took on a myriad of phenotypic forms that have sometimes been as startling as the Wizard itself.

The UClinks phase of the project, which is still in progress, has added new understanding to the potentials and pitfalls involved when the 5th Dimension began to receive funding tied to the goal of increasing college enrollments of under-served youth. To begin with, such change was to be cheered. UClinks has enormously broadened our ideas about core 5th Dimension Project concerns.

When combined with the advent of Web 2.0 and youth that ranged upwards from 12–18 (where twelve had been upper limit for 5th Dimension design), the new adaptations of the 5th Dimension opened up a whole new set of possibilities to achieve goals we had only fleetingly experienced (dense kid-to-kid communication, for example). At the same time, it meant submitting our programs to evaluation through a system of categories and criteria far narrower than was consistent with our core principles. Reconciling that contradiction is a work in progress.

In the collective monograph published in 2006 (Cole & DLC, 2006), the Distributed Literacy Consortium took up the lessons of sustainability, including all of the systems that had come into being throughout the world at the time. They divided the threats to sustainability into factors operating within the community system, factors operating within the university/college system, and the factors operating in the modes of exchange between the two partners in conducting the 5th Dimension, their common object. They can be summarized in a few words:

> *University Challenges*: Steady flow of students, support for small classes, support for classes that run all year long on a quarter or semester cycle.
> *Community Challenges*: Staff turnover and consequent lack of expertise, upkeep of facilities.
> *Relationship Challenges*: The impact of disruption of student provision or staff turnover at the site on each other (the show had to go on) and what the authors refer to as "a gradual erosion of common goals and understanding."

The kinds of work that sustainability of 5th Dimension-like, University-Community partnerships require for their maintenance at the level of the local system was neatly summarized by Nocon as the "Four Cs Model of Sustainability":

> This case study of a community-based after-school educational innovation suggests that sustainability is reasonably and productively viewed as a process of expanding and sustaining. The study also suggests that when productive, the process of sustainability is collaborative, communicative, creative, and continuing. It is collaborative in that participants have strong relationships and direct involvement in planning and implementing the educational innovation. They also participate actively in on-going evaluation and refinement of the innovation. The process is communicative in that participants have voice and opportunities to make visible needs, concerns, and potential solutions to the shared problems of productive integration of the reform. The process is creative in that it remains open to change in the educational innovation and attentive to changes in the local and structural contexts of implementation. It is a continuing process in that innovations are sustained through long-term commitment.
>
> NOCON, 2004, p. 729

Clearly, one needs an attractive object and an unusually attentive social ecology to attain and sustain such levels of attention. Amazingly, the 5th Dimension, and its diverse kin, have attracted that attention, as well as, in many cases, the endurance to sustain it.

In sum, what has emerged over a 30+ year history is an enormous range of activities that fulfill the initial goals of the 5th Dimension project: thousands of young people have engaged in "more time on task" alongside of college buddies who themselves have benefited from the experience of social science field-based laboratory courses. The program has spread across social class, ethnic, and national boundaries.

The unanticipated level of diffusion and variety spawned by the Fifth Dimension project has led to us continuing to examine our notion of what it means to sustain such modes of activity. Our tentative conclusion at the present time is that the term, "sustainability," as implied by Nocon's Four Cs, must be extended far beyond our initial assumption of a single, unchanging, activity continuing over time as part of a single, unchanging, relationship between the cooperating partners. Nor can we assume that just because our research demonstrates that the 5th Dimension promotes valued literacy, numeracy and digital technology skills that all communities will consider it a good thing for their children to engage in. We have now encountered too many cases where, given an opportunity to watch the 5th Dimension in action, responsible adult participants on either the University or Community sides decide it would *not* be a good thing to continue because aspects of the 5th Dimension are not good for the future of children, as the adults in question view that future. In communities where social hierarchy and instructionalism are the valued norms, the 5th Dimension is going to be under great pressure. So long as institutions of higher learning do not sufficiently value laboratory/field experience for their undergraduates to support practicum courses, Fifth Dimensions will suffer. So long as high stakes, standardized testing is the only currency of valuable education, Fifth Dimensions will suffer.

To future implementers of projects intended to be sustainable, our advice is to be prepared to endure. From our experience, some of the factors that will rise up to kill off a local project will be completely out of your control because they are part of long term secular flows in society which were invisible to you when you began. The Boys and Girls Club Fifth Dimension survived for 16 years and was eventually undone because the town in which it was located increased enormously in wealth, so the need for an educational component to its after-school program was no longer valued by its directors. At the same time, in the same town, La Clase Mágica, the bi-cultural, bi-lingual adaptation of the Fifth Dimension begun in 1990 to serve the poor, Latino population is still running strong, with local community and university support. The Fifth Dimensions at UCLA and Appalachian State Universities survived the departure of their originators, and live today in ways that have transformed in synchrony with their social ecological contexts. But the very successful 5th Dimensions at a local elementary school closed because of the triumph of neighborhood schooling over desegregation.

You will not be able to solve the problem of social inequality or ethnic bigotry or the sorting mechanisms of national systems of schooling. For researchers, we have argued, the long term nature of a project such as the Fifth Dimension provides unprecedented opportunities to study learning and development in their sociocultural, historical contexts.

As is true of all projects, the 5th Dimension confronts an uncertain future associated with the uncertainties of its times and places. But it were ever so, as John Dewey reminded us in *Education and Experience,* quoting Tennyson:

> Experience is an arch where through
> Gleams that untravelled world, whose margin fades
> For ever and for ever when I move.
>
> DEWEY, 1938, p. 35, from *Ulysses*, TENNYSON, 1840

Only time will tell. But for now, we can reflect on a relatively long stretch of experience directed along the same road.

Perhaps all that remains to be said is that inhabiting a Fifth Dimension, even for an afternoon, can be a developmental experience as well as a pleasant and interesting way to be part of a community of learners, having a good time. So we, at least, are in favor of enduring the Fifth Dimension in the years to come.

References

American Association for the Advancement of Science (AAAS) (1984). *Equity and Excellence: Compatible Goals. As assessment of programs that facilitate increased access and achievement of females and minorities in K-12 mathematics and science education.* Washington DC: Office of Opportunities and Science.

Anderson, A., Diaz, E., & Moll, L. (1984). Community Educational Resource and Research Center. *The Quarterly Newsletter of the Laboratory of Comparative Human Cognition, 6*(3), 70–71. (Work in progress.)

Cole, M. (1996). *Cultural Psychology: A Once and Future Discipline.* Cambridge: Harvard University Press.

Cole, M. & The Distributed Literacy Consortium (2006). *The 5th Dimension: An After-School Program Built on Diversity.* New York: Russell Sage.

Cole, M., & Traupmann, K. (1981). Comparative cognitive research: Learning from a learning disabled child. In W.A. Collins (Ed.), *Minnesota Symposium on Child Development* (Vol. 14). Hillsdale, NJ: Erlbaum.

Cremins, L. (1976). *Public Education*, New York: Basic Books.

Denham, C., & Lieberman, A. (1980). *Time to Learn.* Washington, DC: National Institute of Education.

Dewey, J. (1938). *Experience and Education.* New York: Macmillan Co.

Fantini, A.E. (1985). *Language Acquisition of a Bilingual Child*, San Diego, CA: College Hill Press.

Frederick, W.C. & Wahlberg, H.J. (1980). Learning as a function of time. *Journal of Educational Research, 73*(4), 183–194.

Goodlad, J. (1984). *A Place Called School: Prospects for the Future*, New York: McGraw-Hill.

Griffin, P., Belyaeva, A., Soldatova, G., & the Velikhov-Hamburg Collective (1993). Review of 'Creating and Reconstituting Contexts for Educational Interactions, Including a Computer Program'. In Forman, E.A., Minick, N., and Stone, C.A. (Eds.), *Contexts for Learning: Sociocultural Dynamics in Children's Development*, 1993, New York, Oxford University Press, 120–152.

Hood, L., McDermott, R., Cole, M. (1980). "Let's try to make it a good day" – Some not so simple ways. *Discourse Processes, 3*(2), 155–168.

LCHC (Laboratory of Comparative Human Cognition) (1982). A model system for the study of learning difficulties. *Quarterly Newsletter of the Laboratory of Comparative Human Cognition, 4*. 39–66.

Levin, J.A., Riel, M., Rowe, R.D., & Boruta, M.J. (1984). Muktuk meets jacuzzi: Computer networks and elementary school writers. In S.W. Freedman (Ed.), *The acquisition of written language*, Hillsdale, NJ: Ablex, 160–171.

Nicolopolou, A. & Cole, M. (1993). The 5th Dimension, its play world, and its instructional contexts: The generation and transmission of shared knowledge in the culture of collaborative learning. In N. Minnick & E. Forman (Eds.), *The Institutional and Social Context of Mind: New Directions in Vygotskian Theory and Research* (pp. 283–314). New York: Oxford University Press.

Nilsson, M. & Nocon, H. (2005). *Teaching and Technology in Local and Global Communities*. Oxford: Peter Lang.

Nocon, H. (2004). Sustainability as process: Community education and productive expansion. *Educational Policy, 28*(5), 710–732.

Rogoff, B. (2003). *The Cultural Nature of Human Development*. New York: Oxford University Press.

Sannino, A. Daniels, H. Gutiérrez, K. (2009). *Learning and Expanding with Activity Theory*. New York: Cambridge university Press.

Toulmin, S. (1978). *The Mozart of Psychology*. New York Review of Books. September 28, 1978, 25(14).

Vasquez, O.A. (2003). *La Clase Mágica*. Mahwah, NJ: Lawrence Erlbaum.

Wertsch, J. (1985). *Vygotsky and the Social Formation of Mind*. Cambridge, MA: Harvard University Press.

CHAPTER 6

Formation of the Concept of "Collaborative Learning Space"

Andy Blunden and Michael Arnold

Introduction

The authors collaborated in a project at the University of Melbourne in 1999–2000, and this report is based on electronic records from the time and interviews with those involved conducted in 2011.

In January 2000, in the midst of the events described, management moved the first author (AB) to a new "office," a disused store room off an underground, secure machine room, accessible only via security swipe card, and removed from AB all responsibility for supervision of staff. These measures, evidently aimed at isolating AB from other staff, are to be seen in the context that AB was the union representative for general staff and had been prominent in a recent strike.

Quite separately from his union work, as supervisor of the Audio-Visual Unit since 1994, AB had also actively agitated against the efforts of the Vice-Chancellor to divest the University's central management of responsibility for provision and maintenance of teaching spaces. The concept whose formation is described in this chapter is predicated on a reversal of this decentralization policy: the central allocation, design, construction and maintenance of all teaching spaces. The concept of "CATS" – Centrally Allocated Teaching Spaces for which the Centre is also deemed responsible for provision and maintenance – imposed itself on the management of the university despite themselves and remains university policy more than a decade later. However, we have not dealt with the emergence of the concept of CATS in the paper as the issues involved are distinct and complex.

Narrative

A new concept arises within some social practice in the form of a problem, and a solution (Vygotsky 1987, p. 123–124; 1994, p. 257–258). In other social situations the identification of a "solution" gives rise to the identification of a "problem." The problem-solution relation is thus bi-directional, at least in principle.

The social situation we have in mind here is the university, specifically in the 1990s in Australia. Universities are institutions which, as a key part of their activity, provide rooms to teachers and students for the purpose of teaching and learning. However, those in the university responsible for designing, building and allocating teaching spaces, on the whole had an understanding of teaching and learning which reflected a centuries-old, unchanging conception of how university education is done, objectified in the University's buildings and the configuration of their teaching spaces (c.f. Leontiev 1978, p. 66). The teachers on the other hand had diverse views on how to teach, which responded not only to tradition but also to continuously changing views on learning, and had a variety of opinions on what might constitute a suitable space for teaching. Most teachers found the existing infrastructure for teaching unsatisfactory in various respects and to various degrees, but had no means of addressing the problem, as teaching space was largely provided by the central bureaucracy, and there was no position within the bureaucracy responsible for planning and supply of teaching spaces. At the time, there was almost no research literature on the problem of design of physical spaces for teaching and learning. In 2002, a monograph was published in the US (Van Note Chism & Bickford, 2002) raising the same concerns, including a literature summary which confirms that research on university classroom design was embryonic even in 2002.

The first author was at the time the supervisor of the Audio-Visual Unit, whose technical staff assisted teachers using the equipment in the lecture theatres. He thus became aware of the considerable dissatisfaction amongst teachers, who frequently vented their frustration on the technical staff who came to their aid when equipment failed to work for them.

In March 1999, AB began visiting teaching staff and:

> collecting descriptions of how people would like to educate if they had teaching space infrastructure of their own desire, and aiming to develop plans to build and equip some central teaching spaces to provide for that. I'm looking at the 20–70 seat capacity range.
>
> email to JG, 25 March 1999

On 30 March, AB reported to management on the results of these consultations:

> I get the impression that there is widespread need for spaces to accommodate "collaborative learning," always keeping in mind that this activity

> would supplement large lectures, individual computer-lab work, private study and library access. There would be a lead time between provision of spaces for this type of work, and adjustment of curricula to orient towards the opportunity.
>
> http://wayback.archive-it.org/2927/20120105030512/http://trs.unimelb.edu.au/archive/seminar1.html

On 15 April 1999, AB informed his collaborators:

> Having spoken to a number of members of University teaching staff about requirements for *collaborative learning spaces*, we have identified the need for a means of freely moving the video from one computer to another or displaying it for all to see.
>
> email from AB, emphasis added

On 11 May 1999, in response to submissions drafted by AB, the Dep. V.–C. (Resources) announced an allocation of funds "for the development of Collaborative Learning and Teaching Spaces as part of the 2000 Lecture Theatre Upgrade Program" including $165,000 for the Cecil Scutt Room, attaching an equipment list.

We see here how the term "collaborative learning space" was invented by teaching staff who were frustrated by the implicit assumption, evident in the configuration of teaching spaces, that all teaching and learning at the University is didactic (teacher-centered) delivery of information. AB provided a vehicle to mediate between the need and a means of its resolution, so that the word "collaborative learning space" first became objectified in AB's communications, and eventually in an allocation of funds by the University for the construction of "Collaborative Learning and Teaching Spaces." Initially, no-one knew what such a space would look like, only that it would meet a certain deficit in the university's infrastructure, by supporting specific modes of activity, that is, concepts of teaching and learning; and none of those responsible for the provision of teaching infrastructure had even heard of the concept of "collaborative learning." The problem now was to concretize the concept and institutionalize a solution within the university's material fabric, self-consciousness and practices.

In April 1999, AB had identified a candidate room in the Arts Building, the Cecil Scutt Room, and acquired from the Timetable Office a list of room allocations and identified History and Philosophy of Science as the Department in the Arts Faculty with the largest share of small-group teaching. He asked the Head of that department who was the most innovative and active member of the teaching staff and was directed to the co-author of this paper, MA. MA was perhaps nominated by the Head as an innovative teacher because the Head shared a widespread misconception that equates innovation with new technology, and MA's research background and teaching practices focused on new technologies Innovative or not, MA accepted the brief, but not without initial reluctance. As the Head explained it to MA, the task was to represent a teacher's perspective in the design of a new teaching space. MA anticipated endless hours of consulting with other teaching staff, reconciling contrasting demands and desires, arguing the merits of different pedagogies, bickering over aesthetics, prioritizing desired features, finally negotiating an uneasy set of compromises, then doing it all over again with AB, who would no doubt need to squeeze all of the above into a set of budgetary constraints, health and safety considerations, heritage overlays and the like.

However, MA's first meeting with AB set out a scenario that put these fears to rest. In what MA took to be a very radical move, AB explained that the University would build a Collaborative Learning Space designed to meet his, MA's, needs alone, and even more surprisingly, that money was no object. The thinking was that a "broad" design strategy built around wide consultation and compromise among users is not the only way to develop and deploy innovative ideas, and that a "narrow" strategy eschewing consultation and compromise was a viable alternative. This move took the design of the space out of the architectural-engineering-industrial design paradigm, which emphasizes satisficing the imagined or empirically determined desires of a defined group of client users, to an "art" paradigm, which emphasizes an authentic expression of the vision of the creator, without regard for the opinions of a potential market. AB believed that meeting the needs of just one of the 3000 teaching staff perfectly, would be bound to meet the needs of a sufficient number of others to fully utilize the room. If successful, the remaining 470 rooms could be subject to a similar process, building excellence through diversity rather than convergence – that is by supporting a range of exemplar concepts of teaching, rather than a single prototype or ideal of teaching. This approach enabled effective collaboration between one teacher and one architect with a clear concept of what was needed, rather than a compromise between numerous stakeholders with the concomitant danger of meeting no-one's needs. Negotiations amongst a large group of the teaching staff who would use the room was in this scheme, neither necessary nor desirable. Of course, all concepts are formed collaboratively insofar as the concepts are socially, historically and culturally interpolated, but collaboration is not always an overtly deliberative process.

The absence of a budgetary ceiling meant that the space might be imagined without being in any way constrained by considerations of cost. The problem of fitting into a budget would be confronted at a later stage once the ideal solution had been clearly conceived.

At this first meeting AB and MA quickly agreed that collaboration was a key concept that would inform the design of this small teaching space. This was to be a non-controversial anchor for our thinking. The Cecil Scutt room was a small teaching space used for many decades to accommodate tutorials and seminars. Tutorials and seminars are by tradition collaborative, involving relatively small numbers of students (say 12–25) in conversation, questioning, debate, small-group work, and other forms of interactive and communal activities. Despite the ubiquity of these practices, rooms at the time were most commonly configured for didactic, teacher-centered instruction only, with desks and chairs in straight rows facing the teacher at the front. The question for MA was not therefore, how to overthrow a style of collaborative pedagogy which teachers were using despite the fit-out, but rather how to better configure a room to better facilitate a longstanding pedagogical strategy, as well as providing for more developed strategies.

From there, numerous discussions took place between AB and MA, during which MA set out the conceptual bones of the concept, and AB suggested ways that flesh might be put on those bones, through input from architects, furniture designers, and equipment suppliers. This marked the first phase of "advancing from the abstract to the concrete" (Marx, 1986/1857, p. 38) – building the first space designed for collaborative learning. The process of conceptualizing the space was not laborious, and quickly settled around a number of needs.

The first and most obvious is that the space should remain convivial for group discussion involving all the room's occupants. The dimensions and volume of the room set a good foundation for this, providing good lines of sight and good acoustics, and while the furniture was inflexible, tatty and run-down, the space itself was a good venue for discussion, and the room was consequently a popular one. Whatever we might do to alter the room, it should not reduce its capacity to enable 20 people to engage with one another as a group.

A second tradition that needed to be maintained was that the room remain convivial for didactic teaching and learning. Tutorials and seminars frequently require that one person take the floor, lead the discussion, field the questions, set the agenda, and so on. The existing configuration met this need when the person taking the lead was the tutor, but met the need less well when the person taking the lead was a student. Any tension between support for collaborative methods and didactic methods had to be resolved.

A third need to be met was that the space facilitate collaboration among small groups of students – say 4 or 5 groups of 4 or 5 students. Enabling students to participate in discussion in small groups was seen to be important in ensuring that all students were active participants in the proceedings, and actively engaged with the questions and issues at hand. Facilitating convivial small-group collaboration requires that participants are positioned in the space in a certain way, and the fore-mentioned whole-of-group collaboration requires a different configuration. The space therefore needed to enable the occupants to make a painless shift from a whole-of-group configuration to a small-group configuration and vice versa.

None of the above ambitions for a collaborative space was particularly novel, and all have been tackled in one way or another many times before, using traditional furnishings and equipment. However, MA was of the view that digital equipment had the potential to extend collaborative practices to new domains.

The first was to furnish the room with equipment that would enable tutorial groups to interact with tutorial groups in other countries, or in other Australian universities. At that time, Internet-based asynchronous document exchanges and emailing were well established practices, and synchronous text messaging, voice over internet protocols and video conferencing were emerging, and seemed to be moving from the exotic to the routine. The capacity to mediate collaboration beyond the tutorial, and in particular to engage students from other countries in real-time interaction, was seen to be a significant move.

The second more novel manifestation of collaboration was to furnish the room with equipment to enable collaborative activity to be anchored to texts. The centrality of text to pedagogy is a practice that extends back to the medieval university, but through the application of digital texts in the place of paper texts, it was thought that text might play a still more important role. It was thought that this could be the case if students and tutors were able to access published digital texts via the Internet, on an as-needs basis. The group would still have access to set readings during the tutorial, but would also have access to what was at the time a rapidly increasing international repository of digitized scholarly publications. In addition to vastly increasing the pool of scholarly texts available to the tutorial, students would also have access to popular media, available through countless numbers of websites. In addition to these scholarly and popular publications, it was thought that students might also have access to their own writing, and might be able to share it around the whole group (or beyond), and work collaboratively in small groups to edit or author their texts. Digital texts of various kinds were therefore cast in a central role in providing a material and performative basis for collaboration in the room. (Other media, such as video and music, were not cast in an important role, and were not specifically catered for, and needed to be retrofitted at the request of other teachers.)

A third desire for the room was that it somehow enable the tutorial activities to escape the time and place set aside for the tutorial on the timetable. That is, the activities of the tutorial – the issues raised, the key elements of discussion, the texts referred to, edited or authored – should be available to the tutorial members outside of the confines of the tutorial itself. In a real sense, tutorials are precious resources. A typical Australian university will only offer 12 weekly tutorials in any given subject – scarcely time enough to engage with the ideas and to engage with others around those ideas. It was thought that considerable benefits might accrue if ways could be found to move beyond the confines of the weekly meeting.

A lot was therefore demanded of the furnishings and equipment to be fitted in the room, and over a period of weeks and months, through collaboration between AB and MA, and between AB and architects, furniture suppliers, and digital equipment suppliers, the following design features emerged.

The first mentioned need for how the room might perform was to be met by furnishing the room with 5 oval shaped tables, each capable seating 4 or 5 students, in order to facilitate small-group collaboration. The tables were in turn arranged in a semi-circle, and chairs were on castors, to facilitate whole-group discussion. This configuration of table shape, table placement, and swivel chairs, enabled a seamless move from small-group work to whole-of-group work without having to rearrange furniture.

The need to also facilitate didactic teaching and learning methods was met by placing one table front and center, and handy to white-boards and an Interactive WhiteBoard (IWB). This table was to be used by the tutor, and was symbolically privileged by its particular location in the room.

The need to place digital text at the center of tutorial activities was met by equipping each of the tables with an Internet connected computer, through which scholarly texts and other web-based media might be accessed, all the computers being linked by local networking software. The shape of the tables, and the position of the screen on the table, provided each of the students around the table with a line of sight to the shared screen. One student at each table needed to operate the keyboard and mouse, and the students at each table therefore needed to agree on the use of the keyboard and mouse, what words were to be typed, what documents accessed, and so on.

The position of the screen on each table posed the difficulty of reconciling a need for clear lines of sight from each table to the screen, while not blocking clear lines of sight from one table to another. The "money is no object" design solution was to equip each table with a hinged flat screen, to be raised for small group work at the table, and to be lowered to give students clear lines of sight from one table to another. But while the design was not constrained by money, the build was, and CRT screens (far cheaper than flat screens in year 2000) were installed instead, compromising lines of sight across the room.

Each table of students was able to search, browse and access their chosen digital texts via the Internet, discuss the texts among themselves, edit the text if in read-write format, or annotate the text if in read-only format. Collaboration between tables of students and among all tables of students was facilitated by the networking software that enabled the display of each screen to switch its source of input. So for example, Table 4 might switch its view to mirror the view of Table 2. Those two tables of students, or all five tables, might then discuss the same document, using conversation at the table and across the room, and using on-screen text editing and annotation. Software on the tutor's computer could also be used to direct the source of each screen's input, so for example, all tables might mirror the tutor's computer, then pass to Table 3, then 2, and so on. The room was also equipped with a projector, and input could be taken from any computer in the room to be projected to a large format display screen at the front of the room.

This large-format display screen was an IWB – at that time becoming popular in board rooms and commercial conference rooms, but this IWB was the first to be used in an educational setting in Australia. The IWB enabled the tutor or a student to display content supplied from any of the room's computers, and to annotate that display using a keyboard, or by hand, using four colored "pens." The displayed text, now annotated by the tutor and the students, might then be captured and saved, and emailed to a subject website, to all students in the subject, or to any subgroup of students. In this way the work of the tutorial is not only recorded, but might then continue at other times and in other places.

In early 1999, at the same time as AB was lobbying for funds for Collaborative Learning Spaces, the library had received a bequest from the Percy Baxter Trust of $600,000 for library development. Interviews conducted in 2011 brought out the fact that the then-newly appointed VP (Information) had just returned from the US with the idea of an "Information Commons" and a project was underway to use the funds to create an Information Commons in the library. However, as a result of conversations with the Dep. V.-C. (Resources) in April 1999, she decided that rather than being seen to copy an idea from the US, the funds should be used to create the "Percy Baxter Collaborative Learning Centre." KK, who led the project team, reported that "this name caused the working group to reflect on what the role of the Percy Baxter space would be? What would be meaningful to students? How will students use the space?

The idea of a "Collaborative Learning Space" crystallized these reflections, and from that time on the aim of the working group was to create a space for collaborative learning" (Interview with KK 18 March 2011). The Medical Faculty, where AD was engaged in creating a suite of Problem Based Learning (PBL) rooms to support a total restructure of their curriculum, also lobbied for the idea of a "Collaborative Learning Space" to be implemented in the library.

The Centre opened in June 2000, but due to shortage of funds, no tables suitable for student collaboration were purchased until later. However, 60 computers were installed, all placed either in individual study carrels which made it difficult for more than one person at a time to use the computer, or at large tables in two training rooms, with students obscured behind a VDU screen while addressed by a trainer at an elevated podium. The suite of software installed did not include any software designed for collaboration. These mishaps in the design of the Centre, demonstrated a failure by the designers to grasp the notion of collaborative learning, as the concept of building for collaborative learning was new at the time. Nonetheless, students made use of the space and its extended opening hours for collaborative study and the limitations of the fit-out were gradually overcome (Interview with DE 11 March 2011). Since then, the Library has created an ever-increasing number of spaces in branch libraries, providing an attractive environment for lap-top use and student collaboration, all equipped with wireless LAN and marked by café-style furniture with machines for students to buy drinks and sweets nearby. Library staff still (in 2011) refer to these spaces as "Collaborative Learning Spaces." Students use the spaces to study together in groups, using shared computers and electronic resources. They are unsupervised and at this point (in 2011) do not involve the use of IWBs.

Over the three years before AB retired in 2002, a further 24 CLSs were built using University central funds and others using departmental funds. The single common feature of the various designs was round, oval or long boat-shaped tables[1] to facilitate student collaboration. It transpired that the oval table was the "germ-cell" (Marx, 1996/1867, p. 8) – the simplest, empirically given thing which encapsulated the concept of building for collaborative learning – but this was not clear at the time of the first phase of ascent from abstract to concrete with the design of the Cecil Scutt Room. This only began to emerge in the second phase of "ascent from the abstract to the concrete" with the process of *proliferation*, in the second year of the program.

1 The ideal table shape for collaboration varies with the group-size; 3 or 4 students collaborate best with small round tables; 5 to8 students require an oval table; larger groups work best with a long refectory table.

In the first year of operation however, the Cecil Scutt Room was grossly under-utilized, because no measures had been taken to see that the Timetable Office allocated the room to teachers who wanted to do collaborative learning. In 2000, this was corrected by adding a new fourth type, "CLS" to the set of "Room_Types" used by the *SyllabusPlus* room allocation software (Theatre, Seminar/Tutorial Room or Laboratory). Teachers could then specifically request that they wanted a space for collaborative learning.

Demand for Collaborative Learning Spaces soon overtook supply, and according to the pro-VC (Teaching & Learning) still outstrips supply a decade later (Interview 8 April 2011). In May 2001, a Teaching Infrastructure Committee was created to mediate between the needs of teaching and the staff responsible for creating and maintaining the infrastructure, overseeing the capital program for the construction of Collaborative Learning Spaces and Lecture Theatres. Faculties such as Medicine and Engineering were already committed to collaborative learning and CLSs could not be built fast enough to meet their needs.

The University administration had been committed at the time to decentralization of responsibility for maintenance and construction of teaching spaces, but the creation of CLSs was predicated on a reversal of this decentralization policy. Despite this, the CLSs were almost all built with central funding and allocated centrally by the TimeTable Office. The necessity of central production, maintenance and distribution of teaching spaces imposed itself on the university leadership despite themselves and remains university policy to this day.

Further, "laboratory" was a concept at the university which not only entailed a room being characterized by its equipment, but implied that the room was "owned" by a Department for whose discipline the equipment was designed. Throughout the process of establishing the concept of "Collaborative Learning Space" a constant struggle had to be fought against the conception of teaching spaces as containers of equipment. Because most of the CLSs had installed computers, many staff referred to them as "Computer Labs." This not only misrepresented the function and conception of the rooms, but implied that the local departments had control over their use and were responsible for their maintenance. For example, in 2001, when two Collaborative Learning Spaces were commissioned near to the Psychology Departmental office, the Department tried to put signs on the door naming them "Computer Labs." Installing and maintaining multiple computers in CLSs had considerable cost implications and as Centrally Allocated Teaching Spaces, this cost accrued to the center, and central staff had to be employed for the work. This struggle over the implications of "Collaborative Learning Space" as opposed to "Computer

Laboratory" took about a year to resolve, but once the central administration agreed to continue picking up the cost of computers (not formerly included in building project costs), the battle was won. These kind of policy issues were resolved within the University's structure by a combination of lobbying of committees and "grass roots" agitation. They were never decided by top-down direction, though in the end, new policies were implemented in this manner.

Different implementations of the idea were developed with teaching staff in different disciplines. The size of tables and the number of students per group varied from one discipline to another. Education, for example, favored groups of 7 per table and made generous allowances for space; the science disciplines favored even numbers while the humanities favored odd numbers. Philosophy preferred around 10 to a group. Some disciplines required audio-visual equipment of various kinds to be available, some used IWBs and some didn't. But the oval tables were a constant feature. Lately, the tables have been built at bench height so that, rather than sitting, students can stand and move around with even greater ease.

All this architectural work was driven by the efforts of teaching staff. Some years would pass before the Vice-Chancellor's office would learn what "collaborative learning" meant. It should be noted however, that the University's administration was never in any respect a homogeneous bloc in relation to any of the questions discussed above.

The Current Position

Of 39 Australian universities, 27 now (2011) have Collaborative Learning Spaces, 5 more have Collaborative Suites or Studios or Rooms, and only 7 have not explicitly applied the term.

At Melbourne, 65 of the 192 classrooms are CLSs, but this term is now a generic name for four types of room, categorized according to whether there is student-only access and according to the level of equipment installed. Some have computers for shared student use, some have IWBs, most have Wireless LAN for laptops, but some also have only furniture to facilitate student collaboration, and no electronic equipment. Nonetheless, "Collaborative Learning Space" still designates a family of room types whose only common equipment feature is oval tables, and this term is used by maintenance staff, senior management, library staff and teaching staff. For a number of years the objectification of the concept in the words "Collaborative Learning Space" on signage outside of rooms, their listing as "Collaborative Learning Spaces" on web pages, and their classification within the *SyllabusPlus* database, constituted an effective objectification of the words "Collaborative Learning Space." With changes of personnel in various administrative positions, these forms of objectification have disappeared in the last few years. Nonetheless, the material form of the rooms themselves has proved to be extremely persistent – just as the rank-and-file room design which had dominated university classrooms since time immemorial had firmly objectified a didactic, information-delivery mode of teaching. "Collaborative Learning Space" is now part of the language and the life of the university.

Currently, the TimeTable Office no longer have "CLS" as a Room_Type in the *SyllabusPlus* database; a mere 5 are of type "Electronic Learning Studio" alongside 293 "Lecture Theatres" and 187 "Classrooms." It appears that the operators who do the classroom allocations, use their knowledge and that of their clients to allocate the 65 CLSs to those requiring them. The *SyllabusPlus* database uses only a small number of Room_Types which represent *true concepts*. In general, the database supports a concept of teaching space according to a list of "suitabilities," invariably interpreted as a check list of the installed equipment, i.e. *pseudoconcepts* (Vygotsky, 1987, p. 141). This conception of a concept as a list of contingent attributes is almost ubiquitous within bureaucratic and information system processes, as this impoverished conception of concepts facilitates large-scale automated procedures.

There is one *mis*conception which has arisen from the 1999 initiative which is instructive. A key feature of the original design was the IWB, which allowed direct manipulation of and shared eye contact with an electronic text by the whole class. The software initially used to facilitate data sharing has now been superseded by hardware switching which allows the tutor to better manage the collaboration, but collaboration remains the *raison d'être* of the IWBs in the CLSs. However, in the decade since this first application of an IWB in an educational setting, the IWB has spread to both universities and schools throughout Australia and New Zealand, to the extent the four companies supplying them sell 80–90 new boards into the educational market every week and approximately 150,000 teachers have been trained in their use, according to the suppliers. But the IWBs are used as *presentation devices*, and rarely used for collaboration. It is widely perceived (Sweeney, 2010), that despite the real value of the technology as a teaching aid, they are usually installed for prestige purposes (see also Arnold, 1996), and it takes at least two years for teachers to overcome the difficulty in using them, before they add value to teaching and learning. During those first two years, learning is markedly *less* collaborative. It seems that an idea which is objectified in an iconic piece of branded equipment, marketed by its suppliers, may take hold and spread far more easily than the form of activity which the equipment may support. Nowadays, technology changes quickly, cultural practices slowly.

It could be said that just as the oval tables were the germ-cell of the concept of Collaborative Learning Space, the IWB was the germ-cell of a *mis*conception, namely the concept of a teaching space provided with advanced electronic equipment, represented by such terms as "Digital Classroom." Perhaps if Collaborative Learning Spaces were branded and purchasable *prêt-à-porter*, then the concept may have been institutionalized even more firmly.

This also raises the question of the role and power of prestige in the institutionalization of a concept. Not all universities in Australia have adopted the term "Collaborative Learning Space." Every University that has gone through the same process of inventing new designs of classroom to meet their pedagogical needs, or to meet their need to position themselves favorably in the education market, has branded their infrastructure with a new name: "Advanced Concept Teaching Space," "eLearning Studio," "Flexible Teaching Space," "Digital Classroom" and so on. Every institution highlights its innovation with its own brand name. The same factor has been involved in the purchase of expensive electronic equipment for prestige purposes. The competitive drive for status recognition militates against the entry of a word into *general* currency. The concept of designing university classrooms to support collaborative learning is now mainstream, though the spaces are not called "collaborative learning spaces" in every institution. Nonetheless, it is clear that through the creation of the concept of "Collaborative Learning Space" and its instrumental, practical and symbolic objectifications have ensured the transition of the project launched in March 1999 to institutionalization.

As the history of science has demonstrated over centuries, a new idea is the product of its times, and when a new concept emerges, it invariably does so in more than one place at the same time. As Goethe put it: "the greatest discoveries are made not so much by individuals as by the age" (Goethe 2006/1823). In the mid-1990s, CLSs were created at the North Carolina State University (see Beichner & Cevetello, 2013), and were later emulated at MIT and the University of Iowa. At the University of Dayton, Ohio, in 2002, teaching staff confronted exactly the situation described above, their response was almost identical, and has been recorded in a book: "The Importance of Physical Space in Creating Supportive Learning Environments" (Van Note Chism & Bickford, 2002), still available on their website: http://spacesforlearning.udayton.edu. As of 2011, demand for CLSs at the University of Dayton has increased. The book outlines principles for the design of Collaborative Learning Spaces and the procedures and structures to support the spaces, that are remarkably similar to the concepts adopted at Melbourne. Issues like these led to the founding of Educause in 1998, a not-for-profit organization which has played the leading role in generating the burgeoning research literature which has grown up on this subject (Oblinger, 2006). This literature rests, in one way or another, on the principle that physical spaces for teaching and learning should be designed to support specific, contemporary modes of teaching and learning. Likewise, at just the time AB was intervening in the design of teaching spaces at Melbourne, the technical managers who were his opposite numbers in British universities set up an email group to discuss the problems of technology in teaching spaces, leading to parallel processes of innovation.

Discussion

It will be observed that the formation of the concept of CLS was far from complete when the first exemplar was built. A protracted struggle had to be fought on several fronts to objectify the concept in University procedures and attention had to be paid even to signage in order to ensure that the Collaborative Learning Space would prove to be a sustainable project. For this reason we believe that the seven actions that Engeström et al. (2012) claim form an "expansive cycle" characteristic of concept formation fall short in taking reflection and evaluation as the final stage. In fact, Engeström observes that the *Helsinki Health Centre Strategy and Balanced Score Card* document for 2011–2013 refers to the relevant concept. We would see this as not simply *evidence* of the sustainability of the concept, but itself an important part of the objectification of the concept, an action which should have been anticipated in the "expansive cycle." A concept is a unit of a social formation and cannot be said to exist until it has achieved a degree of stability and interconnectedness within that form of life. Further, a concept is subject to modification in the course of its objectification which must be taken as part of the concept formation, and not simply the "registration" of the concept.

Hall & Horn (2012) remarks that "Not surprisingly, innovations in teaching often collapse after a few years of intense effort..." and it is our experience that there is a huge difference between a good idea which turns out to be an illusory flash in the pan, and a concept which enters into the culture of the relevant institution, because it represents a viable solution to a recognized problem. Attention to the processes of instrumental and symbolic objectification is the key issue here. It may even be that only in the course of concretization, meeting the various objections and counterproposals, etc., that the germ cell of the concept itself becomes clear.

Virkkuninen observe (Virkkuninen & Ristimäki, 2012) that "A ratchet effect that enables cultural learning is created when a generalization or idea is objectified in an artifact. The artifact stays in place in the community long enough to become a platform for future innovations." Our experience has confirmed that instrumental objectification may have this effect, but we have also found that symbolic objectification (i.e., inscription in documents, laws, signage, literature, etc.) or practical objectification (i.e. normalization of use in actions) can be decisive.

We have noted that although the oval table was created with the completion of the very first CLS, it was more than a year later before the oval table was recognized as the germ cell. When Blunden (2000) gave a lunchtime talk to staff on CLSs in October 2000, the audience questions focused almost exclusively on the oval tables: where to buy them, how much they cost, what size, shape, etc. It was only at that point that it became clear that the oval table was the "germ cell" of the CLS. But developments over the succeeding decade have shown that indeed the germ cell was the oval table, despite the fact that the table design continues to be refined to this day.

We said at the beginning that a concept is a problem-solution arising within some institution. Over time, this essential character of a concept becomes blurred as it is incorporated into the entire culture of a society, but we cannot agree with Bazerman (2012; emphasis added) who says that concepts "both identify the phenomena or objects that are *worth attention* and are to be reported, and also identify procedures by which particulars in a class are to be identified." This is an abstract-empirical conception which fails to grasp the contradictory developmental process which generates new concepts as forms of activity.

Conclusion

We have sought to clarify the conditions under which a new concept emerges and takes an on-going place within the discourse of a community, as well as the factors which tend to militate against the institutionalization of a concept.

A concept originates in a problem or in an opportunity which arises within the social practices of some institution, positing a new need, designating either the problem or a solution. But such a concept will remain "unreal" unless it is objectified. The most robust and enduring mode of objectification is instantiation as a material artifact, such as the masonry and furniture of a building as was the case here. But such an instrumental objectification supports a new concept only to the extent that novel forms of activity constitute and reconstitute the artifact as an exemplar of the concept. Thus the original problem-solving (Nersessian, 2008) has to be continued by some sort of social movement, broadly so-called, which continuously affirms the "problem" and consolidates the reality of the concept by continuously objectifying the "solution," advocating for it and constituting it in practice.

But the objectification of the concept as an instance of itself is not the sole form of objectification. The word which acts as a bearer of the concept and its sign, has to enter the language, and in particular has to enter the formal and objectified language of the institution in the form of signage and its use in the statutes, procedures and databases of the institution, thus ensuring an enduring place for the concept in verbal discourse. This symbolic objectification is important since if a concept is to be maintained, its meaning has to be embedded in the practices and knowledge of the entire institution.

We have not entered here into the conditions which led to the concept of designing rooms to support collaborative learning in universities on opposite corners of the globe in about 1999, 25 years after much the same issue had arisen in school education. Universities across the globe participate in a common discourse, and share the problems that arise within that discourse. We have chosen instead to focus closely on the microgenetic process by means of which this was realized in one institution. To quote Goethe again: "At all times, it has been only individuals who have furthered science, not the age" (Goethe, 1964/1826).

Nonetheless the following observations could be made. Following upon the failure of Keynesian and Monetarist policies, the October 1987 stock market crash initiated a decisive turn away from macro-economic policies towards micro-economic reform and corporate restructure as the strategy of choice of global capitalism. This penetrated the academy in number of ways.

Politically, microeconomic policies initiated a sustained campaign against centralization and in favor of devolution in numerous aspects of economic and bureaucratic life, including both in the university itself and in educational theory. This delegitimized the large bureaucracies managing the universities and provided openings for criticism from outside the hierarchy. The new workplace training and change management industries also penetrated the universities and these people were much more innovative in their approaches to teaching and learning, which were often manifested in novel office design and communications, for example, and likewise the advanced computer and software firms.

The neo-liberal model of student-as-customer did not favor collaborative learning in and of itself, but its critique of teacher-centered pedagogy provided an opening in which collaborative learning could occupy an attractive third position. In the "real world" of 1990s private enterprise, hierarchical chains of line management and sharp divisions between decision making and labor were out of favor, and firms were devolving authority and responsibility for outcomes from middle-management to self-managed teams of multi-skilled front-line workers. In this *Zeitgeist*, devolving responsibility for learning from teacher to students made perfect sense.

We believe that these factors contributed to the promotion of the idea of "collaborative learning." A survey of academic journals using Google Scholar, shows that articles concerning "collaborative learning," as a percentage of articles concerned with "learning," remained at about 0.22% throughout the period 1965 to 1989 but rose to 4% through the 1990s. The global factors mentioned further contributed to the formation of a concept of Collaborative Learning Space, such that the concept emerged in the late 1990s.

The main factor which militates against the institutionalization of the concept is the need, characteristic of late modernity, for institutions to brand their activity and property. Very often, adoption of a term arising in another institution is a form of community which runs counter to the dominant spirit of competitiveness. In this situation, a concept is most easily maintained and proliferated if it is promoted as the exclusive product of a distinct organization or project which promotes it, or, is adopted by a prestigious institution which others are inclined to emulate.

A tour of the teaching and library spaces at the University of Melbourne in 2011 showed a stunning diversity of built forms and fit-out, invariably oriented to the support of a wide variety of learning activities. This stands in sharp contrast to the position in 1999, typical of all universities across the world, of lecture theatres, laboratories and classrooms which objectified an outdated teacher-centered, information-delivery mode of pedagogy. The concept of Collaborative Learning Space has been mainstreamed at the University of Melbourne and entered as an integral part of the mainstream educational discourse of universities across the world.

References

Arnold, M. (1996). The high-tech post-Fordist School. *Interchange 27* (3 and 4), p. 225–250, New York: Springer.

Bazerman, C. (2012). Writing with concepts: communal, internalized and externalized, *Mind Culture and Activity*, *19*(3), Philadelphia, PA: Taylor & Francis.

Beichner, R.J. and Cevetello J. (2013). *7 Things You Should Know About Collaborative Learning Spaces*, Educause, http://www.educause.edu/library/-should-know-about-collaborative-learning-spaces.

Blunden, A. (2000). *Building for Collaborative Learning, Talk for Staff at the University of Melbourne*, http://wayback.archive-it.org/2927/20120105030408/http://trs.unimelb.edu.au/archive/18Oct.html, 18 October 2000. See also images at http://wayback.archive-it.org/2927/20120105030406/http://trs.unimelb.edu.au/archive/cls2.html.

Engeström, Y., Nummijoki, J. & Sannino, A. (2012). Embodied Germ Cell at Work: Building an Expansive Concept of Physical Mobility in Home Care, *Mind Culture and Activity*, *19*(3), Philadelphia, PA: Taylor & Francis.

Goethe, J.W. v. (1964/1826). *Goethe: Wisdom and Experience. Selections by Ludwig Curtis*, New York, Frederick Ungar Publishing.

Goethe, J.W. v. (2006/1823). *Goethe on Science, An Anthology of Goethe's Scientific Writings, Selected and Introduced by Jeremy Naydler With a Foreword by Henri Bortoft*, Edinburgh, Floris Books.

Hall, R. & Horn, I.S. (2012). Talk and Conceptual Change at Work: Adequate Representation and Epistemic Stance in a Comparative Analysis of Statistical Consulting and Teacher Workgroups, *Mind Culture and Activity*, *19*(3), Philadelphia, PA: Taylor & Francis.

Leontiev, A.N. (1978). *Activity, Consciousness, and Personality*, Prentice-Hall.

Marx, K. (1986/1857). Method of Political Economy, *MECW* Volume 28, Lawrence & Wishart.

Marx, K. (1996/1867). Preface to the First German Edition of *Capital*, *MECW* Volume 35, Lawrence & Wishart.

Nersessian, N. (2008). *Creating Scientific Concepts*, Cambridge, MA, The MIT Press.

Oblinger, Diane G. (2006). Ed., *Learning Spaces*, Lexington KY: Educause.

Sweeney, Trudy (2010). Transforming pedagogy through interactive whiteboards: Using activity theory to understand tensions in practice. *ACCE* Volume 24, Number 2, February 2010, Australian Educational Computing.

Van Note Chism, N. & Bickford, D.J. (2002). The importance of physical space in creating supportive environments, *New Directions for Teaching and Learning*, No. 92, 2002: Jossey-Bass, Ann Arbor, MI, Wiley.

Virkkuninen, J. & Ristimäki, P. (2012). Double stimulation in strategic concept formation – an activity theoretical analysis of business planning in a small technology firm, *Mind Culture and Activity*, *19*(3), Philadelphia, PA: Taylor & Francis.

Vygotsky, L.S. (1987). Thinking and speech, *Collected Works, Volume 1*, New York: Plenum Press.

Vygotsky, L.S. (1994). The development of thinking and concept formation in adolescence, *Vygotsky Reader*, Hoboken NJ: Blackwell.

CHAPTER 7

Mayslake: Starting from Scratch

Helena Worthen

There are old industries where social relationships among and between workers and employers have evolved for generations and exist in a rich context of precedent, custom, legal agreements and practice. In such workplaces, these social relationships have been communicated and systematized and to a certain extent, taken for granted. This does not mean that they lack conflict. They have conflict, but they also have processes to resolve conflict. Especially in workplaces where there is union representation, there is a participant structure which acts as the carrier of experience and knowledge on both sides. Continuity is found in individual people, in the knowledge they have accumulated and shared, and the documents that testify to the history of the social relationships of the workplace. Within the participant structure people play different roles and learn from and teach each other, willingly or not. The garment and apparel industry in the US was such an industry. Heavily unionized, it employed thousands of workers until the middle of the 1900s when employers began to relocate first to Mexico and Central America and then to India and Asia. The practice of representation enabled an accumulation and transmission of knowledge about the social relations of work in that industry that was broad, systematic, detailed, teachable and practical. It was charged with the history of the workplace struggles through which it had emerged and was available for immediate use by a worker who needed help. Without the practice of representation, that knowledge would not have existed.

In a workplace where no such participant structure exists, some knowledge may be possessed by individuals but it is not formally shared. It is typically oral, handshake knowledge – private agreements, not collective public agreements. It leaves when they leave, so there is no continuity across generations of workers. In effect, the kind of knowledge that could be found in a unionized garment shop in the 1980s in Philadelphia could never exist in a workplace without representation or at least an established participant structure that accomplished the same thing.

Heartland Human Services in Mayslake, Illinois, was a workplace where nothing was written down. Instead, there was rumor, custom, and habit, guessing about what the boss wanted, and "our way of doing things." In 2006, when this story begins, there was no union, no contract, no structure of representation, no history of consult and confer, and no written policy that couldn't be changed unilaterally by management when it wanted to. The jobs overall were decent jobs, however. People stayed at this place for a lifetime. That made a difference. One woman had worked at a union factory and knew something about what ought to happen; that made a difference, too. Of course, there aren't many jobs in Central Illinois, so one reason why they stayed was because there weren't many other places to go.

The good news is that the people at Heartland Health Services made a transition from a situation where nothing could be taken for granted to one where there was at least a framework in place, in this case a union contract, all in four years. The transition was a rough ride and the outcome was never assured; when it began, people on both labor and management side were taking a step off a cliff. Furthermore, figuring out what winning would really mean was not easy or obvious. The whole fight was an intense learning experience, often painful, for everyone involved.

The bad news is that the pain has lingered on, years after the struggle itself was over. In *Memoirs of A Wobbly*, Henry McGuckin asks, "I wonder: Is a strike lost because those who fought to change conditions do not get to enjoy them? I think not. I think a strike is a part of the total struggle, and where it has forced better conditions which are enjoyed by other members of the working class, it cannot be called a defeat" (McGuckin, 1987, p. 46). Or, as one of the key organizers, Gail Warner, said, looking back on the experience, "We won but I lost." This experience is characteristic of all projects which set out to make a permanent change in the life status of a whole class of people – feminists, disability and public health campaigners, civil rights and national liberation fighters will all tell the same lament.

Three Important Terms: Public Sector, Private Sector, and Service Sector

The National Labor Relations Act of 1935, which came into being to provide a legal framework for collective bargaining, only covered workplaces in the private sector, and not even all of those. For example, agricultural workers and domestic workers were left out. Workplaces in the public sector were not covered by labor law until the 1960s or later, and this took place state-by-state and not in every state. "Public sector," in the US, means places where people work that are supported by tax revenue, like city, state and county offices, public schools or hospitals, transportation authorities, police and fire departments or public colleges and universities. It does not mean companies that have "gone public" in the sense of offering to sell shares in the stock market. This is important background to the Heartland story because we are going to talk about work that historically belonged to the public sector and that became part of the private sector; in other words, it was "privatized." In this case the industry is healthcare; examples of other industries that are undergoing privatization are education, transportation and incarceration. This was part of a long-term capitalist project to shift public assets and services into the private sector, in part to gain efficiency but in part to make them profitable.

The term "service sector" is also important. "Service" is usually contrasted with "industrial" sector, or manufacturing. "Service" jobs are jobs where people take care of, wait on, or help other people rather than building houses or making cars. They are usually low-wage jobs. During the first waves of globalization, back in the 1980s, people saw the danger that as we lost our manufacturing and industrial base, we risked becoming an economy based on service jobs. However, there was optimism that we might become a "knowledge" or "information" economy, drawing on our solid education system and tradition of innovation and entrepreneurship (Reich, 1992). Then, as the U.S. economy became more and more integrated into the global flow of finance, high-skill workers with good education emerged in countries all over the world and "knowledge" – by then, it was clear that this meant "tech" – jobs flowed towards them. The majority of the jobs that stayed in the US were the low-wage service jobs. These jobs stay here because they serve people who are here. They may be jobs in hotels and restaurants, retail, beauty salons or prisons, among others, and many are jobs in health and human services, like the jobs at Heartland.

Yet these are "knowledge" jobs, too, although not in the way the word was being used when it meant high-tech and data management. The knowledge of the people who work in service jobs, in this case healthcare jobs, consists not only in knowing what can or cannot be done, legally, ethically or medically, but also in knowing how to relate to the people whom they serve. These people whom they serve are often disturbed or distressed, in a crisis. The client's relationship with their service provider is part of their treatment. The right or wrong way to conduct this relationship is part of the provider's professional knowledge, learned not only in whatever training he or she may have had but also on the job by doing the job.

Before I tell what happened at Heartland, here are two brief stories about this kind of "professional" knowledge. I use this word intentionally because the status of these workers would not ordinarily position them as "professionals." A student in one of my classes told how he had worked in a residential home for the developmentally disabled and liked to read the newspaper out loud every day to a man who was in his care. Over time, the resident learned something about the world and started to learn to read himself. But the reader got suspended for reading the newspaper on work time. The supervisor did not want to hear about any benefit to the resident from listening to someone read the newspaper. Management owned the right to decide what was appropriate use of the worker's time. The "professional" knowledge of the worker had no power in this instance.

That happened to an individual. His co-workers did not make it a collective project and, for example, challenge the supervisor by having everyone read newspapers to all the residents. In a workplace with a different participant structure, a group of welfare caseworkers handled this differently. These people worked in an office in Chicago. As part of their work, they conducted intake interviews with clients that often meant listening to long, very personal, sometimes horrifying stories. These interviews were conducted in the cubicles of the caseworkers, where clients could have a modicum of privacy. The privacy was an aspect of the professional relationship between the caseworker and the client. The office supervisor, under pressure to increase case completion numbers, decided that to save the time spent by clients walking from the waiting area to the caseworkers' cubicles, all interviews would take place in the waiting area. This meant not only a loss of privacy for the client but also required the caseworker to handle many pieces of paper while sitting in a molded plastic chair without a desk.

There was a union in this workplace, but the union did not file a grievance because there was no actual contract violation involved. Instead, they made up T-shirts for all the caseworkers in the office with the word "RESPECT" in big letters written across the back and the front. The union representative then went and explained to the supervisor what they were doing, and why. After this, wearing the T-shirts, they continued to conduct intake interviews in their cubicles. The supervisor, faced with the spectacle of an office full of T-shirts all saying RESPECT, backed off and dropped the issue.

In both cases, the issue that moved the workers was one of their respect for the clients contrasted with management's disrespect for their professional knowledge about how to do the job. In the first case, the worker objected alone and was ignored. In the second, the workers took the issue up as a collective project and succeeded in rebalancing the social relationships of the workplace. But using the second strategy is not just a simple matter of choice. It does not emerge from nothing. It requires preparation and collaboration. Gaining control over one's own life, *always* involves working with others to achieve that self-determination.

Now, keeping in mind the tension between efficiency and service, and the issue of whose professional knowledge deserves respect, and the necessity for laying the groundwork for a collaborative project, we can turn to the story of Heartland.

A Four-Year Struggle: Mayslake

Mayslake, Illinois, is a town of 12,000 people near where Interstate 57 (Chicago to Memphis) intersects with Interstate 70 (Utah to Maryland), just over 200 miles south of Chicago. East and west of the town is level agricultural land drained by small rivers. Around the overpasses at the intersection there are motels, gas stations and chain food places and a Wal-Mart. There is also a giant white cross, 198 feet high, visible from the freeway, for miles around and on YouTube. A mile north of the freeway interchange, two railroads cross each other, one going east–west and the other north–south, just like the freeways. This was the previous generation of transportation and the railroad crossing is where the original town was built.

Like many towns in Central Illinois, Mayslake was once a mining town. Back in the 1930s, during the mining wars when the Progressive Miners broke away from the United Mine Workers in protest against the undemocratic leadership of John L. Lewis, this railroad was blown up – some say by Peabody, the mining company, itself. Peabody is still the main owner and operator of coal mines in Illinois, although they are now all non-union. They were recently in the news for spinning off their retirees' pension obligations into a small sub-company, which then went bankrupt. The region is conservative, Catholic, Lutheran, and Baptist. It is also like many such towns in that it was a "sundown" town, where it was widely known that black people were not welcome after sundown. Today, Mayslake is very white. It is not a poor town: there is quite a bit of money in it, but it is old money and it's in the hands of people referred to by the workers as "the town fathers." These people do not rely on public services: they can afford to go elsewhere for vacations, education and healthcare. They go to the Mayo Clinic, not to Heartland.

A lot of the businesses are passed down through families and carry family names, mostly German, not chain store names. In fact, the small suburb to the east of Mayslake is named Teutopolis, settled by German Catholics in the 1840s. Being German still corresponds with relative wealth: median household income is $47,450 per year in Teutopolis compared to Mayslake's $34,750 per year.

Mayslake is a combination of isolation by geography and isolated by intention. It is not a "union-based community." The public schools, the railroad and the Post Office are the only union jobs in town. “Bringing a union in is like breaking a holy law,” says one of the women who worked at the health center. “The city fathers have got the unions out and kept them out.”

Previously unionized workplaces have left Mayslake – Worldcolor Press, Crossroads Press, and Fedder’s Air Conditioning are gone. Kingery Printing went bankrupt. If someone has enough money to run a business here, he can also afford to say that if a union comes in, he’ll shut the doors. A worker who eventually went on strike during this struggle at Heartland Human Services said, “He’s made his money. He can close his place of business and go home and live off the interest of his investments.” The same person confirmed that Toyota was going to locate there but “the city fathers kept it out because, they knew it would raise salaries.” Another story told how there was a company that made airplane brakes, that was going to train their own people and would pay $20 an hour. Even though it wasn’t union, the city fathers kept it out. They didn’t want a high-wage company coming into town and drawing workers away from low-wage jobs.

It’s worth noting that so many of the stories people told when asked to describe Mayslake were about good jobs that went away or were kept away by the town fathers. This mattered not only to the workers at Heartland who went on strike but also to their clients, who needed jobs.

While this division of the town into two classes, “the city fathers” and the working class, was known to the workers before they began their fight, it was perceived as background history and culture. Before the strike, they did not understand how far this division would reach into their workplace or anticipate the lengths to which the city fathers, especially those who sat on the Board of Heartland, would go to keep them from winning.

Heartland Human Services

Heartland is a not-for-profit full-service four-county mental health agency, the only agency of its kind in town and for 50 miles around. It provides the full gamut of services. During the period in the 1970s when public health services were spun off into community-based operations, Heartland was set up as a private non-profit and therefore at the time of this story, fell under private sector labor law, the National Labor Relations Act of 1935. Although it is privately owned, it is funded entirely by fees, grants and public money, state and local: Department of Human Services, Social Security, Medicaid and Medicare. Heartland operates on a sliding fee scale, and has a Community Development Program to provide free services to the indigent. There is one other social service agency in town that has a program for the developmentally disabled, but it can only handle a few clients.

Heartland serves the working class of Mayslake, or, as Lucille Musser, who later became president of the union, put it, "The poor and the near-poor." Heartland has a reputation of serving the ne'er-do-wells, the people on public aid, the jail docket and the drinkers. It has a group home for boys, a residential home for male and female mentally ill, services for the developmentally disabled, and counseling for county probation, state parole and federal probation systems. It does AIDS training, substance abuse prevention, child abuse prevention, classes in anger management, teen pregnancy prevention and services for children of divorcing parents.

At the time that the events in this story happened, Heartland was overseen by a Board of Directors consisting of seven people, four men and three women. They were businessmen, an Assistant Superintendent of Schools, President of a Baptist Church, a minister, a retired teacher and a nurse who manages a hospital. They were "town fathers." They hired the Director. In turn, in circular fashion, the Director picked them.

The Boss is the Best Organizer

In October 2005, the Director of Heartland, a woman who had worked for Heartland herself for over twenty years, called a meeting of everyone who worked at Heartland. At that time, it employed about 160 people. According to several Heartland workers whom I interviewed during and after the strike, they all went down to the basement meeting room, where there were chairs set up. The Director announced that she would take no questions. She passed out a sheet of paper. She said they were in a financial crisis. She told the employees what she was going to do in order to resolve this crisis. Then she "dropped this bomb" as one worker put it, walked out of the room and went to Europe on vacation. She had previously arranged to have police outside the building, as if she was afraid that there would be a violent reaction from her employees when she made this announcement.

This "bomb" meant drastic changes in how workers would do their work. It involved wage cuts, loss of benefits, work hour increases, and reductions in holidays. The whole agency would shift from funding whole programs to fee-for-service billing. The work week increased from 35 hours to 40 hours. All the benefits for part-time workers were taken away. Before the Director's announcement, people had vacation, holidays, sick days and personal days. One woman who had worked there 35 years had accumulated 20 vacation days, 12 holidays, 12 sick days and 3 personal days. After the Director was done with this announcement, that same woman had 20 "personal time off" days per year – period.

There were also two particularly problematic changes: the establishment of productivity standards and a new on-call system. A productivity standard has similarities to piece-rate, which was the compensation system for workers such that pay is tied to the amount of work that gets done. A standard is set that establishes a goal for the amount of work done. Then workers attempt to meet that goal. Case managers, counselors and therapists were all going to have to meet productivity standards, as would anyone else who did billable work. The issue usually arises over what the unit of measurement of the work should be. Should the work of a therapist, for example, be measured by hours spent, by phone calls answered, patients met, patients referred, or patients cured?

According to Lucille Musser, if you met your productivity goal, you would get a bonus. But meeting it was not going to be easy. You had to be seeing people face to face or doing case management on the phone in order for an interaction to be billable, and 65% of your time had to be billable. Your paperwork had to be finished within 24 hours. You had to make two marketing calls on your own time. If a patient didn't show up or missed an appointment, you didn't get credit, even if you were in your office, waiting for the patient. You could get fired if you didn't "do productivity." The productivity standards created paranoia and encouraged cheating. Some hourly workers dealt with it by trying to help people who were "on productivity" work. This was an attempt to work together to benefit each other. But that was not a long-term solution.

The new on-call arrangement was especially burdensome. An on-call rotation was established. You would be on call at night. You had to use your own cell phone, assuming you had one. For being on call, you would get $1.75 per hour. If you got called out, you got time and a half based on your pay rate. You would not have a choice about being on call. If you were called out at night and were out all night, you still had to work the next day, or else take one of your personal time off days. If you were too tired to work it would be an "unexcused absence." One worker who had been there 15 years soon got fired. He said he couldn't do the beeper/cell phone on-call routine. He had a doctor's note saying that he had to get a good night's sleep. The Director fired him, saying, "You can't do the job."

There were a lot of other new rules as well. Some of them seemed capricious, such as requiring employees to walk residents from their rooms to group meetings but then also accompany them to the bathroom, which meant leaving the group alone. The workers were angry, frustrated and insulted. The knowledge they had created about doing the work by doing the work was being disregarded. They felt that they could not go over the Director's head to the Board. They knew they'd get fired if they sent a message and signed their own names.

It was general knowledge that the cost of healthcare had been rising and that state and federal funding for all kinds of programs was being cut and could disappear completely in the next few years. At the time of this struggle, no healthcare reform legislation had been passed. Therefore agencies like Heartland, in order to keep going at all, had to find ways to cut costs. All over the state, healthcare agencies were trying to control costs, especially labor costs. Strategies for cutting costs are well-known and well publicized. However, the Director of Heartland appears to have tried to implement them all, all at once, unilaterally.

This was a workplace with no union. The first reaction of many of the workers was, "Can she do that?" The answer is, of course, yes.

Starting to Organize

Mayslake is a small town. People talked with each other, with their families, at their churches and with friends. According to Lucille Messer, four of the Heartland workers started thinking about organizing a union right after the October bombshell meeting. They were two men and two women. One, Anna Beck, had worked in a union workplace before. Another, Gail Warner, had a brother who was a union electrician. The other two knew people who worked in union workplaces. This meant that they had a general idea that being in a union would give them some protection against capricious changes in their working conditions, but their level of experience was in no way comparable to the union representatives found in established union workplaces, who carried out their work in the context of a richly elaborated practice that was well-known, if not consented to, by both union and management. Yet these four were the most experienced of the whole 160-person workforce. So the situation was that these four had to start from scratch. Like most Americans, the other workers had never really understood what a union was. Many simply accepted without question the opinion of the town fathers that unions were mob-driven, third-party nuisances that would attract lawyers and cause businesses to leave town. Since most unions had offices in Chicago, the word "union" also meant "Chicago" which meant "mobsters" or, if the truth be told, black.

Therefore at the beginning, the education was on an each-one-teach-one basis. The content of what was being taught and learned changed with every new problem that cropped up. How should workers respond to the part-time workers who had suddenly lost their benefits? How should they deal with co-workers who were on this new productivity standard and would lose money if a client failed to show up? What national union represented workers like them? When the time came, who should make the phone call to a national union asking for help, and what should they tell them? Who should come to the first meeting, and where should it be held, and who should know about it? What should they expect? Then, how should they treat people who crossed the line and went back to work? How should they treat their clients, many of whom relied desperately on getting their medication, therapy, or other kinds of treatment, whom they were likely to encounter in a grocery store or at church or on the street? What would they say when the client asked, "Where are you and what are you doing?" How would they explain what was going on?

But the team of four made telephone calls, held discussions and meetings over coffee and amazingly enough, by December, 2005, the organizers were confident that 98% of the workers were on board. While the team did not know much about unions, they did know that what the Director had imposed on them was intolerable. They decided it was time to get in touch with an "official" union and called AFSCME, (pronounced aff-skmee) the American Federation of State, County and Municipal Employees that represents mostly public sector workers throughout the US. AFSCME responded. This does not always happen; there are national unions that will decline to work with a small, isolated workforce even if they seem ready to organize. However, AFSCME's big strength is in the public sector and as public work gets privatized out, it has become critical for the union to follow the work no matter where it goes. AFSCME sent one full-time and several part-time staff down to Mayslake, opened an office in the center of town, and got to work. The Heartland workers had an election in February 2006. Anger was more powerful than fear. Between voting for "no union" or for representation by AFSCME, the workers at Heartland voted for representation.

Curiously, the Director never really fought the organizing campaign. According to Heartland workers, she didn't think it would happen. There were two main programs at Heartland, residential and outpatient, and the Director never anticipated that the employees in one program would talk with employees in the other. Of course, they did. What was a conspiracy among four people had become a social movement which could not be stopped.

Bargaining Begins

Once a workforce has had an election and brings in a union, they still don't have a contract. To get a contract, you have to bargain with the employer. Now that they had learned how to organize, they had to learn how to bargain.

Since I am interested in the kind of learning that happens at work when people take, as their collective project, the protection of their jobs, their self-respect and each other, this is a good moment to talk about the kind of learning that had happened thus far. How to organize a union is not something that is taught in high school or in community colleges, where most people are working and going to school at the same time. How to organize a union is information that is as often distorted as it is suppressed. So the learning that took place among these workers in Mayslake, a city where "You're breaking a holy law" when you bring in a union, a city where the only workers with union representation are teachers, postal workers, and railroad workers and where unionized workplaces have been run out of town, is learning that has taken place in a context of fighting, fear and worry. But like any battle, people who are in it together become close friends. The participant structure is warm, informal and personal. This means that the knowledge that is being created when these people call each other up, talk in the parking lot, run into each other at church or talk over family dinners, is very emotionally charged.

It's impossible, for example, for someone to ask, "How are things going at work?" without the other person thinking about the part-time employee who has suddenly lost her health insurance, or the residents who are affected by the preoccupation of the workers with their new working conditions. This means that not only are the workers learning a great deal about the legal and historic context of employment relations in the US, including things like how to run a union election under the National Labor Relations Board and who this strangely-named national union called AFSCME actually is, but this knowledge that they are all taking a crash course in is emotionally charged because people are having to take sides, look at the town fathers through different eyes, make friends and trust people who were just co-workers only a few months ago, and speak up in ways that they have not ever done before. There will be people who are scared to death, sure that they are going to get fired or harassed. There will be people whose paychecks support a whole family or extended family (this was becoming increasingly common in central Illinois at that time) and who are risking not only their own income but money that others depend on. The knowledge that they acquire in the process of organizing is infused with this emotion.

But they now have to move forward, which means that they have to get a contract. A contract is an agreement between workers, as a collectivity, and their employer. The contract will govern the new social relationships of their workplace, which in the past were ungoverned – were at the will, or whim, of their employer, as they found out when she dropped "the bomb." The union staffers who were assigned to Mayslake were knowledgeable about how this was supposed to happen, and provided the workers with a map and told them what to expect.

Then they tried to bargain, and the Director simply refused to bargain. She either failed to show up for meetings, postponed meetings, or came to the table unprepared, saying that she had not read their materials. The negotiating committee kept coming back and coming back. The AFSCME staffers talked the members through the stalemate, over and over. A core article in the

National Labor Relations Act (and in all the public sector bargaining laws that are based on it) says that parties have to "bargain in good faith." "Bargaining" means moving past your starting position, making concessions, coming up with new ideas, compromising, finding common ground and being creative. Good bargainers do all this. The "in good faith" part means showing up on time, doing your homework, sincerely committing to the process, making yourself available, sharing information. "Bad faith bargaining" – in which a party does not do these things – is a violation of the NLRA. Once you are in the universe of having a union, and under the purview of a Labor Board, violating that law creates a flow of problems for you.

The bargaining at Heartland proceeded in ways that looked like bad faith bargaining. The Director and the management team failed to do all those things listed above. Then the union invited a mediator to come in. A mediator is someone with advanced training in the bargaining process who is officially neutral. They come from the Federal Mediation and Conciliation Service (FMCS) that was established as part of the 1948 legislation known as Taft-Hartley, for the purpose of creating more paths to negotiated agreements. Their service is federally-funded and free to users; the idea is that the money is saved overall, to an economy that depends on people having jobs and going to work, by expediting an agreement is worth the cost of providing a mediator. The mediator made a contract proposal which was acceptable to the Heartland workers but which the Heartland management rejected.

Because of Heartland's evident failure to bargain in good faith, the union filed charges of unfair labor practices at the National Labor Relations Board. However, the charges were rejected by the regional Board in St. Louis. When I asked why these charges, which seemed strong to me, were rejected, the union was not able to speculate why, except that under President George Bush, appointments to the NLRB had become extremely politicized and openly anti-union. So the attempts to bargain continued; no muscle was applied from the NRLB to move them faster toward a contract.

Finally, in July, 2007, over a year after they had launched their organizing project, the workers gave the Director thirty days to come to the table, warning her that if she didn't come, they would go on strike. She didn't show up. They went on strike.

Strike

This is a workforce of people who are fundamentally caregivers, not fighters. In the span of less than two years, however, driven by the shock of "the bomb" and the astonishing contempt shown toward them by the Director and the Board, they were picketing.

Throughout this whole process, most workers stayed involved. No more than five people crossed the line and went back to work. Some had to get other jobs and participated in the strike activity only sparingly. Others made it the central project of their lives. They held rallies, spoke with the local media, got on the radio, passed out flyers, went door-knocking. Teachers from the teachers' union (the Illinois Education Association) walked their picket line, let them use the bathroom in their union office and gave them money. Some of the workers practiced public speaking and learned to make presentations. They went to other unions, to conferences and union conventions in other cities and spoke from the podium to audiences of thousands. They talked on the radio and on TV. They wrote letters to the editor and did interviews.

As it got colder, workers set up a strike hut in front of Heartland Human Services and staffed it. The few employees who crossed the line, plus some who were hired after the strike started, had to drive past them. The strikers went out to the street and tried to talk to them as they drove past. When the snow fell, the strikers sat in the strike hut and warmed themselves at a propane burner. This was the point at which I met them. I had come down to Mayslake to talk with a railroad worker about a labor education class for railroad safety representatives. The railroad worker took me on a walk along the Illinois Central tracks and showed me what good and bad ballast looked like, and explained how a signal post two hundred miles away, in Indiana, could be a fatal hazard to someone riding a train through Mayslake. Then I asked him if he knew about the Heartland workers. He immediately said he did, and added that he had spoken brusquely on their behalf to one of the members of the Board of Directors, the Baptist minister, while playing golf with him only a few days before. He told me where their strike hut was.

There they were, in deep snow, huddled in a white tent over a propane gas heater. There were three women inside. Several more were walking up and down outside the tent picketing. Our conversation was quick, since they had no idea who I was or why I was dropping in on them, except that I was a labor educator from the University. I asked if they'd come to a women's conference I was organizing later in the spring and they agreed to come; luckily, the conference, the Regina Polk conference, was fully funded by money raised in honor of a young woman who had been a Teamster business agent and got killed while working, so there was scholarship money that could support their attendance. My plan was to build a curriculum for the conference around their experience with Heartland. They did come, and we did build the whole conference around their experience, but that is another story. That would happen in the coming May 2008 and this was November 2007.

By midsummer 2008, one year after the strike began, with no movement at all taking place at the bargaining table, the workers faced a choice. According to law, if a union and an employer cannot come to agreement and bargain a contract successfully within one year of the union getting organized, the employer can call for another vote by employees on whether or not they want union representation. This is called a decertification vote. The people who would be able to vote would be the workers who were currently employed at Heartland – that is, the five who had crossed the picket line plus those who had been hired after the strike began. It would be highly likely that they would decertify the union.

The Heartland strikers, in other words, were likely to find that their union was gone. Therefore, after a year of being on strike, they decided to go back in and offer to return to work, unconditionally. The meeting in which they agreed to do this and talked about how they would act and what they would say to the people who had crossed the line or been hired since the strike was intense. Then, on the last day possible, they walked back in together and stood in the lobby, waiting to see what would happen. The current employees walked past them as they came in to work.

Lockout

The response of the Director was to lock them out – that is, she said no, they could not come back to work; they had to leave the premises. They stood there, ready to go back to work in their old workplace, looking at the workers who had taken their places, and the Director came and told them all to leave. Therefore by August 2008, the workers were no longer technically on strike, they were on "lockout." That means that they had unconditionally offered to go back to work but had been refused.

They did not give up. They continued to picket and staff the strike hut, which was frequently vandalized and painted with obscene graffiti. This kept them visible in the community and especially to people coming in and out of Heartland. In the summer, large contingents of AFSCME members came down from Chicago to Mayslake in busloads and picketed. For a community that was famous for being white, if not actually Teutonic, the sudden presence of a big, loud crowd of racially diverse Chicago union activists was a shock.

During the lockout, strategies moved to another level and were extended in many directions. One strategy was to try to find another community health organization that would take over the workload from Heartland. Another was to appeal to the State of Illinois to stop funding an agency that was refusing to honor labor laws. The state in fact did an audit and discovered bad accounting and substantial amounts of missing money. The state then withheld some funding. All of this made news.

In November 2008, they received a visit from Richard Trumka, Secretary-Treasurer of the AFL-CIO, and were promised national publicity as the "poster child for EFCA," the Employee Free Choice Act. The most obvious way that EFCA would have made a difference for these workers is that instead of fighting, then striking, and then getting locked out in order to get a contract, they would have gone to first contract arbitration and an arbitrator would have made both sides agree to a contract. It probably would have looked a lot like the one proposed by the mediator (and a lot like the one that was ultimately agreed to). However, this law never was brought to a vote in Congress as the Obama administration, facing a short timeline before the mid-term elections, put all its muscle into getting healthcare reform passed instead.

Finally, in the summer of 2009, nearly four years after the Director "dropped the bomb" that began this intense and drawn-out campaign, the relentless pressure by the union and the high visibility of the struggle in the Mayslake community added a straw that broke the camel's back. *The Board fired the Director*. She was then replaced by a man who had been the President of the Board and who had let it be known that he was willing to bargain.

Very soon after that, in late August, the new Board agreed to sign a contract with the union.

Back to Work after Four Years

So in early September, 2009, the workers went back to work. Not all of them; at the time they went back to work, there were a little over 20 of the original workers left who wanted to go back. Some had moved away, some had taken other jobs, some had found other ways to scrape together a living. Some had had, on the one hand, "the greatest experience of my life," but on the other hand, were burned out and suffering from stress.

The ones who did go back now had to work side-by-side with people whom they had been calling "scabs" for the past two years, and this was difficult. One woman could not forget the filthy words that had been spray-painted onto the strike hut walls. Now scabs and strikers met in the cafeteria. Who was going to make coffee for whom? Who was going to sit at a table with someone who had crossed the picket line? Who was going to teach the job to someone who had been doing it for a year but doing it wrong? But over time, they managed to make the place function.

The vice-president, the young woman named Gail Warner who had invested enormous amounts of energy in the strike, found that her job had been divided among many other people and in effect, no longer existed. She wrote me this message about the day they returned to work:

> To let you know how walking back into work went. I heard the local newscast as I drove in the parking lot at 7:30 a.m. and of course the lead story was about our return to work. I jotted down the exact words of the interim president of Heartland's Board for ya! It disgusted me. [He] said, 'This is a sensitive process, we have a group of people who have been heroic in their efforts the past couple of years in terms of stepping up to make sure that clients of this community continued to receive the services they need and we owe them a great debt of gratitude'. OF COURSE he was speaking about the scabs. It sickened me then and sickens me all over again to actually write it down. We entered the building, met all in one large room. Their HR person offered introductions etc. and asked if we had any comments. ...The other workers got to go into quiet rooms to take their online essential learning tests needed in order to return to work. I on the other hand was taken into the reception area, told to try and do my testing while working and I began working as if I had never left. It was odd! The scab I worked with seemed okay for two hours, then she told me to go to lunch; which I did, then when I returned from lunch, she lost her mind! She began to scream at me, curse at me and ultimately walked out. They offered her early lay off and she never came back. ... I can elaborate on what was said sometime in person with you. Thursday and Friday went well, I haven't received much training, I just do the things I remember from 26 months ago and when something has changed (procedure wise) people pop in and tell me to change this or that. So, I think maybe the worst is over as far as 'scab' altercations, but who knows. The Board will choose a Director by the end of the year, and if they choose someone similar to [the previous Director] nothing will change. I dearly hope they make a wiser decision or working at Heartland will be impossible for me. The whole need for our struggle was to make Heartland better, and if that doesn't happen, it will be difficult for me to watch it remain about money and power and not about helping people. Time will tell. Azure and I are going to Chicago to speak at the Labor Day event at Pullman. I will let you know that goes as well.
>
> GAIL

Only a few days later, however, Gail quit in order to spend time with her daughter. The stress of returning to work in that place was just too much.

Another leader, Anna Beck, took over the union VP position. In January 2010 she reported that the hardest thing about going back in was getting the management to agree that there actually was a contract in place and that they had to read it and acknowledge what it said – and that it would be a good idea for them to agree on what it said. Anna Beck had previous union experience and knew what a grievance looked like and what taking something to arbitration meant, so she put a lot of energy into maintaining the union consciousness on the floor. But it was a different kind of place, now.

Four years is a long, long time to be involved in a struggle. One of the remarkable things about this story is that the union, AFSCME, invested a tremendous amount of staff time and support in this small, isolated workforce. They rented an office in downtown Mayslake and kept it staffed with at least one full-time staffer and a few part-time staffers, as well as the frequent presence of the regional director, Jeff Bigelow. They trained the workers. They encouraged and supported things that the workers came up with. Real leaders emerged from among these workers. The union picked up these emerging leaders and made them the face of the struggle and let them pass on their experience to workers in other struggles. To use terms from learning theory, they supported the creation of a *community of practice* (Lave & Wenger, 1991) and developed a participant structure that gave many, if not all, of the strikers things to learn and real work to do.

When I asked an AFSCME leader, Mike Newman, why AFSCME had been willing to spend so much money, staff time and so much political capital to back up this little group of women (mostly) at a private sector facility in deep Central Illinois, he smiled and said, "AFSCME has never lost a strike." Whether this is true of the whole national union or just of Illinois I don't know, but it is consistent with what AFSCME's probable evaluation of the difficulties were to begin with. It was far from being an obvious win.

When people have been through an organizing effort, especially one that is extremely painful and tears a town apart, they have learned something that can't be unlearned. This then becomes a problem for the town. In the case of Mayslake, while the town fathers were able to keep away the brake lining company that would have paid $20 an hour, it was going to be hard to get rid of these workers at Heartland, who were not likely to unlearn the lessons of their organizing. But even so, consider the difference between the work of representation carried out by the people in the garment factories, where workers and management have been living with contracts for generations, and how the work of representation is carried out when both sides are still learning, and trying to teach each other, what the rules are.

What Did the Struggle Accomplish?

There are many ways to evaluate the results of the struggle at Heartland. They could be a list of friends lost or made, lives ruined or saved, fights, parties, enduring splits in the social world of the town, critical dates and deadlines. One way certainly is, were these workers able to turn bad jobs into good ones?

This can be answered in part by looking at their contract. From a learning perspective, a contract is a map of a participant structure. Paths pass through this structure. Some are dead ends, some create opportunities. There are two areas of the Heartland contract that speak to the question of whether these jobs are now better than before the struggle. Both have to do with the social relationships of work. First has to do with the relationship between the employer and the collectivity of workers, which you could call the union or the bargaining unit. The contract says that work will be assigned to bargaining unit members (not new people hired from outside, but people who are already working at Heartland); that when someone new is hired, the union will be notified of it; the union gets ten days of paid time to send members to conferences and conventions; the union gets to choose four stewards, who get to work on solving problems involving workers (grievances) on paid time, with access to a phone and private meeting space, and that the employer has to meet with them and work on the problems. If the steward and the employer can't work out a solution, then the grievance procedure moves on to mediation and ultimately arbitration, which is enforceable. This means that the union has a legitimate and substantial presence in the workplace. There are also quarterly labor-management meetings, with five persons from each side to be in attendance. These items establish a viable collective presence in the workplace that has the explicit purpose of protecting and advocating for the workers.

The second area has to do with the relationship between the employer and individual workers. The most familiar and standard one is seniority. Assignments, whether to working overtime, working on holidays, asking for paid time off (vacations, for example), promotions, crisis line work or layoffs, are done by seniority or reverse seniority. This prevents favoritism and acknowledges that workers learn while working and senior workers know something newer workers don't know. Discipline, in the sense of punishment, is progressive under this contract, meaning that the punishments progress from mild to severe: an oral reprimand, a written reprimand, suspension, and then discharge. Violations of these contract items is something that an employee can grieve, which means to file a complaint about. This shifts the balance of power between worker and management toward the center and reduces the role of fear and intimidation. The contract also explicitly says that discipline must be carried out "in a manner that will not embarrass the employee."

Part-time workers also got at least some of their health insurance back and there is, not accidentally, a no strike/no lockout clause, in effect for the duration of this contract. And they got a raise.

How do the workers feel? Did the struggle improve the jobs? Azure Newman said, "I think we're doing better than before. The turnover rate before the strike was enormous. It used to be that they'd make us sign a paper with the job description including the words 'at will'. Now, clients know we are going to be there. We have a job, we have protection."

Technically, making workers sign a paper that says that employment is "at will," meaning no unions can be organized, is a violation of labor law. But look what it took to make this law of the land operative.

Gail wrote to me when a couple of years had passed:

> Working day and night, putting my reputation on the line, and walking a thin line where this town was concerned as my husband worked for the most ANTI-UNION bank in town, I felt the pressure every day to just walk away and keep my mouth shut. I really didn't want to risk my husband's job (our only income), but in light of all the unfairness at Heartland I HAD to follow through and we HAD to win for everyone involved. We did WIN, but I LOST in the end. I have moved on, but there will always be a rawness to the whole ordeal. I learned so much about my town and the people in it. I wouldn't trade the experience I gained in public speaking or the friends I made. It was sure a learning period in my life! and grateful for it. You do not need to print any of this, I just wanted to give you a better sense of how difficult it was, with management even using our own contract against us, to place a wedge in our solidarity, in our devotion to one another. They didn't succeed, but they did know how to rub salt into the wounds and it was a very difficult time. Oh, and the scab that screamed at me and quit, they later made her their "marketing manager"! They hired her back on when I left and she worked in a very high paying position there for years after I left. She eventually stepped out of line with the Director and found out what they are really like and she walked out for good.

Conclusion

To say that this chapter tells the story of a project that began with nothing is not exactly right. The "bomb" that the Director dropped set into motion a narrative that was based in a legal process. The narrative of how to organize a union functioned like a "plot" in the sense of the Kravtsova and Kravtsov chapter: a sequence of actions that, if carried out, would get them past obstacles to a hoped-for goal. It offered landmarks to look for, responses to anticipate, and a goal to keep an eye on. It made what might have been experienced as a plunge into meaninglessness into a battle that could be fought. Although this process was well known to only two, and partially known to four of the 160 workers, they were able to communicate it because of the urgency of the situation. Another resource of this workforce was the commitment that the workers felt to each other, worrying about the part-timers who lost their health insurance, the workers who were put on "productivity," and the worker who couldn't handle being on-call all night. This was related to, but not the same as, the concern the workers felt for their clients and through them, for the working class community of Mayslake. It also helped them remain unconfused about who was on their side. These were assets that shifted the balance of power to the workers from the start and made their collective activity, and then their collaboration with the professional organizers from AFSCME, a costly but ultimately successful project. Unlike the garment workers mentioned at the beginning of this chapter, they did not have a rich repository of expertise and established practices built up over time through a multi-generational participant structure. From the point of view of the Director, who didn't even bother to discourage the initial organizing campaign, their resources apparently looked like nothing. A big mistake; what they had may have been invisible to someone looking at it from her point of view, but it was enough to do the job.

References

Lave, J. & Wenger, E. (1991). *Situated Learning: Legitimate Peripheral Participation.* Cambridge, UK: Cambridge University Press.

McGuckin, H. (1987/1914). *Memoirs of a Wobbly.* Chicago, IL: Charles H. Kerr Publishing.

Reich, Robert (1992). *The Work of Nations: Preparing ourselves for 21st Century Capitalism*, New York, NY: Random House.

CHAPTER 8

The Collaborative Project of Public Deliberation

Ron Lubensky

Introduction

In local autonomous settings like trade union meetings or in the past when populations were sparse as exemplified in the 18th century Town Meetings in America's New England states, whole communities have assembled to talk out problems and consent to solutions. But such directly democratic forums are impractical for large communities and states. Representative democracy offered a scaled-up solution that passes the decision-making power to politicians through the majoritarian aggregation of votes in periodic elections. The representative system worked well when societal change was slow and incremental, culture was relatively homogeneous and communication technologies were primitive.

Now, there is a disconnect between the prescriptions of executive power and the dynamic and increasingly complex needs and demands of the people they serve. The rise of political parties and lobbying have obfuscated the relation between ordinary people and the policies under which they must live. Also, public servants do not typically answer directly to the people except to the extent that their roles are limited by the legislation and regulations sanctioned by elected officials. This is exacerbated when authorities fail to live up to their obligations or misrepresent their constituencies. This *democratic deficit* is the most common motivation cited for increasing public participation in governance.

For several decades political theorists have been advocating a new approach to public policy decision-making under the banner of *deliberative democracy*. This approach is most easily presented by extending the mainstream concept of a *jury*, which draws a microcosm of the community with the binary remit of judging a criminal charge against the presented evidence and the law. But unlike a jury, a deliberative panel is recruited with the more active task of exploring a policy issue and making recommendations for take-up by authority. Such a panel is called a *mini-public*, which indexes both its broad representation of perspectives and interests in the community, and the style of discourse it involves. Many mini-publics are recruited from the citizenry at least in part by stratified random selection to ensure representativeness and inclusion, to redress the domination of activists and "the usual suspects" in civil matters. Discourse is conducted in small groups who are professionally facilitated to be constructive, productive and to avoid conversational pathologies. Mini-publics range in size from about 20 participants, for example in a process design called a Citizens' Jury, to large panels like the 160-member British Columbia Citizens' Assembly for Electoral Reform (BCCAER) to recommend a new electoral system (Warren & Pearse, 2008), and the 150-member Australian Citizens' Parliament (ACP) to explore improvements to the operation of government (Carson et al., 2013). Participatory Budgeting is occurring in several countries, inviting residents to nominate and then prioritize taxpayer-funded projects in their local region. All mini-publics are invited into *deliberation*, which includes open and generous exploration of an issue, identification of common ground positions across difference, and agreement on policy approaches and settings that the whole community can live with.

A Citizens' Jury about a local issue can typically complete its work over two weekends. The larger ACP was engaged online for several weeks, then met for four days in Canberra. The BCCAER took eight months to complete, including monthly meetings in Vancouver and regional consultations with citizens. So deliberative designs occur over a range of time scales, depending on the complexity of their considerations and the logistics of bringing them together. New online platforms developed specifically for dialogue and deliberation are bridging distance and time constraints.

While many mini-publics are facilitated, convened and studied by academic teams, deliberative democracy is an innovation in governance, not a research method for political scientists. Unlike focus groups, mini-publics should be empowered to set the agenda of their proceedings, including reshaping the scope and purpose of their investigation and choosing their sources of information. The processes and dialogic methods are designed and led by a new cottage industry of public participation practitioners and facilitators.[1]

Opinion surveys are useful for ascertaining the range of attitudes to which residents are predisposed, but often citizens do not have shared understandings or considered beliefs about the questions being asked of them. A question can mean different things to different people. Furthermore, a social survey inevitably carries the framing biases of its authors.

In a mini-public, on the other hand, participants learn from each other and are able to see policy options empathetically from perspectives beyond their

1 International Association for Public Participation (IAP2) and National Coalition for Dialogue & Deliberation (NCDD) are membership groups that represent the interests of public engagement practitioners.

own. They listen carefully and speak so that they may be well-understood by others. They often invest substantial effort to gain a deeper understanding of the questions that have seeded their engagement. They are aided in recognizing media-fuelled scaremongering and misinformation for its coercive intent.

Mini-publics are convened most often at the local government level, especially for the purpose of envisioning future community growth and setting the priorities for development and spending. Even where representative governance enjoys public trust, deliberative democracy offers more timely and substantial engagement between public officials and their constituencies. Local governments have the best record so far of pre-committing to honor the recommendations of mini-publics.

Mini-Public as Collaborative Project

Andy Blunden's foundational concept which he calls a *collaborative project* (henceforth, just *project* because it can only be collaborative), described in the Introduction of this book, provides an alternative starting point for understanding and presenting public deliberation. This chapter will demonstrate that a mini-public is an *archetypal project.* Furthermore, the interdisciplinary project orientation advances Activity Theory from its roots in developmental psychology (Blunden, 2010) to open new pathways for narrative accounts and improvement of public deliberation. The project orientation will also inform the whole enterprise of advocating deliberative democracy, to understand its contradictions and opportunities.

The first task is to cast a mini-public as a project. This means recognizing it primarily as *an activity* rather than as a model of individuals, as a group, or as a functional system engineered to generate recommendations. The individualized (cognitive) perspective fails to provide the basis for conceptualizing collaboration and the collective emergence of new recommendations. Communication between individuals is often treated as a medium or channel for transferring packets of meaning. Models of deliberation based on individual preferences, autonomous agency and needs are typically driven by self-interest and competition, the antithesis of collaboration. The group perspective is tied up with identity, cohesiveness and boundary-setting which are distractions to the object of a mini-public. The group perspective is agnostic towards the emancipatory potential of a mini-public. The functional perspective portrays the activity of a mini-public as a sequence of interaction tasks that should be conducted efficiently (Hirokawa & Salazar, 1999, p. 169). The functional approach categorizes prerequisites and goals as inevitable rather than emergent from cultural-historical development. All of these other approaches are informed by empirical methods that focus on predicting and validating outcomes. The activity approach applies critical methods to explore and even instigate social action. A mini-public develops its mission, which may be far from clear at the outset.

The mini-public was originally theorized as a microcosm of how citizens should ideally talk to each other in the wild about an issue, but generally lack the vocabulary, information and methods to do so effectively on their own (Chambers, 2009; Fung, 2007). The presumption is that any random selection of people in the community would come to similar recommendations if they had the same opportunity to become well-informed and deliberate calmly about the issues. In this light, a mini-public is a simple instance of community-wide dialogue, a *germ cell* that at its small scale can be directly mediated by face-to-face facilitation. The smallest working germ cell for deliberation is a single oval table (see Blunden & Arnold chapter) comprising 7–10 participants and a facilitator.

Early deliberative theorists such as Habermas, Rawls and Bohman described that communicative ideal in the rational terms of "exchanging reasons." Bohman (1996, p. 25) insists that deliberation is about the formation of *public* reasons, which refers to "the *way* citizens deliberate [and] the *type of reasons* they give," which must be at least understood and acceptable by the community at large. The ideal has expanded further as practical experience has shown that a variety of communicative action types are useful in deliberation, including story-telling and rhetoric (Young, 2000). In addition, the procedural requirement for adherence to valid argument forms is now overshadowed by the normative requirement for broad inclusion in the mini-public, with facilitation intended to help participants bridge any gaps in deliberative capacity. It is the recognition of the diverse range of experience and perspectives that is important to the activity, not that the participants are customarily proper and articulate according to certain privileged norms (Dryzek, 2000, p. 73–76).

The central tenet of Activity Theory, articulated early by Vygotsky (1930/1982), is that the transformation of subjective intent to action necessarily requires some form of mediation that draws on cultural-historical resources. That mediating tool is objectified in the particular language, conventions, constructions and instruments of evolving practice and culture. Under the rubric of *reciprocity*, each participant in deliberative activity is expected to treat others in the dignified manner in which he or she would expect to be treated in return, to listen attentively and to talk with the aim of being well understood. These rules of reciprocity, and any corrective facilitation required, mediate the activity.

The table facilitators in public deliberation are very visible mediators to help improve the potential capacity of the dialogue and deliberation and the confidence that participants have in it. Facilitation structures the dialogue with exercises and turn-taking, and opens the dialogue with questions that drive it wider and deeper than it would otherwise go on its own. Participants ought to nurture respectful relationships between each other, regardless of their differences. Facilitators help participants clarify what they mean and summarize their conversational development, especially when plateaus of understanding (or misunderstanding) are sensed. Public deliberation by a mini-public presents as a mediated shortcut to the development of a community as a whole.

Often, mini-publics face the challenge of participants wanting to be understood by other participants who come from quite different backgrounds. They speak in different ways and draw on different kinds of cultural resources to help make themselves understood. Deliberation presumes that participants have the capacity to learn and explore an issue. The first stimulus to their activity is their gathering to address a particular problem or issue, which will reproduce some of the barriers to joint understanding evident in the community. Facilitators then intervene by encouraging storytelling, list-making and clarifying. This is Vygotsky's method of *double stimulation* scaled up from individual developmental intervention to project facilitation.

In the calm and unthreatening environment of the ACP, everyone spoke frankly and without anger or frustration. As the process unfolded, it dawned on most participants that they were having a transformative experience of public participation. As a result, two of their top proposals included the institutionalization and routinization of deliberative public engagement in political decision making, and the inclusion of education about dialogic and deliberative methods in the national school curriculum.

Analogous to Vygotsky's *zone of proximal development*, the development of a mini-public can be seen to be bounded by a *zone of deliberative confidence*. This is the gap that facilitation bridges in helping participants incrementally make good sense of each other across difference, which they cannot do on their own. Confidence refers to a social relation that binds participants to each other and the process, ranging from cynicism to full trust. Process design and facilitation help participants fulfill their potential to reach further into each others' lives and understandings to find common ground. As they continue to practice effective deliberation, their zone of deliberative confidence shifts outwards to afford the emergence of new concepts for action.

Some practitioners describe public deliberation as a method of harnessing a *collective* or *co-intelligence* to create an action plan (Hartz-Karp & Carson,

2008). Ignoring the cognitive overtones of these terms, they are synonymous with collaboration which presumes that participants build willingly on each others' wisdom. The co-created outcomes of public deliberation are sometimes surprising to the participants themselves and their benefits over other options may be clarified in new ways.

Participants who accept their invitations to attend a mini-public are typically motivated by a desire to learn about the policy context and to contribute to the policy debate. When the participants in the ACP began their process, they thought they were going to generate and judge proposals for democratic improvement in Australia. They did that, but research that closely examined the conversational record showed that they devoted most of their effort to learning about each other. Although they could have done more of it, they did raise questions about what facts and terms really mean, which was revealed to vary across the country. They shifted tables a few times and met other citizens who expressed both similarities and differences in ways that were unexpected. For example, some believe public education means increasing children's capacity to learn and live in a future society, while others view it as inculcating established knowledge and conventions (Lubensky, 2013).

The participants of the BCCAER invested substantial time exploring "representativeness" in an electoral system with multi-member electorates. Participants from the large and sparsely-populated northern electorates of BC formed an informal group that articulated quite a distinct concept of representativeness compared to the others. They wanted direct access to Members of Parliament, but just the minimum number to do the job. Due to their cultural homogeneity, they were happy to be represented by as few as two elected MPs (from different political parties) who would be expected to cover the whole electorate, live there, and be very familiar with its people and activities. This variation of concept led to an innovative refinement of the chosen STV (Single Transferable Vote) electoral system, to use population *density* to determine the number of MPs in each multi-member electorate (Lang, 2008, p. 96–98).

For the ACP, ten thousand invitations were sent to random households around Australia, and from those, 2763 applications to participate were received. Based on a survey they completed, 150 were randomly selected, but stratified by demographic categories (and one per electorate), to gain a proportional microcosm of the Australian population (Lubensky & Carson, 2013). The random selection was treated like a lottery win, and participants arrived for the 3-day event feeling fortunate to be granted a great responsibility. Some behaved initially like delegates to a conference, representing the views of their electorate as if they were elected politicians. But as the process unfolded, their care extended to the country as a whole.

In discussions at the ACP, it became apparent that people in different parts of the country valued disparate policy options for good reasons that respected local conventions, attitudes and practices. Often, these were tensions between rural and urban settings as with the BCCAER. It is typical for such options to be presented as mutually-exclusive, advanced one way or the other by political maneuvering and argument. The participants at the ACP accepted early that the best policy options benefit *both* sides of such divides, while avoiding unjust consequences to any camp. Of course, identifying options that satisfy this "common good" ethic is challenging, but the participants were able to cut through in a couple of policy areas.

While individual and special interests build a mosaic of competing aspirations that should be respected, the overall well-being of the community inevitably rises to become a shared objective of the mini-public. This mutual understanding grows session by session, expressed in terms of fairness, inclusion, freedom and other democratic ideals applied to the concrete options that are being weighed up. Participants in public deliberation neither change their fundamental political or philosophical convictions, nor are they expected to. However, they might alter their orientation to a situation after hearing new stories from residents who have quite different relations to its issues.

ACP participants recognized some differences as tensions that would never go away, as these are deeply seated in regional and organizational cultures and their historical development. The conversational record shows many instances of participants expressing this *dialectic* stance. Their mission became the identification of policy options which would stabilize those tensions rather than necessarily eradicating them to the detriment of particular interests.

The term *community* is bandied about too easily by politicians to mean nothing more than their voters. But many participants at the ACP demonstrated through their communicative actions that their concept of community lifted beyond the unreflectively insular or abstract to embrace the larger cohorts of state and country who necessarily have to get along with one another and conduct their activity alongside each other under a common policy framework. So in addition to their activity, as indicated earlier, the mini-public exemplifies a concrete germ cell of that larger concept of community. The participants come to a concrete understanding of community by the very *practice* of it, albeit on a small scale.

The emergence of a shared concept of community differentiates public deliberation from the common antagonistic approaches which stifle mutual regard and reinforce disharmony. This does not imply that public deliberation necessarily leads to communitarian outcomes. It is important that mini-publics recruit as many participants who value socialist as those who value free-market ethics. Activity Theorists see this as a dialectic tension in a community that has its analogue in individual psychology, in which the need to be "a part of" and being "apart from" constitute contradictory drivers. When conducted well, public deliberation encourages respect for both sides of such tensions, with outcomes that do not privilege one or the other. The underlying assumption is that these tensions will not ultimately be solved, nor should they be. They are fundamental to the human condition. Instead, a project of public deliberation finds ways for happy and tolerant co-existence.

A well-formed and successful mini-public does pass through the four project stages described in the Introduction. (1) The project is convened around a policy issue that should be addressed. The participants live in the community and have a relation to the issue, whether directly impacted or indirectly associated. They should care about the issue, but neither be politically involved nor have a vested interest in it. They gather with a commitment to collaborate rather than compete, and often do not yet have a clear concept about what they will do. (2) There would have been false-starts in the past, with the policy issue addressed in different political ways that were less than successful. For example, policy could have been set authoritatively, and then defended in angry public consultations. Also, past decisions may have favored certain special interests or political parties which then become untenable after a change of government. (3) A mini-public is convened as a reasonable method of stabilizing the situation, expanding the possibilities and recommending a policy solution that can be accepted by the whole community. The object of the activity is the deliberative determination of a just and viable policy, which takes shape as participants learn from each other and become more adept at and committed to their collaboration. (4) Finally, the outcome is implemented by the designated government or agency, venerating the developing work of the mini-public and the mechanism that launched it. These stages are complete for the BCCAER up to the first referendum. The ACP did not exercise the final stage as in the end it had no direct influence on government policy or operation.

A mini-public is an *archetypal project* because it serves as a prototype activity to mediate social movements. As described above, all the ideals of a project are found in a well-formed mini-public. Other chapters in this book describe social change projects of people collaborating to shift prevailing conceptual frameworks and their structures of power. In each of these projects, collaborators are motivated from the start with a particular shared problem or need and a hope of being able to do something about it. They develop plans by deliberating about the issues and reconstructing their project in response to advancing political and environmental events. Their missions gain momentum when the communities and institutions they generate become larger and more inclusive. But this expansion is limited when oppositions continue to constitute projects of resistance and competing aspirations. A mini-public can be convened as a super-project to compel voices from all sides into the deliberative tent, including those who subscribe to those competing projects. Mini-publics are an alternative to political problem solving and contestation, setting out to innovate a distinct shared concept of peaceful co-existence by cross-cutting prevailing project boundaries, especially those with strongly-held norms established historically in cultural development.

Barriers to Public Deliberation

Unfortunately, the advance towards widespread adoption of deliberative democratic practices is not faring well. It is failing to gain broad public and official attention and appreciation. Both theorists and practitioners are more concerned respectively with the ideals and pragmatics of deliberation than the social movement required to institutionalize it. They are generally poor at public promotion, especially in the political arena. Meanwhile, commentators and the public continue to jostle with authorities about policy settings without considering alternate ways of generating them.

The BCCAER demonstrates how even an exemplary, well-funded process needs advocacy to sustain its success. With single-member electorates, first-past-the-post (FPTP) voting and three major political parties, successive majority governments in British Columbia were formed with the mandate of barely 30% of the popular vote. True to his election promise, the provincial premier endorsed a citizens' assembly process in 2004 to recommend a new electoral system, to be then approved by provincial referendum. There were many newspaper reports about the progress of the assembly, who learned much about voting systems and their effects from academic experts and from the public through public hearings convened around the province. The assembly recommended the Single Transferable Vote (STV) preferential system, with a variation that suited the urban–rural divide in the province. The assembly was respected in mainstream media reports, and their recommendation was taken up favorably in published commentary. But the Government did not formally endorse the recommendation and demanded a super-majority of votes and electorates (i.e. 60%) for the referendum to succeed. It turned out to be successful in 77 of 79 electorates, but achieved just 57.7% of the popular vote, thereby falling short by only a tiny margin. Because it came so close, the referendum was repeated in the following provincial election three years later. By that time, few were defending the fine work of the BCCAER. Little public funding was allocated for advocating their recommendation and the politically-funded "No" campaign led the news with misinformation and scare-mongering. The second referendum failed badly.

The second round of public discourse, influenced negatively by mainstream media commentary, was about the outcome of the process rather than the process itself. If they were talked about at all in the end, the very capable citizens of the BCCAER were ridiculed and discredited because they were merely citizens, even though they gained considerable expertise about different electoral systems, and represented confidently the disparate interests across the province.

The common view prevails incorrectly that mini-publics are mere talk-fests by uninformed people. Many believe that nothing more is to be learned about long-standing issues characterized by polarization. No distinction is made between the constructive civil discourse in deliberation and the heated bickering in typical public meetings and consultations controlled by authorities.

Public deliberation constitutes a variety of designs and practices. Practitioners subscribe to several member organizations through which methods and experiences are shared. But there are few hard and fast rules about how mini-publics should operate or who should convene them. Some practitioners identify as change agents and promote deliberation as a progressive method of mediating social and political change. Some NGOs that convene public deliberation maintain specific ethical and ideological stances. Academic involvement in research or support of mini-publics is popularly accused incorrectly of a leftist agenda, even though the processes do not privilege communitarian over free-market outcomes. This perception of systemic bias may deter participation by conservatives, adding to the common challenge for mini-public organizers to attract attendance by young people and ethnic minorities (Lubensky & Carson, 2013, p. 46–47).

Since there are no laws in any jurisdiction to compel participation in a mini-public as with a trial jury conscription, many discredit the representative legitimacy of mini-publics, even though deliberation is not a numbers game. This is a difficult problem because for some only the participation of an entire community, as with the universal franchise of voting, is acceptable as a democratic act of decision-making. It is for this reason that the most notable mini-publics so far have fed their recommendations into a referendum.

Too often, politicians are accused of a lack of decision-making leadership when they suggest public consultation. Therefore, most officials believe that mini-publics erode their authority even though it has been demonstrated repeatedly that respect for officials actually increases when they engage the public deliberatively. For some highly contested issues, any unilateral political decision is fraught because the prevailing options leave a large section of the community out in the cold. Yet the short-term fix seems more acceptable than the more considered solution that can be sustained longer than an election cycle.

The expense and logistical effort required to convene a mini-public is often used as a reason not to do it, especially if it is at least partly publicly-funded. The cost of convening a mini-public may be relatively low compared to the high ongoing public and privately-incurred cost of a troublesome issue that is allowed to fester. Today, it is non-government organizations that raise the funds for most mini-publics, as with the ACP.

Many people are wary of participating in group activity. They remember their school projects when they were bullied by others. These patterns continue into the adult workplace, where boards and teams are often politically dominated by the loudest and most self-centered players. Stories of committees that suffer either from decision paralysis or group-think are generalized as typical. It seems that solutions to problems must always be "fought" over. In a culture that privileges the individual rather than the collective perspective, the verb *to compromise* now means "to lose an argument."

Residents' associations have formed in many local government areas as lobby groups to advocate for certain kinds of political decisions, especially relating to local planning and development. At the national level, media-savvy organizations like Avaaz.org (UK), MoveOn.org (USA) and GetUp! (Australia) have huge online subscription bases that raise funds to support activism towards policy change. The executives of these groups are successful in attracting media attention and present themselves as the genuine representatives of community sentiment. This claim is supported when they demonstrate themselves to be more in touch with their membership than the elected officials are with their constituencies. Other associations take strong positions that may not be shared so stridently throughout the community, such as towards heritage or environmental conservation. This might be tolerated if industry groups did not corrupt the system by inserting unethical financial inducements into the political pressure pot. Regardless of their representativeness, these forms of aggressive activism are accepted as the usual way to influence government policy, especially between elections. The introduction of a deliberative citizens' jury, for example, faces not only resistance from authority and public ignorance about its operation, but also the anger of activist groups that perceive their power to be usurped.

Two recent examples show the way forward. In Oregon, Prof. John Gastil has successfully established a periodic mini-public to review the ballots of citizens' initiatives and provide written statements to guide the voting public in the lead-up to referenda. Note that this is an example of deliberation in support of direct democracy (Gastil & Richards, 2013). In Tuscany Italy, Prof. Rodolfo Lewanski has been the authority in charge of government funded mini-publics convened by public petition (Lewanski, 2013). In the latter case, the agency called to account in any process must answer substantially to the recommendations of the mini-public, or be prosecuted. These are the most advanced instances yet of institutionalized deliberative democracy, in which real influence is vested in the mini-public and its application is promoted as the normal way of addressing political problems.

Improving the Activity of a Mini-Public

Approaching a mini-public as a collaborative project opens new opportunities for analyzing its limitations and for prescribing improvements to the practices. Most of the barriers described above arise because of distractions and contradictions to the emerging object of the mini-public.

Public deliberation should always be convened by non-government organizations that have no vested interest in the outcome. When politicians initiate processes of public participation, such as the Citizens' Assembly proposed by the Australian Labor Party during their 2010 federal election campaign or the Citizens' Juries about health policy in the United Kingdom under Prime Minister Gordon Brown in 2007, they are hijacked for pre-determined political ends and the distorted process is lampooned at the outset by commentators (Carson, 2013). When a government is the host of a mini-public, there may be the perception that it is influencing the outcome by biasing proceedings. While participants are able to re-center the dialogue with the help of facilitation to produce a balanced response, this self-corrective capacity is not evident to the public and its commentators who would discredit the outcome.

Governments should advocate and help fund mini-publics. When a mini-public is established by an NGO, but the government does not then celebrate its activity as with the BCCAER, the public may lose trust in both the final recommendations and the government. It is crucial that key stakeholders in a political issue, including the government, make public statements in support of the mini-public, preferably unconditionally in advance of the final recommendations, which may differ from what was promoted earlier.

While the design and activity of mini-publics are intended to be transparent, the experience of being a public deliberator is rarely told as a narrative. This is a holdover from the rules of a trial jury, which once empaneled is devoted to the process in anonymity. But this is not necessary in a mini-public. Through the use of retrospective documentary and special news reports, the activity of mini-publics should be conveyed in a sympathetic and honest light to the community. If most of the public cannot participate in a mini-public to understand its dynamics, then they should at least be able to witness it vicariously. Following consenting participants through a process can demonstrate how they learn and adapt to the unfolding situation, and show that they are never cornered or coerced. It should be made obvious how mini-publics work to adequately represent all relevant points of view, even some that are not directly represented by participants, in making competent and acceptable recommendations.

Too often, a mini-public is presented to the community as "an experiment in democracy." Such tentative language should no longer be used because it introduces doubt into public acceptance of the process and its outcomes, as if its concept is not full-fledged. It also discredits the many hundreds of initiatives over several decades from which practitioners have learnt a great deal about making it work well. Furthermore, excessive study of mini-public participants, such as repeated attitude surveys and interviews, distracts them from their mission.

A mini-public should be presented less like an academic research sample and more like the community's research team, fully responsible to the community rather than to the conveners for their tasks and the methods they apply. For example, regional community hearings were conducted by participants of the BCCAER themselves – *they* were choosing the objects of research (Ratner, 2004).

One of the most important acts in convening a mini-public is determining the headline question to be addressed. This provides an initial frame for the proceedings. It is always advertised in advance to inform prospective participants of the intended scope of their deliberations. It should be about an issue that concerns most people in a community, who should care about resolving it. For the BCCAER, the quest was straightforward: choose an electoral system. The Oregon CIR Panel was entrusted to study ballot initiatives and identify the strengths and weaknesses of various positions about them. Many other mini-publics are presented as a "visioning" exercise to prioritize the future agenda of a government body. For example, Participatory Budgeting ranks various capital projects nominated for implementation by a local government.

The ACP set out to answer the question, "How can Australia's political system be strengthened to serve us better?" The question was designed to avoid a framing bias for change, but its abstractness made it a challenge for the organizers to design a process that would mediate a pathway to recommendations.

All registered participants were invited to nominate proposals online. These were then taken up as the starting point for face-to-face discussion. Unfortunately, the meaning of the starting question was not investigated fully, so concerns about power and government structure were rarely visited – power is a challenging concept for political scientists, let alone deliberating citizens. The failures of government were almost always blamed on its agents rather than to the institutions of government that shape their activity. Most people could not even imagine a democratic government working in any other way than it does, and simply presumed that the version of democracy they knew was the best system on offer. Therefore, the opening question given to a mini-public must be meaningful and tangible to the community, where there should already be a shared desire for an answer.

The headline question serves as a symbolic beacon to draw the project forward. A mini-public should return often to the headline question to make further sense of it, to reframe it if necessary and to generate subordinate questions which, once addressed, help answer the main question, as with the BCCAER exploring the meaning of representativeness.

Some mini-publics convene citizens who live in distant localities and cannot afford the time away from their busy lives to participate. Online technology platforms for deliberation are steadily improving to include some of the social benefits and structure of facilitated face-to-face gatherings. As with the ACP, online assembly can be used as a preamble to a more intense face-to-face gathering of the mini-public.

Good facilitation is crucial in the success a mini-public. A tradition has developed for mini-public facilitators to take a low-key approach in running the procedure and to only intervene to quell problems like dominating behavior and unproductive diversions from the topic. The project approach suggests that facilitators should take a more forward role in assisting participants to learn from and make sense of each other better, which is what they do most. The mediating facilitator should be oriented more strongly towards the developing object of the mini-public by being more overtly supportive of whatever direction it collectively takes.

For example, as participants advance towards the conclusion of their process, they should be confident in the soundness of their collective argument. Therefore, facilitation should stimulate a logical dialogue that discounts rhetorical amplifications like over-generalizations and false dichotomies.

People often conflate normative and truth claims. In other words, what "should be" is treated incorrectly as fact, leading to fierce arguments between sections of a community with competing normative ambitions. Therefore, facilitation should also stimulate the recognition of normative and ethical distinctions. Many facilitators will require further education in these philosophical concerns to be able to guide deliberating participants.

Finally, facilitators should encourage more story-telling by participants that sets their beliefs, values and attitudes in a cultural and historical context (Black & Lubensky, 2013). This enhances mutual understanding and joint conceptual development.

The Project of Institutionalizing Public Deliberation

The above accounts are mainly about projects of particular mini-publics rather than the project of institutionalizing deliberative democracy as a whole, although they are connected (and clearly so with the ACP). Academic and deliberative democrat Peter Levine writes frankly that the work of deliberative practitioners "remains scattered and local because it is contrary to mainstream national policy. Civic engagement cannot achieve sufficient scale and power without reforms to our most powerful institutions. The way to achieve such reforms is to organize the…most active citizens into a self-conscious movement for civic renewal" (Levine, 2013, p. 4).

Why is the positive and true story of public deliberation unable to cut through the malevolent prejudice? Part of the reason lies in the institutions that spawned the concept of deliberative democracy: universities. The ease of winning research funding for "evidence-based science" over interpretive studies has seeded empirical work into *proving* the benefits and efficacy of public deliberation to legitimize its application. Although there have been some research successes, it is rare for results to be clear-cut. Political philosopher Hélène Landemore also offers the view that the risk of bitter consequences from a recommendation by a diverse mini-public is less than by a unilateral authority (Landemore, 2008). Nonetheless, public acceptance of the deliberative enterprise will rise on normative aspirations and pragmatism, rather than epistemic claims alone. The public *should* be more involved more often and sooner in policy generation, and the deliberative approach offers reasonable methods to do it.

For public deliberation to become commonplace, a social movement for it needs to form. That project needs to engage a critical mass of the population, including those who are able to exercise power through existing political structures and culture. In America, the term *civic renewal* is increasingly being used to name this project, in reference as much to the issues that need to be addressed such as inner-city decline, as to the active citizenship required to make deliberative democracy a reality.

The challenge is that public participation is often expressed in terms of methods that have been used in the past and have been demonstrated to be ineffective, or have been compromised by power. Positive stories from participants and organizers in current initiatives have to be shared more, bringing new language and ideas into public discourse. More historically intransigent problems need to be solved through public deliberation, and these success stories must be broadcast.

The participants in a mini-public are usually given an early pep-talk by organizers about expectations of civil behavior. Aside from a few people who are compulsive talkers, or who arrogantly treat anyone who disagrees with them as quite *wrong*, the vast majority of participants act into the convivial social world of dialogue and deliberation without reminder (Pearce, 2007, 29–56). The actions of kitchen-table hubris, angry letters to newspaper editors, vitriol on talk-back radio, heckling at public meetings and demonstrations, and all the other rhetorical habits are willingly set aside. For the most part, participants speak with each other in the manner that they would always prefer to be spoken to: calm, sensible, creative and unthreatening. In other words, they collaborate willingly and enthusiastically. It surprises them that they can remain actively engaged and acknowledged as contributors without struggle. This is what most people want to do, and the satisfaction of doing it in the context of political issues spurs them to want to do more of it. In exit surveys, participants in public deliberation often remember with delight the moments when the conversation flowed effortlessly, with new ideas and insights arising for everyone. Thus the motivation for the activity of public deliberation arises immanently through their evolving experience of it. Unfortunately, as with so many aspects of life, one must experience it to fully appreciate it. This is the cart-before-the-horse problem faced by the whole project of public deliberation.

In British Columbia, the excellent work of the BCCAER has faded into the past. The ACP did not gain enough media attention and government influence to have much impact. In Tuscany, the legislation institutionalizing their deliberative processes has a sunset clause and may not be made permanent. Citizens' juries generally have only local impact and occur only sporadically. None of these initiatives could bootstrap a social movement, which by any definition implies a groundswell of public enthusiasm for a different paradigm of social and political activity. Cementing public deliberation in political structures remains an elusive objective for deliberative democrats.

Because the deliberative approach is not generally accepted or understood, any project which works on the back of it has difficulty gaining internal traction. The ACP, for example, received only tokenistic endorsement from the Federal Government, and participants gradually realized they were never destined to influence real policy formation. Consequently, many participants treated their activity as the fulfillment of research goals and little more. Nonetheless, they still went about their activity with diligence and dignity. Both deliberative practitioners and participants need to know that their object is taken seriously by power.

It remains debatable whether or not a *true* concept of public deliberation was formed in the examples given here and elsewhere. It may be that the public accepts the outcomes of mini-publics not because of a growing understanding of the method, but because they occasionally trust the authorities who champion the approach. That is not bad in itself, but suggests the tentative nature of the institutionalization which deliberative democracy has achieved and suggests that many more high-profile deliberative projects will be required before mini-publics are accepted as mainstream practice.

Conducting mini-publics as isolated "events" stymies its institutionalization. Some local governments in Australia maintain a roll of residents who are willing to be called up randomly to deliberate about local issues. While individual participants may change, the mini-public itself is seen in this configuration as a more enduring fixture in governance.

Even with public participation institutionalized in the form of criminal court juries, over time the concept which was truly formed around it and cemented into our culture has eroded. Today, many people mistakenly believe that a jury is empanelled to decide the guilt or innocence of the accused, as a moral decision. So when a jury acquits due to poor prosecuting procedure, which is actually what they are there to assess, the public lambastes the jury for making the *wrong* decision, rather than the police for not carrying out their charge properly. Central to the concept of criminal juries was the protection of citizens from unwarranted power exerted by police and the state. But that is forgotten, and increasingly people mistakenly discredit the jury system as its original concept evaporates. To take a project for granted is to lose sight of its concept.

Similarly, the recommendation of the BCCAER was knocked back in the second referendum because the concept of that project was no longer being reinforced. The public largely forgot that they were solving the particular problem of unjust electoral wins in a single-member first-past-the-post system (Fournier et al, 2011, p. 155). With reference to the four project stages described in the Introduction, projects can be seen as having an evolutionary life cycle, with a (5) fifth stage in which ongoing development in the project leads to new issues that need repair, revision and repetition of actions. This may spawn new projects or a rejuvenation of the existing one. In the case of the BCCAER, there was no fifth stage as the project was left to whither. The conventional approaches of media-fuelled contestation returned.

Mainstream broadcast and print media accentuate conflict and rarely highlight collaboration. For public deliberation to become successfully embedded as a collaborative project, media coverage needs to change its spots. This is a project in itself that will require pressure derived from another social movement. Perhaps mini-publics can assemble to address this specific problem.

To be successful, the project for deliberative democracy needs to succeed in resolving some notably difficult policy impasses with the collaboration of activists and stakeholders. The projects of mini-publics must align in their objectives to the projects in the wider community for change and improvement. Some deliberative theorists are calling for a *deliberative system* that connects these various scales of deliberative activity (Mansbridge, 2011; Ferejohn, 2008, p. 204–209), the achievement of which may be aided by the collaborative project approach.

The nuanced concept-building and socially-cohesive ethic that defines a collaborative project is in sharp contrast to the individuated and bluntly competitive ethic that dominates contemporary culture. A world of more collaborative projects calls for leaders and champions who can *mediate* rather than command development. This is a different picture of power that shifts from coercion and persuasion to a more civilized and socially constructive stance. Power is not removed from the situation, but revealed for its detrimental effect of promoting partisan interests.

In reality and in the public eye, mini-publics need to be granted wider responsibility. Lang suggests that, "Deliberative forums would do well to build in mechanisms that enhance participants' agency within discussions. In particular, forums should enable participants to more openly and equitably construct both formal and informal agendas for deliberation.... In sum, more explicit focus on processes of agenda-setting may result in a more varied and responsive discussion among participants, and increase the legitimacy of deliberative forums as institutions for public decision-making" (Lang, 2008, p. 105).

At the heart of the problem of institutionalizing deliberative processes is the prevailing belief of many citizens, politicians and public servants that most people (the "masses") are stupid and policy decision-making should be performed exclusively by elites. Every day the mainstream media reports on "leadership" issues and accusations of its deficiency. Our representative system has been distorted to focus voters on the persons rather than the ideas and commitments that are being represented. At each election voters are encouraged to choose the most charismatic super-human, and then are surprised afterwards when the rhetoric and hyperbole do not translate to appropriate action.

More budding politicians should present themselves to the electorate as mediators rather than saviors of community development. This has already occurred in countless neighborhoods, but those brave individuals who have been re-elected after activating their communities have not been connected to a national or international movement aimed at shifting our democratic practices (Leighninger, 2006, p. 240).

Public deliberation as a collaborative project focuses attention on activity and subsequent outcomes with more widespread benefit and consent. Leadership power is still required to turn the aspiration of institutionalizing public deliberation into reality, especially in shifting existing structures and conventions. The challenge for the deliberative enterprise is to re-frame leaders as mediators of project collaboration rather than as political fighters.

Well before calling for a Citizens' Assembly about climate change in the lead-up to the 2010 federal election, the Australian Labor Party should have embedded a public engagement policy that would require the early convening of mini-publics in all major policy initiatives. The demand for this must come from a grass-roots movement that safely relieves politicians of always having to act authoritatively.

Mini-publics will enter the mainstream once its advocates recognize the need for a social movement that builds a broad social collaboration for it. A concept of the activity required to kick-start that project has yet to materialize. More stories about the actual activity of mini-publics from the perspective of participants should be told, especially through broadcast media. Through such narratives, the public should be able to imagine themselves as mini-public participants, feel confident they can contribute usefully, and accept that the enterprise of deliberative democracy is worthwhile. As Activity Theorists, we should communicate publicly and more often using the language of collaborative projects, especially in the context of public deliberation.

References

Black, L. & Lubensky, R. (2013). Deliberative design and storytelling in the Australian Citizens' Parliament. In Carson, L., Gastil, J., Hartz-Karp, J. & Lubensky, R. (Eds.). *The Australian Citizens' Parliament and the Future of Deliberative Democracy.* Pennsylvania State University Press. 81–94.

Blunden, A. (2010). *An Interdisciplinary Theory of Activity.* Brill.

Bohman, J. (1996). *Public Deliberation: Pluralism, Complexity and Democracy.* The MIT Press.

Dryzek, J.S. (2000). *Deliberative Democracy and Beyond: Liberals, Critics, Contestations.* Oxford University Press.

Carson, L. (2013). How not to introduce deliberative democracy: the 2010 citizens' assembly on climate change proposal. In Carson, L., Gastil, J., Hartz-Karp, J. &

Lubensky, R. (Eds.). *The Australian Citizens' Parliament and the Future of Deliberative Democracy.* Pennsylvania State University Press. pp. 274–288.

Carson, L., Gastil, J., Hartz-Karp, J. & Lubensky, R. (Eds.) (2013). *The Australian Citizens' Parliament and the Future of Deliberative Democracy.* Pennsylvania State University Press.

Chambers, S. (2009). Rhetoric and the Public Sphere: Has Deliberative Democracy Abandoned Mass Democracy? *Political Theory* 37:323–350.

Ferejohn, J. (2008). Conclusion: the citizens' assembly model. In Warren, M. & Pearse, H. (Eds.) *Designing Deliberative Democracy: The British Columbia Citizens' Assembly.* Cambridge University Press. pp. 192–213.

Fournier, P., van der Kolk, H., Carty, R.K., Blais, A., & Rose, J. (2011). *When Citizens Decide: Lessons from Citizen Assemblies on Electoral Reform.* Oxford University Press.

Fung, A. (2007). Minipublics: Deliberative designs and their consequences. In Rosenberg, S. (Ed.). *Deliberation, Participation and Democracy: Can the People Govern?* Palgrave Macmillan. pp. 159–183.

Gastil, J. & Richards, R. (2013). Making direct democracy deliberative through random assemblies. *Politics & Society.* 41(2).

Hartz-Karp, J. & Carson, L. (2008). Putting the people into politics: The Australian Citizens' Parliament. *International Journal of Public Participation,* 3(1).

Hirokawa, R. & Salazar, A. (1999). Task-group communication and decision-making performance. In Frey, L., Gouran, D. & Poole, M.S. (Eds.). *The Handbook of Group Communication Theory and Research.* Sage Publications. pp. 167–191.

Landemore, H. E. (2008). *Democratic Reason: Politics, Collective Intelligence, and the Rule of the Many.* Ph.D. Thesis. Harvard University.

Lang, A. (2008). Agenda-setting in deliberative forums: expert influence and citizen autonomy in the British Columbia Citizens' Assembly. In Warren, M. & Pearse, H. (Eds.) *Designing Deliberative Democracy: The British Columbia Citizens' Assembly.* Cambridge University Press. pp. 85–105.

Leighninger, M. (2006). *The Next Form of Democracy: How Expert Rule is Giving Way to Shared Governance...and Why Politics Will Never Be The Same.* Vanderbilt University Press.

Levine, P. (2013). *We Are the Ones We Have Been Waiting for, The Promise of Civic Renewal in America.* Oxford University Press.

Lewanski, R. (2013). Institutionalizing deliberative democracy: the 'Tuscany laboratory'. *Journal of Public Deliberation.* 9(1).

Lubensky, R. (2013). Listening carefully to the Citizens' Parliament: A Narrative Account. In Carson, L., Gastil, J., Hartz-Karp, J. & Lubensky, R. (Eds.). *The Australian Citizens' Parliament and the Future of Deliberative Democracy.* Pennsylvania State University Press. pp. 65–80.

Lubensky, R. & Carson L. (2013). Choose me: The challenges of random selection. In Carson, L., Gastil, J., Hartz-Karp, J. & Lubensky, R. (Eds.). *The Australian Citizens' Parliament and the Future of Deliberative Democracy.* Pennsylvania State University Press. pp. 35–48.

Mansbridge, J. (2011). A systemic approach to deliberative democracy. *Frontiers in Deliberative Democracy*, ECPR Joint Sessions. St Gallen.

Pearce, W.B. (2007). *Making Social Worlds: A Communication Perspective.* Blackwell Publishing.

Ratner, R.S. (2004). British Columbia Citizens' Assembly: The learning phase. *Canadian Parliamentary Review*, 27: 20–26.

Vygotsky, L.S. (1930/1982). *Collected Works of L. S. Vygotsky, Vol. 1.* Moscow: Pedagogica.

Warren, M. & Pearse, H. (Eds.) (2008). *Designing Deliberative Democracy: The British Columbia Citizens' Assembly.* Cambridge University Press.

Young, I.M. (2000). *Inclusion and Democracy.* Oxford University Press.

CHAPTER 9

Vygotskian Collaborative Project of Social Transformation: History, Politics, and Practice in Knowledge Construction*

Anna Stetsenko and Igor M. Arievitch

In this paper, we contest the currently prevalent portrayals of Vygotsky's work that present it from the viewpoint of traditional – cognitivist and individualist – notions of knowledge and science. These portrayals typically exclude analysis of moral, practical, and political dimensions and relevance of knowledge. In this sense, Vygotsky, not unlike Paolo Freire after him (cf. Glass, 2001), can be said to have been domesticated to suit the politics-neutral ideology that dominates psychology and education today. An alternative view offered in this chapter is that the Vygotsky's project represents far more than a set of neutral theoretical principles and instead, goes beyond the confines of a mentalistically understood enterprise of science. This alternative view has been initially inspired by observations of a uniquely collaborative history of the Vygotskian project and the impossibility to interpret it outside of the broader context of collaboration and practice (e.g. Stetsenko, 1988, 1993). Indeed, from its inception by Vygotsky and his colleagues in the early 1920s, this project has defied the traditional individualist and mentalist (and ultimately idealist) notions of science. Instead, evolving as a value-laden collaborative project immersed in the sociopolitical and cultural-historical practice of its time, it came to embody this practice, and ultimately contributed to it through an active participatory stance and civic-scholarly activism by its participants. Moreover, the Vygotskian project stretched beyond the confines of science as such (in its traditional mentalist guise) and instead blended the dimensions of theory and practice in its history, life, and products. A further constitutive feature of this project is its liberating potential rooted in ideals of social justice, equality, and transformation. Perhaps the most striking and unique feature of this project, launched by Vygotsky almost 100 years ago, is the close rapport between the history of how it has been conceived, brought to life, and carried out, on the one hand, and the core principles advanced and

* Reprinted with amendment from *International Journal of Critical Psychology*, 12 (4), 2004, pp. 58–80.

propagated by it, on the other. The social collaborative nature of the human mind, the paramount role of social context and history in the production of psychological processes and outcomes such as knowledge, the embeddedness of knowledge in practical transformative engagements with the world, and the inextricable link between practical and theoretical, material and mental, political and intellectual, social and individual – all of these principles characterize both the real life history of the Vygotskian project and the very gist of a theory developed in it. In this sense, the congruence between the creation of the Vygotskian project and the foundational principles developed in it provides a living proof of a direct connection between intellectual constructions and the practice of which these constructions are a part.

Revealing and reflecting upon this mirror congruency between the real life of the Vygotskian project and the knowledge produced in it can be beneficial for a deeper understanding of both of these dimensions of science. First and foremost, such an analysis can help to better understand that theory and science at large are not separate from life in all the complex unity of its dimensions such as practical goals, conceptual tools, political agendas, moral challenges, and ideological commitments. Such analysis can also help to strengthen and further advance the newly emerging trend in social studies, feminist anthropologies, and history of science that reject rote positivism and instead capitalize on science as a socially determined and historically contingent practice or culture. The potential contribution of the Vygotskian project to this line of reasoning is that it laid foundations for and itself embodied the notion of knowledge as a form of active transformative engagement (=meaningful activity) of people with their world – aimed at changing this world (including oneself), conducted in view of social goals and agendas, while making use of and contributing to culturally evolved cultural tools and practices.

Paradoxically, there is little evidence that the newly emerging trends in understanding theory and science are in any way informed by ideas and ideals developed by the Vygotskian school. There is equally little evidence that the Vygotskian heritage is being approached from the standpoint of the new culture and practice-bound understanding of science and theory. This paper aims to make up for these unfortunate gaps by highlighting a number of core principles that guided the history of Vygotsky's project and by revealing the congruency between its history and its core principles. Specifically, Vygotsky's approach (and the respective notion of knowledge and science) will be revealed as (a) a direct outcome of and contributor to social practice, (b) entwined with the practical, political, and value-laden contexts of its creation, (b) embodying this practice in the very fabric of its knowledge,

(c) entailing directionality, that is, a commitment to fostering a social equality-based view on human development and society as its essential and ineluctable ingredient, and (d) moving beyond the confines of science as a purist 'thought odyssey', and instead representing a transformative pursuit of new forms of social life. The ultimate goal of this paper is to join the discussion on the status and role of psychological knowledge in today's society and on the ways of making psychology relevant to concerns and needs of this society.

The Traditional Portrayal of Vygotsky's Theory

It is not a secret that psychology has never been at the forefront of either developing or applying advanced principles of meta-theoretical and historical analysis. Psychologists writing on history often employ outdated modes of analysis developed in reconstructions of the nineteenth-century physics based on individualist, mentalist, and context-independency assumptions about knowledge and science (cf. Danziger, 1990).

This is not surprising given that such assumptions comfortably complement the analytical schemes developed in psychology itself, dominated by positivist and cognitivist views on the nature of knowledge and mind. Equipped with the notion of knowledge as an outcome of internal processes in individual solitary minds, psychologists inevitably reconstruct history as being a succession of value-, culture- and politics-free individual pursuits carried out in a sociocultural and sociopolitical vacuum. Vygotskian theory too has been for the most part approached from such a perspective, resulting in a limited portrayal of both the history and the content of this project.

First, quite a prominent feature of many portrayals of cultural-historical theory is an assertion that it has been 'single-handedly' created by Vygotsky – a solitary and visionary genius neither influenced nor supported by any significant collaboration with colleagues and even misunderstood and betrayed by many of them (e.g. Kozulin, 1990; Valsiner & van der Veer, 2000). These portrayals of knowledge as products of solitary individuals follow well with the established manner in which history of psychology is presented in most textbooks – as 'Great Man' histories in which lonely 'giants' stood apart from his (always his, with no women among them) time and peers (cf. Leahy, 2002), making unique contributions due to unusual personal creativity, insight, or intelligence. This view is at odds with the abundant evidence of the truly collaborative nature of the Vygotskian project (to be discussed in the last section of this paper) in how it has been brought to life, worked out, and implemented by a group of people sharing a common research agenda and commitments.

Second, the portrayal of Vygotsky as a solitary genius is only partially mitigated by the notion of dialogues and communication of ideas as underpinning the development of science. From this perspective, theories are seen as influenced by communications among members of intellectual communities, whose voices 'enter' the knowledge construction. For example, Valsiner & van der Veer (2000) view knowledge construction as a dialogical process of relating to voices and views of others and thus acknowledge a certain social embeddedness in contrast to more traditional, extremely individualized frameworks. However, they focus on purely intellectual, mentalist forms of interdependency among scholars and inevitably end up with accounts that are social only in a limited sense. Indeed, when knowledge systems are viewed as systems of ideas and cognitive products of mind, then such knowledge systems turn out to be restricted in principle – that is, in their origins, mechanisms of change, and development – to individual subjectivities. Such individual subjectivities inevitably appear as separate from, though not completely independent of, the social realities. As a result, knowledge is reduced to individual creativity and style as the ultimate factors of 'primary relevance' (ibid, p. 34). This perspective reinforces the elitist myth, especially promulgated since Kuhn's influential works on science (cf. Fuller, 2000), about scholars as a self-perpetuating group existing in an ivory tower of academic pursuits whose views do not concern and are not shaped by any political underpinnings and ramifications of their work.

Third, historical analysis of psychological theories has not been untouched by the new winds in psychology, and like the discipline itself, this analysis too increasingly concerns the role of contexts and culture. A number of historical reconstructions of Vygotsky's theory reflect this trend and include a thorough analysis of cultural and social circumstances surrounding its development (e.g. Feigenberg, 1996; Kozulin, 1990; Valsiner & Van der Veer, 2000; Van der Veer & Valsiner, 1991; Yaroshevsky, 1989).

The laudable motivation to integrate contextual factors into accounts of Vygotsky's theory mostly turns into painstaking descriptions of sometimes even minute details and vicissitudes of his life and work, including accounts of his family history and all sorts of personal quirks. This is typically complemented by descriptions of various facets of the political and sociocultural contexts surrounding Vygotsky. Notwithstanding all the importance of such reconstructions (and their considerable difficulty, including meticulous work in archives), and the credit they deserve for expanding our knowledge of Vygotsky, an important element remains missing from this analysis. Namely, missing is an explication of the very mechanisms and processes through which sociopolitical, sociocultural, and personal life contexts can and eventually do make an impact on theories. That is, although this approach pays attention to sociocultural contexts in the production of knowledge, it does not (paralleling the discipline of psychology) rise above simply describing various aspects of these contexts, in often fortuitous combinations, and continues to view them as factors external to knowledge itself. Culture, history, politics, and other contexts remain to be thought of as external factors that somehow influence the process of knowledge construction but do not belong to it.

This is very clear in accounts of Vygotsky's theory that make no attempt to reveal whether, and how, the very content and major thrust of Vygotsky's theory are related to the way in which he ideologically and politically positioned himself vis-à-vis the turbulent, grandiose societal changes taking place at a time he was working out his approach. Notably, even this political stance itself is ignored and Vygotsky is portrayed as a mere 'sympathetic bystander' (Valsiner & van der Veer, 2000, p. 330; see also Feigenberg, 1996), never engaged in 'building a Marxist psychology' (Kozulin, 1996, p. 328), and instead pursuing abstract issues such as that of nature versus nurture. This goes against Vygotsky's staunch calls for psychology to create its own 'Capital' and his conclusion in one of his most fundamental works that 'Marxist psychology is not a school amidst schools, but the only genuine psychology as a science' (Vygotsky, 1997, p. 341). This also goes against abundant evidence of Vygotsky's truly remarkable political activism and first-hand participation in socialist changes throughout his life, documented by his membership, of a high rank and status, in many structures of power after the Revolution (e.g. in the Committee of Socialist Upbringing, the prestigious Academy of Communist Upbringing, etc., see Vygodskaya & Lifanova, pp. 60, 81). Thus, what is disregarded in these accounts is that Vygotsky (with his colleagues) was developing his approach from the midst of deep political involvement in the broad societal project of establishing a new psychology and the new society itself and that these involvements became transposed into the body of knowledge that he produced (see details in the last section). In other words, disregarded is the context itself, understood not as a compendium of external influences, but as a historical social practice (of which science is only a part), instantiated by people (including scholars) as agents shaped by history and shaping it.

Construction of Knowledge as a Collaborative Social Activity Imbued with Practical Relevance and Ideology

An approach to knowledge much more inclusive of history, politics, ideology, and practices of knowledge production has been recently evolving in psychology and other social sciences (e.g. Danziger, 1990; Walkerdine, 2002; Morawski,

1997, 2001; Narayan & Harding, 2000), as well as in the participatory approach that places issues of power and politics at the center (e.g. Fine & Harris, 2001). These works build upon many previous elaborations on the theory-ladenness of facts and observations, on the role of social factors in shaping science, and on the non-essentialist and historicized nature of knowledge. In this approach, science is revealed to be much more than an intellectual enterprise separate from the practical 'life' of theories and the contexts of their creation. The works that employ this practice-geared view of science are still the exception rather than the rule in psychology. In addition, these works do not include any accounts of Vygotsky. This needs to be amended not only to fill the gap in these otherwise extremely illuminating accounts of science and history, but also to do justice to the Vygotskian project that, perhaps as no other in psychology, directly embodied and implicated the placing of practice at the foundation of analyzing and doing science.

Broad Foundations of the Vygotskian Project

Although Vygotsky did not explicitly conceptualize knowledge as being a form of a practical collaborative activity that relates people to each other and to the world around them, aimed at meaningfully transforming the world in accordance with ideology-driven goals and agendas, his works and the works of his colleagues laid important foundations for such a conceptualization.

One of the pillars of the Vygotskian project was the idea that human development is based on the active transformations of existing environments and the creation of new ones through collaborative processes of producing and deploying tools. This idea is reflected in Vygotsky's creative assimilation of the Marxist premise that '…[the] base for human thinking is precisely *man changing nature* and not nature alone as such, and the mind developed according to how man learned to change nature' (Engels quoted in Vygotsky, 1997, p. 56; Engels' italics). This position set the Vygotskian project far apart from approaches prevalent in his time (and today) that place biological adaptation at the center of human development (e.g. Piaget). The collaborative processes of social practice (involving development and passing on from generation to generation, the collective experiences of people reified in tools, including language) represent a form of exchange with the world that is unique to humans – the social practice of labor, or human activity. In these social and historically specific processes people not only constantly transform and create their environment; they also create and constantly transform their very life, consequently changing themselves in fundamental ways and, in the process, gaining self-knowledge and knowledge about the world. Therefore, human activity – material, practical, and always, by necessity, social collaborative processes aimed at transforming the world and people themselves – is the basic form of human life that lies at the very foundation and is formative of everything that is human in humans, including knowledge produced by them.[1]

Because human labor inevitably entails the collective efforts of people, its development gives rise to increasingly complex social exchanges and to individual mechanisms allowing for these exchanges to be carried out. Both forms emerge precisely because they are needed to regulate the collective material production of human life. It was arguably the greatest insight of Marx that the social (inter-subjective) and the individual (intra-subjective) forms of social life became demystified as being derivative from (though not reducible to) the processes of material production of life. However, whereas Marx focused primarily on the dynamics, contradictions within, and transformations between the material production of human existence, on the one hand, and the emerging collective forms of its regulation (i.e., human society) – on the other, the Vygotskian project addressed two other forms of interdependency critical for human development.

Specifically, Vygotsky focused on exploring the functioning and transformations between the societal and the individual forms of life, relatively (and inevitably) neglected in Marxist philosophical and economic analyses. The idea that became pivotal for Vygotsky was that the social exchanges between people were at the foundation of all intra-subjective processes, as the latter ones originate from the intersubjective ones in both the history of civilization and of individual life (cf. the famous law of development, Vygotsky, 1999, p. 41). For Vygotsky, the transitions from inter-subjective to intra-subjective psychological processes by means of cultural mediation became the focus of analysis. Leontiev and other colleagues of Vygotsky focused relatively more on how the material forms of activity and practice are transformed into intra-psychological processes (in what came to be termed 'activity theory').

Thus, Vygotsky and his colleagues were arguably the first psychologists to expand the Marxist approach to further unravel the centuries-old mystery of human subjectivity – by revealing its origination in the processes of material

1 This theme can be derived from Vygotsky's (1997) ideas that '...an *active change in the nature of man* is essential. It is the basis of all human history'; and '[e]ach specific stage in mastering the forces of nature necessarily corresponds to a certain stage in mastering behavior' (1997, p. 55), with novel human development shaped by 'the fact of social life and interaction of people' (1997, p. 56).

production and social exchanges instead of viewing it as ephemeral phenomena detached from these exchanges and evolving on their own mentalist grounds. In the Vygotskian project, the genuinely constructive practical material processes as they evolve in history were shown to be implicated in producing the dialogical realm of human interactions, subjectivity, and social life itself, expanding the Vygotskian notion of knowledge as a collaborative activity. As just described, Vygotsky and his colleagues' approach is based on a thoroughly historicized account of human development as derivative from the processes of material production that engender both the social relations among people and the individual subjectivity, including knowledge. This view provides a non-reductionist ontological foundation for conceptualizing knowledge as emerging within the broader reality of transformative social practices and signifies a break with 'ontological mutism' typical of so many alternative accounts.

If this approach is expanded by an emphasis on the reciprocally constitutive role of human subjectivity in the emergent reality of social practice and dialogical interactions, then knowledge can be theorized in its practical relevance – as being immanently present in activities that people carry out to contribute to meaningfully changing the world. This also helps to mitigate a certain imbalance in the Vygotskian project in that it capitalized on individuals acquiring cultural practices and addressed less the agentive role of people in contributing to and transforming these practices. Central to this expansion is the idea that the human subjectivity, the collective processes of material production, and the social interactions all co-evolve as parts of a unified system constitutive of human social life, interpenetrating and influencing each other, while never becoming completely detached from each other. In this case, a continuum is outlined – from material to mental and from individual to social – with human subjectivity not only stemming from but also participating in and contributing to collective material practice, enacting this practice, at the same time as this practice enacts it. Then the processes and products of human development, including knowledge, self and society, knowledge and science – all appear as emergent properties of the same reality of collaborative human practices, albeit differing in degree of generality, power, and role in the genesis of social life.

This conceptualization opens ways to address the dialectical manifold transitions and mutual penetrations among all of these facets of a unified system of human social life, including transitions between knowledge and practice that take place in a constant, never-ending dynamical flow of collective practices. It also allows a clear role to be ascribed to the processes and products of human subjectivity, such as knowledge systems and theories, in the larger contexts of social practices.

First, in this perspective, knowledge can be explicated in terms of its ontology, that is, the very type of reality that it belongs to. Based on the Vygotskian project, the phenomena traditionally termed as ideas, theories, and knowledge do not appear as a separate mental realm detached from processes of 'doing science' in the world. Neither are these processes understood as merely being a precondition existing apart from theories and ideas – as is assumed in the mentalist view of science with its insurmountable split between knowledge and practice. Instead, the processes of doing science, on the one hand, and theories and ideas, on the other, appear as being of essentially the same nature, as made up of the same 'fabric' – as different levels of the same reality of human collaborative transformative activity. What is characteristic of theories and knowledge is that they come to reify these activities in the specific medium of concepts, models, and other discursive devices. That is, the seemingly separate realms of theories and practice are seen as differing only in details such as their level of generalization and the specific means that they employ in dealing with reality.

Furthermore, the processes of doing science are conceptualized not at a microgenetic level of actions, as in some models of science (e.g. Latour, 1999), but as transformative activities of people who ultimately pursue real-life practical and ideology-driven projects in society beyond the laboratory world. The procedures ('action') and the theory ('knowledge') are different in details but share a great deal of more important things – common roots, history, mission, orientation – in one word, a firm grounding in the world that they stand for, contribute to, and generally instantiate or perform.

Second, in view of knowledge existing only in the ongoing and never-ending collaborative practices of transforming the world, knowledge too appears to be a process rather than a product, a dynamical phenomenon that needs to be performed and enacted, rather than stored and then retrieved from some space 'in the mind'. That is, knowledge appears as neither an end-product, nor a separate 'destination' of ever expanding human practices. Even when the subjective pole of activity appears to be the final goal, such as in a scholarly activity of theory-building, seemingly detached from mundane practices, this subjective 'theoretical' pole is an important participant in and contributor to social practices and collaborative exchanges between scholars and the world. In this sense, knowledge and theories have agency and practical relevance in the world in that they inevitably enact, bring about, and foster certain practices in and visions of the world. Even theories that change nothing in and about the world do actually contribute to it, albeit only by preserving the status quo and preventing changes in it. In this sense, knowledge has an ineluctable practical relevance, always contributing to processes and practices in the world, always coming out of the world and returning to it (cf. Morawski, 2001). In this sense, knowledge can be said to have meaning and other 'inherent' features (e.g. objectivity, validity, certainty) only within these practices and relative to them.

When knowledge is conceptualized as a form of a collaborative social activity aimed at transforming the world, as a form of changing and engaging the world, it becomes particularly clear that knowledge is always value-laden and moral, produced and achieved only from a certain standpoint that inevitably is taken by those who produce it (cf. Harding, 1991). These moral standpoints and commitments are most visibly channeled into the body of knowledge in the process of establishing and elaborating specific goals of research agendas that scientists pursue. Research goals inevitably reflect moral commitments and standpoints of their creators because they address the questions as to how, what for, and especially for whose benefit each research agenda is carried out. This perspective implicates not only the answerability of human subjectivity to certain contexts and conditions that existed in the past or exist now, but also its addressivity, as each research answers to past and presently-given conditions and also envisions future conditions (and worlds), thereby by extension contributing to the creation of these future human conditions. Importantly, by being channeled into research goals, the personalized (but simultaneously social, in view of an inevitably collective authoring of knowledge) commitments and moral stands, through their representation in research goals, become reflected also in each and every aspect of research – from the more theoretical down to more technical ones, such as the selection of "data sources," research sites, methodology, forums of presentation, and so on.

Thus, in view of the primacy of ongoing transformative engagements with the world, the subjective elements of these engagements, including knowledge, never merely reflect, embody, or reify the world. Instead, knowledge embodies past practices, at a given point in history and in a given sociopolitical space, to only momentarily reflect these past practices in a form that can be put to further use in view of commitments to future practices and visions of the world. Individual constructs such as personal styles as elements in knowledge construction are not denied in this perspective. Neither are contexts and circumstances of knowledge production. However, both of these 'elements' are assigned a role that differs from traditional accounts and they are not seen as determining per se the process of knowledge production. Because knowledge systems are conceptualized neither as direct products of a mental machinery, nor as replicas of external influences, the mechanisms of knowledge production, in the Vygotskian account, are sought elsewhere. Namely, knowledge is conceptualized as constituted by a realm that stretches beyond individual minds and external worlds taken apart from each other – by the realm of activities (always social, collaborative, practical) that relate scholars to the world around them and to themselves. It is only these activities that produce, impart meaning to, and ultimately determine such social products as knowledge. In other words, knowledge is seen as collectively achieved in the process of activities by groups of collaborating individuals – projects that relate them to their world and, as such, come to reflect and embody, in an inseparable blend, both the socio-political and cultural-historical contexts that individuals are immersed in on the one hand, and the unique positioning, answerability, and agency of these individuals vis-à-vis their contexts, on the other.

Finally, seeing science and knowledge as social collaborative activities aimed at transforming the world is the platform from which to counter the now popular relativist stance of social constructionism (e.g. Gergen, 1994), according to which theory and knowledge are indeterminate as to their truth and value. The Vygotskian-based view, in contrast, establishes the ineluctable determinacy and certainty of science (in all of its instruments and constituents), including in its objectivity, value-, moral- and truth-related dimensions. This determinacy and certainty, however, have to do not with anything inherent to science and knowledge per se, but rather with them being elements in, and instantiations of, the broader realities of transformative practices in the world. Since the ultimate purpose and meaning of science are seen as grounded in its role and ability to contribute to inevitably determinate pursuits undertaken in a certain direction and with certain goals of creating changes in the world, knowledge too turns out to be determinate and directional. This is not an old-fashioned, positivist-type, ahistorical determinacy of science that purportedly can be established irrespective of a broader practice from which the conclusions about truth and value are reached. Neither is it the complete indeterminacy and uncertainty of constructivist accounts. Instead, it is a kind of historically and culturally foregrounded determinacy of science that has to do with it being a practical, goal-oriented, and therefore, transformative and value-laden pursuit of always determinate versions of the world. This inevitably marks science and knowledge with determinacy, directionality, and commitment.

In general then, knowledge can be seen as a practical act in the world because it always comes out of active transformative practices and always returns into them, serving as an important step in carrying out these practices and having its grounding, its mode of existence, and its ultimate raison d'être in its practical relevance within these broader transformative (inevitably political, moral, and ideology-ridden) practices. Moreover, knowledge not only provides accounts of the world, ascribing value by virtue of a selective emphasis on certain features of the world (cf. Morawski, 2001), but in addition – and simultaneously – embodies past practices and entails future ones in hierarchical multilayered patterns, thus directing these practices according to moral and political agendas and versions of reality aspired to. In this sense, knowledge is a living, generative, and deeply historical process imbued with human values and also linking the past, the present, and the future. That knowledge may appear as an abstract and autonomous reality detached from issues of real life practice, history, and politics is the vestige of a thinking shaped by the centuries-old split not only between mind and body, but also between knowledge and action, social and individual. This split is underpinned by a lack of understanding that all of these phenomena are just different dynamical instantiations of practice that form and realize this practice, as they are simultaneously formed and realized by practice in a continuous flow of social life.

Knowledge as a Collaborative Practice: Embodiment in the Vygotskian Project

The presented conceptualization of science and knowledge, derived from the cultural-historical approach, can be seen directly embodied in the very life and history of this approach. Below we briefly discuss this mirror congruency.

Collaborative Nature

Firstly, the profoundly collaborative nature of Vygotsky's project (to a large extent ignored in previous accounts[2]), congruent with the notion of knowledge and mind as collaborative processes, needs to be underscored. This project represented fruits of a work by a group of enthusiastic colleagues and followers of Vygotsky – Alexander Luria, Alexey Leontiev, Lydia Bozhovich, Alexander Zaporozhets, Natalia Morozova, Daniil Elkonin, Liya Slavina, Rosa Levina, and several others – who participated in discussing, spelling out, and writing up the initial assumptions of what is termed Vygotsky's cultural-historical theory. There are numerous first-hand accounts of how these researchers (first the famous 'troika' – Vygotsky, Luria, and Leontiev, later joined by the

2 For example, van der Veer and Valsiner state that 'Vygotsky's vision of a large collective working for a common cause was never realized' (1991, p. 289). Although they mention that Vygotsky cooperated with some people, this is not accorded with any significant role and, moreover, is de facto dismissed by characterizing this cooperation as 'religious movement' (ibid, p. 13) with 'Messianic tones' (ibid, p. 290).

other 5 to form the circle of 'eight' and then expanded further) engaged in group discussions, developing many ideas in a truly collective dialogue. For example, Luria directly states that many ideas have been developed in discussions and debates (quoted in E.A. Luria, 1994, p. 42). Vygotsky mirrors this perception when he speaks of 'the common path' in science and refers to this theory as 'our theory' in letters to his colleagues (e.g. to Leontiev, in 1929; quoted in Vygodskaya & Lifanova, 1996, pp. 210–211). A quote from Vygotsky's letter to Luria, responding to Luria's report on his expedition to Asia, is particularly telling.

> Dear Alexander Romanovich,
> I am writing literally in such an excitement that is rare to be experienced in life. I cannot remember a day with more joy and light. This is literally a key to so many problems in psychology… That this study is of primary significance is out of doubt, and our new path is now asserted by you not merely theoretically but also practically and experimentally.
>
> see E. LURIA, 1994, p. 65; emphasis added – AS and IA

One particular form of such group discussions was the so-called conferences where participants presented their research and exchanged views (e.g. Vygodskaya & Lifanova, 1996). Even when direct discussions were difficult to organize (due to turbulent times, participants often had to change locations, working sometimes far from Moscow), their cooperation continued through frequent visits to each other (A.A. Leontiev, 2003).

One further form of cooperation is represented by correspondence among members of the group (e.g. published in E. Luria, 1994; Vygodskaya & Lifanova, 1996), through which many ideas and arguments were refined, negotiated, and developed.

These letters (and memoirs, e.g. Elkonin, 1989; Luria, 1982) reveal another unique feature of Vygotsky's school, namely that its private and professional dimensions were often merged. Participants saw themselves as not merely colleagues, but as one 'collective' of friends, working and personally growing together, open to and even co-responsible for each other (e.g. Vygotsky's letter to Morozova of 1930 and Luria's commemoration of Vygotsky in 1935; both quoted in Vygodskaya & Lifanova, 1996, pp. 165–166, 330). These letters exemplify a unique blending of professional with private, intellectual with emotional, warm and confidential with determined and goal-oriented. They also reveal their authors' strikingly clear awareness of the collaborative nature of their efforts and their common path in science.

Co-operation within Vygotsky's school was far from being merely intellectual also in the sense that its members not only exchanged and co-developed ideas, but also engaged in a collaborative practical work. For example, they together carried out the first and often critically significant empirical tests of the new theory, such as Leontiev's study on memory and Luria's expedition to Asia to explore cultural-historical origins of thinking. They also worked together in clinics and schools, developing their ideas in and through practical work, for example, with handicapped children. Perhaps even more importantly, this group of people also went on to develop and broadly disseminate Vygotsky's theory during decades after his death in 1934. Although there was a lengthy gap in publications of Vygotsky's works from mid-1930s till 1956, his approach, contrary to a common misunderstanding, never disappeared from the psychological 'scene' in Russia. These works were taken as a foundation in numerous research projects, including the founding of research laboratories (i.e. at the Institute of Defectology and of General and Pedagogical Psychology in Moscow), which continue to be largely based on Vygotsky's theory. Vygotsky's early published works and unpublished manuscripts were in wide circulation among psychologists (e.g. the latter were available at the Moscow State University library and taught as the centerpiece of psychology at least since 1960s) and never stopped playing a formative role for several generations of psychologists in that country.

Continuing with Vygotsky's legacy was far than merely an intellectual feat. It was also a feat of courage in that his colleagues withstood the ordeals of a turbulent epoch, continuing this tradition even during the darkest years of Stalinist repression when this theory was under attack. Whereas there were many scholars, including psychologists, denouncing each other and confessing various 'sins' under political pressure, the absence of such denunciations by Vygotsky's immediate followers in the sinister atmosphere of the time (and the likely related amazing fact that none of them was persecuted, in sharp contrast to other scientific schools) is a token of their commitment and morale.

Quite revealing of the collaborative nature of Vygotsky's school is that even the authorship of its central works such as *Tool and Sign* is not easy to determine: because historical records are unclear, this work has been published with varying authorship (i.e., Vygotsky, 1999; Vygotsky and Luria, 1994). The collaborative nature of the Vygotskian project sheds light on why so few interpretations of his texts have been written after his death – likely because his followers did not see them as the remnants of the past that needed to be interpreted, instead employing them as the working tool for furthering the same research agenda.

The development of the cultural-historical theory after Vygotsky often included thorough critical reflections on and re-working of many initial assumptions Leaving aside the intricacies of conceptual differences among various branches of this theory (which remain vastly under-investigated and misunderstood), we can only mention that its foundational ideas, in our view, were preserved in later versions such as Leontiev's activity theory, Luria's neuropsychology, Galperin's and Davydov's approach in education and others.

We do not want to create a rosy picture of the Vygotskian school. Like any other collective, this one, in all probability, did not avoid conflicts and tensions (historical accounts provide some hints but are rather murky). All of these notwithstanding, this school seems to have been representative of what a development of genuine scientific schools might be – full of struggle and contradictions, mutual respect and disagreements, devotion and doubts (perhaps even betrayals), conflicts and challenges, continuities and disruptions, leaps forward and periods of stagnation. Reconstructing the full scope of the cultural-historical puzzle of the Vygotskian school remains to be the task for the future, demanding collaborative efforts by many scholars. However, what already appears clear is that the profoundly collaborative nature of Vygotsky's project and its many unique qualities as discussed above (e.g. the blending of personal and professional; the interpenetration of a life-long friendship and a commitment to a common cause; stark awareness of sharing common path) was not simply an outcome of their somehow unique individualities (if these are conceptualized as existing before and separately from the work of their life) but had everything to do with the kind of project they were developing. This is the topic of the next section.

Knowledge as an Ideology-Driven Practice

Just as knowledge can be described, in the Vygotskian project, as an outcome and vehicle of ultimately practical, inevitably ideological, collaborative engagements with the world, so Vygotsky and his colleagues' own intellectual products were by no means outcomes of their merely intellectual processes. Their approach and knowledge developed in it were part and parcel of the practical, and simultaneously deeply ideological and passionate, project that came out of drama of life, not of ideas, and that also returned to this life to transform it. This knowledge was a product, and simultaneously a vehicle, of their collaborative practical engagements with a unique socio-historical context that presented them with an unprecedented challenge – and opportunity! – to devise a new system of psychology in parallel with creating a new society itself.

As mentioned in the previous sections, Vygotsky and his followers were deeply engaged in practical endeavors and pursuits, first and foremost, in reorganizing the whole national system of education and devising special rehabilitation programs for homeless and handicapped children. Reorganizing and de facto creating anew this system of education – literally from scratch, overcoming strong opposition from old structures and attuning it to the totally new sociopolitical realities and ideology – inevitably was a deeply political endeavor. Given that the new political regime proclaimed education to be among its absolute priorities, Vygotsky was literally in the middle of sociopolitical processes, not just as its participant but as an important actor (e.g. likely associated with and supported by Krupskaya, a top party official in education and Lenin's widow; cf. Prawat, 2000). This civic engagement and socio-political activism were so central to Vygotsky and his followers, that these activities literally interpenetrated their academic pursuits turning them into a truly unique blend of theory, knowledge, practice, ideology, and politics.

Any theory always comes out of, participates in, and contributes to specific forms of life and society. Psychometric theories of intelligence are also part and parcel of social practices, namely those in which people are ranked along a continuum of purportedly inborn and unchangeable capacities of minds and on these grounds ascribed an unequal access to societal resources such as education. These theories, as most other psychological frameworks developed in the twentieth century, were also geared to the goals of social control in societies with an entrenched ideology of preserving the status quo rather than pursuing social transformations (cf. Danziger, 1990). Therefore, it is impossible to see and appreciate the unique blending of theory, practice, and politics in the Vygotskian project without addressing the difficult question about the ideology that its members were obviously so closely associated with. Too often this question is either excluded (in the narrowly mentalist expositions of Vygotsky) or presumed to have a clear-cut answer delivered from the Olympian heights of today's democracy presented as the ultimate model for a just society. This is a difficult question particularly for those who are superficially familiar with history of Russia and the Soviet Union or are personally invested in opposite ideologies. What is overlooked in these cases is that the ideology introduced by the revolution of 1917 could and in reality did appeal to many progressive thinkers, including Vygotsky, due to its emphasis on social equality, liberation of the oppressed (workers, ethnic minorities), women's emancipation, and social transformation through equal access to education (i.e., mass literacy). These features are not eliminated even in light of tragic failings of this ideology, as it became highjacked by a totalitarian regime (turning the Vygotskian project, similarly to the fate of other paradigms, into an arrested social movement, cf. Fuller, 2000). Therefore, perhaps the best way to capture Vygotsky's political stance is to compare it to Paolo Freire's pedagogy of the oppressed, except that Freire's ideas revolved around the need for a social revolution while Vygotsky wrote from within a society in which such revolution had already taken place.[3]

Here also lies an important and so far overlooked difference between Vygotsky and other progressivist thinkers, such as John Dewey. Whereas Vygotsky (like Freire after him) developed his approach from within his practical pursuits with a clear political-ideological agenda grounded in a socialist view of democracy, Dewey's works are marked by uncertainty. Dewey, though admittedly a more radical voice than generally assumed (cf. Westbrook, 1991), posits the centrality of inquiries to explore differences and conflicts with an ultimate goal of nurturing pluralism, diversity, and responsiveness. For Dewey, human action and knowledge evolve in the present, as living events that exist here and now, with neither much grounding in the past (cf. Diggins, 1994),[4] nor continuity between the past, the present, and the future. Moreover, Dewey's theory, though linked to and formative of a progressive view of participatory democracy, is less grounded in a program of actions with a clear ideological and political direction. Deweyan reliance on self-evolving adaptations resulting from inquiries and open-ended quests thus can be usefully expanded by goal-directedness, directionality, and certainty of Vygotsky and Freire.

Comparisons of Dewey, Freire, and Vygotsky are potentially important for understanding the present state of democracy and the role of psychology in charting policies and practices in response to the mounting challenges of a continuing inequality, especially on the global scale. In particular, the present dominant trend in social sciences to embrace the uncertainties and pluralism of knowledge and of ideology claims (e.g. in social constructionism and other postmodern frameworks), though important, need not to be the final goal. Instead, it needs to be expanded by the science of commitments and directionality to avoid the separation of theory and practice, knowledge and action, that

3 It is a mystery to us why these scholars have not been analyzed together. The similarity of their positions is so profound that it is hard not to impute (Freire's knowledge of at least some works from Vygotsky's circle. We have no material to support this hypothesis, except a little known fact that Helena Antipoff (1892–1974), a psychologist educated in Russia and likely familiar with Vygotskian works, later became an important figure in education in Brazil (de Freitas Campos, 2001) and thus might have influenced Freire.

4 Dewey's speech in December of 1941 is revealing when he says: 'I have nothing, had nothing, and have nothing now, to say directly about the war' (cited in Diggins, 1994, p. 1). Dewey went on to add that philosophy can neither discern the direction of events as they develop nor judge their meaning afterward.

inadvertently impedes progress in devising science and education aimed at liberation and social justice.

Returning to Vygotsky's project, the goals of creating a new psychology for a society that itself needed to be created, and the interpenetration of the two, guided this project and turned it into an instrument of social transformation and change. This interpenetration also defined each and all of this project's constitutive elements – its research questions and goals, its epistemology and criteria of justification, its methodology and concepts. This project can thus be seen as a novel type of psychology with a new mission, devoted not to pursuit of knowledge but to creating new forms of social life and practice. In carrying out this project of social transformation, through a direct linkage to creating new radical alternatives in the conditions of social existence, its participants produced knowledge of a radical sort and, in the process, changed and liberated themselves.

All major concepts and ideas of Vygotsky's project reflect its unique orientation toward freedom and social transformation and can be reinterpreted in this light. Human development as the social and historical process; psychological processes as collaborative pursuits of meaningful transformative tasks; teaching-and-learning as a social transformative practice that leads development; the zone of proximal development as a social endeavor in which new horizons of development are collaboratively co-created; new revolutionary methods of treatment through alternating social conditions of life; practice being the linchpin of theory – these all are examples of a direct mirror congruency between Vygotsky's project's own grounding in social transformative practice on the one hand, and the ideas and practice it produced – on the other. The key question of the Vygotskian project is telling in this respect – how to create psychological processes that set individuals free, rather than how to observe the existing processes.

Thus, knowledge about development of freedom and agency was derived from practical pursuits by Vygotsky and his colleagues to create the conditions for freedom in real life. This knowledge simultaneously was put to work and enriched in these pursuits to then guide new cycles of social transformations, thus closing the gap between theory and practice by integrating them in one ongoing never-ending dynamic cycle of transformative social practice, in which knowledge and actions are inseparably blended, enacting and generating each other. In a similar vein, understanding Vygotsky's work is arguably best achieved in pursuits of meaningful socio-practical tasks beyond Vygotsky. That is, the best way to understand Vygotskian project is to turn it into an instrument of social practice. This would continue the life of Vygotskian project and thus constitute a new turn in the constant, never-ending flow of human knowledge/practice understood as an active transformation of the world in the unity of its theoretical and practical dimensions. Kurt Lewin's famous expression that there is nothing more practical than a good theory could thus be expanded, in the spirit of Vygotskian approach, by the mirror expression – that there is nothing more theoretically rich than a good practice. The works by Vygotsky and his colleagues are a living embodiment of such a two-fold view, suggesting an alternative to psychology's outdated image and dubious social role in perpetuating the status quo in society. Instead, they help to open this discipline to the challenges of creating a new, free and equal – society for all – the challenges that are as urgent today as they were a century ago.

Postscriptum

This chapter is based on a paper that was originally published in 2004. No changes have been made other than to the first paragraph and minor editorial corrections. To explicate connections to the present book's topic, the following terminological clarification might be helpful. In this chapter, activities are taken as units of individual and social life, as they were in the Vygotsky-Leontiev-Luria school. Our take on this is that activities exist as broad social endeavors such as the Russian revolution – at the macro-level. They are instantiated in groups of people undertaking their specific collaborative activities (projects) within these broader endeavors – such as the Vygotsky's project of creating new psychology for a new society within the Russian revolution – at the meso-level. They also become instantiated in individual life endeavors, at the micro-level, as individuals participate in the activities at the above levels. Specific instances of activities at any of the above levels can be described as *projects*. An additional specification is that at the individual level, they can be described also as leading activities – or individual planes of participating in broader projects at the micro- and meso- levels. All levels are understood to be not separate but mutually embedded and co-evolving (for details, see Stetsenko, 2003, 2005, 2010, 2012, 2013; Stetsenko & Arievitch, 2004).

References

Danziger, K. (1990). *Constructing the Subject: Historical Origins of Psychological Research*. Cambridge, NY: Cambridge University Press.

Diggins, J.P. (1994). *The Promise of Pragmatism*. Chicago: The University of Chicago.

de Freitas Campos, R.H. (2001). 'Helena Antipoff (1892 to 1974): A synthesis of Swiss and Soviet psychology in the context of Brazilian education'. *History of Psychology, 4* (2).

Elkonin, D.B. (1989). Ocherk nauchnogo tvorchestva Vygotskogo [An essay on Vygotsky's scholarly work]. Davydov, V. & V. Zinchenko (Eds). Elkonin, D. *Izbrannie trudi* [Selected works]: Moscow: Pedagogika. pp. 406–433.

Feigenberg, I. (1996). *L.S. Vygotskij: Nachalo Puti.* Jerusalem: Jerusalem Publishing Centre.

Fine, M., and A. Harris (2001). (Guest eds.). Under the covers: Theorizing the politics of counter stories. *Critical Psychology 4*.

Fuller, S. (2000). *Thomas Kuhn: A Philosophical History of Our Times.* Chicago, IL: University of Chicago.

Gergen, K.J. (1994). *Realities and Relationships. Soundings in Social Construction.* Cambridge, MA and London: Harvard University.

Glass, R.D. (2001). On Paulo Freire's philosophy of praxis and the foundations of liberation education. *Educational Researcher 30*, pp. 15–25.

Harding, S.G. (1991). *Whose science? Whose knowledge? Thinking from Women's Lives.* Ithaca. NY: Cornell University.

Kozulin, A. (1990). *Vygotsky's Psychology: A Biography of Ideas.* Cambridge, MA: Harvard University.

Kozulin, A. (1996). 'Commentary'. *Human Development 39*, pp. 328–329.

Latour, B. (1999). *Pandora's Hope: Essays on the Reality of Science Studies.* Cambridge MA: Harvard University.

Leahy, T.H. (2002). History without the past. Pickern, W.E. & D.A. Dewsbury. (Eds). *Evolving Perspectives on the History of Psychology.* Washington, DC: American Psychological Association. pp. 15–20.

Leontiev, A.A. (2003). *Life and Work of A. N. Leontiev* [Zhiznennij i tvorcheskij put Leontieva]. Moscow: Smisl.

Luria, A.R. (1982). *Etapi projdennogo puti: Nauchnaja avtobiografija.* [The stages of the path: A scholarly autobiography]. Moscow: Moscow University Press.

Luria, E.A. (1994). *My Father A. R. Luria.* Moscow: Gnosis.

Morawski, J. (1997). The science behind feminist research methods. *Journal of Social Issues* 53: pp. 667–683.

Morawski, J. (2001). Gifts bestowed, gifts withheld: Assessing psychological theory with a Kochian attitude. *American Psychologist 56*, pp. 433–440. Narayan, U., and S. Harding. (Eds). (2000). *Decentering the Center: Philosophy for a Multicultural, Postcolonial, and Feminist World.* Indiana University Press.

Narayan, U. & Harding, S. (2000). (Eds.), *Decentering the Center: Philosophy for a Multicultural, Postcolonial, and Feminist World*, Bloomington, IN: Indiana University Press.

Prawat, R.S. (2000). Dewey meets the "Mozart of psychology" in Moscow: The untold story. *American Educational Research Journal, 37*, 663–936. Stetsenko, A. (1988). 'O diahrinicheskom printsipe istoriko-psihologicheskogo analisa nauchnih kontsepsij' [The diachronical principle in the historical analysis of psychological theories]. Zhdan, A. (Ed.). *Izuchenije nauchnih shkol v istorii sovetskoj psihologii* [Scientific schools in the history of Soviet psychology]: pp. 46–52. Moscow: Moscow University.

Stetsenko, A. (1988). O diahronicheskom printsipe istoriko-psihologicheskogo analiza nauchnih kontsepsij [On the diachronical principle in the historical analysis of psychological conceptions]. In A. Zhdan (Ed.), *Izuchenije traditsij i nauchnih shkol v istorii sovetskoj psihologii* [Scientific schools and traditions in the history of Soviet psychology] (pp.46–51). Moscow: Moscow University Press.

Stetsenko, A. (1993). Vygotsky: Reflections on the reception and further development of his thought. *Multidisciplinary Newsletter on Activity Theory, 13*, 38–45.

Stetsenko, A. (2003). Alexander Luria and the cultural-historical activity theory: Pieces for the history of an outstanding collaborative project in psychology. Review of E. D. Homskaya (2001), Alexander Romanovich Luria: A scientific biography. *Mind, Culture, and Activity, 10* (1), 93–97.

Stetsenko, A. (2005). Activity as object-related: Resolving the dichotomy of individual and collective types of activity. *Mind, Culture, & Activity, 12* (1), 70–88.

Stetsenko, A. (2010). Teaching-learning and development as activist projects of historical becoming: Expanding Vygotsky's approach to pedagogy. *Pedagogies: An International Journal, 5*, 6–16.

Stetsenko, A. (2012). Personhood: An activist project of historical becoming through collaborative pursuits of social transformation. *New Ideas in Psychology, 30*, 144–153.

Stetsenko, A. (2013). Theorizing personhood for the world in transition and change: Reflections from a transformative activist stance. In J. Martin and M.H. Bickhard (Eds.), *The Psychology of personhood* (pp. 181–202). Cambridge, UK: Cambridge University.

Stetsenko, A., & Arievitch, I. (2004). The self in cultural-historical activity theory: Reclaiming the unity of social and individual dimensions of human development. *Theory & Psychology, 14* (4), 475–503.

Valsiner, J., and R. Van der Veer. (2000). *The Social Mind: Construction of the Idea.* Cambridge: Cambridge University.

Van der Veer, R. & Valsiner, J. (1991). *Understanding Vygotsky: A Quest for Synthesis.* Oxford: Blackwell.

Vygotsky, L.S. (1997). The history of the development of higher mental functions. In R. Rieber (Ed.), *The Collected Works of L. S. Vygotsky, Vol. 4*, pp. 1–278. New York: Plenum.

Vygotsky, L.S. (1999). 'Tool and sign in the development of the child'. R.W. Rieber. (Ed.). *The Collected Works of L. S. Vygotsky. Vol. 6*, pp. 3–68. New York: Kluwer/Plenum.

Vygodskaya, G.L. & Lifanova, T.M. (1996). *Lev Semenovich Vygotsky: Zhizn, dejatelnost i shtrikhi k portrety* [Lev Semenovich Vygotsky: Life, activity, and some touches of the portrait]. Moscow, Russia: Smisl.

Vygotsky, L.S. & A.R. Luria. (1994). Tool and symbol in child development. J. Valsiner & R. van der Veer (Eds.), *The Vygotsky Reader*. pp. 99–175. Oxford: Blackwell.

Walkerdine, V. (Ed.). (2002). *Challenging Subjects: Critical Psychology for a New Millennium*. London: Palgrave.

Westbrook, D. (1991). *John Dewey and American Democracy*. Ithaca: Cornell University.

Yaroshevsky, M.G. (1989). *Lev Vygotsky*. Moscow: Progress.

CHAPTER 10

Change through Collaboration: Gay Activism and HIV/AIDS in Australia

Jennifer Power

The first formal diagnosis of AIDS (Acquired Immune Deficiency Syndrome) in Australia occurred in October 1982. A gay man visiting Sydney from New York had become unwell and doctors at St Vincent's Hospital recognized his illness as the 'mystery virus' afflicting increasing numbers of gay men in the USA (Editorial, (Menadue, 2003; Menadue, 2003a) 'Twenty Years', *Positive Living*, November–December 2002, http://www.afao.com.au; Menadue, 2003).

Gay men have been affected by HIV/AIDS more than any other population group in Australia. While the rate of HIV (Human Immuno-deficiency Virus) transmission among heterosexuals has increased slightly in recent years, the majority of HIV infections have occurred through male-to-male sexual transmission (National Centre in HIV Epidemiology and Clinical Research 2006; WHO, 2002; National Centre in HIV Epidemiology and Clinical Research, 2010). This pattern differs from that seen in other Western countries where HIV has moved much more widely into the heterosexual population and a greater proportion of intravenous drug users have been affected (Wilkinson & Dore, 2000; Centers for Disease Control 1985; Centers for Disease Control 2005). It also differs substantially from the global pattern of HIV, where HIV/AIDS has become a disease associated with poverty and underdevelopment (UNAIDS, 2010).

When AIDS first emerged in Australia many people suspected that it was a disease exclusive to gay men. Before HIV was identified as the virus causing AIDS, and before the term AIDS was established, the syndrome was being called Gay Related Immune Deficiency (GRID), the 'homosexual cancer' or the more derogatory 'gay plague'. Early theories regarding the cause of AIDS pointed to factors such as excessive semen in the bloodstream from anal sex or the 'fast-paced' lifestyle of many gay men (Seidman, 2002). Although it was not long into the 1980s when the first cases of AIDS among heterosexual people began to appear in Australia, the belief that there was an inherent association between AIDS and the lifestyle and sexual choices of gay men was entrenched in Australian public consciousness.

There were indications, and fears, that the contagious nature of AIDS would provide license for a formal crackdown on the recently won social freedoms of gay men, such as the decriminalization of homosexual sex in some States and

Territories of Australia. As well as threatening lives, AIDS made vulnerable the civil liberties and public acceptance of lesbians and gay men that had been slowly expanding throughout the 1970s.

It was in this context that AIDS activism first emerged. AIDS activism emerged as a 'project' responding to a crisis affecting gay men. The fact that there was an existing gay and lesbian media and a history of organized activism among the gay and lesbian community meant that gay men were in a strong position to respond to AIDS politically and collectively.[1] Activists began to organize not only to protect people afflicted with AIDS and draw attention to their needs, but to defend the broader social rights of gay men and lesbians.

Alongside this, however, AIDS activism developed into a powerful health advocacy movement that over time proved to be hugely influential within two other projects, the Australian medical research system and with respect to government directed public health activity.[2]

From the 1970s onward there was a rise in consumer-based health movements both in Australia and across the Western world. This occurred within the framework of 'new public health', a philosophy gaining ground in public health at the time that emphasized social justice responses to, and preventative action around, illness (Bates & Linder-Pelz, 1990; Crichton, 1990; Woolcock, 1999). But when AIDS first appeared in the early 1980s, the sophistication and breadth of the organized response to it by the gay community were unheralded. Over the course of the 1980s and '90s the Australian AIDS movement, which represented a highly stigmatized and marginalized sector of the community, was able to achieve a level of legitimacy and influence within both the Australian health system and Government that no other community or consumer-based health movement had attained previously.[3] This chapter

1 This point has been made by several authors writing on the Australian response to AIDS. (See, for example, Altman, 1988; Ballard, 1989; Misztal, 1991; Sendziuk, 2003).

2 A number of organizations were active in the response to HIV/AIDS including drug and alcohol agencies, the Haemophilia Foundation of Australia and groups that represented sex workers. This piece focuses on the work of gay activists in response to HIV/AIDS. The intention of this is not to disregard the important role played by other activists, particularly women, in the response to HIV/AIDS in Australia. Rather, the paper has this focus because it comes out of a broader piece of research looked specifically at issues of homosexuality and gay male responses to HIV/AIDS in Australia (see Power, 2011). For a broader discussion on the Australian response to AIDS, see Sendziuk, 2003.

3 While it is common to refer to HIV and AIDS in conjunction with each other, as in 'HIV/AIDS', to signify the medical and social association between the two, I have chosen to use the terms 'AIDS activism' or 'AIDS movement' rather than 'HIV/AIDS activism'. This is, in part, a stylistic decision. AIDS activism is shorter and more readable; however, it is also indicative of the fact

offers an account of the ways in which the Australian AIDS movement achieved a continuing legacy within Australian Government and health systems by creating new space for the involvement of people outside the medical professions, and demonstrating a role for communities, in public health.

Competition or Cooperation? Three Projects

Kevin White and Evan Willis argue that throughout the 1980s and '90s in Australia – and in other Western countries – there were three core *groups* competing to 'enforce their definition of the HIV/AIDS and the political and medical response to it' (White & Willis, 1992). The first of these groups was the 'inner circle' of doctors, scientists and medical researchers working in the HIV/AIDS sector, both government and private. White and Willis describe the second as the 'dissenting enclave' – those non-governmental groups such as the AIDS movement who worked in parallel with the inner circle, but also challenged their scientific autonomy. The third group is the 'exoteric' body of lay-people surrounding both the inner circle and the dissenting enclave. This 'exoteric body' tends to support the knowledge and values of the inner circle, and seeks to minimize the impact of the dissenting enclave. In the case of HIV/AIDS, the exoteric body was usually people with an anti-gay, pro-nuclear-family agenda – often religious organizations or conservative public commentators.

Robert Ariss (1997) similarly conceptualizes the Australian socio-political environment within which responses to HIV/AIDS played out as the state-medicine-community triad. Ariss saw that there were three key *fields*: the interventionist Australian state, institutions which supported biomedical definitions of homosexuality, and gay activists.

As White and Willis and Ariss lay out, the social, political and cultural response to HIV/AIDS played out through the actions of people from these different social and cultural locations – with different interests. White and Willis construct this as differing *groups*, each group holding their own set of values, their own power base. Ariss describes it as three different *fields*, incorporating

that AIDS activism in Australia emerged before HIV had been diagnosed and named. As such it is historically accurate to refer to early activism as AIDS activism. Further, before the antibody test for HIV became available, the only way of knowing that someone was infected were the symptoms of AIDS. Hence much of the stigma around AIDS in the early 1980s was associated with the visible attributes that came to signify AIDS-related conditions such as Karposi's sarcoma.

not just the players and their actions but their discursive/cultural framework in which the actions of these players operated (the structure of the state, the language of biomedicine).

What is common to both of these analyses however is the notion of both tension as well as collaboration between these different interests. AIDS activists, medical professionals and government were often in contest with each other. At many points they had contrasting perspectives on how the response to HIV/AIDS should play out. There were divisions and argument over where funding should be directed or what the 'best' response to HIV/AIDS should be. But ultimately each group had similar objectives regarding preventing a broader epidemic of HIV/AIDS and, in reality, the history of HIV/AIDS is much more a story of productive collaborations emerging between object-oriented groups which previously had very different interests (Ballard, 1992; Ariss, 1997). For this reason the conception of the social action which arose in response to the HIV/AIDS crisis can be conceptualized well in terms of *collaborative projects* being a focus of social action through which change occurs. It is an example not just of the emergence of a collaborative project in the form of collective action on behalf of like-minded activists, with shared goals, but a process of three quite distinct projects (medical profession, government, activists) establishing a basis for collaboration *between* projects.

The history of HIV/AIDS in Australia shows the way in which multiple projects within a community each have a different history, norms and cultural perspective, but that these shift over time in part due to the contradictions and tensions between these projects but also in part through their collaboration.

A Movement Emerges

AIDS found its way into Australian public consciousness in 1984 when it became known that people could acquire the virus through blood transfusions or donated blood products.[4] The first newspaper report on the possibility that the Australian blood supply could be infected appeared in *The Australian* on 2 May 1983, with an article discussing concerns of the British Health Authority that blood being imported from the United States might contain AIDS. As Australia did not rely on imported blood products, this article did not receive much

4 This occurred before the antigen for HIV was identified – although at the time there was a general medical consensus that AIDS must be a blood-borne virus due to the number of people who appeared to have acquired AIDS through intravenous drug use.

attention (Cook, 1983; Ballard, 1989; Sendziuk, 2001). But a short while later Dr Gordon Archer, Director of the Sydney Blood Transfusion Service (BTS), put out a public call for 'promiscuous' homosexual men to voluntarily stop donating blood.[5]

Archer made his call at a time when there was no test available to screen blood for HIV; indeed, HIV had not yet been identified as a virus. The only step authorities could take to prevent infection was to stop people who might be at higher risk of having AIDS from donating. Despite this, many members of the Sydney gay community were angered by Archer's announcement – not because they opposed having a policy on restricting blood donation, but because they felt those most affected by such a policy should be consulted about its terms and potential impact (Baxter, 1993).

Following Archer's rejection of an offer to meet with them, a small activist organization, the Gay Rights Lobby (GRL), organized a picket of the offices of the Sydney Blood Bank.[6] Held on 13 May 1983, protestors waved placards and leaflets demanding 'Ban the Bigots, Not the Blood' (Sendziuk, 2003).

The picket turned out to be a bit of a disaster for the gay community from a public relations point of view. Gay men were portrayed in the media as putting their own interests and needs above public health. However, a few months later a much bigger group of activists – including members of the Gay Rights Lobby, the Gay Counselling Service, the Gay Solidarity Group, the Metropolitan Community Church[7] and the Gay Business Association – met to discuss the next steps in the 'AIDS campaign'. From this meeting, the NSW AIDS Action Committee (AAC) was established (Baxter, 1993; Sendziuk, 2003). Other states soon followed, establishing their own community-led AIDS committees and groups.

---

5 Some within the BTS did not support Archer in his assertions. For example, the chair of the National Blood Transfusion Service (NBTS), David Penington, publicly responded that there was no risk of Australia's blood supply being infected with HIV because blood donation in Australia had always been entirely voluntary (apart from a short-lived experiment with a professional donor panel in 1938) (Ballard, 1999, p. 245). Penington was obviously making the assumption that the type of people who would be inclined to sell their blood for cash would be drug users or other people at greater risk of HIV.

6 The Melbourne Blood Bank did agree to a meeting with gay community activists. There were no similar protests to those that took place in Sydney (Phil Carswell, Personal communication, 25 October 2006, Melbourne).

7 Metropolitan Community Church (MCC) Sydney is a Christian church that operates specifically to reach people excluded by established religious groups on the basis of sexuality. The MCC was an active part of the gay and lesbian community in the 1980s (and still is today) and participated in AIDS-movement initiatives.

The issue of blood donation bans set the focus of AIDS activism because it played into concerns that homophobia and discrimination against gay men would influence medical and government responses to HIV. It also demonstrated that gay men were unlikely to be consulted about decisions affecting them unless they were politically organized to intervene. In this respect, the blood bank picket turned out to be the first important action of the AIDS movement in Australia, marking the birth of this project.

The first success of the Sydney AAC was convincing the NSW Minister for Health to establish a ministerial advisory committee: the AIDS Consultative Committee. Membership of this committee included NSW Department of Health staff, medical specialists and representatives of the Sydney AAC (Menadue, 2003a). Activist Ken Davis, who was involved in the ACC, recalls: 'That was the genesis of AIDS activism, that small (inappropriate) picket of the blood bank that I wasn't at...that precipitated the State Government having to have a meeting between government, medical people and gay men'.[8]

Establishing Legitimacy

The AIDS movement had been well organized from the early 1980s, with the establishment of several State-based collectives: the Victorian AIDS Action Committee (VAAC), the NSW AIDS Action Committee (NSW AAC) and similar groups in other States.[9] By the mid-1980s several of these groups had made the decision to create more formalized structures, in large part so they would be eligible to receive government funding for their health-education campaigns but also to establish a more 'legitimate' public face for their action. The Victorian AIDS Action Committee became the Victorian AIDS Council

8 Ken Davis, Interview with the author, 4 November 2004.

9 This analysis focuses predominantly on Sydney and Melbourne as ACON and the VAC were the largest AIDS organizations and both provide a clear example of the strategies undertaken by the AIDS movement. There were, however, organizations similar to VAC and ACON that received government funding in Perth, Adelaide and Canberra. The Queensland story is a little different as this State was subject to the reign of ultra-conservative Premier Joh Bjelke-Petersen throughout much of the 1980s. The Queensland Government for many years actively campaigned against the involvement of the gay community in the AIDS response. Homosexuality remained on the criminal code in that State until 1990. Nonetheless, there was a community response to AIDS in Queensland. The Federal Government was able to override Bjelke-Petersen to some extent by funneling money to the Queensland AIDS Council through a religious charity (Phil Carswell, Interview with the author, 23 July 2005).

(VAC) in 1984[10] and the NSW AAC was reformed into the AIDS Council of New South Wales (ACON) in February 1985 (Sendziuk, 2003). Other states and territories soon followed a similar process. Historian Graham Willett observed that AIDS activism, 'was transforming the activists as much as they were transforming the world'. Willet writes that,

> It is not an accident that a shift from 'action committee' to 'AIDS Council' took place in late 1984 and early 1985 as the government and gay activists started to work more closely together. The shift in nomenclature marked a shift in outlook by the organizations and those running them. Adam Carr, who first proposed the change, saw 'council' as evoking respectability and authority, a gathering of experts and their expertise, appealing more to governments, bureaucracies and medical professionals than action committees.
>
> WILLETT, 2000

Building a working relationship with the Federal Government proved to be an extremely important tactic of the AIDS movement in terms of gaining access to funding and political power, and establishing the public profile of activists.[11] For instance, in late 1984, representatives from the Victorian and NSW AIDS Action Committees, Phil Carswell and Lex Watson, were invited to join the new

---

10 Phil Carswell, Interview with the author, 23 July 2005; Phil Carswell, Excerpt from personal notes made for a presentation on the history of the AIDS epidemic at Sydney University, 2005c; Altman, 1990.

11 Despite the political authority afforded by the AIDS movement's relationship with the Federal Government, questions began to be raised about the limitations imposed on the movement once they were operating with government funds and had activists sitting on official advisory boards. There were fears that the movement had become 'coopted' by government and therefore less able to advocate independently the interests of the gay community. Although I do not discuss these issues further in this text, they are important considerations in terms of studying movement building in the longer term. In Australia, concerns that government funding had the potential to demobilize collective action were, to some degree, justified when the Liberal Party won the federal election in 1996, under the leadership of John Howard. The Howard regime began a program of cutting funds to non-governmental organizations. Organizations that publicly criticized the Government, or were actively campaigning against government initiatives, began to feel that their funding was under threat. Many argue that the political efficacy of non-governmental agencies was significantly hampered in this political climate in a way that it was not under the Labor Governments of the 1980s and early 1990s. As AIDS organizations were still partially funded by the Federal Government, some argued that the capacity of the AIDS movement was undermined by the reliance of these organizations on government funds. Even if activists not affiliated with a formal AIDS organization were to

National Advisory Committee on AIDS (NACAIDS). In the mid-1980s the Federal Government agreed to follow the recommendations of a strategy paper devised by the Victorian AIDS Action Council and support a community-based model of HIV prevention (Ballard, 1992). A cost-sharing agreement was enacted between the Federal and State governments through which the Victorian AIDS Council and the AIDS Council of NSW received establishment grants of $56,000 and $74,000, respectively. This gave the AIDS movement funds with which to create increasingly sophisticated HIV/AIDS education materials and programs (Ballard, 1992; Sendziuk, 2003). The government *as well* was taking an unprecedented initiative in providing funds and formal legitimacy to such a stigmatized and previously informal group of activists. So important moves towards collaboration came from both sides at this point.

What was significant about this is not just that the AIDS movement received money and political power, but that for the first time gay community organizations had both resources and a legitimate public profile. In the past when people spoke about homosexuality in the media or government, they generally consulted legal or psychological experts about the 'condition' of homosexuality. It would have been very rare prior to HIV/AIDS for gay men or lesbians themselves to be consulted about 'gay issues'. When HIV/AIDS emerged it became clear to members of the gay community that not being consulted could have devastating implications for gay and lesbian rights. Creating a public profile for the gay community as 'experts' on homosexuality therefore became imperative for the AIDS movement. The legitimacy offered by both access to public funds and the newfound financial capacity to promote themselves as important contributors to government discourse and policy about HIV/AIDS provided a platform for activists to establish themselves as expert commentators on both homosexuality and HIV/AIDS.

De-Medicalization of AIDS?

The first HIV antibody test – the ELISA[12] test – began to be used in Australia in April 1985. As this was some years before any effective antiviral treatments

take action against the Government around AIDS, it arguably could threaten the funds of organizations such as ACON and VAC (Staples, 2006; Tabone, 2004). That said, most people interviewed for this text who were involved with ACON and VAC in the early 1980s acknowledged that the partnership with the Labor Federal Government in the 1980s was politically advantageous and progressive – even radical – for its time (Ken Davis, Interview with the author, 4 November 2004).

12 ELISA is an abbreviation for 'enzyme-linked immunosorbent assay'.

were available,[13] the arrival of the ELISA test meant that people could be diagnosed as HIV positive but not treated for the virus. For individuals who tested positive, doctors could do little besides advising on healthy lifestyle and nutrition choices and provide ongoing surveillance of related illnesses. An early diagnosis of HIV was not likely to change an individual's long-term prognosis. Despite this, medical authorities and many individual doctors strongly advocated the HIV test, with the Albion Street Clinic in Sydney (a prominent HIV/AIDS and sexual health clinic) releasing a pamphlet that proclaimed 'A Simple Blood Test Could Save Your Life' (Sendziuk, 2003).

Testing became the subject of much debate among AIDS activists. For many people in the gay community, the reasons *not* to submit to an HIV test far outweighed the reasons for testing. As well as unease about the stress and emotional trauma that would likely be associated with a positive diagnosis, people were concerned about the discrimination they might face if they were known to have HIV. Conversely, other members of the community felt that encouraging testing would help build knowledge about the illness.

As with the blood bank bans, apprehension about testing was indicative of fears that the marginalized status of gay men would allow for more punitive public health measures than would be considered acceptable for other groups in the population. There were concerns that the perception that gay men were somehow responsible for HIV/AIDS would lead to calls for public identification of people with HIV, or other restrictive measures such as quarantining.

Concerns about HIV testing were magnified when, in 1985, the NSW Government proposed legislation that would make it mandatory for doctors to supply the Government with the names of all people testing positive to HIV (commonly referred to as compulsory notification legislation). This raised alarm, with many gay men cancelling appointments for testing or demanding their medical records be destroyed (McDonnell, 1985; Green, 1985). AIDS activists voiced opposition to the proposal, announcing publicly that they did not trust the NSW health authorities to retain the confidentiality of medical records (Lex Watson cited in Sanderson, 1985).

This proposal had come on the back of a 1984 containment strategy released by the Federal Government AIDS Task Force that involved the establishment of wide-scale HIV-testing programs and a system of compulsory notification to the Health Department of positive results so the epidemic could be monitored (Sendziuk, 2003).

13 The first breed of HIV medications – a drug known as Zidovudine (or more commonly AZT) – began to be trialed in the United States in 1986 but did not become widely available in Australia until the 1990s. (Sendziuk, 2003).

The AIDS Task Force was an advisory group established by the Federal Health Minister to prepare advice for the Government on scientific matters relating to HIV/AIDS. The committee comprised practising and academic medical professionals. It was chaired by Professor David Penington, a haematologist working in academia and former Chair of the National Blood Transfusion Service (NBTS) (Ariss, 1997). Some in the medical field, including Penington, began to investigate methods by which identified 'at risk' populations, such as gay men, injecting drug users and prison inmates, could be compelled to submit for testing (Sendziuk, 2003). While this action didn't move beyond the 'investigation' stage, the fact that AIDS Task Force members held a high level of public authority meant the issue maintained a profile in media and government. For instance, the issue was picked up by media in 1985 with some commentators likening HIV testing to the compulsory chest X-rays used to screen for tuberculosis in the 1950s. It was argued that as Australia had used compulsory medical screening before there could be no claims of discrimination by the gay community if it were once again adopted for AIDS. As a journalist writing in *The Age* put it: 'Compulsion is never attractive in a "rights" minded society, but we have come to accept it in many areas of public health and safety where the alternatives may be considered worse' (Barnard, 1985).

The idea of wide-scale mandatory HIV testing was never adopted by the Australian Government due to the enormous cost of such a venture, as well as the legal and logistical barriers. However, in July 1986, Health Minister Blewett, realizing the issue was gaining attention, invited a range of stakeholders – community activists, medical professionals and government representatives – to attend a summit, with the aim of achieving consensus on processes for HIV testing in Australia. At the summit, it was agreed that testing should remain voluntary and take place only with informed consent and with pre- and post-test patient counseling (Ballard, 1992).

This outcome did not entirely resolve the issue. In early 1987, the Victorian Government proposed changes to infectious diseases legislation that would have made testing of individuals participating in 'high risk' behavior mandatory. The Victorian AIDS Council mounted a campaign against this, arguing that the delineation of 'high risk' behavior was a highly subjective exercise – one that had potential to be an exercise in moral persecution rather than sensible public health. Following an intensive lobbying effort, this section of the legislation was eventually dropped from the draft bill (Carr, 1987). However, the issue was raised again in 1988 with the release of a Federal Government discussion paper on the response to HIV/AIDS, which was essentially a draft of the First National AIDS Strategy. In response to the draft strategy, the Federal Opposition

Liberal Party published an alternative discussion paper that advocated a medicalized, conventional public health approach to HIV and proposed mandatory HIV testing of all people with sexually transmitted infections and those showing symptoms of AIDS. The paper also recommended diverting AIDS funds away from community education in favor of much broader testing regimes (McCauley, 1988).

Community education, however, was the approach adopted by the AIDS movement. Throughout the 1980s (and still today) the AIDS Councils took a lead in developing HIV education and prevention campaigns targeting the gay community. Largely through their efforts – and those of similar groups in other countries – the catch-cry of 'safe-sex'[14] came to define the AIDS era (Altman, 1994). The AIDS councils and other gay-led groups promoted safe-sex as erotic and pleasurable, often using explicit imagery in their campaigns to encourage condom use and normalize it as part of sexual practice. Humor and parody were also important in these campaigns, allowing for a less serious and more engaging approach to the issues, even in a climate that had been dominated by fear and illness (Sendziuk, 2003).

While safe-sex promotion is today a commonly accepted approach to HIV prevention, in the 1980s it was an approach that had little scientific evidence supporting its efficacy in disease prevention. Some members of the medical community were not convinced that safe sex alone would be an effective HIV-prevention strategy (Ariss, 1997). They considered community education to be a risky and unscientific approach to HIV prevention, referring to government funding for gay community groups as the 'de-medicalization' of AIDS. These doctors advocated more conventional public health measures that relied on strict observation of clinical symptoms of AIDS, facilitated by patient monitoring and testing, and money to be dedicated to research on medical treatments and vaccines (Emke, 1992).

At the Third National Conference on AIDS in 1988, Dr Bryce Phillips, the Federal President of the Australian Medical Association (AMA), addressed the meeting. In his speech, he criticized the separation of the 'medical model' and the 'community education model', expressing concern that this kept medical professionals out of the loop in terms of provision of information and education on HIV/AIDS. He stated:

14 During the 1990s, health education workers and community groups began to use the term 'safer sex' instead of 'safe sex', acknowledging that there is some risk of STI and HIV transmission involved in all sexual encounters, although this is minimal if safer-sex practices are adopted.

> The 'demedicalization' of AIDS in Australia over the past four years must be redressed immediately. AIDS has major social and moral implications, but it is an infectious disease and the medical profession has a central role [to play] in its prevention and management. In carrying out this role the doctor has a responsibility both to the individual and [to] the community.
>
> PHILLIPS, 1988

Phillips campaigned publicly on this issue, informing an article published in *The Bulletin* magazine in April 1989, which stated: 'Australian doctors want a much greater emphasis on testing for the virus. And they want the disease to be notifiable. They see the government's emphasis on counseling and advertising as providing social solutions to medical problems' (Barnett, 1989). Phillips was joined in this campaign by the AMA Vice-President, Bruce Shepherd (who went on to become AMA President in May 1990) and the President of the Australian Association of Surgeons (AAS), Dr David McNicol, who in 1989 began to campaign for compulsory HIV testing of all surgical patients. Both were openly critical of the Federal Government's response to HIV/AIDS. The AMA and the AAS clearly wanted HIV/AIDS to be viewed as a biomedical problem that neither politicians nor community activists had the expertise, or right, to be involved with.

Debates about HIV testing and the '(de-)medicalization' of HIV were fundamentally a fight for influence and funding as each side sought a greater share of available government money to shape the HIV/AIDS response in their vision (as is the nature of politics). But these debates were also part of a struggle around who would or should be considered a legitimate 'expert' on HIV/AIDS (Misztal, 1990; Ballard, 1998). As Dennis Altman has written:

> In the early developments around AIDS one can see the outlines of a struggle for control, in which medical professionals, government officials, affected communities, and traditional sources of moral authority, particularly churches, vied to be seen as the 'experts' on the new disease. How AIDS was conceptualized was an essential tool in a sometimes very bitter struggle: was it to be understood as a primarily bio-medical problem, in which case its control should be under that of the medical establishment, or was it rather as most community-based groups argued a social and political issue, which required a much greater variety of expertise.
>
> ALTMAN, 1994, P. 26

The more conservative medical authorities and the AIDS movement represented two ends of a spectrum of opinion on how best to respond to HIV/AIDS.

However, the then Australian Government was committed to incorporating them both into funding and policy decisions. This was central to shaping the ongoing impact that HIV/AIDS has had within the Australian public health system by encouraging collaborations.

An alliance between doctors and the gay community (or other health activists) had no historical precedent. Indeed, many gay men had a long history of mistrusting medical authorities due to the role medicine and psychiatry had played in pathologizing and punishing homosexuality over previous decades. But despite their criticisms of medical authorities, AIDS activists knew that medical authorities had a central role to play in the response to HIV/AIDS – they needed them for medical care and medical research. Similarly, medical professionals would not have previously been in a position where they had to work professionally with either activists or the gay community. Yet AIDS activists had strategically positioned themselves, with support from the Federal Government, as central to the Australian AIDS response. They were part of government committees such as the National Advisory Committee on AIDS, and had a high profile in public discourse on AIDS. Medical professionals were in a position of having to engage with activists.

The collaborative project that emerged in response to HIV/AIDS over time transformed the frameworks in which both activists and medical professionals, including researchers, operated. AIDS activists worked hard to become astute medical advocates, working within medical and government systems, while medical professions accepted and incorporated a role for activists in medical and public health processes – something that radically challenged the long held autonomy of the medical professions.

The Expertise of Experience: People Living with AIDS

The National People Living with AIDS Coalition (commonly referred to by its catchy acronym, NPLWAC, pronounced 'nipple-wack'), was formed in Australia in 1988, later to be renamed the National Association of People with AIDS (NAPWA). Several state-based coalitions were established alongside this (Menadue, 2003b; Woolcock, 1999; McQuarrie, 1993).

NPLWAC/NAPWA formed as advocacy bodies, promoting the rights and interests of people living with HIV/AIDS. But they also sought to influence the nature of medical and social research being conducted around HIV/AIDS. Activists argued that medical research often occurred without input from patients and that the experiences of people living with HIV/AIDS were not well documented. It was on this basis that NAPWA began to put forward the argument that 'expertise' about HIV/AIDS should come from personal experiences of living with the virus as much as it should come from formal Western medical expertise.

The position of NPLWAC/NAPWA is articulated well in the following quotation taken from a presentation by a former convener of NAPWA, Peter Canavan:

> Sometimes, just being present as a positive person can in itself function as a reminder that research deals with flesh-and-blood people, who live daily with the reality that is HIV. We know about lipodystrophy not necessarily because we understand how or why it develops – but because we are the ones who have stood in front of the mirror, and observed the changes over time to the bodies in which we live. When a piece of research involves a high number of hospital visits, or that we are hooked up to an intravenous drug delivery machine, we are the ones who know what that means and what that will feel like, or how various treatments might affect your capacity to work or play or have sex or generally get on with the business of life. It's not that doctors and clinicians aren't aware of it or haven't thought of it: mostly, they are really sensitive towards this stuff, especially in HIV – which in itself is a testament to the power of a partnership between community and researchers for which we have fought and struggled. But the research process involves people whose perspectives and priorities are not always coincidental with our own, at least in the practical sense. I am not suggesting here that anyone wants to do bad or harmful research. But all research disciplines – whether social or clinical science – require people to conform to certain principles about research design, or 'how things get done', or indeed, to answer to particular political, academic or cultural agendas, and these may not always sit comfortably with how HIV positive people see their lives.
>
> CANAVAN, 2003

It was on this basis, that PLWHA groups began to agitate for greater control over the processes in which clinical trials for new HIV medications were undertaken.[15] Australia provided a unique context in which these groups proved to be highly successful. Firstly, the relatively small number of HIV-positive people in Australia meant that there was only a small pool of possible research

15 In 1996, Highly Active Anti-Retroviral Therapy (HAART) was introduced. HAART involves the use of several antiviral medications in combination. The rate of mortality and morbidity associated with AIDS dropped dramatically with the introduction of HAART. (Stewart, 1998).

participants for any HIV drug trial. If patients were unhappy with trial protocols, they could elect not to participate or withdraw from the study, and there were not necessarily other people to replace them. Secondly, many potential trial participants were also connected to an organized social movement with a vested interest in the outcomes of those trials and an increasing expectation that they should be consulted on medical aspects of HIV/AIDS. Much of the advocacy work conducted by PLWA organizations was directed towards supporting people involved in HIV trials. These organizations lobbied for increased involvement of people with HIV/AIDS in the design and implementation of clinical research.

One major issue that brought activists into conflict with the medical profession was the use of placebos in randomized control trials (RCTs). There were concerns that the use of placebos meant some people enrolled in the trial missed out on potentially life-saving medication.[16] Many activists insisted that placebos were unjustified in the case of drugs which overseas trials had demonstrated to be effective well before Australian trials were concluded. This situation had occurred with one of the first potential anti-viral treatments for HIV, Azidothymidine/Zidovudine (AZT) (ACT UP, 1990). There were several occasions where activists undermined the validity of placebo-based RCTs by having their pills tested to see if they were active or not. Those with active doses would halve theirs in order to share it with people on the placebo (Ballard, 1993). Through actions such as this, or the refusal of large numbers of people with AIDS to participate in a trial, community support became virtually a basic requirement if a trial was to go ahead. Hence, the medical community in Australia was pushed into a position where they had to accept greater community involvement in HIV clinical research, although there were many researchers who were supportive of this. As a result, by the end of the 1990s, both NAPWA and AFAO had representatives on the National Centre in HIV

---

16 Randomized control trials (RCT) were initially developed in the 1940s to test the effects of various drugs on tuberculosis. In RCTs, patients are randomly assigned either to the trial group, where they receive the medication being tested, or to the control group, where they receive a placebo pill. To control for any possible 'placebo effect', patients do not know to which group they have been assigned (in a double-blind trial, the clinician does not know this either). The idea of clinical trials is to remove uncertainty – including that which might come from human emotion or subjectivity – from the process of testing therapies. RCTs are claimed to remove any 'guesswork' from scientific assessment. They are still considered the 'gold standard' in biomedical research – the most effective method of accurately and objectively assessing the efficacy of a treatment regime. (Epstein, 1996; Willis, 1989).

Epidemiology and Clinical Research (NCHECR) Protocol Working Group. They also participated regularly in various NCHECR working groups and advisory committees (Canavan, 2003). This achievement of the AIDS movement brought about a permanent change in the conduct of medical research in Australia.

Activists had transformed themselves into medical advocates from early on in the AIDS epidemic. Rather than waiting for health information to be provided to them from medical authorities, they researched, produced and disseminated clinical reports about HIV/AIDS. From the early 1980s, activists had regularly disseminated detailed medical information about AIDS (as much as it was available at the time) to the gay community through the gay street-press and community-produced brochures. Not surprisingly, the massive impact HIV/AIDS had on the Australian gay community was of personal interest to gay men with medical training. These doctors became active participants in both HIV/AIDS medical treatment and community activism, facilitating much of the development and dissemination of medical information about AIDS.[17] Alongside this, many AIDS activists were skilled in other areas such as journalism or law, and made efforts to become knowledgeable in medical science relating to AIDS so they could communicate on this level.[18] Activists did not see 'medical knowledge' as outside their domain. Nor did they view medical authorities as having an inherent right to control the flow of medical knowledge and information to gay communities.[19]

When the first antiviral medications became available in the late 1980s, AIDS information published through the gay community press became much more detailed and focused on providing information about treatment options. In 1988, activist Terry Bell established the *AIDS Advocate*, a treatment information and advocacy newsletter. Bell's philosophy was one of empowerment through education. His objective was to ensure people with HIV had enough knowledge to be able to ask questions of doctors and determine their own course of treatment. In part, this was a strategy of shifting the power imbalance between doctors and patients. But also Bell was aware that, at the time, most GPs

---

17 David Lowe, Interview with the author, 12 July 2005.

18 Adam Carr was a journalist who, from the early 1980s, began to write articles on HIV/AIDS for the gay press. Carr read all the medical literature he could find on HIV/AIDS and followed all information being published through US sources, translating this into language that would be easily understood by the general public. Carr is regularly cited as one of the key sources of information about HIV/AIDS for the gay community throughout the 1980s and 1990s. Many of these articles can still be viewed on Carr's personal web site: http://www.adam-carr.net/.

19 David Plummer, Interview with the author, 30 August 2004; Ariss, 1997; Misztal, 1990; Ballard, 1989.

themselves did not have a great deal of knowledge about HIV treatment, so patients simply had to do their own research (Ariss, 1997). Around the same time, another treatment information magazine, *Talkabout*, began to be published by People Living With HIV/AIDS (PLWHA) in New South Wales. Following this, in the early 1990s, the national peak body, AFAO, established a treatment information program with assistance from Federal Government funding. The project produced a regular publication, the *HIV Herald*, which was distributed nationally. The *HIV Herald* provided information about available treatments as well as continuing and upcoming drug trials. AFAO also began work with the National Association of People With AIDS (NAPWA) to produce *Positive Living*, a publication that was first released in 1995 and quickly became one of the major sources of information about HIV treatments in Australia.

Publishing treatment information such as this was intended to endow people with enough knowledge to determine their own course of HIV treatment. It also encouraged people to adopt an inquisitive and critical approach to medicine and science, and to the advice of their doctors. There was no real precedent in Australia at the time for patient groups taking charge of medical advice in this way, although it is more commonplace now (particularly with the emergence of the internet). But certainly in the 1980s and 1990s, the notion that patients should be encouraged to take a critical approach to their doctor's advice, or pursue a collaborative rather than hierarchical approach to medical care, was not commonly promoted (Hurley, 2001). As activist Ian Rankin observed: 'Some issues such [as] how a patient should go about choosing a GP or their right to have a say in their own treatment had never been [debated] before in Australia'.[20]

Conclusions

In the 1980s there was an emerging philosophy across the public health sector that supported community involvement in healthcare. At the international level, the 1978 Alma-Ata Conference of the World Health Organization had adopted 'new public health' principles which focused on the social causes of ill health and the important role of community development and empowerment in fostering good health (Crichton, 1990). HIV/AIDS was the first test of this approach. It was the first time in Australia that an organized community had really demanded the implementation of new public health principles in response to a disease threat – in terms of seeking government support for

20 Ian Rankin, Interview with the author, 26 July 2004.

community-led disease prevention and health promotion initiatives and for community involvement in medical care and research. Few patient advocates had achieved the level of influence within the formal medical system that AIDS activists achieved.[21] Yet today, community or consumer involvement in health is commonly expected and often written into health funding agreements. There are large consumer health and patient rights groups operating across the health sector, including within mental health.

Collaboration between doctors and activists was a distinctive feature of the AIDS movement. This was particularly apparent in the work of organizations led by people living with HIV/AIDS. While activists were strong critics and agitators for change within the Australian medical system, particularly with respect to medical research and clinical trials for new treatments, they also established productive working relationships with medical professionals and researchers – becoming involved in the design and implementation of research and insisting on acknowledgement within this process of their expertise as people most affected by HIV/AIDS.

Brown and colleagues refer to health social movements as 'boundary crossers' (Brown et al., 2004). While health activists generally engage in protest activities such as street demonstrations and lobbying, they also often partake in formal collaboration with scientific and research institutions – both in terms of collaborative policy and advocacy work, but also in more personal doctor/patient relationships. This blurs the traditional boundaries between 'medicine' and 'lay-people'. But by working with medical institutions, health social movements also move beyond commonly agreed definitions of social-movement activity, cooperating with the 'opposition' and adopting an 'expert' identity of their own.

This is perhaps where the concept of 'collaborative projects' has much to offer an analysis of social movements. The AIDS movement didn't operate in isolation. While the movement was a project in its own right, activists worked in collaboration with others, which in turn transformed the processes and cultural perspective of each project. The AIDS movement developed from grassroots community organizing into a set of well-established agencies that engaged professionally within government and the medical system, while also maintaining a strong community base. Activists within the movement became fluent in medical language and skilled in political practice. Meanwhile, the medical system responded to challenges presented by the AIDS movement, incorporating community-led, 'non-medical' expertise into processes of

---

21 The Women's Health Movement in Australia is one exception to this, feminist activists have a long history of lobbying for community-led healthcare, see Gray Jamieson, 2012.

medical care and research. Doctors came to develop strong working relationships with non-medically trained activists and adapt to a community presence in medical research. Looking at the AIDS response as the emergence of a collaborative project enables understanding of how social movements can develop influence with respect to other (sometimes initially opposing) forces and how a movement may achieve social and cultural change across a range of areas or institutions – and indeed influence, and become part of, the mainstream. It also shows how projects develop over time. Institutions such as the medical system or profession are not static or monolithic. They evolve over time in relation to changing social conditions incorporating both challenges by, and collaboration with, other projects, such as the AIDS movement. The history of HIV/AIDS in Australia is an illuminating case study of the ways in which relationships between different projects generate social and cultural change that is permanent, influencing society well beyond the active life of a social movement.

References

ACT UP (1990). *Cut the Red Tape*, Media briefing kit (unpublished resource), AIDS Coalition to Unleash Power, Sydney.

Altman, D. (1988). Legitimation through disaster: AIDS and the gay movement. In Fee, E. & Fox, D. (Eds.), *AIDS: The Burdens of History*, University of California Press, Berkeley.

Altman, D. (1990). Introduction. In Richard Clayton (Ed.), *Gay Now, Play Safe*, Victorian AIDS Council/Gay Men's Community Health Centre, Melbourne.

Altman, D. (1994). *Power and Community: Organizational and Cultural Responses to AIDS*, Taylor & Francis, London.

Ariss, R. (1997). *Against Death: The Practice of Living with AIDS*, Gordon and Breach, Amsterdam.

Ballard, J. (1989). The politics of AIDS. In Heather Gardner (Ed.), *The Politics of Health: The Australian Experience*, Churchill Livingstone, Melbourne.

Ballard, J. (1992). Australia: Participation and innovation in a federal system. In David Kirp and Ronald Bayer (Eds.), *AIDS in the Industrialized Democracies: Passions, Politics and Policies*, Rutgers University Press, New Brunswick, NJ.

Ballard, J. (1993). Interviewed by Professor Peter Baume, *Oral History Project: The Australian Response to AIDS*, TRC 2815/1, NLA.

Ballard, J. (1998). 'The Constitution of AIDS in Australia: Taking Government at a Distance Seriously'. In Mitchell Dean and Barry Hindess (Eds.), *Governing Australia: Studies in Contemporary Rationalities of Government*, Cambridge University Press, Melbourne.

Ballard, J. (1999). HIV contaminated blood and Australian policy. In Eric Feldman and Ronald Bayer (Eds.), *AIDS, Blood and the Politics of Medical Disaster*, Oxford University Press, New York.

Barnard, M. (1985). AIDS: A time to get tough?, *The Age*, 19 March, p. 19.

Barnett, D. (1989). Surgeons alarmed at AIDS risk, *The Bulletin*, 25 April, pp. 38–41.

Bates, E. & Linder-Pelz, S. (1990). *Health Care Issues*, [Second edition], Allen & Unwin, Sydney.

Baxter, D. (1993). Interview with James Waites, 26 November 1993, *Oral History Project: The Australian Response to AIDS*, TRC 2815/75, NLA.

Brown, P., Zavaestoski, S., McCormick, S., Mayer, B., Morello-Frosch, R. & Gasior, R. (2004), Embodied health movements: New approaches to social movements in health, *Sociology of Health and Illness, 26*(1), pp. 50–80.

Canavan, P. (2003). Reflecting on 'Our' Involvement in NAPWA, Presentation to The Art of Living: Ninth Biennial Conference of the National Association of People Living With AIDS, 27–28 October, Cairns, Queensland.

Carr, A. (1987). President's report, *Annual Report*, Victorian AIDS Council, Melbourne.

Centers for Disease Control (1985). *Acquired Immunodeficiency Syndrome (AIDS) Weekly Surveillance Report—December 30*, US AIDS Activity Center for Infectious Diseases, Centers for Disease Control, Atlanta, Ga.

Centers for Disease Control (2005). *HIV/AIDS Surveillance Report 2004*, US Department of Health and Human Services, Centers for Disease Control and Prevention, Atlanta, GA, viewed 21 November 2005, http://www.cdc.gov/hiv/topics/surveillance/resources/reports/2004report/.

Cook, S. (1983). Disease fear leads Red Cross to ban gays as donors, *The Australian*, 10 May, pp. 1–2.

Crichton, A. (1990). *Slowly Taking Control? Australian Government and Healthcare Provision, 1788-1988*, Allen and Unwin, Sydney.

Emke, I. (1992). Medical authority and its discontents: A case of organized non-compliance, *Critical Sociology, 19*(3), pp. 57–80.

Epstein, S. (1996). *Impure Science. AIDS, Activism, and the Politics of Knowledge*, University of California Press, Berkeley.

Gray Jamieson, G. (2012). *Reaching for Health: The Australian women's health movement and public policy*, ANU E-Press, Canberra.

Green, R. (1985). With compulsion, victims go underground, *The Canberra Times*, 6 September, p. 10.

Hurley, M. (2001). *Strategic and Conceptual Issues for Community Based, HIV/AIDS Treatments Media*, Researchers in Residence Program, Working Paper 3, Australian Federation of AIDS Organizations, Newtown, NSW, and Australian Research Centre in Sex, Health and Society, La Trobe University, Melbourne.

McCauley, C. (1988). Opposition looks at mandatory AIDS test, *The Age*, 1 September, p. 4.

McDonnell, D. (1985). Patient panic on AIDS law, *The Sun*, 28 September, p. 13.

McQuarrie, V. (1993). "Keep on acting" says Richardson, *Sydney Star Observer*, 12 November, p. 7.

Menadue, D. (2003). *Positive*, Allen & Unwin, Sydney, www.afao.com.au.

Menadue, D. (2003a). Opening Plenary Session Address, The Art of Living: Ninth Biennial Conference of the National Association of People Living with AIDS, 27–28 October, Cairns, Queensland.

Misztal, B. (1990). AIDS in Australia: Diffusion of power and making of policy. In Barbara Misztal and David Moss (Eds.). *Action on AIDS: National Policies in Comparative Perspective*, Greenwood Press, New York.

Misztal, B. (1991). HIV/AIDS policies in Australia: Bureaucracy and collective action, *International Journal of Sociology and Social Policy, 11*(4), pp. 62–82.

National Centre in HIV Epidemiology and Clinical Research (2006). *Australian HIV Surveillance Report, 22*(2), National Centre in HIV Epidemiology and Clinical Research, University of New South Wales, Sydney, pp. 1–16.

National Centre in HIV Epidemiology and Clinical Research (2010). HIV Viral Hepatitis and Sexually Transmissible Infections in Australia Annual Surveillance Report 2010, National Centre in HIV Epidemiology and Clinical Research, University of NSW, Sydney.

Phillips, B. (1988). The Role of the Australian Medical Association, Presented to Living With AIDS Toward the Year 2000: Third National Conference on AIDS, Department of Community Services and Health, 4–6 August, Hobart, p. 641.

Power, J. (2011). *Movement, Knowledge, Emotion: Gay Activism and HIV/AIDS in Australia*, ANU E-Press, Canberra.

Sanderson, W. (1985). Gays may refuse AIDS test, *Daily Telegraph*, 14 January, p. 5.

Seidman, S. (2002). AIDS and the discursive construction of homosexuality. In Kim Phillips and Barry Reay (Eds.), *Sexualities in History: A Reader*, Routledge, New York.

Sendziuk, P. (2001). Bad blood: The contamination of Australia's blood supply and the emergence of gay activism in the age of AIDS. In Elizabeth Ruinard and Elspeth Tilley (Eds.). *Fresh Cuts: New Talents 2001*, API Network and University of Queensland Press, Sydney.

Sendziuk, P. (2003). *Learning to Trust: Australian Responses to AIDS*, UNSW Press, Sydney.

Staples, J. (2006). *NGOs Out in the Cold: The Howard Government Policy Toward NGOs in Democratic Audit of Australia*, Discussion Paper 19/06, Faculty of Law, University of New South Wales, Sydney, viewed 3 June 2006, http://apo.org.au/research/ngos-out-cold-howard-government-policy-towards-ngos, p. 2.

Stewart, G. (1998). You've gotta have HAART, *Medical Journal of Australia, 169*, pp. 456–457.

Tabone, J. (2004). Australia's Response to HIV/AIDS at Risk Through Lack of Leadership from the Commonwealth Government, Media release, 18 May, AIDS Action Council of the ACT, Canberra.

UNAIDS (2010). *UNAIDS Report on the Global AIDS Epidemic,* UNAIDS, http://www.unaids.org/globalreport/Global_report.htm.

White, K. & Willis, E. (1992). The languages of AIDS, *New Zealand Sociology,* 7(2), pp. 127–149, at p. 127.

Wilkinson, D. & Dore, G. (2000). An unbridgeable gap? Comparing the HIV/AIDS epidemics in Australia and Sub-Saharan Africa. *Australian and New Zealand Journal of Public Health,* 24(3), pp. 276–280.

Willett, G. (2000). *Living Out Loud: A History of Gay and Lesbian Activism in Australia,* Allen & Unwin, Sydney.

Willis, Evan (1989). *Medical Dominance: The Division of Labour in Australian Health Care,* Allen & Unwin, Sydney.

Woolcock, G. (1999). *A Vector of Identity Transmission: AIDS Activism and Social Movement Theory,* Unpublished PhD Thesis, La Trobe University, Melbourne.

World Health Organization (2002). Australia 2002 update, *Epidemiological Fact Sheets on HIV/AIDS and Sexually Transmitted Infections,* viewed 2 June 2003, http://www.unAIDS.org.

CHAPTER 11

The Miracle Fiber Exposed as a Deadly Threat: Some Moments in the Battle to Have Asbestos Banned from Use in Australia

Lynn Beaton and Andy Blunden

The history of the mining, manufacture and use of asbestos in Australia is a history of shameful neglect at best and at worst horrendous promotion of profit over human life. All those in touch with asbestos are at risk of contracting one of the many diseases associated with it. While asbestos was used in Australia from early in the twentieth century its use escalated dramatically after the Second World War. A substance that could withstand extreme conditions without damage was irresistible to those who sought to profit from the unprecedented growth of post-war Australia. In a booming economy the miracle fiber was used extensively in the manufacture of many products and in industrial, commercial and domestic construction. Use of asbestos in Australia was extensive compared with other countries. The legacy of this is that asbestos still lurks in backyards, in sheds, in rubbish dumps, in schools and in hospitals. Everywhere there are buildings or products that pre-date the banning of asbestos in 2003. There are few living Australians who don't know first-hand a person who has died from asbestos related disease. 642 people died of mesothelioma in 2010 (*Sydney Morning Herald*, 5 September 2012), and as the number of victims continues to rise it is predicted that mortality will not peak before 2020.

The asbestos industry in Australia was involved in mining, and manufacture of products which contained asbestos largely for the building industry but also in parts for cars and machinery. There were three mines; Wittenoom in West Australia (WA) produced blue asbestos (crocidolite) from 1943 to 1966; in the seventies there was a mine at Woodsreef, and another at Baryulgil in NSW that mined white asbestos (chrysotile). None of the mines were particularly profitable. Building materials containing asbestos were made by James Hardie Industries, Wunderlich (which was owned by CSR who had also owned the mine at Wittenoom) and Goliath Portland Cement Company in Railton. Hardie were by the far the largest of these companies and their influence on the events in Australia was hegemonic. Other companies that worked with asbestos were in the manufacturing sector and included either spraying asbestos as insulation or using it for friction parts for vehicles.

Conflicted Loyalties

The problem that the history of asbestos poses to all of us interested in social change is this. Some asbestos producers were in possession of the facts of asbestos disease before the end of the second world war and acted effectively to prevent this from becoming public knowledge. In the post war period research uncovered more and more information about more and more health hazards yet this information was largely held captive by the industry. Yet why was it that medical scientists who also knew that asbestos posed lethal dangers did not communicate this fact to the general public until the 1960s, and many participated in spreading disinformation to the end? Why was it that government authorities, also long in possession of the facts, failed to put an end to asbestos production and importation until 2003, despite thousands of deaths? And even when the dangers of asbestos became public knowledge in the 1960s, on the whole, people who were exposed to asbestos fibers continued working in unsafe conditions refusing to believe that they were in danger, often until the number of deaths in their locality and among coworkers and family became overwhelming? And how was it possible for even senior managers of asbestos companies to see members of their own family die of exposure to asbestos, and yet continue to deny the dangers of asbestos and expose others to the risk? Why did low-paid, exploited asbestos workers go on exposing themselves to asbestos long after the dangers of asbestos were public knowledge, even when other jobs were available?

Neither structuralist sociology nor naïve theories of economic self-interest provide an adequate explanation of these facts. But even more significantly, such theories cannot explain how it came about that asbestos mining, importation and use, which had gone on in Australia for a century, *was eventually banned*, and asbestos is now universally recognized as a lethal danger and its discovery in old buildings frequently the cause of panic.

What this story brings to light is that the behavior, loyalties and beliefs found in the world of work in a capitalist economy cannot be grasped solely in terms of economic categories or theories of social reproduction. In the order of Nature, so to speak, individuals occupying the same economic position are in *competition* with one another. Solidarity between workers and class consciousness arise in the face of exploitation, only thanks to projects launched by activists promoting a solidaristic ideal which mitigates the exploitation and *creates* class consciousness, mutual aid and the commitment of workers to the class project. Employees are neither blind and loyal servants of their firm, nor uniformly imbued with class hatred of their bosses, nor solely driven by individual, family or community concerns. The extent to which one or another loyalty prevails depends on the outcome of social struggles. Employers work hard to foster the loyalty of their employees to their own project, and usually enjoy a degree of success.

Likewise, different firms fighting for a larger share of the social wealth by means of asbestos production are in competition with one another. But faced with an existential threat to their entire activity, the competitors formed an 'Industry', that is, a project, a self-conscious social agent which defends the interests of asbestos producers by any means available, side by side with firms' mutual competition in the market.

There are a plethora of sociological and psychological theories which explain how cultures and institutions maintain themselves by means of various kinds of reward-and-punishment, sanctions for noncompliance to norms of various kinds, myths, legends and moral codes – fields, traditions, frames, narratives, discourses, customs, paradigms, ideological apparatuses and so on. It is well known that members of a social group share beliefs and mutual solidarity, but *how* people are constituted in such groups, and *what* beliefs are shared still remain to be explained. Such theories explain, for example, how scientific consensus is resistant to change, how peer review and arrangements for promotion function to defend entrenched views in science. But what these theories fail (on the whole) to explain is how, under the hegemony of the Asbestos Industry, medical science which failed to warn the community of the danger of asbestos, and government health regulators who failed to protect the community, and courts which failed to award punitive damages and compensation to victims, and media which failed to disseminate important facts to the community *eventually* were obliged to fulfill their mission and collaborate in the complete elimination of the use of asbestos in Australia.

History of the Campaign against Asbestos in Australia

The project to stop asbestos mining, manufacture, importation and use in Australia was mostly carried out by health professionals and trade unionists and was most enthusiastically fought when these two streams met and formed an alliance in the Workers Health movement. The battle has been long and arduous. It has also been sporadic, as one of the most potent of the weapons used by Asbestos Industry and their supporters was their ability to derail progress toward regulation that would have saved lives. The Anti-Asbestos Movement – the Workers Health movement and the scattering of victim's groups, legal firms, journalists and others – involved thousands of small actions in numerous settings around the country and without any coordination and very little communication between them. As identified cases of asbestos disease increased, the battle for compensation for victims emerged and became the dominant objective of the Movement as a whole. The battle to have asbestos *banned* required information, for the first step was to prove the extent to which it was a hazard. Litigation required copious amounts of detailed information, and the resulting research provided the movement for banning the substance with its basic weapon.

The project which began seeking compensation, and expanded to seek the banning of asbestos in Australia could not at any stage be called a mass movement. Rather it has been groups of interested health and legal professionals, trade unionists, and victim support groups who, at various times, have made headway. Even this was erratic and inconsistent and often gains made were lost, forcing the same ground to be covered again and again. For the majority of the twentieth century, the campaign aims were to have health and safety measures adopted that it was hoped would reduce harm, rather than have the substance banned altogether. While the dangers have been known at least since the Romans made slaves working with asbestos wear masks so as to prolong their lives, leaps in scientific investigation have exposed the nature of the substance and examined its propensity to cause a wide range of diseases. As information became available, and as the death rate grew, increasingly the lethal nature of asbestos could not be ignored and calls for a complete banning of the substance also grew.

Both the campaign to have asbestos banned and the battle for acceptable levels of compensation for victims have been obstructed at every point by the Industry which has continually argued that handled with care, asbestos is not dangerous.

> The growth of evidence linking asbestos and disease was marked by the play of competing interests which shaped both the research process and the reception of knowledge.
>
> MCCULLOCH & TWEEDALE, 2008

And yet in Canada and the USA insurance companies were confident enough of its dangers to refuse to provide insurance to those who worked with the substance.

> By 1918 enough was known about the dangers of asbestos to lead to the decision of US and Canadian insurance companies to stop selling life policies to asbestos workers.
>
> EPSTEIN, 1979

Those who campaigned for harm minimization and banning of the substance were reliant on the information available, yet the research itself was often controlled by the Industry. Where research uncovered results that were unfavorable to the Industry, that research was either buried or the researchers were vilified.

Mobilized Industry

> Organized greed always defeats disorganized democracy.
>
> TAIBBI, 2010

In this case it was organized greed against disorganized health professionals and union representatives although it was a far cry from being everyone involved in those projects. While most of those who worked with asbestos were ignorant of its dangers, those who owned and managed the workplaces that depended on asbestos to produce goods were probably not. It is now well documented that the largest and most powerful of the companies involved in the asbestos industry worldwide had the most up to date information about the risks to health. We also know that they went to long and costly lengths to hide this information from those who worked for them, those who would consume their products and the peoples of the world at large. The maintenance of this deception required sophisticated strategies to keep governments, medical, scientific, legal, media, and union communities and activists at bay.

For almost the entire campaign, most health professionals, out of ignorance, denied the presence of asbestos when diagnosing diseased individuals. There were also health professionals who denied in the public debate that there was any danger which could not be controlled. Trade unions were a major player in the story but they also had a difficult road which often led to neglect. Unions which intervened were sometimes met by members who were antagonistic to any activity that might end with the loss of jobs. This led some unions to fight for a penalty (hazard pay) for handling asbestos, rather than banning its handling altogether or fighting for protective handling. Furthermore, union personnel are reliant on the available information and while there was much that exposed the dangers of asbestos this was often buried beneath the mountain of counter-information released by the Industry.

As long ago as 1898, Factory Inspectors in Britain identified the dangers to workers' health and evidence began to mount. In 1931, Dust Control Regulations for the Asbestos Industry were introduced in Britain. In 1946, the toll of known asbestos deaths in Britain reached 235 (ADFA, 2009), at the same time as, in

Australia, the manager of the blue asbestos mine at Wittenoom notified head office of their first known asbestosis case (ADFA, 2009).

Australian asbestos firms were well connected with the Industry internationally. Although competitors in the market place, the risky business of profiting from the production and use of asbestos fostered close bonds of collaboration. At the end of the second world war, as the asbestos industry in Australia expanded rapidly, several hundred scientific papers had already been published around the world detailing the dangers of asbestos that had been established by research and warned of the dangers. Warnings had been published by organizations ranging from the international asbestos industry's internal journal, *The Asbestos Worker*, which reported on a 'new form of chronic pulmonary fibrosis among asbestos workers', to the International Labor Organization which wrote: 'All processes, from extraction onward, unquestionably involve a considerable hazard' (Hills, 1989). This information was publicly available as far back as 1938 when a book titled 'Silicosis and Asbestosis' was published in Australia as well as overseas. The book included detailed descriptions of the symptoms of asbestosis, noted that these were often misdiagnosed and made links between asbestos and lung cancer. The author, Dr. Lanza, was described in the Preface as an adviser on industrial hygiene to the Commonwealth of Australia (McCulloch, 1986).

The Industry's approach was typified by their response to a six-month strike in 1949 by asbestos miners in Thetford, one of the mining areas of Quebec. One of the demands of the strikers was 'some company action to check the spread of lung choking silicosis caused by exposure to asbestos' (Marsh, 2010). Months before the strike, Kenneth Smith, a doctor who worked for Johns Manville, one of the companies involved in the strike, undertook research in the town of Asbestos and found only 4 workers in the whole town with healthy lungs. Smith recommended that men not be told of their condition and wrote to Johns Manville:

> As long as the man is not disabled it is felt he should not be told of his condition so that he can live and work in peace and the company can benefit by his many years of experience. Should the man be told of his condition today there is a very definite possibility that he would become mentally and physically ill simply through the knowledge that he has asbestosis.
>
> PEACOCK, 2009

A situation emerged around the world and in Australia where knowledge of the dangers of asbestos would come to the fore and remedial action would be attempted. Sometimes this action led nowhere and sometimes it led to a tightening of regulations on exposure to asbestos. For many years, the major focus in setting regulations, which was initiated and enthusiastically supported by the Industry, was the setting of 'safe' levels of airborne particles. The difficulties which were involved in setting, measuring and maintaining a 'safe' level kept many well-intentioned people occupied at the expense of providing possibly life-saving information to those who were being exposed.

In 1950, the Third International Conference on Pneumoconiosis was held in Sydney with an agenda that included several papers on the health risks of asbestos (McCulloch, 1986). The same year the WA Commissioner for Public Health reported to his Minister that 'Asbestos dust, if inhaled, constitutes a very grave risk and is, if anything, worse than silicosis' (ADFA, 2009).

Throughout the 1950s a number of significant developments in knowledge of the asbestos health hazard were made and led in many places to health regulations being introduced for the asbestos industry. In 1951, the British medical journal, *The Lancet*, carried an article that discussed cancer of the lung among asbestosis sufferers and within two years the journal had listed asbestos as a carcinogen. In 1955, an epidemiological study of a group of British asbestos workers confirmed the risk of lung cancer (McCulloch, 1986).

An example of the way that a determined, though sporadic struggle to keep workers safe from asbestos can be frustrated is seen in the Victorian Railways. In the mid-1950s, the Victorian Department of Health and a number of unions became concerned about what the newly exposed information about asbestosis meant for those who worked with asbestos. After an initial investigation, Doctor Douglas Shiels of the Victorian Health Department became particularly concerned about asbestosis and commissioned Doctor Leslie Gordon Thomas to undertake further research. Thomas carried out a radiological survey of all workers in the 'dusty trades' and the results showed high levels of disease in those working with asbestos. One third of 300 asbestos workers had asbestos bodies in their sputum and 15% showed lung damage on X-Rays. In one workplace a further examination showed that 20 out of 44 cases were positive for asbestosis. The results were published in *The Age* in January 1956 and a year later a full report of the findings was published in the *Medical Journal of Australia*. Thomas argued in this article that disease was more widespread than had previously been known and was a danger, not only to those involved in the production of asbestos products, but also to those who used the products. He particularly mentioned 'sawing, cutting and finishing', any products containing asbestos such as brake linings, asbestos sheeting and insulation materials (Haigh, 2006).

Disappointed with the lack of action taken by the Industrial Hygiene Department in Victoria, Thomas took it upon himself to inform workers of the risks to health and addressed the Victorian Trades Hall Council. As a result, the Secretary of the Tramways Union intervened in the case of a member who had lung problems. He had been employed as a motor mechanic and had been using a rotary buffing machine to grind down asbestos brake linings. When the union insisted, as a result of Thomas's address, that the man have an extensive series of sputum tests, it was proved without doubt that the man's lungs had been 'dusted with asbestos'. Workers Compensation was paid to him.

However Thomas also informed the Secretary of the Australian Railways Union, J.J. Browne, that in 1954 the Industrial Hygiene Department had conducted tests on railway workers at the Newport Workshops. A report showing that asbestos was a menace in two locations at the Railway Workshops had been secretly given to the Railway Medical Section, but the Union had not been informed. Once this information was disclosed the Union were able to take action which involved fighting for compensation for sufferers. However it also involved a battle over on-going work on railway carriages. It was noticed that the railway carriages were lined with asbestos and that men were knocking holes in the material to put in rivets. Six of the men were given sputum tests and X-Rays and two were found to have asbestos disease. The Union established that neither of these men had worked with asbestos before and the Victorian Railways agreed they should have regular medical tests and that the results of the tests should go to the Union. Later it was agreed that all men working on the carriages were entitled to medical tests without loss of time if they requested them.

The Secretary of the Australian Railways Union, J.J. Brown, then wrote letters to all branches of the union to inform them of the dangers that workers may face. He also wrote to other unions and Labor Party Branches to spread the information. Nevertheless, the information and the warnings were somehow *lost*. Many years later, in 1977, when ABC journalist Matt Peacock publicized the presence of blue asbestos in trains operating on the Melbourne suburban lines on the ABC, the Shadow Transport Minister, Tom Roper, demanded that the trains be removed. However, the Victorian Railways claimed that the train service would grind to a halt if the trains were removed, and instead they were inspected and 'sealed'. In full knowledge of the danger to workers and passengers, the authority kept trains in service until 1988.

As the 1960s dawned, research led to new awareness about the health risks of exposure to asbestos. Research from South Africa threw a spotlight on a previously unknown and highly alarming asbestos-related disease, mesothelioma. It was always fatal, was only caused by exposure to asbestos fibers and it only needed a single fiber to lodge in the wrong place for a person to contract it (McCulloch, 1986). The South African findings were supported by an epidemiological study at the London School of Hygiene and Tropical Medicine which found that of 76 patients who had died from mesothelioma in the London Hospital at least 40 had worked with asbestos or had lived in the same house as an asbestos worker (Byrne, 1965).

Landmark research was also taking place in the USA. Irving Selikoff had led a team that investigated the files of union members in the insulation and asbestos industries who had died in the Mount Sinai Hospital in New York. The results were published in medical journals and then released at an international conference held in New York in October 1964 which shook the industry and threatened its future. The health records of men who were on the union files in 1943 were traced up to 1962.

> ...they showed that insulators had an excess death rate of 25 per cent, with a heavier mortality than normal not only of asbestosis, but also lung cancer, mesothelioma, and stomach/colon/rectal cancer.
>
> MCCULLOCH & TWEEDALE, 2008

These results were corroborated as the findings of further studies became available. Selikoff's research had proved, beyond doubt, that asbestos was a killer and potentially lethal to everyone who was exposed to it. Selikoff's collaboration with the IAHFIAW, the union representing insulators, laggers and asbestos workers, proved to be the archetype of the Anti-Asbestos Movement.

In Australia, the regulatory bodies were closely allied to the asbestos industry whose activity they were supposed to be regulating. Likewise, when the National Health and Medical Research Council established an occupational carcinogens sub-committee, it included Terry McCullough of Hardies and Gersh Major whose institute received funding from Hardies. This committee published recommendations for 'safe' levels of asbestos dust. They also recommended that all employees exposed to asbestos dust should have pre-employment X-Rays and regular X-Rays throughout the period of employment (Council, 1961). In 1962, one of the first clinical case reports connecting mesothelioma and asbestos exposure was published in the *Medical Journal of Australia.* Between 1961 and 1965 more than 100 cases of lung disease were diagnosed among current and former Wittenoom mineworkers. This was more than for all other mines in Western Australia put together and publicity about the dangers of asbestos mining now began to seep into the public sphere (ADFA, 2009).

One of the most successful strategies of the Industry was to create confusion in the minds of regulators. This was relatively easy. The distribution of information was fragile and interested parties often received sporadic and fragmented pieces of the whole. This left gaps which could be easily filled with contradictory or divergent information that caused regulators to doubt the information they had. Secondly, confusion was sown by the distribution of highly technical information that was difficult to confirm or refute. The Industry framed the problem of one of developing 'safe' working environments, and the science of dust monitoring became a pervasive preoccupation, diverting attention from epidemiological and medical findings that *no* level of dust was safe. Employers maintained that they could provide a safe workplace by controlling the concentration of fiber in the air.

These strategies of the Industry were so successful that opposition to the use of asbestos was easily marginalized. However, the work of Selikoff gradually began to receive more and more exposure and was taken up by the trade union movement. In 1968, *The Australian* newspaper published a detailed article about the Selikoff research beginning: 'The Australian Council of Trade Unions might have better cause than it imagines for asking for an investigation into the harmful effects of asbestos on those who work with it.' The article went on to outline the types of disease associated with asbestos exposure, gave a history of asbestos research, particularly the work of Selikoff and listed the uses of asbestos. The article ended: 'today's children are almost certainly inhaling more asbestos than their parents did and we now know that if a person inhales significant amounts of asbestos dust, he carries a burden that will provide a latent potential for the development of cancer for the rest of his life' (GPCC). Similar articles were duly published in other newspapers around the country.

In 1974, the first major mass media story about the dangers of blue asbestos was published in *The Bulletin*. It was called: 'Is this Killer in Your Home?' and written by Tim Hall. Surely, by now anyone who worked with asbestos would be aware of the lethal danger they faced.

Isolated but powerful bits of information circulated around the trade union movement and as it was exposed it often led to industrial action and policy development that began to change the way asbestos was viewed in the workplace. A trade union trainer in Western Australia, Bill Deller, provides an example of how this took place. He remembers first hearing about the dangers of asbestos.

> In 1975, I was shown a documentary that had been made about Dr. Irving Selikoff for the Canadian Steel Workers Union. At the end of that documentary I no longer had any doubts about the dangers of asbestos.
>
> DELLER, 2013

After this Deller made a presentation and showed the video to the National Executive of the Builders Laborers Federation which was meeting in Perth. A motion was immediately adopted to have the spraying of asbestos banned by all union members. This reverberated around the country. One year later, Deller provided trade union training to a group of workers from a James Hardie factory in Perth. As a result of the information he provided they began industrial action have protective clothing and harm minimization practices put in place.

In 1977, ABC reporter Matt Peacock became aware of the dangers of asbestos and, with Mark Aarons, produced a series of radio programs that were quickly taken up by other media outlets (Peacock, 2009). These broadcasts became landmark exposures which began by discussing the dangers and quickly moved to exposing the Industry's involvement in the concealment of those dangers.

One of the radio programs discussed the need for labeling of products to warn consumers of the dangers. This call was taken up by Workers Health Action Groups around the country. In Sydney and Melbourne they printed bright yellow stickers warning: 'Danger: dust from this product can cause cancer' (Peacock, 2009).

The consumer magazine *Choice*, called for regulations to warn do-it-yourself and domestic users of products like asbestos cement sheets of their potential cancer hazard. The magazine published a large color photograph of the warning label used in the UK (Peacock, 2009).

Pressure was building around the world to have ever-tighter restrictions on asbestos use. In 1978, the Lidcombe Workers Health Action Group in Sydney published a Fact Sheet on asbestos which outlined the dangers was widely circulated throughout the union movement around the country.

Another group of workers who had become concerned when faced by the effects of asbestos on the health of their members was the Waterside Workers Federation. The conditions under which wharf laborers handled asbestos were extremely hazardous. Originally, the raw material arrived in paper bags which were often pierced with the hooks used for unloading ships. Dust would waft out of the torn bags and over the workers. The Union made several local agreements but at the end 1979 they called for national action to tighten restrictions on transport methods. Industrial action took place in Victoria and the Waterside Employers group issued a policy:

> ...that from 1st January 1980, no asbestos imports will be handled by Melbourne Branch members unless the asbestos is totally enclosed in airtight containers.

By 1980, exposure of the realities of the health hazard had become widespread and governments, unions, industry bodies, and consumer groups introduced policies, bans and regulations, designed to counter the hazard. At Goliath, sales were deteriorating while consumers and the workforce were asking questions about the safety of asbestos fiber. Asbestos product manufacturers began to phase out the use of asbestos and union bans increased. Regulations were tightened in various states.

Until the 1990s, Occupational Health and Safety regulations were largely state matters. With the first OH&S Act introduced in Victoria in 1985, and there was inconsistency from state to state. By the mid-1990s, a Federal government registration agency for new chemicals was established – the National Industrial Chemicals Notification and Scheme (NICNAS). This body oversaw the regulation of asbestos on a national level.

Regulations continued to be tightened at both national and state levels, but fell short of a total ban.

The End of Asbestos Use in Australia: the Case Study of Asbestos Brakes

Australian Manufacturing Workers Union (AMWU) Occupation Health and Safety Officer, Deborah Vallance who was involved in these activities throughout said:

> The history in terms of the actual ban was much more located within the union movement and the health and safety bureaucracy. Most of the work was done behind the scenes, individuals in the union and in the health bureaucracy researched tirelessly to find out how many parts were being imported, how overseas countries were dealing with similar situations. This was all done by people behind the scenes, not high profile, but trudging away doing the preparatory work. Unless that work happens, nothing happens but it isn't public, it just bubbles along.
>
> VALLANCE, 2013

While the building industry, under pressure from the building workers' unions had legislated and regulated against the use of asbestos it was still being used in other, less obvious ways and this wasn't stopped until 2003 when the Federal Government finally passed legislation that totally banned the importation of all asbestos and products which contained asbestos. While it might seem that this event would have been a simple matter of creating consistency across all industries and as such a formality, the legislation was only enacted after a campaign by unions and the Anti-Asbestos Movement generally.

The AMWU represents maintenance workers and tradespeople in a range of industries where the use of asbestos lagging and friction products was entrenched. Asbestos was used extensively as insulation in the power industry and in shipbuilding and also in the manufacture of brakes, clutches, and gaskets. As the manufacturing sector in Australia declined, the jobs of these workers were fragile. Their employment depended on the importation of raw chrysotile which continued long after it was stopped for the manufacture of asbestos cement sheeting and insulation. Similar products were manufactured overseas and so for the members of the AMWU, banning the raw substances only would cost them jobs as imported asbestos-containing brakes and clutches would command market dominance. AMWU members were concerned that they would suffer job losses if there was a phase-out of the use of raw asbestos without a ban also on the importation of asbestos-containing products from overseas. As well as this, requests from unions for a phase-out of all importation was met by Industry claims that non-asbestos products were not as safe and would put Australian motorists at risk.

A NICNAS report was released that called for changes to the labeling of products, employee induction training, an increase in control measures to decrease the exposure of workers to chrysotile and health surveillance of these workers. However the recommendations were not acted on by the National Occupational Health and Safety Commission (NOHSC). For the next years, the trade union movement continued to lobby to have action taken. In November 2000, the ACTU resolved to work towards a ban on the importation of asbestos *and* asbestos products, rather than simply a ban on manufacture of asbestos products.

During that time the trade union movement resolved to bring attention to the fact that asbestos was still being imported. A community campaign was initiated by the AMWU that reached out to the asbestos support groups, sympathetic labor lawyers and other interested community members.

> The support groups and labor lawyers had more appeal than the unions did. The asbestos support groups have always been groups of people who come and go, self-help groups often are, that's partly their nature. We knew who those people were, we had good links with good legal companies who do the asbestos litigation so we were able to organize public events. People who had 'meso' [mesothelioma] were involved in public action and those people have since died and they were amazing, because this wasn't about their health, but about the health of other people. There

> were existing links because our members are part of those groups, unions have been on the committees of those groups.
>
> We had a post card and a T-shirt campaign. The post cards were signed by different people and sent to Tony Abbott who was Minister for Employment and Workplace Relations at the time. The T-shirts were designed to bring attention to the issue. We did stuff during Asbestos Awareness Week which is in November, and also for International Workers Memorial Day which is April 28. In 2001 the ACTU hosted the international trade union official function for Workers Memorial Day. We held a public ceremony on the steps of the state library. We called on people to sign the post cards and then we listened to speakers from the Latrobe Valley Asbestos Support Group. There was also little events, little media events. Once we went to the Department of Employment and Workplace relations and laid wreaths. We had asbestos removal workers in their gear and we sent post cards. One of the people who laid a wreath was an asbestos disease sufferer and that's very powerful.
>
> In my opinion there are a lot of unsung heroes. The Workers Health movement was essential in the first place. It was a group of health activists and trade unionists.
>
> VALLANCE, 2013

Towards the end of 2000, the matter was raised at an ACTU Executive meeting. The Secretary of the Maritime Union was present and was confident that all asbestos importation had ceased. But once it was established that chrysotile was still coming in through the ports, packed in such a way that waterside workers had not identified it, the Maritime Union threatened immediate industrial action to ensure that Canadian chrysotile was no longer imported into the country.

This was problematic for the AMWU whose members would certainly lose jobs if the ban was placed only on raw asbestos. However, at the same time the strength of the threatened industrial action was such that if the ban had gone ahead, the industry would have been without asbestos within a matter of weeks. This forced all parties to the table and in May 2001 negotiations led to an agreement for a phase out of asbestos to be completed by the end of 2003.

> Despite a high incidence of asbestos-related disease, it was the threat of industrial action that eventually persuaded Australian governments to impose a ban.
>
> VALLANCE, 2004

On 31 December 2003, the importation of chrysotile asbestos and asbestos containing products was finally banned by the Federal Government. This action followed a long campaign by the Australian Manufacturing Workers Union, and would never have happened except for the militancy of the union campaign and the strong support that the unions enjoyed in workplaces and in the community at large.

The Life-Course of the Project

The life-course of the Anti-Asbestos Movement is typical of that of any project.

For a long period of time until the alliance between the trade union and medical scientists was forged, there were only isolated cases in which workers sought compensation and were either silenced or died before succeeding. There was no social movement, although the conditions were crying out for such a movement.

Once the medical scientists, who had acquired the knowledge, and the unions, who could take that knowledge to the shop floor workers who needed it, entered into a collaborative relationship with each other, a social movement, albeit fragmented and discontinuous, was launched. Despite the extensive knowledge and commitment of the activists in the Anti-Asbestos Movement from the beginning, the objective of the project went through a series of stages before realizing its ultimate objective.

- At first the object was to win compensation for victims, which involved proving the lethal nature of asbestos. This provided the evidence needed to take the project further.
- Once asbestos was exposed as a dangerous substance, the Industry found common ground with Anti-Asbestos Movement in seeking 'safe levels' of exposure and other measures typical of the OH&S approach at the time.
- Then claims for punitive compensation were taken up, which required proving that the employer *knew* the dangers they were exposing workers to. This provided the impetus to demonstrate the ineffectiveness of regulation.
- Demands were then taken up for the banning of the mining of asbestos and production of asbestos products altogether.
- A ban on the importation of asbestos and the production of asbestos products was demanded, and
- ultimately, the importation of asbestos products as well as raw asbestos was to be banned.

As each new goal came forward, this did not mean that earlier goals were abandoned. On the contrary, the battle for suitable or adequate compensation continued long after the final total ban on asbestos production and importation was in place.

Finally, no kind of 'social movement', even one as diverse as the Anti-Asbestos Movement could exist once the total ban was legislated. Because of the existence of asbestos in old buildings, constant vigilance is required to protect workers and the public, and many of the former campaigners are now occupied in 'policing' the safe eradication of asbestos. But this work is now supported by legislation and regulation, rather than being aimed at changing the law. Just as the residue of the industry's product – lethal fibers tucked away in public buildings, telecom trenches and homes will be with us for a century, thousands more will suffer a painful death from mesothelioma and other asbestos-related disease. But the *eternal* legacy of the Anti-Asbestos Movement is the new *concept* of asbestos which is now part of our culture, legislated and objectified in new laws and regulations and a new range of work skills and knowledge about asbestos and new solutions to the applications formerly used by asbestos. Many of the activists, notably members of the victim support groups, never lived to see the benefits of their struggle to expose the real nature of asbestos. *C'est la vie*. But asbestos, is now almost universally regarded not as a 'miracle fiber', but as a lethal threat, a concept so engrained in the community that discovery of old asbestos during renovations or public works may trigger panic.

We say 'almost universally', because, for instance, the town of Wittenoom, in remotest outback of Western Australia, until 2006 when public utilities were turned off, still had 37 inhabitants who continued to live in what is no more than a giant dump of blue asbestos 140 kilometers from anywhere, still in dogged denial of the lethal nature of asbestos. This brings us to the next issue.

Dying for the Boss

Long after the lethal nature of asbestos was public knowledge, workers in the asbestos plants continued to work in dense clouds of lethal dust, and took their work clothes home to be cleaned, thereby spreading the disease to their wives and children, all the time denying the dangers and viewing union officials, journalists or even fellow-workers who warned of the dangers as troublemakers. Eventually, unfortunately often when it was too late to avoid a painful death by mesothelioma, most were won to the cause of the Anti-Asbestos

Movement. But a couple of cases will illustrate how the loyalty of these workers to their employers deserve the Victoria Cross for 'the most conspicuous bravery, daring or pre-eminent acts of valor or self-sacrifice, and extreme devotion to duty.'

Consider the case of Ozzie Allan, Mine Manager at Wittenoom. In 1959, Dr. Jim McNulty, Head of WA's Pubic Health Department, had told CSR's managers to stop allowing tailings to be dumped around Wittenoom, but was ignored. McNulty succeeded in bringing the matter before the WA Parliament, but nothing was done. He also advised at least 100 of the miners that their X-Rays showed evidence of asbestos disease, and advised them to leave Wittenoom. Not one miner took his advice. Ozzie Allen was manager of the mine for most of his later life, and was among those who McNulty advised to leave. Allen was told in no uncertain terms of the dangers, but colluded in ensuring that the full extent of the health risks was kept from the men. He died of mesothelioma in 1987, a few days after wheezing his way through cross-examination in the Supreme Court, perjuring himself to defend CSR's claim that they had no knowledge of the dangers of asbestos exposure in Wittenoom (Hills, 1989, pp. 48, 54–55, 113–114, 169).

Likewise, Paul Thomas, Mine Superintendent at Wittenoom from 1966 to 1979, did not even seek (no fault) workers compensation for the asbestosis of which he died in 1988. According to McCulloch & Tweedale (2008, p. 199): 'At James Hardie, a number of managers, safety officers and personnel directors died from the disease'. It is remarkable that the owners and directors of these companies have escaped charges of manslaughter, but under Australian law (ComLaw, 1995, 1995a; Blunden, 2012), while a *company* can be deemed responsible for such deaths due to a 'culture' of criminal negligence, the *directors* of such companies are deemed to be as much victims of that culture as employees and not deemed personally responsible for the creation and maintenance of a culture of criminal negligence. Companies like Hardies can hide behind the corporate veil, move off-shore as they have, and put down compensation to the costs of doing business. Hardies remains a very profitable firm to this day, though it is questionable whether their asbestos business has contributed to that profitability.

What is evident is that when workers go to work in an Industry they make a commitment to the norms and conventional wisdom of that Industry. They may become as loyal to the Industry and their mates as any soldier, even to the point of sacrificing their life. This even extends to loyalty to a firm, a project whose only object is the accumulation of capital. Hardies for example, easily diversified out of asbestos production in Australia when it became profitable to do so, but many of their employees remained loyal. It was only the intervention of the Anti-Asbestos movement which after a long and arduous struggle, shook that loyalty and made knowledge of asbestos disease accessible and believable for those who worked with asbestos.

Tolerance of Risks with a Long Latency Period

There is no doubt that if asbestos dust had been as immediately active as nerve gas, asbestos production would never have happened. But the long latency period associated with asbestos disease does not by itself explain people's willingness to tolerate the risk of asbestos disease. A broad literature on moral panics (e.g. Douglas & Wildavsky, 1983) and on risk-taking behavior (Lightfoot, 1997) has established that *belief* or access to evidence is not the predominant issue in determining what people fear and what risks they tolerate. Tolerance or avoidance is predominantly a function of ethical commitment or disgust. An asbestos worker's indifference to the danger of mesothelioma is not due so much to ignorance of the mechanism of the disease, but rather to their commitment to their firm, the Industry and their community (often company towns) and the trust which accompanies commitment. These commitments can lead them to regard scientists, union officials and journalists who warn of the dangers of asbestos as trouble-makers and scaremongers. Acceptance of the lethal danger of asbestos meant not only the loss of their job (although frequently it did not) but abandonment of a way of life and commitments to profession, family and community. In the order of Nature, so to speak, asbestos workers would work themselves to death. It was only the determined intervention of the Anti-Asbestos Movement, and in particular the collaborative project formed by the union movement and medical science, and their penetration of the justice system, the press and the government bureaucracies, that created conditions under which asbestos workers could be won to the cause of Anti-Asbestos. Irving Selikoff (McCulloch & Tweedale, 2008, p. 275) said that knowledge can only be effective if it is in the hands of the people who work with dangerous materials. Many arms of the Anti-Asbestos movement contributed to placing that knowledge into the hands of the workers themselves, but the trade union arm of the Movement was key. Nonetheless, those workers also have to be made ready to accept that knowledge. Public information of scientific matters is never enough to change someone's mind when science runs contrary to ethical, religious, political or even professional and work commitments.

But Deborah Vallance also points to the difficult conditions for workers who have to decide on who to trust in making these decisions:

> [A]t Bintex Mentix, [t]he union opposed the use of asbestos but the workers were told, which was true, that the substitutes had dangers as well i.e., a mixture of lead and synthetic mineral fibers that meant they would have had to have regular blood lead levels done – lead is probably one of the oldest known industrial poisons – and during the 1980s the union movement was also raising grave concerns about some synthetic mineral fibers. So…the workers were rather in an invidious position. I do not wish people to judge workers without any understanding of the lack of choices people felt they had, despite the dangers of asbestos. It's easy not being the person having to make a choice between safety, health and food on the table.
>
> VALLANCE, 2013b

Conflict and Collaboration

The history of asbestos is one of the formation of and collaboration and conflict between projects, by which a cultural belief in the benefits of the 'miracle fiber' was transformed into revulsion at the residue of the asbestos industry left hidden in our buildings. Having been legally designated a lethal threat to public health, asbestos is never to be produced or imported and is remediated with the utmost care.

How did the Industry nobble its potential enemies? In the first place, competing firms formed a collaborative Industry project to protect themselves from regulation. Three main tactics were then used. In the first place, the Industry worked very hard at fostering the loyalty of their employees and the residents of company towns. They were also active contributors to the local community (while poisoning them to death). Usually, they employed new immigrants or Aboriginal people, grateful for the employment but lacking political muscle, or older workers who would retire by the time they became ill. Secondly, they systematically interfered with the dissemination of knowledge about asbestos. In particular, the focus on 'safe' levels of dust and adapting to a rising culture of Occupational Health and Safety (itself a gain finally institutionalized in the 1980s by trade union action). This had the effect of subverting the objective of the Anti-asbestos Movement, recruiting many well-meaning activists into the fake project of achieving 'safe' levels of exposure. Thirdly, they bought off potential opponents, sometimes with monetary rewards, but usually with rewards of prestige and recognition.

How did the Anti-Asbestos Movement achieve its aims? As Deborah Vallance outlines, it involved long and arduous 'back room' work, assembling evidence and winning over individuals. In particular, it meant collaboration between the two main existing projects – the trade union movement, whose mission was to defend the working conditions of working class people, and institutions of the medical science, whose mission included the discovery of the real causes of disease. Only by means of the collaboration of these two projects was it possible to form a collaborative project which could overthrow the hegemony of the Industry. The collaborative project created by the alliance of unions and medical scientists was then able to recruit individuals from the regulatory authorities, a few members of government, individual journalists, victims and their families and labor law firms into the Anti-Asbestos Movement even while the majority of their associates remained passive. This *counter-hegemony* established by the Anti-Asbestos Movement eventually prevailed.

Where did individual workers and their families stand in this? There were some who already had a strong commitment to the Union Movement and they played an important role. But for most of them, their life-project entailed raising a family, leading a good life in their community, with a respectable job in a good industry. The struggle over asbestos entailed a battle for the loyalty of these people above all. Public information was never enough; for a long time these workers and their families were cruelly and tragically deceived and their lives destroyed.

But alliances were formed, and minds changed by a successful collaborative project. The world we live in is the product of such collaborative projects, whose products are institutionalized in the concepts, institutions, customs, laws, land and infrastructure that has been built up over many generations, while all the time threatened by projects of self-enrichment and self-promotion. This cultural world continues to change thanks to the activism of those who commit themselves to right what is wrong and find that they are not alone, but remains threatened by projects like that of the Asbestos Industry.

References

ADFA (2009). *Asbestos History*. Sydney, Australia: Asbestos Diseases Foundation of Australia.

Blunden, A. (2012). *Corporate Manslaughter Laws in Australia*, http://academia.edu/2079565/Corporate_Manslaughter_Laws_in_Australia.

Byrne, D.A. (1965). Urgent probe into 'new' killer dust disease. In *The Sunday Times*: London.

ComLaw (1995). *Criminal Code Act 1995*, Australian Government, http://www.comlaw.gov.au/Details/C2012C00306/.

ComLaw (1995a). *Crimes Amendment Act 1995*. Australian Government, http://www.comlaw.gov.au/Details/C2004A04867.

National Health and Medical Research Council (1961). *Schedule of Recommended Maximum Concentrations of Atmospheric Contaminants for Occupational Exposures*. Canberra, Australia.

Deller, B. (2013). Interview with Lynn Beaton.

Douglas, M. & Wildavsky, A. (1983). *Risk and Culture, An Essay on the Selection of Technological and Environmental Dangers*. Berkeley, CA: University of California Press.

Epstein, S. (1979). *The Politics of Cancer*. New York: Anchor.

GPCC (Goliath Portland Cement Company Ltd.). Internal Files of David Lawrie: Asbestos: Local News Items etc. In BoxAI3F6: Railton, Tasmania.

Haigh, G. (2006). *Asbestos House*. Melbourne, Australia: Scribe Publications.

Hills, B. (1989). *Blue Murder*. Melbourne, Australia: Sun Books.

Lightfoot, C. (1997). *The Culture of Adolescent Risk-Taking*. London, UK: The Guildford Press.

Marsh, M. (2010). Asbestos strike. *The Canadian Encyclopedia*. Quebec Canada: Historica Foundation.

McCulloch, J. (1986). *Asbestos – Its Human Cost*. University of Queensland Press.

McCulloch J. & Tweedale G. (2008). *Defending the Indefensible*. Oxford University Press.

Peacock, M. (2009). *Killer Company*. Sydney, Australia: ABC Books.

Taibbi, M. (2010). *Griftopia*. Kindle ed., New York: Speigel & Grauy.

Vallance, D. (2004). The phase-out of asbestos in the Australian manufacturing environment. *International Journal of Occupation and Environment Health*, 10:209–211.

Vallance, D. (2013). Interview with Lynn Beaton.

Vallance, D. (2013a). Email to Lynn Beaton, 4 July 2013b.

CHAPTER 12

Tahrir: A Project(ion) of Revolutionary Change

Brecht De Smet

The Project of Revolution

On 25 January 2011 a diverse group of Egyptian social media activists, leftists, youth organizations, political opposition forces, human rights proponents, Islamists, and hardcore football supporters (the so-called Ultras) had called for a demonstration in Tahrir Square. The demands of the organizers were relatively modest: "...the sacking of the country's interior minister, the cancelling of Egypt's perpetual emergency law, which suspends basic civil liberties, and a new term limit on the presidency that would bring to an end the 30-year rule of President Hosni Mubarak" (Shenker, 2011). No-one expected the protests to attract tens of thousands of ordinary Egyptians, let alone become the harbinger of revolution. "Before the revolution it was a success to have 100 people demonstrating in the street. So we were laughing: tomorrow we will have a revolution,"[1] leftist journalist Haisam Hassan recalled. "We wanted to challenge the cops by protesting that day. A lot of people were surprised to see that we had more than 25,000 people at Tahrir that day and things escalated from there,"[2] shrugged youth activist Ahmed al-Gourd. Political cartoonist Salah Abd al-Azim had originally planned his wedding on 22 January. When he heard of the protest organized on the 25th, he decided to postpone his marriage to the 26th, so he could participate in the demonstration: "I imagined it would only be one day of protests as usual. So I delayed my wedding to 26 January. So on 25 January we went to the protests. No one of my guests could make it to my wedding on the 26th, because half of them was protesting and the other half was escaping the police!"[3]

The security apparatus was surprised by the massive turn-out and followed the events rather passively at first. In the afternoon, Central Security forces tried to break up the protests with water cannons, sound bombs, batons,

1 Interview with Haisam Hassan, Cairo, 7 March 2011.

2 Interview with Ahmed al-Gourd, Cairo, 24 March 2011.

3 Interview with Salah Abd al-Azim, Cairo, 22 March 2011.

rubber bullets, and tear gas, and the peaceful demonstrations turned violent as protesters retaliated with rocks and bricks. Central Cairo became a war zone with continuous street battles between police forces and tens of thousands of demonstrators. The protests in Cairo sparked off massive demonstrations in Alexandria and in cities in the Delta, the Canal Zone, and Upper Egypt. The next 18 days saw an ebb and flood of mass protests and violent countermeasures, throughout which the original tame demands were transformed into the revolutionary slogans of "the people want the fall of the regime," and "bread, freedom, and social justice," Tahrir Square in Cairo was occupied, and in the whole country police stations and the party offices of the ruling National Democratic Party (NDP) were burned down. Suddenly people realized they were making a revolution and that there was no way back. Their mass uprising eventually pressured Hosni Mubarak, who had been Egypt's President since 1981, to step down.

In this chapter I investigate the process of the 25 January uprising as a collaborative project. On the one hand, by deploying the concept of project, I hope to disentangle some of the theoretical knots in the study of revolutions and the understanding of the current Egyptian revolution in particular. On the other hand, by confronting the concept of project collaboration with a specific case, I wish to explore the strengths and weaknesses of this approach to the study of revolutionary movements. From this perspective, my discussion of the 25 January Revolution is guided by five important theoretical questions.

Firstly, I address the *developmental* and *historical* dynamic of revolutionary collaboration. Where does a project "begin," where does it "end"? Revolutions are not created ex nihilo: they are the continuation, expansion, replacement, or transformation of collaborations that came before, and, in turn, constitute the building blocks of new projects. I explain that the 25 January Revolution was not only a project of revolution, but it also represented a revolution of existing projects. Secondly, I investigate the *boundaries* of a project. What is internal and external to a specific collaboration? How can we distinguish the object of investigation from its context? I suggest that the notion of a *unit of analysis* offers a way out of this problematic. With regard to the Egyptian uprising, "Tahrir" is taken up as a unit of analysis of the whole process, a "nested" project within the wider project of revolution. Thirdly, how is the life-process of projects organized? Projects are not static "things," but they grow, degenerate, and/or die in the course of their development. Some projects remain brief, ad hoc collaborations, while others may exist, in one shape or another, for hundreds of years. The project of Tahrir saw a rapid and non-linear sequence of *leading collaborations* – demonstration, occupation, festival, and governance – which each determined the further development of the whole process. Fourthly, Tahrir was not only a project, but also a *projection*, in the sense that its saliency interpellated and shaped other collaborations. Tahrir was able to step outside its own boundaries – the physically shared social space of hundreds of thousands people – because it was literally projected in the living rooms of the whole world, inspiring movements from Occupy Wall Street in New York to the Indignados in Madrid. Fifthly, how are the *activities* and *goals* of a project interconnected? With regard to the 25 January Revolution, it was the original goal of contesting the corrupt regime that brought together tens of thousands of people. However, it was the development of the various actions interpellated by this goal that created new, revolutionary goals, which in turn constituted new forms of collaboration. As goal-driven collaborations, projects are found to exist at the crossroads of *teleology* and *immanence*. Finally, I discuss how the conceptual limits of using Tahrir as the cell-form of the whole revolution also illustrate the real developmental pathologies of and challenges for the revolution.

Past and Present

Seeing that little had changed over the course of two years after the fall of Mubarak, labor historian Joel Beinin claimed that: "The January 25 Revolution is not over. Rather, it has not yet occurred" (Beinin, 2013). The authoritarian state apparatus was largely untouched by the mass protests and there was no fundamental transformation of the political and economic relations of power in Egypt. Beinin rightly pointed out that revolutions are "…social, political, and economic transformations involving social movements and political mobilizations, one or more moments of popular uprising, and a longer-term process of reconstructing a new socio-political order involving the replacement of the former ruling coalition with new forces of a substantially different social character and interests" (Beinin, 2013). The popular uprising of 25 January did not represent the whole process of revolution, and the palace coup by the Supreme Council of Armed Forces (SCAF) was all but the end of the reconstruction of a new order. As the *outcomes* of the uprising at the level of state power were not (yet) revolutionary, Beinin refrained from categorizing the whole process as a revolution. This outcome-centered approach echoed the works of Theda Skocpol (1979) and Samuel Huntington (2006), who emphasized rapid transformations in the structure of societies as a key element of revolutions. This perspective turns a particular outcome of the revolutionary process into a primary determinant of its categorization, rendering the notion of a failed revolution problematic, as its success – i.e. the conquest, break-up, and transformation of state power (c.f. Lenin, 1976) – becomes a precondition of its definition. Thus, in the case of Egypt, the success of the counter-revolution after the fall of Mubarak was interpreted as evidence that there was no authentic revolution taking place. This, in turn, meant that the protagonists of the 25 January uprising fell victim to a cruel self-deception when they called their own mass activity during the 18 days a "revolution."[4]

The conundrum is a difficult one. On the one hand, by labeling the process as a revolution, its current, unsatisfactory outcomes are legitimated. On the other hand, by rejecting that there is, in fact, a revolution unfolding, the agency and self-consciousness of the masses are diminished. In order to solve this problem, I argue that it is much more productive to conceive of the January 25 Revolution as an *unfinished process that has always been there*. As Beinin (2013) emphasized, the mass uprising of 25 January was but one moment within a chain of diverse protests that preceded it. It was, however, a *crucial* moment because what had been already there, in an undeveloped, implicit, and hidden form, was rendered explicit and salient. The 18 Days represented a sapling of which both its past, as a seed, and its potential future, as a tree, were hidden from immediate observation. Nevertheless, these moments are part of the same developmental process. A project approach allows us to recognize within the 25 January uprising the development of collaborations that existed before 2011, and, conversely, to recognize the undeveloped form of "revolution" within collaborations that paved the way for the insurrection.

Labor leader Fatma Ramadan commented that she was "…not measuring the revolution since 25 January, but since the year 2000, since the anti-imperialist movements and the social movements and the strikes. All the worker strikes, the continuous strikes since 2006 were a prelude to the revolution."[5] The Egyptian uprising was not created ex nihilo, nor was it simply initiated by the Tunisian protests, but it constituted a development of earlier projects. As Ramadan explained, since the 2000s there emerged a diversity of collaborations among human and civil rights activists, among pro-democracy forces, among workers, among farmers, among the urban poor, et cetera. These different projects emerged from problems particular to the life of their participants. Workers moved against their crumbling purchasing power, the rise of unemployment, and the precarious working conditions induced by policies of privatization and liberalization. They came increasingly into conflict with the General Federation of Egyptian Trade Unions (GFETU), the official state-led syndicate that monopolized labor conflicts, which forced them to develop

4 See De Smet 2014.

5 Interview with Fatma Ramadan, Cairo, 15 March 2011.

their own, independent and democratic strike committees and trade unions (De Smet, 2012; Zemni, De Smet & Bogaert 2012). Together with experienced militants from every ideological pedigree, a new generation of young activists organized demonstrations in solidarity with the Second Palestinian Intifada of 2000, and protests against the wars in Afghanistan, Iraq, and Lebanon. From these collaborations emerged new projects such as the democratic movement Kefaya (Enough) between 2004 and 2006, which, for the first time, contested the legitimacy of the Egyptian regime, and especially the possible succession of the elderly Hosni Mubarak by his son, Gamal (Zemni, De Smet & Bogaert, 2012). This democratic movement "on the ground" was supported and stimulated by the advent of "virtual" political activism by bloggers, Facebook users, and Twitterers. In the countryside, farmers struggled against increasing land rents because of the deregulation of prices and markets and the concentration of landed property by occupying their lands and organizing cooperatives. Villagers cut off roads, railroads, and waterways to protest a lack of potable water or electricity. And so on.

Rather than conceiving of the 25 January uprising as a separate phenomenon, it should be integrated within an understanding of the development of a tangle of previous protests, which, each from their particular angle, contested an aspect of *al-nizam*, the "regime" or "system." What the uprising represented was a moment in which this molecular accumulation of economic strikes and protests, and political sit-ins and demonstrations was forged into a meaningful, salient, and explicit whole – into a quantitatively and qualitatively new project of revolutionary change.

But the 25 January revolution was already present within forms of collaboration that were even less explicit and developed. With regard to labor activism, for example, Asef Bayat observed that: "Under repressive conditions, labor resistance may take the form of absenteeism, sabotage, disturbances, theft, religious practice, and poor quality production. Labor activism of this nature is not necessarily unplanned or purely 'spontaneous'..." (Bayat, 1996, p. 180). Before January 25, discontent with *al-nizam* was not restricted to organized protests – which remained, after all, relatively small in the context of a population of more than 80 million – but it surfaced in the shape of cynical jokes about the president and such forms of "hidden" and "everyday" forms of resistance that Bayat discussed. The shared practices and signs of subterfuge and humor were probably the most primitive shapes of the revolution, and constituted revolutionary collaboration at its minimal level. At that point, activities that were merely *survival* or *coping strategies*, were indiscernible from *everyday forms of resistance*. In fact, calling an individual or collective act of destruction, "laziness," or sarcasm a form of resistance imputes a much more advanced consciousness and intentionality to the actor. (See Abbink & van Walraven, 2003, pp. 1–10.) Although the participants of such a collaboration may *objectively* undermine the political legitimacy or economic base of *al-nizam*, they are themselves not conscious of their activity *as* resistance. The solution, again, is to conceive of these primitive collaborations as an actuality of an open-ended process of contestation with a potentiality to develop into a project of resistance – in the words of Robin Cohen: "The hidden forms are at a lower level of consciousness but can be seen as part of an incremental chain of consciousness leading towards a 'higher', more politicized, form of consciousness...though any incremental process cannot be viewed deterministically" (Cohen, 1980, p. 21).

Within the 25 January uprising, these forms of collaboration, ranging from pro-democracy sit-ins and strikes for higher wages to sabotage and cynical humor, reappeared, but in a much more developed and mass-based form. The famous occupation of *Midan Tahrir* had been anticipated by a large demonstration in the Square in 2001 and a brief occupation in March 2003, when 20,000 protesters protested against the U.S. military intervention in Iraq (Howeidy, 2005). The strike wave that started from 8 and 9 February 2011 – and which continued unabated after Mubarak's resignation – was foreshadowed by the upturn of workers' struggles since the mid-2000s (Zemni, De Smet & Bogaert, 2012). The inventive ways in which protesters organized and defended themselves against the attacks of the security forces, or drained electricity from the net to power up speaker systems in Tahrir, were rooted in their daily survival strategies. Concerning humor, journalist Ashraf Khalil remarked that the Egyptian revolution was possibly the most funny revolution ever, such as the self-made placard reading "Just leave already, my arm hurts!" (Khalil, 2012, p. 246). When all these different threads are taken together, the 25 January uprising appears not only as a revolutionary project in its own right, but also as a revolution of projects, in which existing collaborations develop new forms and goals.

Inside and Outside

Conceiving of the entire process of the 25 January Revolution as a single project, calls forth a series of methodological challenges. A major obstacle is the simple problem of "where to begin?" This is not only a diachronic question – i.e. of which moment in the development of the project the investigation should take as its starting point – but also a synchronic issue: how can the essential be distinguished from the non-essential within a given process, and what is the relation between "the thing" and its "context"? How can a specific project be disentangled from other forms of collaboration?

Beginning a study of a phenomenon requires a "point of entrance" into the subject matter, from where the whole problem can be approached. In the *Grundrisse*, Marx gave the example of taking "the population" as the starting point of "economics." Although the population is *ontologically* "…the real and concrete…the foundation and the subject of the entire social act of production…" (Marx, 1973, p. 101), as an *epistemological category* it is a general abstraction, because it leaves out the specific elements that constitute it *as* a population. In order to grasp the multi-determinateness of a phenomenon, Marx suggested a double movement of scientific investigation. Firstly, a descending movement of abstraction: "…if I were to begin with the population, this would be a chaotic conception of the whole, and I would then, by means of further determination, move analytically towards ever more simple concepts, from the imagined concrete towards ever thinner abstractions until I had arrived at the simplest determinations" (Marx, 1973, p. 101). These simplest of determinations were the cell-forms of the phenomenon: "From there the journey would have to be retraced until I had finally arrived at the population again, but this time not as the chaotic conception of a whole, but as a rich totality of many determinations and relations" (Marx, 1973, p. 101). This ascending movement discloses the subject matter as a concrete phenomenon, i.e. not merely in the abstract as "population," but as a population *of* classes, division of labor, capital, et cetera.

Vygotsky appropriated this methodology with regard to the study of human action, based on finding a suitable unit of analysis as a point of entry into such a complex phenomenon: "This form of analysis relies on the partitioning of the complex whole into units. In contrast to the term 'element', the term 'unit' designates a product of analysis that possesses all the basic characteristics of the whole. The unit is a vital and irreducible part of the whole. The key to the explanation of the characteristics of water lies not in the investigation of its chemical formula but in the investigation of its molecular movements. In precisely the same sense, the living cell is the real unit of biological analysis because it preserves the basic characteristics of life that are inherent in the living organism" (Vygotsky, 1987a, p. 46). Likewise, Blunden listed three requirements. Firstly: "It is the conception of a singular, indivisible thing" (Blunden, 2010, p. 190). A unit of analysis is the most primitive and simple appearance of a particular phenomenon. Secondly: "It exhibits the essential properties of a class of more developed phenomena" (2010, p. 190). The primitive concept, the simplest determination, displays a capacity to be developed into a mature and concrete form of thought. Thirdly: "It is itself an existent phenomenon (not a principle or axiom or hypothetical force or such like non-observable)" (2010, p. 190). A unit of analysis should be "both a concept and an existent reality" that "…must be conceived and chosen so as to provide the building block for conception as well as actuality" (2010, p. 191).

From the perspective of an interdisciplinary and emancipatory social science, Blunden proposed collaborative project as a unit of analysis of human activity. Project collaboration is a shared system of human actions and mediating artifacts, which projects itself forward to a certain goal or ideal (2010, p. 313, and Introduction to this book). Although the whole Egyptian revolution constitutes a project by itself, it is, much like Marx's "population," too extensive a phenomenon to be grasped immediately in its full complexity. Our understanding of the revolutionary process has to be mediated by a unit of analysis; a point of entry from where we can investigate the many determinants of the project. In order to make sense of revolution as a concrete phenomenon, we need to find a project *within* this project that functions as its cell-form, both "in conception" and "in actuality." There is no magic formula to find such a unit of analysis. Rather than a straightforward process of deduction, a unit of analysis emerges from the engagement of the researcher with the subject matter, and what Althusser called its 'problematic';[6] when intuitions about a phenomenon, either gradually or by a sudden *aperçu* (Blunden, 2012) or *Aha-Erlebnis*, crystallize into a scientific concept.

Here I suggest the project of Tahrir as a unit of analysis of the 25 January Revolution. "Tahrir" became almost synonymous with the 25 January Revolution, although it constituted a discrete collaboration within the wider process, which pushed forward the development of the entire struggle. After the defeat of the police on Friday 28 January: "…Tahrir…became the epicenter of a revolution. Protesters not only transformed it, they were themselves transformed by their presence in it. Tahrir became a revolutionary organism unto itself…" (Khalil, 2012, p. 5). The collaboration of Tahrir gave the revolution a focal point, a history, and a future. Firstly, Tahrir presented itself as a spatial center of Cairo, and in turn of the whole of Egypt, as it represented: "…a major transport hub surrounded by vital elements of the state apparatus: the parliament, several ministerial buildings, and the imposing Mogamma'…" (Rashed, 2011, p. 23). Secondly, "Liberation Square" referred to the 1919 revolutionary uprising against the British, which secured partial independence. Thus it became a favorite gathering place for national events: "Egyptians have poured into Tahrir to celebrate soccer victories, to mourn the passing of national icons,

6 A problematic is the theoretical framework in which a new idea takes shape as a recognition *of* and an answer *to* conceptual absences and lacunae. See Althusser & Balibar 1970, p. 316.

and to protest injustice" (Shokr, 2012, p. 41). In 2003, as discussed above, the Square became the symbolic locale of political mobilization, when demonstrators occupied the square for ten hours in protest against the war in Iraq. Thirdly, the project of Tahrir developed much faster than the revolution as a whole, constituting its collaborative vanguard, and projecting a potential line of development for the whole process: "When protesters arrived at Tahrir on January 29, they did not come with the intention of creating a radical utopia... As the revolution unfolded, Tahrir was elevated from a rally site to a model for an alternative society" (Shokr, 2012, p. 42).

Taking the project of Tahrir as a unit of analysis offers a solution to the problem of finding an entry point into the subject matter of the Egyptian revolution. Moreover, it also renders the relation concrete between, on the one hand, "the revolution" and, on the other, "its context." Within the particular collaboration of Tahrir "structure" and "agency," "objective" and "subjective" factors, external forces and internal dynamics, came together as concrete constitutive elements of the revolutionary project. In the spirit of Vygotsky's approach, I conceive of the "context" of Tahrir as a *social situation of development*: a *predicament* from which the project *emancipates* itself by *making a development*, to paraphrase Blunden (2010, pp. 154–158). For example, "the regime" is not merely an external force or the background of Tahrir, it is continuously *present* within and against the project, physically embodied in the security forces, emotionally materialized in the fear and the anger of the masses, culturally reproduced in the patriarchal prejudices towards women, et cetera – all of which constitute predicaments from which the revolutionary collaboration has to emancipate itself if it wants to survive, progress, and prosper. The successful development of a revolutionary project thus not only appears as the story of its "own" life form, but also as an index of "its" context, as the negation of the constraints that fetter its growth. In other words, the study of Tahrir also reveals a lot about *al-nizam* as a problem that the revolution tries to overcome, just as an analysis of the regime discloses the predicaments confronting the revolutionary project.

It was an important insight of Vygotsky's that the social situation of development does not offer new psychological structures and forms of mediation on a plate to the child; on the contrary, the infant has to create these necessary neoformations on its own, in order to make a qualitative development to overcome the predicaments it faces. The conflict between, on the one hand, the child's desire and will to overcome its current social situation of development, and, on the other, the constraints of its condition, is the motor behind the creation of new psychological functions and mental development as a whole (Blunden, 2010, pp. 154–158). Below I argue that Vygotsky's approach to ontogenesis as "development from predicament by neoformations" offers a productive conceptual instrument to investigate the developmental process of a project. I engage with this notion through a close analysis of the 18 Days.

Demonstration and Occupation

Vygotsky observed that for each stage of development, one "neoformation" and one "line of development" play a central part in developing the entire mental structure. Central or leading neoformations and lines of development of a previous phase continue to exist in the current stage, but lose their decisive role in the maturation of the whole (Blunden, 2010, p. 157; Vygotsky, 1987a; Wertsch, 1985, p. 19). For example, the development of memory as a psychological function pushes forward the maturation of the whole mental structure, opening up a new social situation of development for the child. In early school years the child "thinks" by remembering. When this line of development has run its course, another neoformation takes over this leading role, and, continuing the example, the child remembers by thinking (Vygotsky, 1987b, p. 309).

Transposing this understanding of development to the domain of social collaboration, I suggest that projects also go through a formation process, in which specific activities and organizational structures take up a leading role, while others sink into the background. This is especially obvious with regard to long-term, systemic, and relatively stable projects such as a family, the Church, a political party, a football club, et cetera. But such a pattern is also recognizable in the short-lived 25 January uprising. I contend that there were four main lines of development during the 18 Days in Tahrir, expressed by specific forms of collaboration: demonstration; occupation; festival; and governance.[7]

"Demonstration" was the first form of collaboration that emerged in the Square on Tuesday 25 January. A political *demonstration* is literally a *showing* of discontent: a message directed at those in power and a rallying call towards potential supporters. Because of widespread popular resentment towards the increased violence and authoritarianism of the Mubarak regime and the powerful projection of the Tunisian Revolution against Ben Ali (Khalil, 2012, p. 123), activist groups called for demonstrations on National Police Day, which commemorated the progressive role of the Egyptian police in the struggle against

7 These lines do not represent a real linear sequence of forms of collaboration – e.g. when the Square was attacked its "festival" activity fell back to a militarized "occupation" – but it stands to reason that "demonstration" was the practical premise of "occupation" and "occupation," in turn, of both "festival" and "governance" as forms of collaboration.

British occupation forces in 1952, and had recently became a national holiday. Ironically, by 2011, the honored liberators of 1952 had turned into loathed epitomes of the oppressive state (Al-Bendary, 2011).

Although various small-scale grassroots organizations and social media activists organized the first protests, leftist activist Wael Tawfiq remarked that: "The reason why 25 January became a mass protest was that it started from below, from the popular neighborhoods."[8] This tactic of gathering protesters in working-class and poor neighborhoods had already been developed during the anti-war demonstrations of 2003.[9] There, activists would collect a critical mass of demonstrators before heading towards Tahrir, as groups of only tens of protesters would get arrested easily by the police before they were able to make it to the Square (Al-Ghobashy, 2011). Because of the accumulation of discontent since the past years, and the example projected by the Tunisian revolution, suddenly activists were able to convince huge numbers of non-politicized citizens into showing their displeasure with the regime (Khalil, 2012, p. 143–144).

The massive turnout of the demonstrations took the riot police by surprise. Egypt's Central Security Forces (CSF) were organized for a large-scale, but short-term and focused deployment, striking swift and hard at a single point of resistance by overwhelming protesters by pure numbers. However, as on January 25 the quantitative balance shifted in the favor of the demonstrators, the CSF was no longer able to simply "surround" and subdue protesters (Colla, 2011; Khalil, 2012, p. 140–142). Heavy street fighting broke out between demonstrators and the CSF, and in order to exercise their right to demonstrate and show their discontent, protesters attempted to hold Tahrir Square in order to make a stand against the riot police.

At this point, the activity of occupation was merely instrumental to the leading collaboration of demonstration – a way to solve the problem of the police preventing them from demonstrating. Moreover, during the late evening and the night, the emerging revolutionary project bumped into another obstacle. Tuesday had been a national holiday, but now people began to leave Tahrir for their homes. The remaining "hard core" of activists had to keep the fire burning until the next big moment of popular mobilization, Friday the 28th, which was dubbed the "Friday of Anger." As the masses thinned out in Tahrir, its first occupation was violently dispersed, and small groups of hundreds of protesters – especially the "Ultras" – threw themselves into a game of cat and mouse with the security forces in nearby streets and neighborhoods (Al-Werdani, 2011; Khalil, 2012, p. 149–153). There was a sense of urgency among

8 Interview with Wael Tawfiq, Cairo, 8 March 2011.

9 Interview with Gihan Shabeen, Cairo, 16 March 2011.

the remaining protesters and an awareness of the leading role of the Tahrir occupation in the whole revolutionary process: "We must hold Tahrir through the night and tomorrow, so that every corner of Egypt can take us as an inspiration and rise up in revolt… It's a matter of life and death now – what happens over the next 24 hours will be vital to the history of this country."[10]

Although the transformation of collaboration into an "urban guerrilla war" was born out of the defeat of the first occupation of Tahrir, its constant, decentralized attacks and withdrawals, played an important role in weakening the security apparatus, as conscripts and petty officers began to suffer from physical and moral fatigue (Al-Ghobashy, 2011; Khalil, 2012, p. 161). However, despite its importance as an activity to keep the engine of the project running – to continue to *project* the revolution to its potential participants, as it were – the urban-guerrilla form of collaboration did not have a *developmental* influence on the maturation of Tahrir as a project. Arguably, this impact emerged only within the leading collaboration of occupation, as only then did it create specific structures and methods of civil defense, which in turn pushed the development of the whole project forward.

Friday 28 January became a key moment for the revolutionary project. The vanguard heroics of the urban guerrilla on Wednesday and Thursday had kept the demands and spirit of the revolution on the minds of the masses, who returned to the streets on their day off. The collaboration of demonstration flowed organically from their participation in the Friday midday prayers. The revolutionary projection transformed this traditional moment of religious collaboration into a political demonstration. Against the protesters stood, again, the obstacle of the CSF, which however, were to be defeated by a mass repetition of Wednesday's and Thursday's urban guerrilla warfare – but this time with a mass character. Whereas the previous guerrilla collaboration had been a defensive strategy of small groups to keep the revolution alive, now it became an offensive of the masses in order to overcome a main obstacle in their revolutionary project: the violent repression of their demonstrations: "The protesters, in the face of such violence, temporarily abandoned their signature cries of *salmeya* (peaceful) and responded with their own storm of rocks, concrete chunks, and, eventually, Molotov cocktails" (Khalil, 2012, p. 1). This time the demonstrators were prepared for the confrontation by their experience of 25 January and advice from their Tunisian comrades: "…a Tunisian friend concluded that we could make a revolution on Friday and he sent us advice on what to do if they started to use tear gas: using cola and vinegar and onions."[11]

10 Ahmed Salah in *Guardian* Egypt Live Blog 2011.

11 Interview with Haisam Hassan, Cairo, 7 March 2011.

From the midday prayers until 6 PM there was an all-out battle in Downtown Cairo between the CSF and tens of thousands of demonstrators who were trying to reach Tahrir. Especially the bridges connecting the west to the east bank of the Nile became the sites of fierce struggles, as the riot police tried to block these passages towards the Square. At a certain point, conscripts and petty officers began to lose consciousness themselves because of the smog of tear gas in the streets, and started to defect.[12] Finally: "After a lot of people were killed with trucks, and after the people who came from Ramsis and other streets had regrouped, there was the biggest demonstration of that day. This was the moment the police chose to surrender and go back to…we still don't know yet,"[13] laughed Wael Tawfiq.

The CSF was replaced by military troops, which, for reasons of their own (See De Smet, 2014), did not confront the protesters head-on, but preferred a war of position, digging "urban trenches" around important regime sites, such as the Parliament, the Maspero Radio and Television Building, the Presidential Palace, the Stock Exchange, et cetera. The withdrawal of the police from the streets allowed the protesters to occupy Tahrir anew, and this continuous collaboration of occupation came to represent the revolution as a whole. Instead of merely being a site to demonstrate discontent, the collaboration of the Square became an instrument of popular power to pressure the President to step down: *we* won't leave until *you* leave. The protesters dug their own trenches around Tahrir, erecting tents and distributing blankets, food and water, and arranging entertainment to keep the spirits of the occupiers high.

Festival and Governance

The occupation of Tahrir swiftly gave way to a new leading development, which articulated the cultural transformation that the revolution inspired. Lenin had emphasized that "Revolutions are the festivals of the oppressed and the exploited. At no other time are the masses of the people in a position to come forward so actively as creators of a new social order as at a time of revolution" (Lenin, 1969, p. 125–126). Although by then the objective of the revolution – the overthrow of *al-nizam* – was grim, occupiers already felt liberated in Liberation Square. People sang, discussed, prayed, told jokes, fell in love, got married, and spent their honeymoon in Tahrir.

---

12 Interview with Haisam Hassan, Cairo, 7 March 2011.

13 Interview with Wael Tawfiq, Cairo, 8 March 2011.

The festival of revolt was supported by established artists who joined the protests, and amateur cartoonists, actors, and singers who emerged from the collaboration of Tahrir itself. As the Square brought together political activists, artists, and the masses in close collaboration, there was a double movement of activists and artists becoming part of "the people," and the people becoming involved in politics and artistic production: "Most Egyptians didn't see any art or know any artists and for many Egyptians it was the first time to see artists in action, and for artists it was the first time to have a mass feedback and audience through the Square."[14] Revolutionary stages were erected where every participant of the project was allowed to act, speak, or sing.[15] Artists not only provided entertainment, but also reflected and refracted the revolutionary project in graffiti, cartoons, slogans, songs, and jokes: objectifications that mocked and discredited the regime. The art of the Square was its material consciousness and constituted a concentrated articulation as well as an active shaper of political awareness.[16]

On Tuesday 1 February there were new mass demonstrations, coming from all over Cairo and, despite military blockades of railroads and highways, even from other places in Egypt, they filled the Square. Whereas demonstrations as a form of revolutionary collaboration remained important throughout the whole 18 Days, they now played a supporting and reinforcing role towards the leading collaboration of occupation. The revolution-as-festival had reached its zenith, as anthropologist Samuli Schielke described it: "This day was one of the most amazing things I have ever experienced. It was perfectly peaceful, perfectly organized by spontaneous volunteers who took care of order, security, cleanliness. The people behaved in a very peaceful and reasonable way, and there was an amazing shared sense of dignity and power... Such pride, such determination, such sense of dignity, such sense of power, and such joy prevailed today in the center of Cairo that I cannot write about it tonight without becoming very emotional. Not a moment for detached analysis" (Schielke, 2011).

In the evening, Mubarak made some vague concessions to the protesters. Whilst the most politically conscious elements of the project derided the President's move, other protesters were satisfied by the proposed reforms, and wanted to return back to "normalcy." This moment had the potential to split the mass movement into a "moderate" and a "radical" wing.[17] Relatively large

14 Interview with Salah Abd al-Azim, Cairo, 22 March 2011.

15 Interview with Muhammad Zaki Murad, Cairo, 30 March 2011.

16 Interview with Menal Khalid, Cairo, 25 March 2011.

17 Interview with Sabry Zaki, Cairo, 10 March 2011.

pro-Mubarak protests were organized to discredit the powerful claim of the revolutionaries that they represented "the people," sowing additional confusion in the ranks of the less politicized protesters. If the regime had restrained itself at that moment, temporarily exchanging the stick for the carrot, it would have considerably weakened the revolutionary project. However, after the soothing speech of Mubarak, the Ministry of Interior initiated a clampdown on the remaining hard core or vanguard of protesters who were camping in Tahrir. Instead of splitting revolutionary collaboration, the vicious attack on Tahrir by Molotov-throwing plainclothes security forces, rock-throwing *baltageyya* (thugs), paramilitary snipers, and – in a surreal episode – charging camel drivers, reunited the masses, and drove them in great numbers back to Tahrir (Shokr, 2012, p. 45).

This dynamic is reminiscent of Marx's alleged aphorism that "…a revolution needs from time to time the whip of the counter-revolution" (Trotsky, 2001, p. 774). It elucidates Vygotsky's insight that a predicament is not merely an obstacle, but a springboard in the course of development, as it forces a project to create practices and structures to overcome it, through which the whole collaborative process is pushed forward. From a "utopian street party" (Khalil, 2012, p. 243), the Square turned into "Fortress Tahrir" (Khalil, 2012, p. 247). "… the Square transformed into organized workgroups. Everyone in the Square was organized: girls, women, even the girls with a niqab… Everyone did what he could to his ability,"[18] revolutionary activist Wael Tawfiq recalled. The "borders" of Tahrir – the Front (Rashed, 2011, p. 25) – had to be defended, which encouraged the formation of a "military" division of labor: a first group outfitted the "warriors" with protective layers; "gatherers" tore rocks from the pavement as ammunition; "foragers" supplied the "warriors" in the frontlines with rocks, water, and food (Khalil, 2012, p. 229).[19] A field hospital was erected in the center of the Square and a "civil prison," where the occupiers held captured plainclothes police officers and security personnel in custody,[20] not least to protect them from the wrath of their co-demonstrators.

The attack also stressed the importance of a continued occupation of Tahrir. Apart from the defense of the Square, the participants of the project had to create a daily life routine: securing food and shelter, treating the wounded, washing clothes, setting up stations for mobile charging, et cetera. As Tahrir became a project of life in almost all its facets, it required some form of governance. As the State was forcefully driven away from the space of the Square,

18 Interview with Wael Tawfiq, Cairo, 8 March 2011.

19 Interview with Wael Tawfiq, Cairo, 8 March 2011.

20 Interview with Wael Tawfiq, Cairo, 8 March 2011.

practices of self-governing emerged from the developed collaboration of occupation: "Daily struggles to hold the space and feed its inhabitants, without the disciplined mechanisms of an organized state, were exercises in democratic process. It was through these everyday practices that Tahrir became a truly radical space" (Shokr, 2012, p. 44).

All the collaborative functions which developed *against the regime*, soon made "the transition from outside inward" (Vygotsky, 1997, p. 106) to meet the needs of the occupation itself, transformed into solidarity and a strong sense of mutual responsibility. The occupation of Tahrir brought Egyptians from diverse backgrounds literally close to one another: "Everyone I talked to echoed similar transformative themes: they highlighted a sense of wonder at how they discovered their neighbor again, how they never knew that they lived in 'society' or the meaning of the word, until this event, and how everyone who yesterday had appeared so distant is now so close..." (Bamyeh, 2011). Schielke commented that: "It is not just a protest against an oppressive regime and a demand for freedom. In itself, it is freedom. It is a real, actual, lived moment of the freedom and dignity that the pro-democracy movement demands" (Schielke, 2011). What emerged was an ethical and political unit of people who created rules and ethical principles for themselves: "Those evidenced themselves in a broadly shared sense of personal responsibility for civilization – voluntary street cleaning, standing in line, the complete disappearance of harassment of women in public, returning stolen and found objects, and countless other ethical decisions that had usually been ignored or left for others to worry about" (Bamyeh, 2011). Already before the regime had been defeated, people began to organize their lives independently from *al-nizam* in the "Republic of Tahrir," which thus represented, in a miniature scale, a potential political future for the whole Egyptian nation.

Projecting the Project

The collaboration of Tahrir not only entailed a *project*, in the sense of people jointly working towards a shared goal, but also a *projection*: an image that shone forth from this activity. Let me first consider a projection as the *outward* appearance of a project to *non-participants*. Through al-Jazeera and other international media outlets Tahrir was literally projected into the living rooms of Egyptians and the global community. This projection offered a powerful, contemporary example of popular revolt and the building of a new society "from below." Moreover, it forcefully dismissed the notion that the Middle East was "...a place where the burden of the past weighed so heavily and the cultural DNA somehow preconditioned those who carried it to feel more at home with tyrants and terror" (Antoon, 2011). Within the dominant paradigm of Middle Eastern studies, the lack of a "democratic transition" in the region was understood through the categories of "persistent authoritarianism," "religious fundamentalism," and "cultural backwardness" (Beinin & Vairel, 2011, p. 1). The Arab population was primarily conceived of as a passive object of regime policies or cultural traditions, instead of an active political subject in its own right. This discourse of powerlessness and passivity was also expressed by local elites and intellectuals who: "...reproduce a pervasive and ongoing divide between the 'educated' and the 'uneducated'... Elites are reproducing the very infantilization of the people that has buttressed colonial, authoritarian, and neo-colonial domination" (Seikaly & Ghazaleh, 2011).

Even after two days of intense protests on 25 and 26 January 2011, an article on the BBC News website downplayed the possibility of a replication of the revolutionary Tunisian scenario in Egypt, because: "...the population of Egypt has a much lower level of education than Tunisia. Illiteracy is high and internet penetration is low."[21] This comment echoed a widespread skepticism about the likelihood of a popular revolution in Egypt (Kinsman, 2011, p. 39). Less than three weeks later, President Mubarak, who had been in power for more than three decades, was ousted by a mass uprising of a scale unseen in the history of the Middle East. Those who had ridiculed the perspective of an Egyptian revolution, had to admit that they had been unable to predict the spectacular events of January and February 2011. Schielke acknowledged that: "...if this revolution has taught me one thing is that the people of Egypt do not need to look up to Europe or America to imagine a better future. They have shown themselves capable of imagining a better future of their own making (with some important help from Tunisia). Compared to our governments with their lip service to democracy and appeasement of dictators, Egyptians have given the world an example in freedom and courage that we all should look up to as an example. This sense of admiration and respect is what has drawn so many foreigners to Tahrir Square in the past days, including myself" (Schielke, 2011). The projection of Tahrir interpellated Egyptians and foreigners, either drawing them towards the actual collaboration on the Square (for example through solidarity), or stimulating them to appropriate the universalized ideals or methods of the project to their own particular circumstances. "Fight like an Egyptian" (Shihade, Flesher & Cox, 2012, p. 5) was heard worldwide, among the Indignados in Madrid, Occupy Wall Street activists in New York, workers

21 BBC News 2011.

striking in Wisconsin, students demonstrating in the UK, and Greeks protesting on Syntagma Square.

The concept of projection denotes the capacity of a project to universalize itself and attract new participants to its cause, and, most importantly, it underscores collaboration as a process of learning and instruction. The Tunisian and Egyptian revolutions illustrated how people learnt to act democratically, not through formal education, but by the lived experience of collaborating towards shared goals of freedom, dignity, and social justice. A revolutionary insurrection is not the mop of history: an abrupt, irrational, instinctive, chaotic, blind force, in which "the people," after decades of passivity, suddenly rise up, destroy the status quo, and clear the path for new political actors. Grassroots democracy, self-determination, self-emancipation, et cetera, are not practices and ideals extrinsic to the revolutionary project, but they are developed *within* the process of revolution. Throughout the 18 Days, Tahrir evolved from an *instrument* of political and human emancipation to emancipation *itself*. The governance of Tahrir projected a concrete alternative to *al-nizam*: "...they agree that together they are Egypt, and they agree that they imagine and demand a better future for themselves and their offspring, and they agree that better means free. The protestors in Liberation Square are not fighting for limited, direct demands – higher salaries, fewer taxes, more perks. They are fighting for values such as freedom and dignity. And they understand this to mean self-rule, democratic representative government, human rights, a dignified life" (Al-Bendary, 2011).

Hence, a projection also constitutes the *inward* appearance of the project to its own participants. Tahrir was not only the actual collaboration of protesters on the Square (project), it was also a glimpse of a better society (projection); an imagination that moved ahead of their current project and instructed and inspired them to develop their activity accordingly. Within the development of revolutionary collaboration, there was a continuous, reciprocal transformation of imagined goals by actual activities and vice versa, which highlights the dual character of a project as both a teleological and immanent movement.

Teleology and Immanence

Are activities constituted teleologically by their goals, or do goals emerge immanently from activities? I suggest that the notion of project collaboration encompasses both movements, i.e. from goal to activity, and from activity to goal. Vygotsky's student and founder of Activity Theory A. N. Leontiev posited that human beings engage in activities to satisfy certain natural and social needs (Leontiev, 1978). Hunger (need) motivated primitive humans to hunt (activity) in order to obtain food (goal). In other words, a need projects a goal, and this imagination exists before the actual activity. This agrees with Marx's observation that: "…what distinguishes the worst architect from the best of bees is that the architect builds the cell in his mind before he constructs it in wax. At the end of every labor process, a result emerges which had already been conceived by the worker at the beginning, hence already existed ideally" (Marx, 1990, p. 284). A goal then is the ideal form of the outcome of an activity, and the outcome is the material shape of the goal. The first rallies on 25 January clearly illustrated this notion, as the activity of demonstrating was directly constituted by the call to protest of the organizing activists. The idea of the protests already existed before the materialization of the demonstrations.

However, from 25 January onward, the goals of the developing collaboration seemed to lag behind its actual activities. Even though some activists had hoped that 25 January would initiate a revolutionary uprising,[22] the organizers only demanded the implementation of basic democratic reforms, rather than the dismissal of Mubarak, let alone a revolutionary change in the relations of power.[23] However, the sheer numbers of protesters in the streets swiftly transformed the goals of the demonstrations "from below." Already at noon it was clear to some participants that the massive protests could be "an opportunity to bring down the Mubarak regime"[24] and the slogan of "the people want the fall of the regime" was heard among some of the demonstrators.[25]

As the actions of the protesters became more radical, their aims followed suit. No-one who came to the protests of 25 January would have dared to dream that in the following days they would torch NDP and state security offices throughout the whole country, and by strength of numbers defeat the dreaded CSF in the streets. In successive waves, elements of the State apparatus were disorganized and defeated by the masses, and with each victory the call for a "regime change" became louder. The Friday of Anger was the moment when the people realized that they were in the process of "making" a revolution.[26] Whereas political activists were still cautiously chanting for the *government* to change, it was non-organized and non-politicized people who shouted for an end to the *regime*.[27] The radical demands of "the people want the fall of the

22 Interview with Khaled al-Balshy, Cairo, 14 March 2011.

23 Interview with Sabry Zaky, Cairo, 10 March 2011.

24 Guardian Egypt Live Blog 2011.

25 Interview with Haisam Hassan, Cairo, 7 March 2011.

26 Interview with Mustafa Bassiouni, Giza, 17 March 2011.

27 Interview with Wael Tawfiq, Cairo, 8 March 2011.

regime," "leave, leave, Hosni Mubarak," and "bread, freedom, and social justice" were the explicit recognition of the masses that, during the past days, they actually had been waging a revolutionary struggle against the State. Here the goal that is rendered explicit is not an external object that constitutes the activity, but, on the contrary, it is a reflection in consciousness of the real collaborative process that is unfolding. *People became conscious of what they were already doing in practice*: creating a revolutionary project.

This observation agrees with Blunden's critique of traditional Soviet Activity Theory, in which activity appeared as just an object-oriented process of gratification. Pace Leontiev, Blunden stressed that the goal of a project emerges from the concrete collaboration of its participants (Blunden, 2010, p. 208–210; 255–257). Accordingly, it was the transformation of the forms of collaboration in Tahrir, from demonstration, through occupation and festival to governance, that stimulated the formation of new goals. Revolution appears not only as the *expression* of an already-present popular democratic will, but also as a *generative process* of self-emancipating practices and ideas. Obviously, in the development of a project, these two movements, from goal to activity and from activity to goal, are interwoven. The trajectory of Tahrir illustrates how the imagination of a project sometimes lags behind its actual collaboration and tries to catch up theoretically with its own radical practice, or sometimes moves ahead of it, pulling the activity towards it, as it were.

Moreover, the conception of this reciprocal, dual movement sheds light on the mysterious phenomenon of "spontaneity" in the Egyptian revolution. Muhammad Bamyeh claimed that: "...spontaneity was responsible, it seems, for the increasing ceiling of the goals of the uprising, from basic reform demands on January 25, to changing the entire regime three days later, to rejecting all concessions made by the regime while Mubarak was in office, to putting Mubarak on trial... Here one found out what was possible through spontaneous movement rather than a fixed program, organization or leadership. Spontaneity thus became the compass of the Revolution and the way by which it found its way to what turned out to be its radical destination" (Bamyeh, 2011). Spontaneity is indeed an important concept for understanding a revolutionary process "...because revolutions do not allow anyone to play the schoolmaster with them," as Rosa Luxemburg (1970, p. 188) observed. Likewise, Trotsky (2001, p. 18) described spontaneity as "...that leaping movement of ideas and passions which seems to the police mind a mere result of the activities of 'demagogues'." In this sense, the notion of spontaneity underlines that revolution is not a collaboration engineered by demagogues, or even parties and political activists, but a project fully belonging to the people itself.

However, when spontaneity is opposed to *organization*, the concept acquires a mystical character. There was nothing unorganized about the committees that defended, cleaned, entertained, and governed Tahrir. If anything, they represented "...spontaneous order out of chaos" (Bamyeh, 2011). The notion of spontaneity does not exclude organization or centralization: it rather addresses the organic, bottom-up origins of the organization, coherence, and systematicity of a project. The Republic of Tahrir was a spontaneous development, because it was unplanned yet organized, unforeseen yet immanent to the collaboration of the Square. Neoformations arose as solutions to specific problems that confronted protesters: "...how to communicate, what to do the next day, what to call that day, how to evacuate the injured, how to repulse *baltagiyya* assaults, and even how to formulate demands – emerged in the field directly and continued to develop in response to new situations" (Bamyeh, 2011). Revolutionary collaboration produced its own division of labor, rules, relations, artifacts, and signs – elements which, in turn, taught the people that they could govern themselves: "...we don't need politicians, this is the people's revolution!" (in Schielke, 2011).

The Limits of Tahrir

From the first Friday of Anger on, there were activists who tried to rally and direct people towards occupying not only the symbolic location of Tahrir, but also "real" spaces of State power such as the Maspero television and radio building, the Parliament, the Presidential Palace, and the army barracks. During the Friday of Departure there was a renewed attempt to orient the masses towards a march on the Presidential Palace, but this call did not materialize. Conversely, the regime, after its disastrous attempts to repress the revolutionary uprising by force, was content to wage a war of position with the protesters.

Friday 5 February was dubbed the Friday of Departure as an ultimatum to Mubarak. This episode expressed both the strength and the weakness of the revolutionary project at that moment. Whereas the movement had been able to set its own concrete timetable and demands, it had not yet developed the means to enforce them. Tunisia's projection of successful revolution, which had been instructive in drawing in participants to the project of Tahrir, now became a brake, as protesters hoped that Mubarak would, like Ben Ali, just leave in the face of their mass demonstrations and occupations alone. State institutions were paralyzed and disorganized due to the demonstrations and sit-ins, but they were not captured and transformed. As long as key sites were protected by the military, the State dug in, enduring the protests in the hope that the demonstrators' physical and mental constitution would wear down quickly. The occupation form of collaboration, which had been the motor of the revolution in the previous week, now became a bottleneck for its development. Whereas the majority of protesters were stuck in the "Tahrir occupation strategy," from Tuesday 8 February onward some participants tried to develop a "second front" of occupation near the Parliament and the Presidential Palace. Moreover, workers opened up a new form of collaboration in the revolutionary struggle by organizing strikes, while peasants mobilized in the countryside, dealing blows to the economic pillars of the regime.

These novel collaborations expressed the potential for a new line of development for the revolution. The Republic of Tahrir had to expand itself beyond its physical borders, not only as an ideal projection, but also as a material form of collaboration, occupying and conquering all the strongholds of power throughout Egypt. However, in order to transform the projection of its collaboration to the nation into a nation-wide collaboration, Tahrir had to negate itself. Its revolutionary "governance" had to be shared with neighborhoods and workplaces all over Egypt. Instead of being just a particular within the revolution, The Republic of Tahrir had to become a universal, connecting its vanguard, projective role in the revolution to the particular struggles waged by the popular masses outside its borders. In other words: Tahrir had to become the active, self-conscious center of the revolution.

From the beginning of the uprising, there had been a continuous exchange between Tahrir and participants from local projects of resistances in other Cairo neighborhoods or even towns and cities. In the Square these "delegations" enjoyed the freedom to debate the strategy of the movement and the future of Egypt. When they returned to their own, particular collaborations, they transposed their participation in the self-governance of the Square to the local sites of protests, sharing and diffusing the experience of the Republic of Tahrir. However, these connections were anything but systematic and coherent. The expansion of Tahrir required a specific neoformation, a grassroots political center of some kind, that represented both the plurality and the concentrated will of the masses.

In the final days of the Mubarak era there was a shy push for such a development. When in his speech on Thursday 10 February the President still refused to step down, out of the anger and confusion among the masses rose "...a feeling that people want to get on the move now. I can hear this chant: We'll go to the palace and tear him out."[28] The absence of a political center that could

28 Guardian Egypt Live Blog 2011.

direct the masses was temporarily compensated for by the presence of artistic forms, which imagined and projected the next step in the development of the revolution. Cartoonist Salah Abd al-Azim recalled: "…I made a cartoon of Mubarak sitting in his chair and a lot of spiders climbing on it. As a symbol to say: 'stay in your palace, don't move, and we will come to you'. I made a lot of copies, small and big ones. Mubarak didn't resign in the first days. After the speech of Mubarak when he said I will remain in the chair, a lot of people carried small copies of the cartoon in a demonstration to Mubarak's palace. The biggest one is four to three meters, they carried it on a car and people wrote on it: don't leave, we're coming to you…"[29]

The movement of the masses towards key sites of State power – in particular the Presidential Palace and the Parliament (Khalil, 2012, p. 259–260) – and the parallel explosion of a nation-wide strike, prompted the military to intervene in the process, cutting short the developmental process. The confusion about the role of the Armed Forces in Egyptian society among many of the protesters, and the absence of a grassroots political center, allowed the military leaders to step in and represent themselves as revolutionary arbiters (See De Smet, 2014). This moment represented a crisis for the revolutionary project, which has not yet been successfully solved at the moment of writing. The failure to expand the Republic of Tahrir to the whole of Egypt reduced the Square to a symbolic site for ritualistic protest. Although Tahrir continued to play a role as a key locale for demonstrations and occupations, it no longer determined the development of the revolutionary process. Political analyst Sabry Zaky posited that "Now, staying in Tahrir is an old game. I think it has brought many successes and gains for us, but we have to be creative, because a revolution by definition is a creative thing…we have to think about other avenues and other ways to spread this revolution."[30]

The military intervention signaled the end of the 18 Days and the Republic of Tahrir, and opened up a new and protracted phase, in which the various projects that were constitutive of the revolution and had been revolutionized themselves – e.g. the particular collaborations of workers, farmers, social media activists, youth revolutionaries, et cetera – were differentiated again from each other, seeking new and sometimes opposing pathways to develop themselves. This episode elucidates the shortcomings of Tahrir as a unit of analysis of the entire Egyptian revolution. Whereas Tahrir was the cell-form of the revolutionary *uprising*, the project was unable to represent the plurality of collaborations that had led up to 25 January. Although within the practices

29 Interview with Salah Abd al-Azim, Cairo, 22 March 2011.

30 Interview with Sabry Zaky, Cairo, 10 March 2011.

and signs of the Square there were elements of the particular struggles of farmers, workers, women, students, et cetera, these were largely subsumed under the banner of the fight for democracy and civil rights. It is hard to say if the Republic of Tahrir would have been able to articulate the class, gender, and socio-geographical[31] dimensions of the popular revolution, if its development had not been interrupted by the "soft coup." On the other hand, the military intervention showed the revolution a new and powerful obstacle that had to be overcome by novel forms of revolutionary collaboration – probably in the shape of an alliance of different projects such as grassroots parties, independent trade unions, and other subaltern networks and organizations. After all, even though many protesters were demobilized from the streets after the soft coup, they still considered themselves as participants in the revolutionary project. In Marx's words: "For a moment active heroes of the revolutionary drama, they could no longer be forced back into the inactive and spineless role of the chorus" (Marx & Engels, 1969, p. 147).

References

Abbink, J. & van Walraven, K. (2003). Rethinking resistance in African history: An introduction. In Abbink, J., de Bruin, M. en van Walraven, K. (Eds.). *Rethinking Resistance: Revolt and Violence in African History*, 1–40: Leiden.

Al-Bendary, A. (2011). Making History in Tahrir, *Jadaliyya*, http://www.jadaliyya.com/pages/index/578/making-history-in-tahrir, published 7 February 2011, last consulted Tuesday 14 February 2012.

Al-Ghobashy, M. (2011). The Praxis of the Egyptian Revolution, *MERIP, 258*(41), http://www.merip.org/mer/mer258/praxis-egyptian-revolution, last consulted 18 June 2012.

Al-Werdani, M. (2011). The Ultras and the Egyptian Revolution, *Jadaliyya*, http://www.jadaliyya.com/pages/index/3759/the-ultras-and-the-egyptian-revolution, published 25 December 2011, last consulted 12 June 2012.

Althusser, L. & Balibar, E. (1970). *Reading Capital*. London: NLB.

Antoon, S. (2011). Impromptu: A word, *Jadaliyya*, http://www.jadaliyya.com/pages/index/485/impromptu_a-word, published January 28 2011, last consulted Monday 13 February 2012.

Bamyeh, M. (2011). The Egyptian Revolution: First Impressions from the Field [Updated], *Jadaliyya*, http://www.jadaliyya.com/pages/index/561/the-egyptian

31 The opposition between urban and rural areas; between the metropolises of Cairo and Alexandria and provincial towns; between Upper and Lower Egypt; et cetera.

-revolution_first-impressions-from-the, published 11 February 2011, last consulted 15 February 2012.

Bayat, A. (1996). Historiography, class, and Iranian workers. In Lockman, Z. (Ed.): *Workers and Working Classes in the Middle East. Struggles, Histories, Historiographies*, 165–203, Albany: New York State University Press.

BBC News (2011). Egypt protests: Three killed in 'day of revolt', http://www.bbc.co.uk/news/world-africa-12272836, last updated 26 January 2011, last consulted 17 June 2012.

Beinin, J. (2013). Was there a January 25 Revolution? *Jadaliyya*, http://www.jadaliyya.com/pages/index/9766/was-there-a-january-25-revolution, published 25 January 2013, last consulted 23 February 2013.

Beinin, J. & Vairel, F. (2011). Introduction: The Middle East and North Africa. Beyond classical social movement theory, 1–23. In Beinin, J. and Vairel, F. (Eds.): *Social Movements, Mobilization, and Contestation in the Middle East and North Africa*, Stanford: Stanford University Press.

Blunden, A. (2010). *An Interdisciplinary Theory of Activity*. Leiden: Brill.

Blunden, A. (2012). *Concepts. A Critical Approach*. Leiden: Brill.

Cohen, R. (1980). Resistance and hidden forms of consciousness amongst African workers, *Review of African Political Economy, 19*(9), 9–22.

Colla, E. (2011). The poetry of revolt, *Jadaliyya*, http://www.jadaliyya.com/pages/index/506/the-poetry-of-revolt, published 31 January 2011, last consulted 13 February 2012.

De Smet, B. (2012). Egyptian workers and "their" intellectuals: The dialectical pedagogy of the Mahalla strike movement. *Mind, Culture, and Activity. 19*(2), 139–155.

De Smet, B. (2014). Lineages of Caesarism and passive revolution in the Egyptian 25 January Revolution. *Science & Society. 78*(1), 11–40.

Guardian Egypt Live Blog. (2011). http://www.guardian.co.uk/world/blog/2011.

Howeidy, A. (2005). A chronology of dissent, *Al-Ahram Weekly*, 748(June), http://weekly.ahram.org.eg/2005/748/eg10.htm, last consulted 18 June 2012.

Huntington, S. (2006). *Political Order in Changing Societies*. New Haven: Yale University Press.

Khalil, A. (2012). *Liberation Square. Inside the Egyptian Revolution and the Rebirth of a Nation*. Cairo: The American University in Cairo Press.

Kinsman, J.(2011). Democracy rising: Tunisia and Egypt, when idealists got it right, *Policy Options*, April, 37–43.

Lenin, V.I. (1969). Two tactics of Social Democracy in the democratic revolution. In *Selected Works Volume 1*, London: Lawrence & Wishart.

Lenin, V.I. (1976). *The State and Revolution. The Marxist Teaching on the State and the Tasks of the Proletariat in the Revolution*. Peking: Foreign Languages Press.

Leontiev, A.N. (1978). *Activity, Consciousness, and Personality*, Englewood Cliffs: Prentice-Hall.

Luxemburg, R. (1970). *Rosa Luxemburg Speaks*, New York: Pathfinder Press.

Marx, K. (1973). Grundrisse: *Foundations of the Critique of Political Economy*, Harmondsworth: Penguin.

Marx, K. (1990). *Capital.* Volume 1, London: Penguin Group.

Marx, K. & Engels, F. (1969). *Marx/Engels Selected Works.* Volume 1, Moscow: Progress Publishers.

Rashed, M.A. (2011). The Egyptian Revolution. A participant's account from Tahrir Square, January and February 2011, *Anthropology Today*, 27(2), 22–27.

Schielke, S. (2011). 'You'll be late for the Revolution!' An anthropologist's diary of the Egyptian Revolution, *Jadaliyya*, http://www.jadaliyya.com/pages/index/580/youll-be-late-for-the-revolution-an-anthropologist, published 8 February 2011, last consulted 14 February 2012.

Seikaly, S. & Ghazaleh, P. (2011). Abduh al-Fallah: Elite Myths and Popular Uprisings, *Jadaliyya*, http://www.jadaliyya.com/pages/index/910/abduh-al-fallah_elite-myths-and-popular-uprisings-, published 15 March 2011, last consulted 17 February.

Shenker, J. (2011). Egypt braced for 'day of revolution' protests. Youth activists, Islamists, workers and football fans to hold rallies and marches against Mubarak government, *Guardian*, http://www.guardian.co.uk/world/2011/jan/24/egypt-day-revolution-protests, published 24 January 2011, last modified 25 January 2011, last consulted 2 February 2012.

Shihade, M., Flesher C.F. & Cox, L. (2012). The season of revolution: the Arab Spring and European mobilizations, *Interface: Journal for and about Social Movements, 4*(1), 1–16.

Shokr, A. (2012). The eighteen days of Tahrir, 41–46. In Sowers, J., and Toensing, C. (Eds.): *The Journey to Tahrir. Revolution, Protest, and Social Change in Egypt*, New York: Verso.

Skocpol, T. (1979). *States and Social Revolutions. A Comparative Analysis of France, Russia, and China.* Cambridge: Cambridge University Press.

Trotsky, L. (2001). *History of the Russian Revolution*, New York: Pathfinder Press.

Vygotsky, L.S. (1987a). Thinking and speech. In *Collected Works. v. 1*, New York: Plenum Press.

Vygotsky, L.S. (1987b). Memory and its development. In *Collected Works. v. 2*, New York: Plenum Press.

Vygotsky, L.S. (1997). Genesis of the Higher Mental Functions. In *Collected Works. v. 4*, New York: Plenum Press.

Wertsch, J.V. (1985). *Vygotsky and the Social Formation of Mind*, Cambridge, Massachusetts and London: Harvard University Press.

Zemni, S., De Smet, Brecht , & Bogaert, K. (2012). Luxemburg on Tahrir Square. Reading the Arab revolutions of 2011 with Rosa Luxemburg's 'The Mass Strike'. *Antipode*, Online first: http://onlinelibrary.wiley.com/doi/10.1111/j.1467-8330.2012.01014.x/abstract.

PART TWO

Reflections

CHAPTER 13

Alterglobalization and the Limits of Prefigurative Politics

Brecht De Smet

Prefiguration and Alterglobalization

Among anarchist and autonomist scholar-activists investigating the alterglobalization movement, the "Arab Spring" revolts, the Indignados, Occupy Wall Street, and other contemporary instances of collective resistance, "prefiguration" has emerged as a key concept for the explanation and evaluation of emancipatory goals, strategies, practices, and forms of collaboration.[1] Prefigurative politics is understood as a practical and immediate *critique* of representative democracy, as an open-ended *strategy* for social change, and as the "...mini form here and now..." (Maeckelbergh, 2013, p. 34) of a better society, offering an *alternative* to oppressive power relations.

Anarchist-inclined alterglobalization activists argue that the collaborative activity of the *movement itself* functions as a critique of hierarchical and authoritarian power relations reproduced by the institutions of representative democracy, corporations, political parties, and even trade unions: "...new forms of organization *are* its ideology" (Graeber, 2002, p. 70). Instead of elaborating an alternative *theory* of social relations, *practices* of "horizontalism," "diversity," and "connectivity" demonstrate how power can be redesigned along emancipatory lines (Maeckelbergh, 2011, p. 13).

Practice as critique also entails a unity of means and ends, between strategy and goals of the movement – a traditional anarchist point of view. Instead of gathering people around a predetermined, shared goal, prefiguration takes the character of the activity itself as its premise. The rationale is that if organizing practices are democratic and emancipatory, the goals of the movement will be articulated along concomitant liberating lines. Prefigurative politics teaches actors "...how to govern the world in a manner that fundamentally redesigns

1 For the sake of argument and brevity this reflection piece abstracts from the many nuances and points of difference in the debate, contrasting an *archetypical* form of "prefiguration," specifically derived from Maeckelbergh (2011, 2013), against "project."

the way power operates" (Maeckelbergh, 2011, p. 15). Conversely, authoritarian and hierarchical organizations tend to reproduce oppressive power relations when they enforce reforms, or after they conquer state power.

Direct Action versus Mediated Development

Direct action could be designated as the "leading activity" of anarchist prefigurative politics, as the end is already present within the means, and as the actors leading the activity are the direct beneficiaries of the action – e.g. the homeless squatting derelict houses, workers occupying and running factories, etc. (Carter 1973). Direct action is *immediate* and *unmediated* and these attributes are considered morally necessary and desirable.

From a collaborative perspective, however, such a concept of prefigurative politics is deeply problematic, as it is unclear what precisely is being *pre*-figured. The only difference between the alternative power relations of the "pre-figuration" and its "figuration" is one of scale, not of substance: it rejects the *qualitative* development of collaboration in favor of a merely *quantitative* expansion of its already existing liberating practices. In the flat world of direct action, prefiguration remains "…a politics of dispersed singularities…" (Carroll, 2006, p. 30) – a series of *anti*-hegemonic *events* instead of the seeds of a *counter*-hegemonic *movement*. Direct action does not *unify* the opposites of means and ends, but *collapses* them into the single, self-identical category of prefiguration. Such a flat identification of means and ends obscures the whole developmental logic that underlies the formation of activities in response to original goals, and the emergence of new goals from activities. Vianna et al. (pp. on page 58–59) emphasize that collaboration is essentially a *transformative* process of both the whole project and its individual participants. With regard to my own investigation (pp. 193–209), I concluded that the means to overthrow the oppressive Mubarak régime – mass mobilization and organization – became a goal in itself, and the original goal of the movement – getting rid of a dictator – became a means for the development of a new society, which was being pre-figured in the "Republic of Tahrir."

From a project perspective, prefiguration is but the first shape or *prototype* (cf. Nissen, p. 66; Cole et al., p. 91) of a developmental process of "figuring out" human collaboration. I suggest that Paul Ricoeur's hermeneutic conception of mimesis or representation offers an interesting thread to weave the concepts of prefiguration and project together. Ricoeur conceived of prefiguration as the first step in a process of representation, followed by configuration and transfiguration. *Prefiguration* is the "emplotment" of stories following "…a preunderstanding of the world of action..." (Ricoeur, 1984, p. 54) Prefiguration then represents the project-in-itself: a collection of actions, which are loosely connected to one another, constituting an amorphous and fluid whole, and "... providing a partial, and perhaps implicit, understanding of their significance" (Zelazo & Lourenco, 2003, pp. 57–58). A new collaboration is prefigured by tools and concepts that are developed within the womb of other projects. In the absence of an authentic concept of their emerging project, participants *imitate* and *borrow* ideas and instruments for their new activity. Children, for example, appropriate the language forms and practices from social settings and reproduce them in their own, discrete activities (cf. John-Steiner, p. 84).

However, there is an immanent contradiction between these imitated concepts and borrowed tools on the one hand, and the developing activity on the other. Activity is not solely the passive *object* of interpretation, but entails an *act* of interpretation itself. When participants begin to "figure out" the difference (and thus identity) of their collaboration vis-à-vis other projects, their activity becomes less *pre*-figurative and increasingly *con*-figurative.

Configuration and Transfiguration

The second moment of mimesis, *configuration* "...joins and relates disparate aspects of the story, including various agents, actions, motivations, and outcomes..." (Vanderhaagen, 2013, p. 195). The participants recognize their shared activity as a distinct project and begin to select, combine, and arrange prefigured relations, structures, symbols, and tools into a coherent and systemic ensemble. With regard to the Mayslake strikers, Worthen remarks that: "The narrative of how to organize a union functioned like a "plot" ...a sequence of actions, that, if carried out, would get them past obstacles to a hoped-for goal" (p. 135). Configuration is the glue that ties individual participants to the project as a whole, for example by a division of labor. Configuration situates the project within a history of similar collaborations, and, conversely, interprets this history from its own perspective. Configuration is the moment of *institutionalization* of the project.

Maeckelbergh correctly identifies such a process as a potential threat for the movement, as it carries the seeds of hierarchy and authoritarianism. She concludes that prefigurative politics principally rejects a distinction between a vanguard of activists and "the public," as such a hierarchy would reproduce unequal power relations between the educators and the educated. (Maeckelbergh 2011, p. 14) However, this admirable mission statement does not solve the real and present problem of the uneven development of practice, experience, and consciousness within a project, which cannot be transcended by simply declaring it undesirable. A technical division of labor does not necessarily lead to a social hierarchy, nor is it the doomed end point of the journey. The *homo universalis* cannot be the *premise* of an emancipatory struggle, but it can be one of its *outcomes*. In the context of a critical learning site, Vianna et al. (p. 45) demonstrate how teachers can become learners and vice versa. Likewise, Worthen (p. 133) stresses that union leadership was not just externally imposed, but it also emerged *organically* from the Mayslake struggle.

The third moment consists of a process of *transfiguration* or *refiguration*.[2] In hermeneutics, it represents the interpretative relation between authorship and readership. The text invites the reader to "inhabit" its world, an active relation that expands both the authored meaning of the story and the horizon of the reader (Vanderhaagen, 2013, p. 198). Whereas configuration turned the project inwards, transfiguration is the externalization or actualization of the collaboration in the wider world of projects. Such a process inevitably contains an ethical and political component, as relations of power determine how participants are "configured" into the project, and how different forms of collaboration relate to one another, as elaborated in the Introduction (p. 12).

The logic of direct action, however, precludes a transfiguring moment. Because a prefiguration already constitutes the future society in a *developed* micro-form, it does not need to learn or to mature, but only to expand or to be repeated. A prefiguration does not enter into a dialogue, but simply encourages non-participants to *imitate* and adopt the prefigured practice (Maeckelbergh, 2011, p.14). Prefigurative politics reduces the organic development of a *project* to the atomistic "connectivity" of a *network*.

Network versus Project

For authors such as Maeckelbergh, the loose relations of a prefigured project do not constitute the beginning, but the normative end point of political collaboration. Homogeneity and a shared political platform, goal, or adversary are considered *threats* to the diversity of the alterglobalization movement (Maeckelbergh, 2013, p. 35). Prefiguration defies a universalist moment in politics and celebrates the particularism of its individual participants. At the core of prefigurative politics stands an atomistic, individualist ontology in which autonomous and independent actors can only come together in a non-binding

2 These three moments do not reflect a linear progression, but they mediate one another throughout the life course of a project.

network that continuously reaffirms their mutual *differences*. Solidarity is merely a deontological relation between individuals, floating on a categorical imperative to support each other's desires: "...everyone has to take responsibility for bringing about the change they desire, and for helping others to achieve what they desire, whether they desire the same things or not" (Maeckelbergh, 2011, p. 14).

In contrast, politics as project stimulates *unity* in thought and action. A "closed" (Dhaliwal, 2012) reading of prefigurative politics collapses the difference between unity and identity; sharing and assimilation; bureaucratization and institutionalization; dialogic convergence and monologic diffusion. Configuration does not *necessarily* mean the assimilation of individual strategies and goals along the lines of a predetermined homogeneous model. The organizational threats of bureaucratization, authoritarianism, and hierarchy cannot be contained by the immediacy of action or a forced plurality of outcomes, but by the joint development of a dialogic and democratic culture. *Ethical* collaboration is the convergence, supersession, and objectification of prefigured practices into *shared* means and ends, by a process of *reciprocity* (cf. Lubensky, p. 139) and *mutual appropriation* (cf. John-Steiner, p. 83).

The collective will and desire represented in a project is more than the sum of the desires of its individual participants. Conversely, the shared goals that emerge from collaboration can offer the means to achieve individual desires. The workers of Mayslake (pp. 128–132) needed unity and organization in order to strike. The survival of their project depended on the agreement of its participants on this shared course of action. Without such a universal moment, political collaborations reinforce their fragmented character and are unable to develop a "problem-solution" or concept (cf. Blunden & Arnold, p. 111) of their social situation or predicament.

Similarly, the ethical transfiguration of the alterglobalization project does not require a politics of imitation, of "many Tahrirs," but of dialogue and alliance with other subaltern forces, such as the coalition between trade unions and health professionals that constituted the Anti-Asbestos Movement in Australia (Beaton & Blunden, pp. 179ff).

References

Carroll, W.K. (2006). Hegemony, counter-hegemony, anti-hegemony, *Socialist Studies*, 2(2), 9–43.

Carter, A. (1973). *Direct Action and Liberal Democracy*, London: Routledge & Kegan Paul.

Dhaliwal, P. (2012). Public squares and resistance: the politics of space in the Indignados movement, *Interface: A Journal for and about Social Movements, 4*(1), 251–273.

Graeber, D. (2002). The new anarchists, *New Left Review, 13*, 61–73.

Maeckelbergh, M. (2011). Doing is believing: Prefiguration as strategic practice in the alterglobalization movement, *Social Movement Studies, 10*(1), 1–20.

Maeckelbergh, M. (2013). Learning from conflict: Innovative approaches to democratic decision making in the alterglobalization movement, *Transforming Anthropology, 21*(1), 27–40.

Ricoeur, P. (1984). *Time and Narrative. Vol. 1*. Chicago: University of Chicago Press.

Vanderhaagen, S.C. (2013). The agential spiral: Reading public memory through Paul Ricoeur, *Philosophy and Rhetoric, 46*(2), 182–206.

Zelazo, P. D.& Lourenco, S.F. (2003). Imitation and the dialectic of representation, *Developmental Review, 23*, 55–78.

CHAPTER 14

A Reflection on the Feminist Movement

Lynn Beaton

> A coherent community is an integral fabric, woven together by projects: not a quilt of multi-colored patches, but a rich and moving tapestry of diverse intertwining threads.
>
> Introduction, p. 18

There is a popular view, perhaps even a dominant view, that young women no longer identify as feminist and this is the reason that the feminist movement has lost momentum and is no longer viable. In extreme cases it is argued that gains won by earlier feminists are being lost. There are two concepts here that I'd like to begin to address. The first is that young women do not identify as feminist and the second that the movement is less viable or has lost momentum. Both of these assertions are so limited in their understanding of the reality that they are false. Both rely on a view that social movements are finite moments in history, separated in time and space as isolated entities. Both views are boosted by a dominant ideology that downplays any social change that might challenge it.

It is easy to accept the view that today's young women are not identifying as feminists. The media loves to promote it and we are constantly bombarded by information that challenges the aims and objectives of feminism; images of women objectified as sexual objects or victims of violence. And for those women, like me, who were activists in the 'second wave' it can be galling to watch young women lapping up the gains we fought for while refusing to identify with our struggles to win them, and refusing to take the struggles forward. We fought for women to have equal access to wealth, jobs, goods and services and the gains we won in all these areas are abundant. Many of us gave many years of our lives so future generations of women would not have to experience the oppression and lack of entitlement that we had experienced.

This view is based on a false assumption that 'second wave feminism' was a mass movement that involved the majority of women in the developed capitalist countries. This was never the case. Those of us who were active in the movement were a tiny minority of women and were treated like a lunatic fringe by the majority. Men in general knew instinctively that we were out to challenge their entitlement to dominance in all things. Their responses were crass: we had no motivation except that we hated them; were jealous of them; mostly because we were a bunch of unattractive freaks who couldn't get a man. What is less understandable perhaps is that many women adopted that idea too. It was more frequent to have women say, often with smug pursed lips: 'Oh I'm happy with the way things are'. than to have women say: 'Oh yes I agree with your aims'.

But while that was the case, even when the movement was most visibly active, women were taking on the gains. For example in Australia one of our early gains was to have a state pension for single mothers. Almost instantly statistics revealed that what was happening was that women were quick to accept the gain. More women were keeping children born outside of relationships rather than giving them up for adoption, and large numbers of women took their children and left unsatisfactory relationships because there was at least minimal financial support available.

On another level women were gaining access to areas that were previously unknown and many of those women were oppositional to the aims and objectives of feminism, yet that didn't stop them utilizing the gains. Two well-known examples of this were Maggie Thatcher, the British Prime Minister and Ita Buttrose, a magazine editor in Australia. Interestingly, while the very existence of the first woman Prime Minister of the UK was clearly a feminist gain, it's occupant was antagonistic to the feminist movement, but most of her opponents, including active feminists, not only denied her status as a role model for the movement, but many denied her womanhood – 'oh but Thatcher's not really a woman'. Buttrose is now celebrated as a feminist icon, but at the time was seen as a woman who had become prominent as a defender of the status quo. Nevertheless she herself set precedents for women in the Australian newspaper industry, had a strong sense of herself as a career woman and a sense that women wanted more than housekeeping, child rearing, cooking and beauty tips.

From my standpoint there are at least as many, and possibly more young women who identify as feminists than there ever were and this has been consistent through the decades of the eighties, nineties and naughties. What is also true is that there are many more young men who identify as feminist and support the movement. For some reason we expect that because nearly all young women in the developed capitalist world have benefitted from the gains of feminism, they should identify with the movement. Yet there never seems to have been a parallel between numbers of women who utilize gains with those who identify. Although I would argue that the proportion of women who identify has been growing consistently.

What we were was *loud* and our activism was highly visible. The attitudes we wanted to change were so deeply embedded in our consciousness that it took years to sort them out. Consciousness raising groups are now laughed at, but they were an amazing concentration of discussion and debate in searching for understanding both on a social level and a personal one. After all as somebody said at the time: it took a lot of social and personal dredging to even understand our situation fully. Women live their lives in the most intimate of relationships with their oppressors.

The sixties and seventies were decades of enormous struggle around the world and the women's movement was a part of that. National liberation struggles, civil rights struggles, labor movement struggles, the massive anti-war movement were all prominent in those decades. In the decades that followed the struggles lessened – largely as a result of the ascendancy of neo-liberal economics and politics.

Still if we look at the political struggles that exist today – women are a prominent part of them all, labor movement struggles, national liberation struggles, student struggles, civil rights struggles, the Occupy Movement, struggles against austerity, all have women active at every level and often in prominent and leadership roles. My observation is that in most cases these women identify as feminist, and in many cases they struggle alongside men who support them. One prominent example has been the mass support around the world for Pussy Riot in their battle for civil rights against the Putin regime. Often the struggles are about the rights of women. For example in recent years no-one can fail to have noticed the world outrage at the plight of Malala Yousafzai the Pakistani schoolgirl shot for demanding education for girls; or the outpouring of grief and anger that an Indian student could be gang-raped and then thrown off a moving bus; and in Australia the support for the woman caught in the so-called Skype scandal at the Australian Defence Force Academy.

In Australia, both the ultimate glass ceilings were broken in 2010 when we had our first female Governor General, closely followed by our first woman Prime Minister. Attitudes to these women were positive. In the case of the Governor General I haven't heard a single doubt of her right to be there or criticism of her capabilities, rather there has been an unspoken national pride that we have broken that glass ceiling. In the case of the Prime Minister, Julia Gillard, the situation is much more complicated because of the controversial manner of her acquiring the job. The ensuing personal attacks on her involved horrendous sexism and misogyny. This was interpreted by some as proof that feminism was losing ground and yet it created a national and very public debate about feminism that has never been seen in Australia. The public debate was mirrored by a million private debates. Men as well as women expressed outrage, horror, disappointment. I'm not arguing at all that sexism has been stamped out – far from it, but the number of people who overtly supported Gillard through that time, as a proportion of the Australian population, was much greater than the number of women who were involved in, or who overtly supported, the second wave feminist movement.

This movement generated changes so enormous, so widespread that not only have they continued to take effect, they have formed a base on which new struggles can be built. While there was a period of heightened activity in the '70s and early '80s, the difference between then and the years that followed is only the amount of publicly audible noise – it's likely in fact that more gains have been made quietly since then. The 'movement' fought successfully for a basic change to ideology. To challenge the gender roles in society is to challenge the most basic tenet of identity. The first thing that is identified in any baby is its gender and from that moment a raft of gender identifiers are applied; name, colors of clothes, aspirations of parents etc.

When I became active in the women's movement there were almost no women doctors, lawyers, journalists, managers, school principals, tram drivers, train drivers, pilots. The list could go on and on. Women were not allowed to drink in the biggest and most active part of any hotel – the public bars. Our opinions were considered unstable, emotional, lacking rationality. It was openly acceptable to say out loud that women's role was in the home, babies and kitchens were our domains. Underlying all of these restrictions on women was a dominant ideology that insisted that women lacked the ability to successfully engage in the public sphere, they were destined for the private, domestic sphere.

The ideology of the women's movement has conquered the dominant ideology so now it is generally accepted that women have the potential to develop capabilities with men in almost all areas of life. Those who still say that women are lesser beings than men or are unable to take on equal responsibilities, or aren't entitled to equal shares of the wealth now speak outside of the dominant ideology. The impact of this ideological change lies underneath the massive changes to social organization that have been taking place ever since. In every workplace, in every home in the advanced capitalist world attitudes to women and their capabilities have changed. These changes in attitude have not been limited to the ideas of women, but to men as well, who have been dragged, often kicking and spluttering, along behind the women. The changes have not been confined to the developed capitalist world but have clearly impacted everywhere. It is also evident that those who want to maintain the old values of men's superiority have to assert their ideas with ever increasing force and violence.

This change in ideology has far-reaching effects. Almost all aspects of life are affected by the expectations associated with gender. The women's movement therefore has affected every aspect of life and the range or scope for further developments is far from exhausted. The empowerment of women has encouraged them to want more and during the last three decades gains have continued to be fought for and won.

Given the enormity of its aims, the project for the emancipation of women has existed as a conscious and active movement for over two centuries. It has seen myriad forms and stages, it has seen some leaps forward and some battering back, but the project has been a steady continuous movement towards its ultimate goal of creating the conditions which give women the capabilities to participate fully in all aspects of their societies. The project of women's emancipation is a road which began long ago as a narrow and perilous track. Each development has improved the road but the second wave feminists built the highway we now travel.

CHAPTER 15

The Peer Activist Learning Community: A Peer Perspective

Mike Rifino, Keiko Matsuura and Francisco Medina

It is no exaggeration to say that we have become radically different persons as we engaged in the Peer Activist Learning Community (PALC). Thus, it is a great joy for us to write about how we transformed our education and ourselves as we created this activist learning community. We each joined PALC for different reasons, as each one of us struggled with different aspects of our college education and future aspirations. We each came from different racial and cultural backgrounds, spoke different languages, and had different ideas about what careers were realistic and worth pursuing. We seemed so different; our ideas, opinions, and values were so divergent that we often doubted, especially in the beginning, if we could ever be a community. However, as we began coming together to talk about our college experiences, our ideals, and our lives, we learned that despite our diversity, we all shared a common struggle to achieve the American dream. At the time, our struggles, especially regarding learning in our college courses, seemed a natural consequence of the price we needed to pay to succeed. What we did not know, or did not want to see, was that our notions of success pretty much meant fitting in with the status quo.

In this reflection we will explain how we came to recognize and liberate ourselves from this conformist burden. Through transformative activist learning in PALC we began to see how the burden of academic achievement in college, requiring competition, individualism, and disconnection from our fellow students, was part and parcel of the burden of adapting to an unjust society. Gradually, all that had seemed the necessary cost to succeed, such as leaving behind "backward" cultures and adopting a professional attitude, was called into question. We began to realize how much we were holding back our critical perspectives, how willing we were to accept our education in order to go with the system, which then began to seem an unbearable cost for our humanity.

Most of us joined PALC either because we were struggling in our courses, due to difficulty learning concepts and mastering academic skills, or because we were pretty lost in terms of our professional paths. Upon entering this project, and for a while after joining PALC, we constructed a narrative about our dissatisfaction with uninspiring professors, bad courses, and incompetent, unmotivated peers. While some members had taken critical courses and had enjoyed and admired some open-minded, accessible instructors, the overall experience was not radically transformative. Moreover, there was a lot of complaining about intractable life circumstances since many of us had to work in low-wage jobs or deal with family issues. In addition, there were many times when some of us doubted our ability to master academic skills, such as how to write a research paper, because many of us thought of our skills as relatively fixed or irrelevant for the jobs we envisioned. Sometimes it just seemed that our peers were passive and lazy, incapable of negotiating mundane tasks with their instructors. At other times the professors seemed unreasonable, incompetent, or unavailable. As a great deal of the things around us seemed impossible to change, many of us felt a sense of resignation to the status quo of our education. This was reinforced by our prejudices about community colleges, and many of us also tended to regard community college students with contempt. Since for many of us (though not all) the primary goal was to transfer to a four-year school as soon as possible, the community college was a transitional place. We did not care to connect or engage with the campus community.

As we continued sharing our struggles and discussing our future aspirations, it became clear that while each of us tried to deal with our struggles individually, these were not isolated but actually collective issues. With the guidance of the group leaders and through critical concepts and theories we began questioning why learning, or studying was, for so many of us only for short-term goals, such as tests and exams. Or, in contrast, how come so many of us felt the opposite, that the development of academic skills was a matter of individualistic upward mobility. The upshot of these discussions was that they opened us to interrogating educational practices, including curricular and pedagogical issues, which led us to read about critical theories of education. Soon, the oppressive nature of the educational system became clear, including the way classes were conducted and course curriculum organized, the pursuit of education for sheer upward mobility, and social inequalities and injustice at large.

It was in this context that we began to engage in critical-theoretical learning in earnest. This was transformative because many of us never really thought of academic concepts and theories as relevant or as having transformational effects in our lives and society. Embracing critical theories helped us become aware of our oppression while equipping us with the language and tools to articulate and critique our current situations and past experiences. One of us recalls the liberating effect upon reading Freire for the first time and his critique of the banking concept of education. Freire revealed to us how alienating traditional teaching practices are, as they aim to produce docile students, which some of us had internalized. Through critical theories we began to question our preconceived assumptions and moved away from our individualistic, decontextualized views of social issues. We began to critically examine the social contexts in which individuals are situated, and see various forms of inequality and oppression as being structural and systemic. The realization that our experiences were not unique to individuals, but part of underlying oppressive patterns in society, was essential to the emergence of our activist stance as a community and as individuals.

The transformations in PALC could not have ensued without the supportive learning community we created among faculty and students. In fact, there were times when we began to doubt whether this pursuit to change the world was possible. Amidst austerity measures in our college and the typically ambivalent stance of our families and friends about the prospect of change, almost inevitably there were moments of resistance on our part. More specifically, we questioned if leading a life committed to social justice was worth our investment and sacrifice. Thanks to the solidarity in PALC, members weighed in on this matter openly and honestly and we continued to inspire and rekindle the passion to pursue social change. In this context, the development of solidarity and our shared emotional connections provided a safe space where we could learn from and influence each other. Part of this process was to challenge one another through constructive, critical arguments about our already-exposed contradictions in our stances and discourses. Oftentimes, our pursuit of knowledge came from wanting to engage each other in critical dialogues that challenged our positions by relating it to intersecting, systematic oppression. One example of this was how one of us, in response to a PALC member's discourse about not believing in social change, drew on his knowledge of the feminist movement, to counter argue that change was possible. Hence, knowledge became a tool to directly challenge a passive and disengaged position in the group. Gradually, a transformative activist stance emerged, leading us to pursue collective activities that aided the creation of the overall curriculum in PALC. This grew organically out of concrete questions that each of us were dealing with or pose to the group.

Increasingly, learning began to hold a meaning beyond our individual, immediate academic goals. Learning became a daily activity in our community that shaped PALC as a unique context at community college. Moreover, we became a group that inspired one another and supported each other with course assignments. This was really empowering because we could directly see that we could make a difference in each other's lives. However, there was still doubt about our power and ability to affect larger institutional change. Then, things began to change as our group kept growing and became a long-term endeavor, which caught the attention of faculty and staff. After a presentation one of us made to the psychology club describing his personal transformation, an invitation to a college-wide presentation and others followed. By this time some of us were posing questions for which there seemed to be no clear or easy answer, such as the meaning of race, and what does it mean to be Latino. Then we came up with the idea of having a psychology student conference, which positioned us as producers of knowledge. As we began collaborating on creating this conference, which we organized, wrote papers for, and participated as discussants, we began to see ourselves as emerging scholars. Afterward, new collaborative projects emerged, such as a Social Science Conference, then a symposium for a professional educational conference, more talks in the college, and contributing our collective efforts to social movements. As PALC grew out of our collaborative efforts in a way that we could directly see how much each of our individual contributions were crucial to the overall endeavor, it began to dawn on us that we indeed mattered. This realization facilitated the shift from a passive to a transformative activist stance toward our learning, society, and life agendas.

One important aspect of collective reconstructing the meaning of our learning and lives had to do with the institutional issues around our education. After learning about the interrelated issues around our education (e.g., the series of tuition hikes being implemented and the deteriorating condition of our education), many of us began to question the nature and politics of institutions and authority, starting in our educational setting. At first, we were not included in the discussion on austerity measures in the institution. Engagement in PALC led us to become acquainted with the institution's history and current conditions of diversity and adversity. From simply accepting these issues and rarely questioning authority or what we were taught, our shift to meaningful learning and the development of a transformative activist stance has provided us with tools to challenge institutional arrangements. For example, we became critical of the psychology department, where students were exposed almost exclusively to the positivist view of psychology. We began writing articles for the psychology magazine to criticize the lack of exposure to various critical views in psychology. In addition, we began collaborating with our peers in creating alternative ways of learning, such as study groups where we could discuss issues that were not touched upon in our classes. We also began participating in social movements at a broader level, such as Occupy Wall Street.

The idea of making a contribution to society made learning more meaningful for all of us. We embraced learning to change the circumstances that perpetuate different modes of oppression in our daily lives. In turn, we began to develop transformative activist agendas connecting what we want to do in the world and our careers.

We feel that the move toward transforming higher education starts with changing educational institutions from sites of passive learning into sites of transformative practices where students have the chance to engage in critical learning that will allow them to locate themselves within history and social practices. Recognizing the dialectical nature of individual and social transformation, higher education needs to aim at producing agents of social change committed to transform social powers that perpetuate injustice through critical learning. Such a critical learning, including a more diverse and inclusive curriculum, needs to be collaboratively co-created by and in negotiation with students. An essential aspect of transforming higher education involves questioning the fundamental assumptions about knowledge by asking where these come from and whose interests they reflect and serve. Lastly, the process of decision-making should be democratized, allowing students to partake in important processes such as changes to the college, tuition costs, and curriculum.

CHAPTER 16

Reflection on Collective and Individual Transformation

Ron Lubensky

During the mid-1970s in western Canada, I was an undergraduate university student in the fledgling discipline of computing science. A handful of us deliberately chose to fail a unit when, after the withdrawal cut-off date, the faculty lecturer continued to spend more time talking about his own research than the listed topic. We complained to the Dean and his contract was not renewed.

Reading the chapter *The Dialectics of Collective and Individual Transformation* by Vianna, Hougaard and Stetsenko brought this memory to the surface for me. Their compelling and emotive narrative about the Peer-supported Activist Learning Community (PALC) that they spawned brings to life the transformation of their students from passive victims to active change agents in the institutional setting of their education, and in wider society.

The irony for me is that in the liberal era of my youth, we were students who were fully engaged with the political forces of our institution. (Several of my peers were mature-age Americans who had earlier fled to Canada to avoid conscription into the Vietnam war.) Unlike the episode above, most of the faculty *did* encourage student empowerment, consistent with their own activism in various pursuits. We were not overly concerned with tests or grades because our mutually positive and engaged activity with faculty inevitably produced a good outcome. We were optimistic about our power as change agents, and we collaborated constantly. We did not have to explicitly learn that we could or should exercise individual and collective agency.

Later, my optimism faded. During the 1980s and 1990s I taught computing and interactive media topics at institutes of technology in Canada and Australia, with multiple yet disparate missions similar to the community colleges described by the chapter authors. Too often when I wanted to open up discussion with share industry experiences and explore issues critically, my students would sit stone-faced and cross-armed with an attitude of, "just tell us what we need to know." As the chapter authors describe, most students today still only see the instrumental value of attaining a college certificate or university degree.

While an echo of Freire (1968/2000) is heard in the ambitious research project described in this chapter, which raised the consciousness of students and expanded their capacity for action, it is revolutionary on several levels. It challenges the supremacy of institutions that frame the objectives and experience of education. It challenges the commodification of knowledge and learning. It challenges the role of faculty instructors. It challenges students to *become* different.

Stetsenko asserts that we have been culturally conditioned to accept models of human development in which the essential motor is *adaptation*. This aligns with the Darwinian notion of evolutionary natural selection and the conservative desire for universalized norms. Goals for everyday judgment and decision-making are routinely reduced to adaptations aimed at economic optimality, expedience and predictability. Furthermore, the adaptation is generally seen to occur in the moment of interaction between subjects and their environment, without historical connection:

> In this conceptualization, humans are viewed as responsive rather than deliberative, with the mind understood as an organ of adaptation to given circumstances. For Piaget and Dewey, humans develop, learn and achieve knowledge—all in the spirit of adapting to existing conditions, to the here and now of their world—in order to 'fit in' better with the world. Mind and knowledge, therefore, are also profoundly saturated with the goals and processes of adaptation, rendering social and political issues that require stepping beyond adaptation impervious to research.
>
> STETSENKO, 2008, p. 482

The chapter authors emphatically reject that passive perspective, recognizing that social and political changes occur when people dislike the present situation, understand how it came about, want something better, and are prepared to do something about it. People do want to live in an ever-improving world. Therefore, education should be designed to help students become "activist" agents for change rather than mere adapters. People should be *pro-active*.

The authors apply the stronger term *transformation* rather than *change*. A transformation is not just a change in superficial behavior or attribute of a person or social object, but a change in self-identity and self-concept. Therefore, the change is not only to their situation or practices, but to the person who is making the change happen and living through it. Stetsenko (2008) calls this perspective of human development the *transformative activist stance* (TAS), which is

> ...a perspective that opens up ways to understand human development that integrates notions of social change and activism into the most basic assumptions of how human beings come to be, to act and to know the world.
>
> p. 61–62

This posture towards transformative activism is also implied in Blunden's *collaborative project* and the activity theory from which it is derived. As Blunden writes in the Introduction to this volume,

> What the notion of [Collaborative] Project is intended to do is to bring the concept of an activity back to a simple concept which can also mobilize everyday meanings, and at the same time give greater emphasis to the dynamic nature of activities and a vision of the social fabric in which the unlimited agency of individual human beings is manifest.
>
> p. 25

So a project is initiated with a concept of a problem or issue framed in a familiar paradigm, and then develops through immanent motivation for improvement. There is no doubt that the unit of analysis for TAS activity is the collaborative project. However, TAS activity constitutes a species of project with the strong ethical premise that people *should* reposition themselves to collectively improve their practices and those to which they are subjected. A TAS project strongly engages a backbone of moral responsibility and commitment:

> People come to know themselves and their world and ultimately come to be human *in and through* (not in addition to) the processes of collaboratively transforming their world in view of their goals and purposes.
>
> p. 62

Of course, the students of PALC did not set out to overthrow the whole institution of college life. By their growing willingness to imagine new possibilities and believe they could be realized, they created prototypes for new formations of activity within the prevailing institutional environment.

The teaching role at the starting point for TAS activity is the facilitation of critical-theoretic inquiry, or what Habermas referred to as "reflexive learning" (Habermas, 1975, p. 15). As critical learning theorist Stephen Brookfield explains, "reflexive learning involves us talking over with others the conflicting evidence available to us regarding whether or not things have been ordered the best way they could be in society, and whether or not corporations, bureaucracies, and governments act with the best interests of the people at heart" (Brookfield, 2005, p. 249). Add colleges to that list.

The early subjects thought they would just receive some helpful hints and counseling about how to cope with college, and examine their goals and aspirations. Instead, the authors invited the students to fearlessly ask hard questions about the institution and their relation to it. Students were encouraged to explore the sources of their personal unhappiness with college life. The door was opened to new shared concepts and vocabulary about power, motivation and strategy, mediated by the authors. The students learned how the college culture developed, and were allowed to develop within the wider community.

The activity approach that underpins TAS provides a critical method to reveal gaps and contradictions that hinder the object of their activity. For example, it is a contradiction for an educational system to profess to advocate the development of creativity and innovation, but then lock students into an administrative and pedagogic framework that is more about inculcation, conformance and assessment.

TAS pedagogy theoretically and practically introduces students to the dialectical relation of individual agency to collective activity. The authors assert that personal and cultural development *can only* occur with the type of learning that exercises aspirational individual agency. The challenge taken up in TAS practice is to build the students' confidence that their collaborative contributions can have historical significance in improving local culture and society, which repositions them as a consequence.

Whereas critical theory tends to be mainly concerned with patterns and framing of discourse, TAS is about invoking innovative action for institutional change. The first wave of change occurred within PALC itself, as students gradually took control of the workshop agenda and began to do presentations and open up dialogue around issues about which they were becoming increasingly knowledgeable, passionate and confident. From these small collaborative projects grew the seminars and conferences which then served as the emancipatory mediation to advance campus culture.

The instructors and researchers who are committed to TAS become full partners in the collaborative projects with which their students and subjects were engaged. This coincides with critical adult learning approaches, in which teachers are unafraid to openly share and explore political perspectives. They are not standoffish observers with privileged authority who would claim (usually incorrectly) that their guidance is value-free and unbiased. As demonstrated in the narratives of this chapter, TAS teaching practice is about broadening the capability for students to become change agents, and participating with them in their activity as hands-on advocates of *their* emergent projects.

I was attracted to the work of the authors because it is compatible with my own advocacy of the practice of public deliberation (see chapter 8). It is the convention for facilitators, who guide participating cohorts of people drawn from a community to discuss public policy issues, to be seen as unbiased and agnostic about the process outcomes. Instead, I implore facilitators to do as advised by the authors of this chapter, to assist participants to reflect critically and generate actions that invoke political and social change. This means helping participants reframe the situation in ways that are not locked into the polarized rhetoric of the day. Furthermore, facilitators should become advocates of the recommended outcomes by directly helping participants become ambassadors of change, such as through promotion and hosting information sessions after the conclusion of their deliberations.

Transformation starts when people step back and reflect on an existing situation and explore related human activity from the unfamiliar perspectives of others. Exercising this *reciprocity* is difficult for people who are self-absorbed, down-trodden or who associate mostly with people who are like themselves. The chapter authors mediated the early transformation by guiding their students in mutual exploration:

> The group empathetically (i.e. non-judgmentally) embraced each member's personal concerns while challenging them to position themselves as agents who make a difference, even on a small scale, in their community practices and relationships.
>
> p. 75

This is the same sort of reciprocity that facilitated deliberation relies upon for constructive progress. People make sense of each other and then by seeing themselves as active members of a dynamic and diverse community can begin to contemplate previously unimagined futures. This is how the seeds for social movements are sown.

This chapter demonstrates how the foundational framework of collaborative projects underscores the activist stance needed to improve the human condition and guide decision-making that is ostensibly in the public's best interests. Having been facilitated to enjoy the activist educational experience that I took for granted in my youth, I hope the students described in this chapter continue to develop as active citizens and ambassadors of the on-going collaborative project of critical-activist education.

References

Brookfield, S.D. (2005). *The Power of Critical Theory: Liberating Adult Learning and Teaching.* San Francisco: Jossey-Bass.

Freire, P. (1968/2000). *Pedagogy of the Oppressed, 30th Anniversary Edition.* Translated by Myra Bergman Ramos. New York: Continuum.

Habermas, J. (1975). *Legitimation Crisis.* Boston: Beacon Press.

Stetsenko, A. (2008). From relational ontology to transformative activist stance: Expanding Vygotsky's (CHAT) project. *Cultural Studies of Science Education,* 3:465–485.

CHAPTER 17

Play through the Prism of Projects

Natalia Gajdamaschko

In this commentary, I've accepted an invitation to look at play activity through the prism of "project." Play in its mature forms is typically a complex collective activity which gives rise not only to the development of the collective's members but also to understanding of the culture around them, both on an individual level (development of higher, cultural, psychological functions) and on the collective level.

Looking at play through the prism of the concept of a project also opens up some possibilities to overcome previous difficulties in analyzing play, especially in a pedagogical realm where it could help to provide a clearer answer to the question of the role of adults in a child's play. It can also assist in a deeper understanding of mechanism of play, and provide new insights for clarification of play vis-à-vis learning and development.

Two main lines of Vygotsky's thinking seem to be promising in such an analysis: the theory of development of higher psychological – cultural – functions and the methodology based on genetic-experimental method of double-stimulation during such development. To study development, according Vygotsky, is to start with analysis of the appearance of a new social situation of development in the life of a child with a view to its internal contradictions, following up with analyses of the genesis of neoformations. His two notions – "social situation of development" and "neoformation" must be considered carefully during the analysis play as a project of childhood. Such analysis also must elucidate the crises, the critical periods that open up at each level of development, as well as the prerequisites of neoformations it contains for the disintegration of the social situation of development. To assist development is to provide conditions for one's development with full understanding of such mechanisms, the laws of development, as Vygotsky called them. Because, in the process of development, the child, "arms and re-arms himself with widely varying tools," (Vygotsky, 1997b, p. 88) it is also necessary to understand development along the cultural line of development.

From the very beginning of his career, Vygotsky insisted that play would be viewed as an activity within cultural development. The motives of play activity for Vygotsky clearly relate to the cultural development of a child and actions in play are always goal-oriented. Unlike Piaget and Freud, Vygotsky maintained that play and imagination are always part of child's cultural experience. As a cultural function, imagination is active. When engaged in artistic creativity, like drawing or storytelling, children direct their imagination towards a creative pursuit – this pursuit is not just a subconscious activity but a particular skill that children access and promote. Even in play that is not directly or explicitly related to creative pursuits, children actively engage their imaginations in constructing a world in which they contextualize their play. Fantasy does not serve as merely a context, but rather is "highly directed."

We cannot determine where a project will "end up" in advance, and the same could be said for play. The role of the plot in mature make-believe play opens an opportunity for a teacher to infuse the play with some curriculum-oriented material but in no way can pre-determine the outcome of the action development of the play. This open-endedness of the individual play and multivariate possibilities of child's creative actions that stems from the child's initiative is the characteristic that unites play and projects. This is also why adults' effort to influence play directly and to infuse it with pre-determined academically-useful actions remain at times problematic, as it is impossible to influence play from the outside of the play-space by a direct instruction without ruining the play.

Other methods are needed to aid play activities. This is exactly what distinguishes genetic-developmental methods, or the projective method as Kravtsova and Kravtsov call it in their chapter, from activity with pre-determined learning outcomes with instruction of a behaviorist nature. The projective method, or the experimental-genetic method does not aim at achieving some preconceived quantifiable results; it aims to model the developmental processes which are replicated in the social situation of development of a child. The projective method represents an approach to determining the highest possible level of cultural development of a child's personality in the form of a future neoformation, and uses "projection" models to help children to develop them with the mediation of adults: "The projective method is aimed at the mechanisms and conditions of origination of the psyche's and the personality's various qualities" (p. 42).

Similarly, Michael Cole echoes the need to create a new methodology – mesogenetic method, as he calls it – that arises from the same Vygotskian proposition that to understand behavior means to understand the history/genesis of behavior. Cole believes that there is a strong need for "a new methodology – a new way of "collecting data," inscribable aspects of the flow of human activities which our theory specifies as relevant to understanding the phenomenon of interest" (p. 333).

The Vygotskian approach is exemplified in both the Golden Key schools (Chapter 1) and in the 5th Dimension program (Chapter 5), where the focus is on the creation of an innovative "social situation of development" as a prerequisite of the development of new formation. Those "play worlds" (Cole, p. 365) and "developmental social space" (Kravtsova & Kravtsov, p. 51) are experimental models of a "social situation of development" that are formed by collectives of multi-aged children and adults, with the goal of sustaining these communities for a life-span of at least three-four years. It is only through this special situation of multi-year engagement by all parties involved in the education project that it becomes possible to focus on the development of all members of such communities, including the researchers. Only in this situation can educators trace the genesis (history) of neoformations and attempt to mediate them in the process of development.

Understanding Play as Project of a Childhood and Some of Its Neoformations

Vygotsky considered the creative imagination of an adult to be of great cultural value: "imagination and creativity connected with free processing of elements of experience, and with their free combination, absolutely require, as a precursor, the internal freedom of thinking, action, and cognition that can be attained only by one who has already mastered the formation of concepts" (Vygotsky, 1997c, p. 153). In contrast, a person with a total lack of imagination is incapable of abstract thought removed from a concrete context. This capacity to be creative does not develop at once, it gradually evolves from more elementary and simpler forms into more complex ones during the play activities. Development of imagination and creativity depends on gaining more experience in those play-projects.

Imagination is an active, conscious process of meaning-making. Along with language, imagination forms a special unity with thinking in order to help the child make sense of his world. Language and imagination develop concurrently, their unity, "is inherent in the very first generalization, in the very first concept people form" (Vygotsky, 1987a, p. 78) The development of imagination is a process that occurs through play activities. The child internalizes different tools, or in Vygotsky's language, "mechanisms of imagination," such as associations, absurdities, and exaggerations. These tools, which have an important role in the development of creative adults, have their roots in play. In agreement with Karl Buhler, Vygotsky argued that the ability to exaggerate, for example, was an important tool of imagination that allowed a child to practice dealing with quantities with which they have no direct experience, which in turn leads to an ability to reason in the abstract, not only during play, but also during serious intellectual pursuits.

However, not all aspects of a child's activity can be understood as mediated by "psychological tools." If something "did not have the capacity to influence behavior, it could not be considered a tool." Thus, the mere existence of an emotion without the subsequent action that allows a child to master that emotion or use it in some fashion does not mean that the emotion develops into a psychological tool. Kravtsova and Kravtsov offer an example of this: two children are shown an image that scares them. One child responds by turning the image away, using her imagination to change the situation while the less imaginative child simply refuses to face the image. The fear exhibited by both children led to two divergent reactions, but only one of those reactions would be aptly described as the use of the "psychological tool" of a mature imagination.

Self-regulation is another important function developed through play and projects. In play, a child is under immense pressure to act on an immediate impulse but through play he develops resistance against this pressure. Rather than running off at once, a child learns to obey the rules of the game and performs within a specific, bound context.

Play activities in childhood, under certain conditions, can serve as projects that help a child to develop, to "arm" and "re-arm" themselves with cultural tools that bring about profound changes in their development. This new take on play as childhood projects requires a new methodology and lots of theoretical re-considerations but seems to be fruitful for future research and can have a profound implications for our pedagogical practices. As we can see from the chapters of Kravtsova and Kravtsov and Cole, the first steps have already been taken in this direction, it is up to us educators to follow the lead.

References

Vygotsky, L.S. (1987). Thinking and speech, *Collected Works, Vol. 1*, pp. 39–285, New York: Plenum Press.

Vygotsky, L.S. (1997a). The history of the development of the higher mental functions, *Collected Works, Vol. 4*, pp. 1–259, New York: Plenum Press.

Vygotsky, L.S. (1997b). The instrumental method in psychology, *Collected Works, Vol. 3*, pp. 85–89, New York: Plenum Press.

Vygotsky, L.S. (1997c). Pedology of the adolescent, *Collected Works, Vol. 5*, pp. 3–184, New York: Plenum Press.

CHAPTER 18

Human Flourishing in Developmental Education Schools: A Collaborative Project Perspective†

Chiel van der Veen and Lynne Wolbert

In the early '80s, various Dutch educational researchers, practitioners, teacher trainers and policy makers got involved in what we came to call a collaborative project. What brought and still brings them together are their critiques of a form of education based on the direct transmission of cultural meanings and rote-like learning, whilst neglecting children's personal sense. From these critiques, a long-term collaboration was begun, leading to an approach to education which promotes 'children's meaningful learning and cultural development in an emancipatory way' (van Oers, 2012a, p. 59). This approach to education is referred to as Developmental Education (van Oers, 2012b). In this chapter, we will reflect on the emergence of the Developmental Education approach in the Netherlands from a project perspective. Firstly, we will distinguish four stages, or phases of projects in describing the foundation and development of Developmental Education. Secondly, we will argue that the Developmental Education project, as both a descriptive and normative conception of good education, promotes the flourishing of teachers and children by creating conditions for children to develop their personalities in a broad sense, acquire agency for participating in cultural activities, and design their own life-projects. Further, teachers in Developmental Education flourish themselves in their project of educating children.

From Shared Problem to Collaborative Project

Developmental Education is an approach for the education of children in pre- and primary school settings (0–12 year olds) and is rooted in Vygotsky's cultural-historical theory. For over three decades, numerous teachers, innovators, researchers, policy makers, etc. have been collaborating in an attempt to develop a

† We thank Bert van Oers and Doret de Ruyter for their helpful comments.

> theoretically well-grounded practice for the education of (young) children that would be inherently pedagogical, that is to say an approach that aims to deliberately promote the cultural development of children, acknowledging the responsibilities and normative choices that educators have to make (and want to make) in helping children to become autonomous and critical agents in society.
>
> VAN OERS, 2012b, p. 13

As for today, a well-organized community is established involving over 300 schools that have implemented the Developmental Education approach, a platform for members organizing conferences, a teacher training center, and more. Tracing back the emergence and development of the Developmental Education approach in the Netherlands, we can undoubtedly see the similarities with the collaborative projects as described in this book. Characteristic of projects is that they embody change on both an individual and societal level, inherently advocating collaboration and promoting human flourishing.

Phase 1: Shared Discontent with the Status Quo of Education in the Netherlands

In educational discourse, there is an ongoing debate on how children's learning and development in the context of formal schooling should be organized. Traditionally, schooling is organized as the transmission of knowledge and skills from teacher to children. Children's personal sense is often neglected. This is considered to be one of the main reasons for children becoming alienated from the practice of schooling (Leontiev, 1981). From the early '70s, several researchers, teachers and educational developers from different institutions in the Netherlands experienced this very problem and shared their discontent with this one-sided focus on transmission. Further, in 1985 the Primary Education Act became effective in which the starting age for compulsory education was lowered from six to five years and separate kindergartens were abolished and integrated into primary schools. Educators involved in the education of the youngest children worried that play would gradually disappear from the curriculum at the cost of formal schooling. It was Frea Janssen-Vos who first developed an approach to education for the youngest children which would promote their development in the context of meaningful play activities. Her work supported the legitimacy of the cultural-historical research program as executed at the VU University Amsterdam. Under conditions of shared discontent among educators over this one-sided focus on transmission of knowledge, the integration of kindergartens into primary schools acted as a trigger for the project to emerge.

Phase 2: Negotiation of Aims and Direction

In the second phase of the development of this project, people became aware of the problem and attempted to clarify it. They 'projected' the ideal situation to reach and negotiated aims and direction. In the start-up of the Developmental Education project, there was an ongoing debate on how pupils should appropriate cultural tools and to what extent this process of appropriation should be personally meaningful for them. Following the work of Davydov (1977), some people involved in the initial phase of the project argued that children should be provided with high quality cultural tools by the teacher, preferably 'scientific concepts'. Others found this approach too instrumental, giving no room for children to (re)construct these tools. Besides, it was argued that providing children with cultural tools alone runs the risk of neglecting their personal sense (i.e. their motives or needs to use these tools). The latter issue was the very problem from which the Developmental Education project emerged. So it was decided by the majority of those involved in the project that the focus should be on promoting children's cultural development, whilst acknowledging their responsibility, agency, motives and needs.

Phase 3: Developmental Education Community

In the third phase, there was a clear conception of the problem at stake and from this problem, a project was launched to change the current educational practice. This project was officially named Developmental Education (in Dutch: Ontwikkelingsgericht Onderwijs). Educators from different practices became involved, and collaboratively they aimed to change educational practices. A community was established, allocating different roles (researcher, developer, teacher) to the people involved in the Developmental Education project. Further, this community promotes and facilitates collaboration between the different roles. Collaboratively, the Developmental Education community aims to change educational practices towards a practice that inherently promotes the flourishing of children and teachers involved.

Phase 4: Steps towards Institutionalization

As for today, Developmental Education has become partially mainstreamed and institutionalized. Over the years, a specific language has been developed to communicate about a conception of good education that follows from the Developmental Education approach. Such concepts as 'the zone of proximal development', 'play-based curriculum' and 'meaningful learning' have become part of the language of the wider, Dutch educational community. In several institutes for primary teacher education, students can specialize in the

Developmental Education approach. However, to some extent Developmental Education remains in a project state. Many schools in the Netherlands still focus on the one-sided transmission of knowledge and skills, there is an ongoing debate about the aims and function of education in Dutch society, and the majority of people involved in education still conceive of Developmental Education as a socio-constructivist approach to education in which children can do whatever they please.

Developmental Education and Flourishing

In (educational) philosophy, there is a renewed interest in Aristotelian virtue ethics. In neo-Aristotelian theory the concept of human flourishing plays a central role. Educational philosophers argue that children should flourish in life and that therefore flourishing should be the ultimate aim of education. To flourish means to have actualized your potential, to do the best in life *you* can (e.g. Rasmussen, 1999). In theories of human flourishing there is often a notion of development implied; to flourish is a process, an activity, a *praxis* (Hurka, 1999). Following Aristotle, a third important aspect of the concept of human flourishing is that it combines both objective and subjective goods (de Ruyter, 2007). We should thus aim for children to live a good life, also in a moral sense; engaging in objective goods, but to also have the feeling they live a good life in a 'happy' sense; enjoying what they are doing. Humans only flourish if they themselves feel or know that they do (de Ruyter, 2007).

Several aspects of the projective method, as explained by Kravtsov and Kravtsova (Chapter 1), and several aspects of Developmental Education, connect with the idea of flourishing. Firstly, the focus of Developmental Education is indeed to develop children's personalities in a broad sense and conceives of the child's education as something that is more than knowledge transmission alone, namely becoming 'well-equipped' for the project that is the child's own life. In the 'Golden Key' program this idea is well described as 'every child having acquired his own golden key from and to the whole world' (p. 39). As such, Developmental Education schools promote children's flourishing and help them to come into the world as unique, singular beings (Biesta, 2011). Secondly, the notion of (never-ending) development is ubiquitous in activity theory, since the framework of Developmental Educational is built around promoting the development of the individual child to be autonomous, critical members of society, and as such helps children to be able to design their own life-projects. Vygotsky's notion of the 'unity of affect and intellect' (p. 37), meaning that the content of education has to be connected to the interests of children and must not have an alien character, goes well with the Aristotelian notion that flourishing combines living a good life and feeling happy about what you do.

Reciprocal Flourishing

Kravtsov and Kravtsova explain in their chapter how the projective method is a developing process for all participants. The major difference between the projective method and all others is 'that the developing work is aimed not at the individual child or group of children but at the whole environment and all spheres of children's and adults' life' (p. 34). Perhaps this is the most important point we can make about human flourishing as an aim of Developmental Education. In Developmental Education the multilevel, multidirectional, multi-environmental approach to human flourishing is of high importance. In the same way as all participants get involved in various collaborative projects, striving for flourishing also influences all parties concerned. And it works both ways. In Developmental Education, the teacher creates and is part of the environment of the pupil, trying to create the best possible environment to flourish, but at the same time the pupil is part of the environment of the teacher and with his behavior contributes to the conditions for the teacher to flourish. The same applies to all other subjects involved in Developmental Education.

Conclusion

In this reflection, we have described the emergence and development of the Developmental Education approach in the Netherlands from a project perspective. Using the concept of collaborative project, we were able to distinguish the different phases in the development of this project. Tracing back the emergence of the Developmental Education project, we can see how it embodies change and collaboration. Furthermore, we have argued that the aim of Developmental Education can be interpreted as promoting the flourishing of children and teachers. Finally, using collaborative project as unit of analysis has contributed to our understanding of collaboration, change and flourishing within the Developmental Education project. As a normative conception of good education, the Developmental Education approach aims to promote the flourishing of children and teachers involved and, thereby, to change not only the individual child or teacher but their whole environment.

References

Biesta, G. (2011). *Good Education in an Age of Measurement. Ethics, Politics, Democracy.* London: Pluto Press.

Davydov, V.V. (1977). *Arten der Verallgemeinerung im Unterricht. Logisch-psychologische Probleme des Aufbaus von Unterrichtsfächern.* Berlin: Volk und Wissen.

Hurka, T. (1999). The three faces of flourishing. In E. Frankel Paul, F.D. Miller, & J. Paul (Eds.), *Human Flourishing* (pp. 44–71). Cambridge: Cambridge University Press.

Leontiev, A.N. (1981). *Problems of the Development of the Mind.* Moscow: Progress Publishers.

van Oers, B. (2012a). Developmental education: Reflections on a CHAT research program in the Netherlands. *Learning, Culture and Social Interaction, 1*(1), 57–65.

van Oers, B. (Ed.)(2012b). *Developmental Education for Young Children: Concept, Practice, and Implementation.* Dordrecht: Springer.

Rasmussen, D.B. (1999). Human flourishing and the appeal to human nature. In E. Frankel Paul, F.D. Miller, & J. Paul (Eds.), *Human Flourishing* (pp. 1–43). Cambridge: Cambridge University Press.

de Ruyter, D.J. (2007). Ideals, education, and happy flourishing. *Educational Theory, 57* (1), 23–35

CHAPTER 19

Reflection on Complementarity and Mutual Appropriation

Vera John-Steiner

The authors of this book on collaborative projects have been successful in overcoming some longstanding dichotomies. One of the most troubling ones is the tension between the social and the individual. Blunden writes in the Introduction, "A person's identity is not just formed *by* collaborative projects, it *is* a collaborative project. Projects create selves at the same time as they create social bonds" (p. 16).

One collaborative project that is universal is the beginning of life, where mother and infant jointly strive toward survival. After birth, the infant undergoes a critical transition from biological interdependence to social interdependence. As infants continue their need for nurturing adults, both caregivers and those who receive care create selves as they create social bonds.

While recognizing the importance of this fundamental "collaborative project," it is not a process that is referred to in contemporary CHAT theory. Childhood, that most pervasive of collaborative projects, is primarily mentioned by those engaged in educational activities. Theoretically, it has largely been neglected in contemporary writings, which focus more on adults and their work and their political projects. Important exceptions in this book include the chapter written by Kravtsova and Kravtsov, who have successfully developed the projective method in helping children to learn through special play situations. Another exception is the chapter on the well-known 5th Dimension program. Cole, Gordon, and Blanton depict the unexpected ways in which a long-term intervention project has flourished (as well as failed) in a variety of US and international contexts. The observational data collected by these authors and their undergraduate collaborators' field notes have yet to be analyzed to provide us with information about the diverse ways in which children participate in technologically-assisted learning and problem solving. At present, we will have to wait for opportunities to mine this rich database, as funds are limited and the prevalent focus in cultural historical research is on adult collaborative projects.

Anna Stetsenko and her collaborators address in this book the dialectical unity of the individual and the social. In developing a theory of collective and individual transformation, these authors highlight how, in project activities, each participant contributes to a widening range of community practices (p. 59). Their formulation supports the role of the self and leads to the question: Are there differences between project participants, and if so, how do they evolve? By opposing biological determinism are we, within the CHAT community, opposing all considerations of individual differences? We have side-stepped this issue, and, by doing so, we minimize the role of mutual appropriations – the way in which people with different histories, skills, and personalities expand each other's possibilities.

But if the texts in this volume are closely scrutinized, examples of mutual appropriation can be identified. One of these is in the account of the Mayslake strike. Helena Worthen mentions how, in general, the workers at Heartland Human Services lacked a written tradition of contractual agreements between workers and employers. Instead, without a union, transactions between the two groups took place based on custom. The Board of the agency had enormous, unchecked power and, when faced with financial challenges, made drastic, disastrous changes in workers' wages and benefits. There was no customary way to challenge them. When four of the workers started to talk about organizing a union, they were the ones who had some previous experience or exposure to union practices. This was in contrast with the rest of the workforce. The organizers' experience was crucial in educating their peers and in approaching a national union for assistance. The role of these four individuals raises important theoretical issues about the way in which we conceptualize collaboration and the central role of complementarity.

Individuals participate in collaborations that differ historically and culturally, and the result is the development of new, diverse skills and knowledge on the part of collaborators. When entering a new collaboration the expertise of those working together manifests itself as individual differences and facilitates a reliance on complementarity. The relevant dimension in Mayslake was being part of (or knowing second hand) about union practices. The four workers who initiated the drive had a different history than their coworkers, and their contribution was crucial to the events in the organization in which they worked, particularly during the early phase of forming a union. Later, with the help of a national union, their expertise was fused with what others, including professional organizers, brought into the collaborative project. New skills, including public speaking, were acquired by an increasingly large number of participants. The relationships which were established among the workers during this struggle were close and supportive. The four persons who started the drive were strengthened by this new atmosphere of mutual support. As the strike developed, other skills surfaced among the participants. I would like to suggest that, unless we pay attention to these potential personal contributions to a project and trace their diffusion among participants, our description of collaborative projects remains too general. In our theories, we posit the importance of participants without detailing the ways in which they achieve the mutual appropriation of information, skills, beliefs, and knowledge essential to a successful outcome. Such complementarity becomes the lived experience, the *perezhivanie*, of collaboration.

While in the account of the Mayslake strike, Worthen highlights the crucial contribution of the four individuals who had previous union experience. Other authors do not explicitly state the impact of specialized knowledge on the joint effort. For instance, during the early history of the 5th Dimension Project, Peg Griffin's extensive experience in reading instruction was a crucial skill. It was later combined with Mike Cole's knowledge of field methodology and familiarity with undergraduates' skills and interests, which helped transform an afterschool meeting program into a complex collaborative project. There were many other research and program participants in this highly successful international program. One of those was Olga Vasquez who adapted the program for Spanish-speaking communities. The roles of these individuals were not isolated. All their innovations were jointly modified and implemented while "they were creating their selves" while also creating social bonds.

When introducing the issue of individual differences, I am not suggesting a genetically determined static self. Instead, I am proposing a changing self, one who is able to complement others as a consequence of the person's previous history and participation in diverse collaborative projects. In addition to the complementarity and mutual appropriation that takes place as individuals join in working toward a shared goal, an interesting parallel occurs at the group level. The interweaving of groups with differing disciplinary training can result in productive complementarity and development on the part of both groups. This is illustrated in Beaton and Blunden's chapter on the fight against the widespread use of asbestos in Australia. In this long and painful struggle, the joining of health professionals with trade unions was decisive. The medical researchers contributed the hard data that were needed to highlight the life threatening danger asbestos posed to the population. But without the organizational skills of the unions, that information would have remained in the hands of specialists. The unions, with the help of some crusading journalists, made the issues public and started on the long road to bring about legal and political change in the face of opposition on the part of the manufacturers (p. 270). The collaboration between these two groups is a further illustration of complementarity as an important part of successful joint efforts.

In his account of the 2011 Egyptian uprising, De Smet provides examples of different mutual appropriations. One of these is intergenerational collaboration where experienced militants shared their knowledge of protest movements with a younger generation of activists, who in turn were able to provide their skills with social media (p. 304). Practical advice was provided by Tunisian militants – they recommended that when participants in Tahrir Square were confronted with tear gas they should use cola, vinegar, and onions (p. 293). An interesting joining of diverse groups during the occupation of Tahrir was when artists joined the protests, who together with amateur cartoonists, actors, and singers, created a festival experience for the protestors. De Smet interviewed Menal Khalid who explained: "Most Egyptians didn't see any art or know any artists and for many Egyptians it was the first time to see artists in action, and for artists it was the first tome to have a mass feedback and audience through the Square" (p. 201). These transformative experiences were coupled with an emergent internal division of labor where people assumed responsibilities for feeding, cleaning, and information sharing and achieved "spontaneous order out of chaos" (p. 302).

In identifying specific instances of mutual appropriation and complementarity in this text, I focus on these crucial processes of knowledge expansion within and across collaborative projects. This provides but a beginning for the collaborative project of specifying the particular dynamics of joint activity, which result in projects creating selves "at the same time as they create social bonds" (p. 16).

CHAPTER 20

Spirited Collaborations

Greg Thompson

In her chapter "Rhythms of Collaboration," John-Steiner points to the problematic dichotomy of individual and society that has run through the relatively short history of science in the West and which undergirds the preference for thinking of the individual scientist in isolation. John-Steiner's research critiquing the pervasive ideology of the isolated individual points to the need for an alternative to the ideology of the isolated individual. She offers a wonderful corrective to this ideology by showing the critical role of collaboration in actual scientific practice.

In this commentary, I first briefly trace the history of the Vygotskian critique of the ideology of the isolated individual, tracing it back through Hegel and Marx to the work of Jean-Jacques Rousseau. I then take up the work of another theorist also influenced by Rousseau, namely, Emile Durkheim, and show how he offered a similar and complementary critique in his social ontology of the subject. Finally, I propose additional directions in which we might take John-Steiner's work using Durkheim's approach.

In Western thought, Rousseau offered an early attempt to reconcile the apparent contradiction between individual and society. Though often misread as simply fetishizing the individual who stands outside of society, as in the infamous "noble savage" (a red herring to be sure), Rousseau was one of the first to articulate a dialectic between individual and society that appreciated how the individual is *constituted* by society. Thus, the individual in society cannot even be compared with the "natural" individual before or outside of society because the two are qualitatively different beings. Yet although Rousseau was one of the first to offer a reconciliation of individual and society, Rousseau did not fully articulate a social ontology of the subject, leaving the force of his insights largely unrealized. Such a social ontology of the subject was more fully developed by the philosopher G.W.F. Hegel and sociologist Emile Durkheim.

In Hegel's *Phenomenology of Spirit*, individual self-consciousness emerges from the individual's relation both to other individuals and to society as a whole, realized in socially mediated forms of recognition and eventually in social labor. Cultural historically, this means that there is no individual or society without the other, the individual is thoroughly social and vice-versa, "An I that is We and a We that is I" (Hegel, 1977, p. 110).

While it has been argued that Vygotsky likely would have read and have been influenced by Hegel and thus would have likely been familiar with Hegel's social ontology of the subject, it is most certainly the case that Vygotsky was familiar with the work of Karl Marx. In his work, Marx echoes Hegel's social ontology of the subject:

> In a sort of way, it is with man as with commodities. Since he comes into the world neither with a looking glass in his hand, nor as a Fichtean philosopher, to whom "I am I" is sufficient, man first sees and recognizes himself in other men. Peter only establishes his own identity as a man by first comparing himself with Paul as being of like kind. And thereby Paul, just as he stands in his Pauline personality, becomes to Peter the type of the *genus homo*.
>
> MARX, 1867, p. 63

And closer to John-Steiner's point, Marx applies this social ontology of the subject to an individual scientist engaged in the practice of science:

> But also when I am active *scientifically*, etc. – an activity which I can seldom perform in direct community with others – then my activity is *social*, because I perform it as a man. Not only is the material of my activity given to me as a social product (as is even the language in which the thinker is active): my own existence is social activity, and therefore that which I make of myself, I make of myself for society and with the consciousness of myself as a social being.
>
> MARX, 1844, p. 298

Vygotsky brings a similar understanding of the subject into his analysis of ontogenetic development. Whereas Hegel provided a cultural-historical social ontology of the subject, Vygotsky provides an ontogenetic social ontology of the subject in which the subject (here the child) is constituted by his interactions with socially significant others. Here we have a theory of development that, like that of Rousseau, Hegel, and Marx before, gets us past the ideology of the isolated individual. I suspect that this is an important part of why so many Vygotskian scholars, particularly in the U.S., have been inspired by Vygotsky's work – it gives us a whole new way of seeing the world that discloses aspects of our lives and ourselves which we previously had difficulty seeing. Most notable among these are the ways in which our individuality is constituted by and through our social context. In their efforts along these lines, I find the work of Vygotsky and Vygotskian scholars like John-Steiner to be invaluable, for they present a critical corrective to the ideology of the isolated individual.

In the interests of further developing this line of thinking, I here turn to the second social ontology of the subject mentioned above, namely that of Emile Durkheim.

In *The Elementary Forms of Religious Life*, which remains as provocative today as it did when it was published in 1912, Durkheim (1912/1995) argues that thinking originated in the highly emotional experience that people have as they periodically came together in sacred religious rituals. During these rituals, the group takes on a spirit that is greater than any of the individuals. In this process, certain symbols, most notably totemic emblems, become infused with the emotional energy that they experience when together.

When this highly emotional collective ritual is over and they disperse and return to their mundane daily lives, the emotional energy is then taken with them in the form of the totemic emblem. Most crucially, the highly emotional experiences of being together with others serve to infuse daily life with a sense of "something more." In other words, these experiences provide the basis for mediation, that is, for the transcendence of immediacy and for the emergence of an understanding of the world as more than just what it presents itself as. For example, the totem is not just a rock with lines carved into it. Rather, as a totem of the clan, it is infused with the emotions associated with the clan and thus is decidedly "something more" than that. This "something more" both launches the participants into the world of mediated conceptualizations and, equally importantly, this "something more" provides emotional energy that motivates participants to become more than they otherwise could have been.

Whereas for Hegel, the critical social factor in the making of subjects was socially mediated recognition and social labor, for Durkheim our subjecthood emerges from the intense emotional energy that is dependent upon the emotional experiences that people have when they come together in collectives.

The reader familiar with Vygotsky will notice some similarities in the social ontology of the subject proposed by both Vygotsky and Durkheim. Both argue that thinking comes from social interaction mediated by the use of symbols. Also similar to Vygotsky, Durkheim points to the importance of the passing on of cultural historical knowledge from generation to generation as mediated by symbolic forms.

I would add that there are also important similarities with John-Steiner's project. First, and similar to John-Steiner's characterization of the rhythms of collaboration, Durkheim argues that the rhythm of life that produces this emotional energy involves the periodic coming together of people in collaborative moments in which both totemic emblems and individuals are infused with the emotional energy of the group that then allows them to return to mundane life and carry out their everyday work. Second, both Durkheim and John-Steiner offer a critique of the "old standing dichotomy between individual and social."

Yet I think we can take Durkheim's project a step further and use it to imagine new directions of research into collaborative projects. Turning to John-Steiner's rather remarkable example of Tim Gowers's *Polymath Collaboration*, Durkheim's work directs our attention to a new set of concerns – collective symbols, totems, emotional energy, and the spirit of the clan. To this end, we might ask: what is the role of the collective symbols, totems even, of this clan of mathematicians? The Fields Medal is the mathematical equivalent of the Nobel Prize, arguably a totemic emblem representing the tribe known as Mathematicians. Could a younger and unrecognized scholar, lacking Gowers's mathematical *mana*, have provoked such a collaboration?

With regard to emotional energy, in what ways are the individual participants as well as the relevant symbols "charged up" by their interactions with other collaborators and the group? How does this math problem take on a sense of being more than just a mundane part of everyday life? In other words, how does the math problem take on a sacred quality?

With regard to the spirit of this particular clan, what was the spirit that developed in the course of the project? How might it have developed such that it could have charged up its members with the emotional energy necessary to go and do the difficult work of spending months working through this math problem? And particularly important for the Gowers example: how did such a spirit develop in the medium of a blog where there is little or no face-to-face contact?

When studying collaborative projects, it is all too easy to elide this "spirited" dimension of collaboration in favor of a more cognitivistic approach that attends primarily to the exchange of information between collaborators. This is particularly true in examples like that of Gowers where the ideational nature of the material can make it seem as if what matters most is the merely the information being exchanged. But attending only to ideational and information exchanges can cause one to miss more basic questions such as: Why did people even bother to show up at Gowers's blog in the first place? And, how does this group of scholars create a kind of collective effervescence which animates the participants such that they go off and work for months on something so removed from the practical concerns of everyday life as a highly abstract mathematics problem?

In short, Durkheim's work suggests that research on collaborative projects could benefit greatly from greater attention to the *spirit* of collaborations.

References

Durkheim, E. (1912/1995). *The Elementary Forms of Religious Life*. (K. E. Fields, Trans.). Free Press.

Hegel, G.W.F. (1977). *Phenomenology of Spirit*, trans. A. V. Miller, Oxford: Oxford University Press.

Marx, K. (1844/1975). *Private Property and Communism*, *MECW*, vol. 3, New York: International Publishers.

Marx, K. (1867/1996). *Capital*, vol. 1, chapter 1, *MECW*, vol. 35, New York: International Publishers.

CHAPTER 21

Emotional Commitment and the Development of Collaborative Projects

Manfred Holodynski

In this book, Andy Blunden introduces a new concept, the "collaborative project." This label and concept serve the purpose of conceptualizing the tension between individual actions and their societal context in an interdisciplinary manner. "'Project' functions explicitly to theorize the connection between human actions and the societal context in which individual actions are meaningful" (p. 23). In my reflection, I want to focus on two points: (1) Reconstructing the development of collaborative projects can be a tool for figuring out the societal and psychological conditions of how projects can be successfully planned and managed. (2) A successful realization of a project does not only depend on its conceptual and operative conditions, but also on the motivational and emotional conditions of how the participants of a project harmonize the project's goals with their personal motives and create a personal sense of their collaboration.

Reconstructing the development of collaborative projects. Although not explicitly formulated, the introductory text of Andy Blunden reveals that collaborative projects have their starting point in collectively experienced social evils for which no suitable conceptual and instrumental tools exist which could remedy the evils and shortcomings. These tools still have to be invented and optimized by the cooperative actions of the persons affected often against massive societal resistance. In the course of a project's development, its goals as well as its tools become fine-tuned. Because of its universality, the concept of collaborative projects can be applied to all domains of the societal life. The projects described in this book with their wide range and heterogeneity, are a convincing illustration of this.

Hence, collaborative projects emerge at those parts of a societal activity at which the already existing tools and norms are not sufficient (any more) for the satisfaction of its societal motive. Collaborative projects are the spearhead of a societal activity as can be inferred from Blunden's stages of a project (p. 8). The starting point is a problem within a given societal activity, goes on to some failed solutions and finally leads to a construction of new and efficient tools that could solve the problem which in turn can become mainstreamed as part of the societal practices of the wider community. Insofar, a project is as a rule only an element of a societal activity in which it is embedded.

When a project focusses on a social evil it is probable that some more projects emerge at the same time that initially are not mutually coordinated. For example, a couple of teaching projects might exist within the institutions of school and university that devote themselves to innovative forms of teaching and learning that may improve the process and results of teaching and learning. This creates the important task of connecting the projects and generalizing them so that they can step out of their original marginal existence and begin influencing the societal mainstream of the activity.

For a productive realization of a collaborative project, it is especially important to know how projects develop, by which actions in relation to which social and societal conditions the participants of a project can successfully expand the project or see it marginalized or even break off. Reconstructing the development of successful vs. unsuccessful projects can contribute important insights for a successful managing of projects. Are there early indicators of success? To what extent does a project rely on trial and error? In many cases, one can only evaluate how generalizable a project really has been in retrospect. For example, some projects emerged in the early 1970s in western countries which criticized the authoritarian education of children at that time, and they propagated and practiced an anti-authoritarian education especially in kindergartens. These projects, however, failed miserably and disappeared very soon. Looking back at these projects, their arguments had been very naïve and misleading because they neglected the differences between adult caregivers and children.

The reconstruction of motivational and emotional aspects of collaborative projects. The contributions in the book contain a bunch of innovative projects which provide very informative details about their conceptual and organizational development. A collaborative project, however, does not consist only of these conceptual and organizational aspects. People do not carry out only actions that are more or less integrated in a societal activity or project. Looking from a psychological perspective, an individual "only" tries to satisfy his or her individual motives which do not really coincide with the societal motives of the collective activity in which the individual actions are embedded. As Blunden pointed out: "Individual participants may be aware of the motive of the activity in which they are participating, but its meaning for them, and their motive for participation in the activity, is individual" (p. 24).

This leads to two important tasks in managing a project. (1) How can people be convinced to engage in the project and act in line with the project's goals, up to the point that they devote themselves to the project and adopt the project's goals as their own motives? (2) How can the motives of a person be diagnosed and identified? Let's start with the second task. Leontiev (1978) figured out that a person's emotions signalize the personal sense he or she attributes to his or her actions. Emotions signalize the relationship between the goal (and result) of an action and the elicited motives of the person (Holodynski, 2013). Commitment to a project is not only expressed by project-serving actions – the personal sense is expressed by the emotions which the protagonist experiences. On a general level, this emotional relationship can be described in line with Blunden's (p. 19) distinction between colonization, external reward and solidarity, but on a personal level it could be more complex.

All contributions in this book have been written from the perspective of the project's protagonists who did not only drive the project forward in a conceptual and organizational way, but who were also very emotionally involved. For example, the report of the Mayslake project (Worthen, pp. 176ff) shows in a very impressive way the highly emotional commitment the protagonists summoned up for pushing the project also against bitter resistance, and the emotional successes, but also emotional defeats and insults that the protagonists had to suffer. One of the main protagonists described her experience with the bitter conclusion: "We did win, but I lost in the end" (p. 194). This remark expresses the tension between the societal meanings which describe the success of a project for the public and the personal sense, which means the commitment to the project for the personal life of a protagonist. It will be very informative for the successful management of projects when it is possible to extract general insights into the motivational and emotional power and the conditions that enabled the protagonists of the described projects to drive their projects forward. But also, how far emotional insults and defeats are an unavoidable downside of an engaged collaboration in a project?

The second abovementioned task of carrying out a project focusses on the problem of how formerly uninvolved people can become engaged in the project because most of the projects are not limited to the protagonists. If the goals of a project are orientated to general goals (for example, the implementation of an innovative learning curriculum at schools or universities) the realization of a project also requires convincing an (ever) larger circle of people of the necessity of the project and to win them as new project members. This is, however, not an easy task. When a project is introduced to outsiders it comes upon people who possess already an established hierarchy of personal motives. On the basis of these motives, a person appraises how far participation in the project may satisfy these motives. The result of this appraisal is shown by emotional reactions towards the project. The result of this appraisal is shown by emotional reactions towards the project, such as sympathy for the victims of a social evil whom the project is going to help, and reactions of indignation about the social evil that the project denounces. Such emotional reactions of an outsider are the first hints that she or he finds the project's goals and content noteworthy and cause him to seek more information about the project.

Indignation is elicited when a person recognizes that a person or a group of people transgressed a generally valid social norm and caused harm to the person themself or to a third party. Sympathy is elicited when a person recognizes the harm of a third party especially when the person has an emotional bond to the third party. These emotions contain an action-readiness to put a stop to the norm violator and to support the victims of the harm. Actions with a low threshold of commitment make it easier for outsiders to get involved in the project and perceivable successes elicit pride and confidence which in turn strengthen the commitment to the project.

Many projects do not focus on the removal of social evils or fateful disasters. Therefore, indignation and sympathy cannot be used as emotional hooks. Projects, however, take up dissatisfaction with an existing (professional) practice. This is the case for many projects within the institutional contexts of kindergartens, schools and universities where the institutional learning and teaching have been judged unproductive and inappropriate. This dissatisfaction makes the persons affected (teachers, students, parents) receptive to a search for innovative and successful teaching and learning strategies and their testing. Taking up dissatisfaction is the starting-point for collaborative projects to demonstrate the superiority of their innovative strategies and to win outsiders as new supporters and members of the project. For example, Blunden and Arnold (pp. 111ff) illustrate this in the description of their project "Collaborative Learning Space." The task is to induce newcomers to engage for a first step and to enable the experience that the innovative strategies of the project are successful. The success does not only manifest itself in a defined result, but also emotionally in pride and joy in the success which in turn strengthens the commitment to the project. So projects succeed only insofar as they enjoy recognition and expand.

When a project begins to step out of its marginal existence and prepares to influence the societal mainstream, the acquisition and distribution of resources, powers and public recognition become important. This entails actions that are also useful for the satisfaction of personal motives which have only a little in common with the original goals of the project or even run counter to them. Let us take, for example, the project "Collaborative Learning Space" again. It is conceivable that the installation of computer-assisted learning rooms becomes so prestigious that the administration of a university or school might install them to profit from their innovative aura, but does not provide further resources required to also changing the climate of learning and teaching by teachers and students. In this way, it is possible that the motivational and emotional commitment of new project members to the original goals of the project gets lost and disappears when the project spreads out and empties the original impetus of the project up to the point of a corruption of the project's goals. Blunden (p. 19) describes these processes as colonization and external reward. One can state as a reversal of the abovementioned quote: "We lost, but I won in the end."

Therefore, when a project spreads out it is necessary not only to establish a socially shared conceptualization of the project and a socially coordinated practice. It is also necessary to establish *a socially shared personal sense* of the project's goals. This personal sense can be expressed in socially shared emotions such as shared indignation about a social evil which removal is the goal of the project, shared enthusiasm for joint successes or the experience of solidarity with project members and emotionally shared symbols. This includes all efforts to establish an emotionally anchored solidarity and identity among the members of a project, especially when the mutual relationships get more and more differentiated and segregated because of the necessary division of labor in a growing project.

Taken together, for a successful organization and development of collaborative projects, it is necessary to know how far conditions of success and failure can be extracted from an analysis of already existing projects. The reconstruction of their emotional aspects in which the personal sense of the project's members comes to light is as necessary as the reconstruction of the conceptual and organizational aspects.

References

Holodynski, M (2013). The internalization theory of emotions: A cultural historical approach to the development of emotions. *Mind, Culture, and Activity*, 20, 4–38.

Leontiev, A.N. (1978). *Activity, Consciousness, and Personality*. Englewood Cliffs: Prentice-Hall.

CHAPTER 22

Projects, Activity Systems: Figuring Out How to Use these Concepts

Helena Worthen

The challenge that this book rises to meet is to place the concept of "project" at the junction of the sciences of the individual, like psychology or social work, and the sciences of society, like sociology, political science, the study of social movements and others. The value of doing this is to make visible the individual's effort in the development of something larger, perhaps much larger, than himself but to keep both in view at the same time.

This book is in itself such a project. It gathers chapters about different experiences of engagement within a society (Lubensky on public deliberation; Power on gay activism, de Smet on Tahrir Square), within an institution (Vianna, Hougaard and Stetsenko, a community college; Cole, an education system; Kravtsova and Kravtsov, a school system; Blunden and Arnold, a university) an industry (Beaton and Blunden on asbestos) or a business or workforce (Worthen, a regional healthcare facility). The contexts range from very broad to fairly narrow, but even the smallest involves several people and over time, more. Each chapter describes a project that is a "social situation of development, a predicament from which the project emancipates itself by making a development" (de Smet, p. 290). The authors are then invited to reflect on each other's work; in other words, to collaborate in the project of the book itself.

The tradition out of which this project developed is the Cultural Historical Activity Theory (CHAT) of which Activity theory, originating in the work of Vygotsky and expanded and defined first by Leontiev and then Engeström, is the main well-known contemporary manifestation. However, the term "activity" in English is not self-explanatory. It can mean meaningless or mindless motion or generic forms of recreation. It primarily separates activity from inactivity. This is by itself an argument in favor of finding a different name for a term to be used to study social phenomena. Unless someone knows what "activity" refers to in Activity Theory, saying those words to someone who is hearing it for the first time tends to draw a puzzled stare. "Activity system" is even more of a problem. It gives us two fuzzy words instead of one. By contrast, using the single word "project," as Andy Blunden proposes, as a way to name collaborative, purposeful effort (which is what is meant by "activity system" and "activity theory") would make talking about it much easier (would "mobilize everyday meanings" – p. 25). However, Blunden also indicates that "collaborative project" could be thought of as a unit of analysis for Activity Theory (p. 11, p. 15). Thus "project" would not replace "activity" but would name the unit of analysis generally referred to as "activity system."

But then there is the problem of the commonness of the word "project." Everyone thinks they know what a project is. Anything a person is planning to do can be called a project. As Blunden notes in the introduction, there is also the project method of John Dewey, familiar to people who study education history. So while "activity" has the problem, in English at least, of meaning something too vague, "project" also has the problem of meaning of anything that a person is planning to work on.

It's probably better to look at the whole book and see what the people writing in it mean by "project." It draws together a range of reports that make a good argument for rethinking what they should be collectively called. Blunden calls them "research," and they are certainly research. But they are also stories. All the chapters are narratives of something that happened. They involve many people and tell about something that happened over time. There are pauses, when the writers reflect on how the narrative is moving along, but above all the story keeps going. In an odd way, while writing history sometimes leans away from telling a narrative towards collecting evidence and putting it into categories, here we have social science telling narratives. The person who describes these projects ranges from a participant or advocate to a neutral-seeming observer who is peering in through a window. Most of the people who are doing these projects (as compared to writing about them) fit the markers of a project proposed by Blunden in the introduction, namely, that they belong to a group of people who are experiencing some problem or constraint on their freedom. They are motivated to respond. Over time, trial and error clarifies the project until it becomes something recognized, named and acknowledged. This gives us a timeline in the development of a project. However, instead of people as individuals performing the role of main character, we have a project performing that role.

In most chapters, there is a point at which some part of the project becomes emblematic of the whole project. It might be the design of the interactions of the students in the Fifth Dimension; it might be the oval table in the Blunden and Arnold chapter about the University of Melbourne; it might be a Mini-public in the Lubensky article on Public Deliberation, the expert status of gay doctors in the Power article on AIDS, the union contract in my article on the Mayslake struggle or Tahrir Square in the de Smet article on the Egyptian revolution. This object becomes something like a molecule of the project, something that embodies the best hopes of the efforts and also signals (or projects, in the sense of displaying or highlighting) the meaning of the effort out to the public and inward to the collaborators.

Blunden acknowledges the similarities between "activity system" and "project," with one difference:

> An "activity system" is a system of actions directed toward some object, with its own norms, tools and division of labor. The concept is essentially the same as that of "project" but is usually understood as some kind of functional institution, which develops as a result of contradictions within its structure.
>
> BLUNDEN, p. 5

Whether or not it is accurate that an activity system is usually understood as a functional institution (and I don't know how to confirm or refute this, but that's not how I think of it), the mention of norms, tools and division of labor is important. Each of these is a category that is rich with ways to surface specifics. This means that one of the things that is easy to do with Activity theory is to link up its components to identify how a change in one component, like a change in regulations, norms or laws; a re-interpretation of a history; a new participant among the subjects/actors in the project; a new tool like a new computer program, a person who speaks a language no one else has been fluent in, or simply money, can shift the relationships among other components. This helps people who are studying ongoing activity systems pay attention to potential change and conflict. It helps them know where to look if a crisis starts rising. It also provides a way to make sure that someone looking back over a completed project will ask all the proper questions and not miss the important role played by something that might, when it's all over, look insignificant.

By drawing the boundary of the activity system clearly by defining it by its purpose, and making visible the components that are inside compared to those that are outside, or lacking, it is also possible to see what the surrounding social context is made up of. What other activity systems are in place in the immediate vicinity? Are they supportive or in conflict with the one under discussion? In the Cole chapter on the Fifth Dimension, there were other activity systems – other projects – at work in the social context of early instances of the project. One project was philosophically diametrically opposed to the aims of the Fifth Dimension, but nonetheless created an opening for it to flourish.

My main concern about theories that explain or model how change happens, whether it is individual or collective learning or organizational development or social change on the broadest level, is, how do you use them? A theory is good for organizing a complex experience or predicting what will happen. In reading through this book, I kept asking myself how I would explain to someone who is not a social scientist how you would use either the project unit of analysis or the whole analytic framework of Activity Theory. Although many theorists (for example, according to Morten Nissen this is true of Jean Lave) dislike the idea that a theory which is imaginatively productive for them might be used prescriptively by someone else, this is highly likely to happen anyway. I think it is quite normal for someone to respond to a description of a theory with the question, "What is that good for?" The answer they are looking for is one that helps them figure out how to do something.

None of the writers who contributed to this book used this Activity theory to work out the details of a project, or at least they don't say so. While they all drew on CHAT in the sense that they knew they needed to pay attention to the concrete social context of a project, and that the project had to be defined by its purpose, none of them – at least in my reading – actually took Activity theory into the daily workings out of the projects they were researching. Yet in order to answer the question, "What is this good for?" I think you would have to be able to say that it was good for more than just awareness of context and purpose. It needs to be good for making comparisons and planning.

Here is an idea of a possible effort where Activity theory, and the project as a unit of analysis, might be made use of in daily, detailed way. I recently was travelling along the route of the Underground Railroad, the several-thousand mile long escape route of fugitives from slavery in the US. It stretches from Mississippi to Canada (even after the Emancipation proclamation, there was no secure freedom for black people in the North). We were only traveling along the few hundred miles between Louisville and Cincinnati, but there were many sites in that area especially above and below the Ohio River, which was the boundary between Kentucky, a slave state, and Indiana and Ohio, which were free states. There are small towns along this borderland where there are museums of the Underground Railroad experience. Some museums are very specific to that town or village: Madison, Indiana, for example, has a walking tour of what was once a black neighborhood, with individual houses marked with plaques saying who lived there and what they did. New Albany is another such town, but they have an actual museum with an exhibit that tells the stories using multi-media of five or ten actual historical people who were involved in the Underground Railroad. While the display is modest, you come away with the feeling of having read a thick historical novel with interwoven threads of stories. Then there is Cincinnati, where corporate sponsors have erected a giant multi-story museum overlooking the Ohio River. This building is surprisingly empty, as if it were designed for major receptions yet to come.

How would someone trying to decide how to design a museum display about the Underground Railroad know what to include or leave out, and why? This is a project that a small town with limited resources but some city pride might very well take on. It is like a project within a project. This would be an example of using the concept of "project" for planning something (doing a project) before it starts, rather than looking back on something and analyzing it after it's finished.

CHAPTER 23

Toward a Mesogenetic Methodology

Michael Cole

Every new theory, Vygotsky asserted, requires a new methodology – a new way of "collecting data," inscribable aspects of the flow of human activities which our theory specifies as relevant to understanding the phenomenon of interest.

The idea of a mesogenetic methodology arises from the general proposition that to understand behavior means to understand the history/genesis of behavior. This proposition has long been acknowledged as a fundamental tenet of cultural-historical approaches to the study of human nature. The actual representation of this idea in the practice of cultural-historical psychologists has, however, been restricted to implementing only parts of the overall paradigm. In place of research programs that include phylogenetic, cultural-historical, ontogenetic, and microgenetic data within a single, integrated field of inquiry, scholars have either focused entirely on a single genetic domain (ontogeny or microgenesis, for the most part) or the relationship between two neighboring domains (e.g., ontogenetic changes in microgenetic processes). The reason for this state of affairs is obvious: phylogenetic and cultural-historical change generally take place at rates so slow with respect to the ontogeny of the investigator that integrated research is impossible. In the relatively few cases where the goal has been to study the relation between phylogeny or cultural/historical development and ontogeny, "cross-species" and cross-cultural methods, with all of their attendant methodological problems, have been used.

What I am referring to as a "mesogenetic" approach to the study of development is one in which the time scale falls between the ontogenetic scale focused on individuals and the macro-genetic societal scale implied by the historical difference between peasant and industrialized societies. The basic strategy for this research exemplified by the 5th Dimension has been to create a system of activities with its own standing rules, artifacts, social roles, and ecological setting, that is, its own culture. The system of activities is implemented in a plausible setting with plausible collaborative intent on the part of the university and community institutions to enter into a long term partnership. Then the developmental history of the activity system in its context is traced to observe "its" struggle to develop and survive.

A basic characteristic of the mesogenetic approach involved in designing, implementing, and seeking to sustain 5th Dimension is that the expected lifespan of such activities is about three years (based on a sample of 120 such efforts in our data base). However, some 5th Dimension-inspired programs continued for a decade or more and some have yet to expire. This range of 5th Dimension longevity means that it is possible to obtain critical data associated not only with the conception, birth and growth of a cultural-historical system of activity, but with the decline and eventual demise of such systems. This point is important because students of development in the Vygotskian tradition argue that the principles of development manifest themselves no less in the process of aging among the elderly and among infants.

A difficulty with critically engaging the study of lifespan development at the ontogenetic level is that researchers themselves and the objects they are studying (other human beings) develop on roughly the same time scale. Birth and death. The same is not true for 5th Dimension activity systems. In so far as they continue for a number of years, and the researcher begins the work when s/he is young enough, it is possible to document the process of the development of "the activity system itself" including the process of its demise.

In what follows, I provide a history of the development of the concept of a mesogenetic methodology. It was not there when we began the research. It developed, as Vygotsky would expect it to, in the process of seeking to overcome the barriers to creating and sustaining our activity system over time.

The Development of the Concept of a Mesogenetic Methodology

While we did not have a self-conscious, articulated concept of a mesogenetic methodology when we began, we did have a tool kit of methods and theoretical ideas. We had designed and implemented activities before but never with the intent to sustain them as long as possible and observe their demise. It is certain that we did not fully understand the implications of our focus on sustainability.

We had come at the problem of sustainability so to speak, backwards – from the shock of discovering that our investigation into the characteristics of successful programs for STEM inclusion had a known answer, stamped with the approval of the AAAS (1984). The issue, as we saw it, was *not* a specification of what was required to induce the kind of academic changes that policy makers were striving for; it was crucially a matter of how to *sustain* already proven effective programs. In the beginning, we really did not know what to expect at the "cultural-historical level," at the level of the programs in their community settings. Our basic strategy was to work as hard as possible to implement multiple 5th Dimensions and support others in attempting to do so. We expected only that each would require site-specific modifications in the process of its implementation.

It was in the course of preparing a final report to the Spencer Foundation that we began to formulate the methodology that I refer to as a "mesogenetic methodology" (see LCHC, 1982; Nicolopolou & Cole, 1993; Cole, 1996, chapter 10).

The End is in the Beginning

The idea that "the end in is in the beginning" is intuitively shared in many philosophical and religious traditions as well as the tenets of modern biology. It underlies the idea of a spiral of development, an idea also influential in theories of ontogenetic development.

We experienced this insight as part of the process that led us to formulate the notion of a mesogenetic methodology. The key experience emerged from the initial research plan. As described in the summary of the project, Cole deliberately absented himself from the "goal formation" process which was carried out by LCHC staff headed by Peg Griffin et al 1993. He did not make contact with people representing the group of community institutions that had elected to participate in the project until August of 1987, a month before he would need to implement the complementary class at UCSD.

The very practical goal of these meetings for Cole was to plan for the resource requirements each site would need, what special bureaucratic procedures, and at least a rough division of labor and responsibility for each of the three initial sites. He tape recorded those first, "commitment sealing" meetings to provide a kind of "starting point" for tracing our understandings later, as the activities emerged. The tape recording having been made, the set of tapes was put in a file and forgotten.

When it came time to write the final project report, the research group had a pretty well worked out narrative of what had transpired in the previous three years. They could call upon not only on their personal memories, but the residue of countless other meetings, fieldnotes, artifacts from the sites, and so on, to create a coherent narrative.

The crucial moment came when we pulled those initial recordings from Cole's meetings with the directresses and directors at each site. The experience of hearing those conversations severely jarred our understanding of the events. What was amazing was the way in which the future fates of each of the three systems, as we subsequently came to experience them, were present in the conversations on those tapes. But we did not recognize them as the fatal factors they turned out to be. We understood from our own knowledge of the social context why the Headmistress of the Day Care Center had been a stickler for insuring that all the students were fingerprinted and health certified. We complied with those requirements, although it was a challenge.

But the legal requirements and the popularity of the system at the Center were not sufficient to compensate for the Headmistress's panic when a whole cadre of new UCSD students turned up the second quarter of the year. We fully sympathized with her choice to end the project, and experienced a marked sense of relief because the strain of conducting three 5th Dimensions at once was weighing on us heavily. Our load lightened, we were free to concentrate on the remaining two programs.

At the Library we knew from the start that integrating the computer based activities into that setting – the "wave of the future for libraries," also required us to deal with a variety of constraints. Making noise and finding space were two leading concerns in the initial meeting. Little discussion occurred around the fact that the Library was located in a shopping mall, so that parents had to drive their children to and from school or home. But when the Library died, it was because the parents had turned out to be unreliable transporters, and the librarians were concerned about issues of liability around supervision and safety that they did not want to have to deal with, and their desire for the library to close precisely at 5 PM when the County stopped paying them for their time.

In both of these cases, the process of decline and demise arose from strains springing from contradictions between the established working norms, practices and concerns of the local community organization that only revealed themselves in the course of implementation. There was nothing the UCSD researcher could do that would solve the problems that emerged.

The tapes from the interview at the youth club focused on the local club norm of allowing children to move from one activity to another more or less as they chose; there were many potentially attractive activities they could engage casually. By contrast, from our experience when the 5th Dimension was initially designed to run in a school after school, we sought deep engagement in the various tasks that comprised the activity. Our experience after three years was that it was very difficult to *implement* the 5th Dimension at the Club. The Club wanted to sustain an activity that we found constantly challenging and problematic!

Hearing the tapes from the three sites after three years of intense engagement, I was deeply impressed by the feeling that I was seeing the future from the perspective of the past. I could now "see" the obstacles that would challenge the activity and eventually lead to difficulties and the potential demise of activities which "in themselves" our partners continued to think a valuable experience for the children. I remember quite clearly a sensation of doing a balancing act, while constantly dodging unanticipated manifestations of the difficulties to come – a sensation that brought strongly to mind the comment of my anthropologist friend, Roy D'Andrade, that "Doing social science is like doing geology in a landslide."

Theorizing the Emerging Methodology

During the early part of the 1990s, our theorizing of the 5th Dimension was heavily focused on the design "of the activity itself," occasions in which children, undergraduates, and research came together within the domain of the Wizard/ess. Inside what might now be called "a play world." Heavy focus was placed on the central role of principles stolen from various cultural historical scholars. For this focus, a particularly central notion was that of an artifact, and particularly Wartofsky's notion of a tertiary artifact:

> which can come to constitute a relatively autonomous 'world', in which rules, conventions and outcomes no longer appear directly practical, or which, indeed, seem to constitute an arena of non-practical, or 'free' play or game activity.
>
> WARTOFSKY, 1973, p. 208

We began to conceive of the 5th Dimension as such an artifact, and recognized ourselves as being intensely focused on the teaching/learning dynamics that we created within the "cultures of collaborative learning" that we sought to embody in the 5th Dimension's design.

Here is how we made the linkage from core ideas of CHAT formulated in the 1920s to the way we were implementing them at this stage in the project.

Implicitly or explicitly, Vygotsky and Luria emphasized the double-sided nature of artifact-mediated actions. The inextricable link between these two moments of human activity are neatly summarized by Vygotsky as follows:

> all processes forming part of that method form a complicated functional and structural unity. This unity is effected, first, by the task which must be solved by the given method, and secondly, by the means by which the method can be followed.... It is precisely the structure which combines all separate processes, which are component parts of the cultural habit of

> behavior, which transforms this habit into a psychological function, and which fulfills its task with respect to behavior as a whole.
>
> 1929, pp. 61–62

The remaining central postulates of this paradigm flow necessarily from the premise of artifact mediation. Historical (genetic) analysis is an essential methodological tenet of this paradigm because culture (the synthesized totality of artifacts available to a group) and mediated action emerged as a single process of hominization. To understand the workings of culturally mediated activity, it is necessary to understand processes of change and transformation that, by definition, take place over time. Theory demands simultaneous analysis on several temporal levels (what Wertsch, 1985, refers to as genetic domains) because any psychological phenomenon emerges from the interaction of processes occurring at all the levels of the human life system: phylogeny, cultural history, ontogeny, and microgenesis.

The emphasis on social origins of human psychological functions in CHAT arises from the same source. As Dewey emphasized, every child is born into a world transformed by the activity of prior generations. It is only enculturated human beings who can organize children's environments and thus afford them the opportunity to appropriate the existing pool of cultural resources. It is only through interactions with other human beings that newcomers can become old-timers.

The overall perspective sketched here is summarized quite succinctly by Vladimir Lektorsky, who wrote the following using activity theory as his point of departure:

> practical activity itself must be understood in its specifically human characteristics, namely as joint or collective activity in which each individual enters into certain relations with other persons; as mediated activity in which man places between himself and an external, naturally emerging object other man-made objects functioning as instruments of activity; and finally, as historically developing activity carrying in itself its own history.
>
> 1980, pp. 136–137

References

Cole, M. (1996). *Cultural Psychology: A Once and Future Discipline*. Cambridge: Harvard University Press.

Griffin, P. Belyaeva, A. Soldatova, G. & the Velikhov-Hamburg Collective (1993). Review of 'Creating and Reconstituting Contexts for Educational Interactions, Including a

Computer Program'. In Forman, E.A. Minick, N. and Stone, C.A. (Eds.), *Contexts for Learning: Sociocultural Dynamics in Children's Development,* 1993, New York, Oxford University Press, pp. 120–152.

LCHC (1982). A model system for the study of learning, *Quarterly Newsletter of the Laboratory of Comparative Human Cognition*, 4(3).

Lektorsky, V. (1980). Subject Object Cognition, Moscow: Progress Publishers.

Nicolopolou, A. & Cole, M. (1993). The Fifth Dimension, its playworld and its institutional context: The generation and transmission of shared knowledge in the culture of collaborative learning. In *Contexts for Learning: Sociocultural Dynamics in Children's Development*, E.A. Foreman, N. Minnick & C.A. Stone eds., New York, Oxford University Press.

Vygotsky, L.S. (1929). The problem of cultural development of the child, in *The Vygotsky Reader*, ed. R. van der Veer & J. Valsiner, Oxford, UK: Blackwell.

Wartofsky, M.W. (1973). *Models*. Dodrecht: Reidel.

Wertsch, J.V. (1985). *Vygotsky and the Social Formation of Mind.* Cambridge, MA: Harvard University Press.

CHAPTER 24

Conclusion: Time and Activity

Andy Blunden

One thing stands out from this collection, in which writers trained in and accustomed to scientific writing were asked to provide articles in which the concept of 'project' was the unit of analysis: as Helena Worthen reflects, 'All the chapters are narratives' and 'while writing history sometimes leans away from telling a narrative towards collecting evidence and putting it into categories, here we have social science telling narratives' (p. 357).

As I discussed in *Concepts* (2012), a number of writers have recognized two 'modes of knowledge' which I will call 'narrative' and 'conceptual' (Bruner, 1990, p. 35). The conceptual is often referred to as 'scientific' but this is erroneous as scientific knowledge is only one of many currents of conceptual knowledge and narrative may be scientific as well as unscientific. Furthermore, these two modes of knowledge do not form a dichotomy. As Lyotard (1979, p. 28–29) was the first to point out, we believe in concepts only insofar as they figure in convincing narratives, and narratives are intelligible only to the extent that they utilize valid concepts. These two modes of knowledge are inextricable and mutually validating. Some (such as Bruner, 1990, p. 45) have speculated that human beings have an innate narrative competence somewhat akin to the ability to distinguish figure and ground. In other words, narrative competence is a basic and essential way of knowing, both in science and elsewhere.

A narrative is not just a chronicle, or even a story line. What Ricoeur calls 'emplotment' entails arranging heterogeneous components together into a plot, in such a way that one situation follows from another in an intelligible and convincing way. Science, which is concerned with what *exists*, requires of its narratives that they are validated by their interconnection with other narratives, just as it makes the same demand of its concepts (Hegel, 1830, §123). The real question is: how does social science manage *without* narratives?

According to Ricoeur (1984), the leading alternative to narrative explanation for historical events is the 'covering law', that is, the subsumption of events or situations under a universal *law*. Restriction to such a mode of explanation in the social sciences is untenable, and until such time as social science were to reduce all the phenomena of social life to 'laws', narrative explanation is going to play a central role. This is all the more true in the case of a relatively young branch of science, such as interdisciplinary Activity Theory.

But there is more than this. What the use of 'project' as a unit of analysis has done is to introduce into the unit of analysis of Activity Theory the element of *time*, which, though perhaps we never noticed, was previously absent. Although, following in the tradition of Vygotsky, Activity Theory has taken ontogenetic development and organizational change as its subject matter, and applied the experimental-genetic methodology (see p. 42), its fundamental concept lacked intrinsic development. A 'system' (CAT&DWR, 2003), like 'structure', is in-itself self-reproducing. But development – time – is intrinsic to the very idea of 'project'.

According to Ricoeur (1984, p. 194), the relationships of 'participatory belonging' which constitute the entities of social science, the quasi-characters of its narratives, mediate between the quasi-plots and quasi-events, and the concepts which form the basis for a conceptual explanation. 'Quasi' because the narratives are not narratives of the actions of individuals but of supra-personal entities, in our case, projects. These narratives flow from the use of *idiographic* as opposed to nomothetic science (Ricoeur 1984, p. 195; Frank 1986), which has a proud place in the CHAT tradition, notably the work of A.R. Luria. As Worthen remarks: 'instead of people as individuals performing the role of main character, we have a project performing that role'. It is also the means by which we escape methodological individualism (Ricoeur 1984, p. 199).

CHAT is characterized by the conviction that human individuals can only be understood in connection with their activity within a cultural and historical situation. As Mike Cole recalls (p. 362), Vygotsky further insisted that the processes of human life can only be grasped through observation of their growth and disintegration. As Cole's reflection makes clear, these demands together oblige us to study both the formation and disintegration of social formations themselves. These considerations inevitably bring us to the notion of projects as units of analysis of human life, and the narrative mode of knowledge and explanation. Hitherto, an 'activity' or 'system of activity' changed only as a result of contradictions in their elements. But since these elements were external to the subject and object of the activity, change and development, whilst not being excluded, were not essential to the very concept of the activity as it is for 'project'. For projects, the principal contradiction is within the object itself.

Worthen (p. 358) also draws our attention to the absence from the chapters describing and analyzing projects of the elements of an activity identified by Engeström – the norms and rules, division of labor, instruments and so on, the contradictions within and between which are seen as the source of both blockages and of change, and also the idea of interactions with other systems of activity in the surrounding social context. This is true to some extent, though partly also because the same issues have been dealt with without the recognizable terminology of Activity Theory. But it has never been the intention of this project to create an *alternative theory*. The aim is to introduce into Activity Theory *one new concept*, the concept of 'project', which is to take the place of the unit of activity. All the past gains of Activity Theory and Cultural-Historical Psychology need to be retained. But the introduction of this new concept of the unit of activity will have not just an additive effect, but a transformative effect on the theory as a whole. The notions of the norms and rules, instruments, community, etc., and the understanding of interaction between activities will be radically changed by the introduction of 'project' as a unit of analysis. But it is early days. This book marks only the very first effort. It is vital that everything we have learnt about the internal structure and dynamics of activities (a.k.a. 'systems of activity' or 'projects') needs to be sublated into the concept of 'project' if it is to become a genuinely useful concept for the human sciences.

However, there are two aspects of the concept of 'project' which suggest a transformative effect on Activity Theory. The first is the element of time already mentioned, and the second is the concept of the object of activity which is quite different for each so-called generation of Activity Theory. These two problems (time and the object of activity) are closely interconnected, but before turning to the problem of the object of activity I want to consider the problems posed by the new unit of activity for developing firstly, the internal dynamics of projects (or systems of activity) and secondly, the interactions between projects, which arise by a reconceptualization of norms and rules, instruments, subject, object and division of labor consequent upon a change of the conception of the unit itself.

The Internal Dynamics of Projects

Two currents of Activity Theory have developed concepts which need to be appropriated for a deeper understanding of the internal dynamics of projects. The first is Engeström's very differentiated concept of 'system of activity'. Projects obviously have a division of labor; in fact, division of labor is meaningful *only* within projects. All the reports in this book have touched on the division of labor within their projects (e.g. Power, p. 254; Beaton, p. 280). The instruments and norms and rules also need consideration (e.g. Cole, p. 135; Power, p. 249). Engeström's expanding triangle logo, for example, is a proven mnemonic reminding researchers to identify and track these elements. But whereas these elements are distinct from subject and object, which are in turn separate from one another, for an Activity Theory based on 'projects', all these elements have to be conceived *integrally*. In particular, the norms and rules have to be understood as objectifications of the object of the project. The object here is not as it is for Engeström, but more like it is for Leontiev, that is, the imagined objective situation attainment of which is the source of motivation for the project and its *self-concept*, which arises from the project activity. More on this below. The subject is not to be taken as an individual or group at some location within the project's division of labor, but rather the project itself is to conceived as a subject-object in the Hegelian sense. In these circumstances, norms are both deontological objectifications of the project concept (Blunden, 2012) and the material by means of which the researcher can determine what the object of the project is. Not something *else*. So reforming Activity Theory for analysis by projects presupposes a considerable amount of work to integrate the notions of norms and division of labor into the conception of a 'formation of consciousness'. Likewise, 'outcome' is not something other than the object, but is the realization or 'unfolding' of the object itself. Scientific study of the internal dynamics of projects presupposes that this conceptual work is done.

The other current of Activity Theory which offers considerable opportunities for the development of an understanding of the internal workings of projects is Jean Lave and Etienne Wenger's (1991) notion of Community of Practice, in particular, Jean Lave's critical work on the various modes of apprenticeship which mediate the interaction between newcomers and old-timers and how newcomers become, over time, old-timers. These ideas must be utilized alongside the 'modes of collaboration' already discussed in the introduction and the chapters above.

Interactions between Projects

The 5th, 7th, 10th, 11th and 12th chapters above explicitly dealt with alliances between distinct projects, and it is implicit in the treatment of relations between child and teacher in the 1st chapter. In relation to such interaction, I have introduced a number of concepts for the prototypical ways in which projects interact with each other, referred to in the Introduction. But Engeström's work on this problem has merit too. Although, in my opinion, his conception of 'systems of activity' and the boundary problems that come with the concept of a closed system is ill-equipped to theorize interactions between projects,

Engeström and his colleagues have done a lot of work on this which should be appropriated.

The basic thesis is that projects may share elements. For example, they may share what Engeström calls the 'object'. But by 'object' is meant here what Marx called the *Arbeitsgegenstand*, that is, the 'the "raw material" or "problem space" at which the activity is directed and which is molded and transformed into outcomes' (CAT&DWR, 2003). So for example, rival political movements in a country share the nation as their *Arbeitsgegenstand*, or 'subject of labor'. They may also share semantic, practical and theoretical norms, and technical and symbolic instruments. These relations are crucial to understanding interactions between projects and we should follow Engeström in paying attention to them where interaction between projects is in play, and developing these observations theoretically.

The question of shared objects (in Leontiev's sense) simply does not arise in Engeström's theory; he is a 'behaviorist' when it comes to collective subjects. But the question of shared or conflicting objects has already been adequately dealt with in several of the chapters.

The Object of Activity

'Object' has broadly the same meaning for projects as it has in Leontiev's psychology, as the imagined objective situation the realization of which provides the motivation for action.

> Only as a result of [a need] 'meeting' with an object that answers it does it first become capable of directing and regulating activity. ..., 'filling' it with content derived from the surrounding world.
>
> 1978, p. 88

Whilst retaining these characteristics, for projects, the object of activity is not something outside the project which is the source of its motivation, but is *immanent* to the project itself.

For Leontiev, a person's actions betray their real, usually hidden or unconscious motive, which is the *personal sense* of the object for them, that is, it is *subjective*. On the other hand, the meaning of the object, which 'everyone very well knows' (1978, p. 129) is *objective*. This works well in a society where the objective meaning of everything is determined by the Politburo but hardly reflects reality in the postmodern, multicultural communities of our times.

The appropriate distinction is not between subjective and objective, but between the individual, particular and universal moments of a concept. In formal logic, the universal is an attribute shared by every individual subsumed under it, but such an abstract general notion is not what is meant here. In dialectical logic, the individual actions are connected to a universal sign by particular practical norms and do not necessarily share any single attribute. The concept is realized only by the eventual reconciliation of the contradictions immanent in the diversity of individual actions and conflicting practical norms.

For projects, the object is taken to be the concept of the object, or *object-concept*. Other projects have other concepts of the same *Arbeitsgegenstand*. The relation between the object-concepts of interacting projects is what Hegel called the *Subjekt-Objekt* relation. This is quite different from the subjective/objective contrast. *Subjekt* and *Objekt* are both independent cognizing, practical subjects (i.e., 'formations of consciousness', or what Marx called *social* formations), and interpenetrate and transform one another in the course of their mutual development, as described in the chapters above on AIDS and Asbestos, and the reflection by the Hunter College students on their own development in seeking changes in their college, for example.

What this allows is that the object-concept of a project, like the object of a design project, undergoes continual revision in response to experience and 'feedback'. People set off to build socialism but end up creating an autocratic state. In the process of realizing an object-concept, the object turns out often quite other than what one expected. As Cole illustrates in his narrative of the 5thD project.

It is important here that 'concept' not be understood in a mentalist sense. In *Thinking and Speech* (1934), Vygotsky made a study of concepts. The method for this study of concepts was the observation of *actions*, in both real-life and laboratory conditions, and the determination of the concept which made sense of the subject's actions. That is, he took concepts to be *forms of activity*, just as he took word meaning to be an artifact-mediated *action*, equally subjective and objective, not a mental object. What this means is that, as mentioned above, it is the actions, in particular those actions which are normative, together with the universal symbols used by a project, which together constitute the object-concept of the project and thus the project itself. The object-concept is not something *outside* the project, motivating it, but is intrinsic, *immanent* to the project itself and is realized as the project's 'end point'. But just like a person, and like history itself, a project is always a work in progress.

References

Blunden, A. (2012). *Concepts. A Critical Approach*, Leiden, Netherlands: Brill.

Bruner, J. (1990), *Acts of Meaning*, Cambridge, MA: Harvard University Press.

CAT&DWR Center for Activity Theory and Developmental Work Research (2003). *The Activity System*. http://www.edu.helsinki.fi/activity/pages/chatanddwr/activity system/.

Frank, I. (1986). 'Psychology as a science: Resolving the idiographic-nomothetic controversy', In *The individual Subject and Scientific Psychology*, edited by J. Valsiner, New York: Springer.

Hegel, G.W.F. (1830/2009). *Hegel's Logic, with a Foreword by Andy Blunden*. Kettering, OH: Erythrós Press.

Lave, J. & Wenger, E. (1991). *Situated Learning. Legitimate Peripheral Participation*. New York, NY: Cambridge University Press.

Leontiev, A.N. (1978). *Activity Consciousness and Personality*, Upper Saddle River, NJ: Prentice-Hall.

Lyotard, J.-F. (1979/1984). *The Postmodern Condition: A Report on Knowledge*. Minneapolis, MN: University of Minnesota Press.

Ricoeur, P. (1984). *Time and Narrative. Vol. I.* Chicago: University of Chicago Press.

Vygotsky, L.S. (1934/1987). Thinking and speech, *Collected Works, Vol. 1*, pp. 39–285, New York: Plenum Press.

Index